HOUGHTON MIFFLIN
math CENTRAL

 HOUGHTON MIFFLIN

Boston • Atlanta • Dallas • Geneva, Illinois • Princeton, New Jersey • Palo Alto

Authors

Kindergarten

Patsy F. Kanter
Consultant, Teacher, Author
New Orleans, Louisiana

Janet G. Gillespie
Title I Specialist, Consultant, Author
Woodlawn Elementary School
Portland, Oregon

Levels 1–6

Laurie Boswell
Profile Jr./Sr. High School
Bethlehem, New Hampshire

Mary Esther Reynosa
Elementary Mathematics Curriculum Specialist
Edgewood School District
San Antonio, Texas

Dr. Juanita V. Copley
Associate Professor of Education
University of Houston
Houston, Texas

Dr. Jean M. Shaw
Professor of Elementary Education
University of Mississippi
University, Mississippi

Audrey L. Jackson
Assistant Principal
Parkway School District
St. Louis, Missouri

Dr. Lee Stiff
Associate Professor of Mathematics Education
North Carolina State University
Raleigh, North Carolina

Edward Manfre
Mathematics Education Consultant
Albuquerque, New Mexico

Dr. Charles Thompson
Professor of Mathematics Education
University of Louisville
Louisville, Kentucky

Consultants and Contributing Authors

Dr. Carole Basile
University of Houston
Houston, Texas

Cindy Chapman
Inez Science and Technology
Magnet School
Albuquerque, New Mexico

Dr. Deborah Ann Chessin
University of Mississippi
University, Mississippi

Dr. Richard Evans
Plymouth State College
Plymouth, New Hampshire

Dr. Robert Gyles
Community School District 4
New York, New York

Dr. Karen Karp
University of Louisville
Louisville, Kentucky

Casilda Pardo
Armijo Elementary School
Albuquerque, New Mexico

Caitlin Robinson
Mitchell Elementary School
Albuquerque, New Mexico

Printed in the U.S.A.

ISBN: 0-395-84739-7

6789-B-03 02 01 00 99 98

Contents

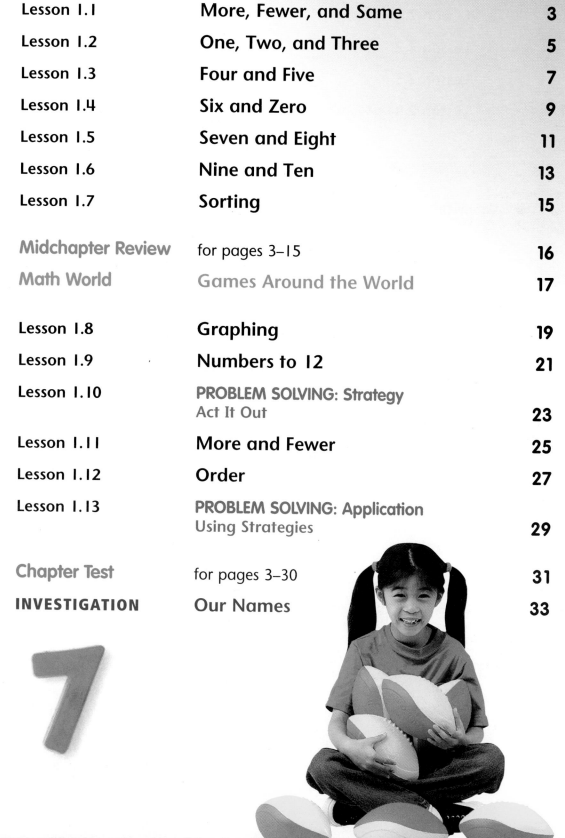

Houghton Mifflin Math CENTRAL

3 Subtraction Facts Through 6 Page 57

6¢

CHAPTER 4
Addition and Subtraction Facts Through 10

Page 81

Theme: Sea Creatures

 **Place Value Through 100**   **Page 117**

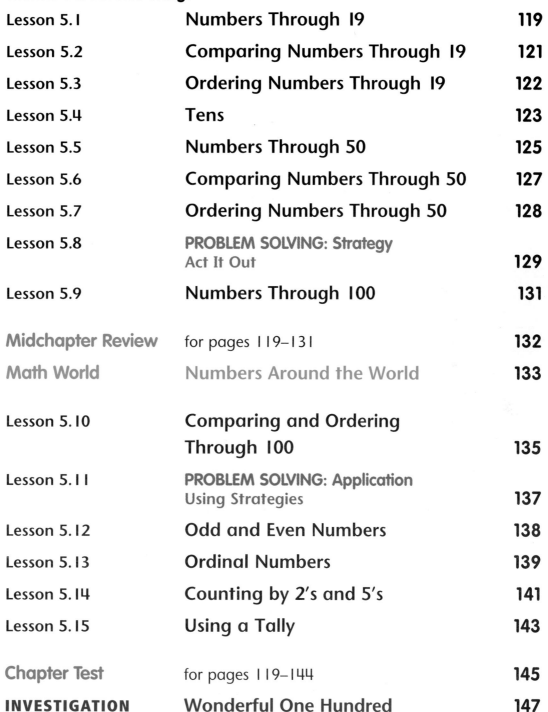

Theme: Good Things to Eat

Geometry and Fractions

Page 225

x

CHAPTER 9

Addition and Subtraction Facts Through 20

Page 261

Theme: Animals, Animals

Readiness for Multiplication and Division

CHAPTER 11

Page 333

Theme: Fun with Friends

Addition and Subtraction of 2-Digit Numbers

Page 361

Super ★ Star

Numbers Through 12

Literature

Ten Little Froggies
By Louise Binder Scott

Read Aloud Anthology p. 2
Theme Connection
Starting School

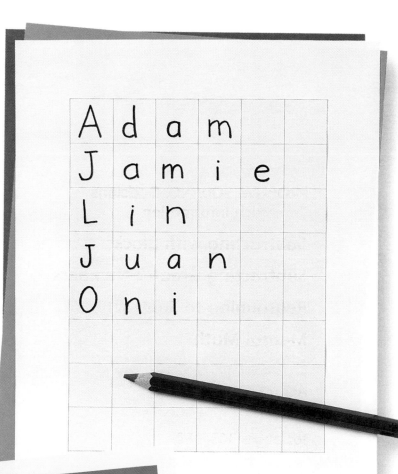

A	d	a	m	
J	a	m	i	e
L	i	n		
J	u	a	n	
O	n	i		

See what I can do by the end of this chapter.

Use What You Know

What are the names of your friends?
Are the names long or short?
How can you tell?

Listen to the poem.
Use counters to act it out.

Dear Family: Practice counting through ten by making up your own froggy tales. Have your child use cut out shapes or dried beans on the workmat to act out the stories.

Cooperative Learning

Very good!

Name _____

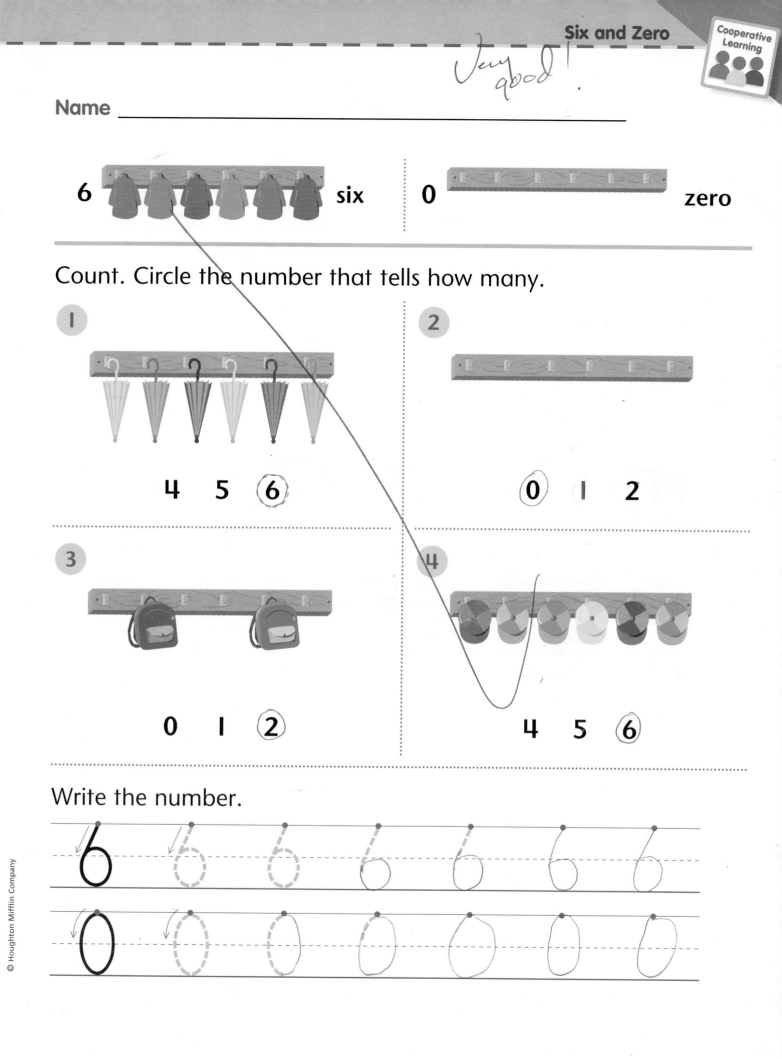

6 six   **0** zero

Count. Circle the number that tells how many.

1

4   5   (6)

2

(0)   1   2

3

0   1   (2)

4

4   5   (6)

Write the number.

6 6 6 6 6 6 6

0 0 0 0 0 0 0

Work with a partner.
Use number cards and a bag.
Pick a number.
Write the number.
Put the card back.

How will you know when
you have taken **6** turns?

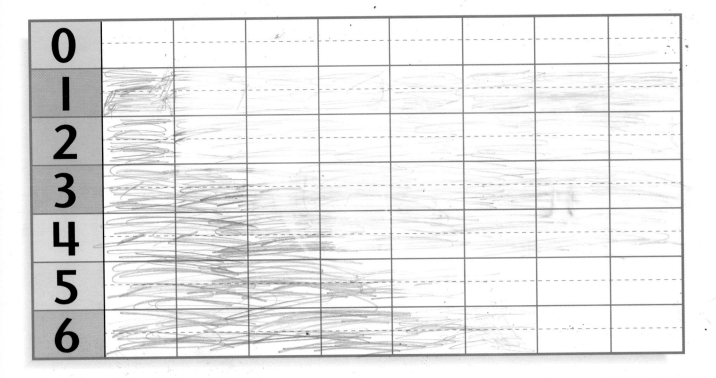

0						
1						
2						
3						
4						
5						
6						

Communication

Talk about it
Compare your chart with your partner's chart.
How are they alike? How are they different?

▶ **More Practice, page 390**

Dear Family: Play the game on this page several
times with your child. Take turns pulling numbers from
a bag. Have your child record the numbers.

Name _____

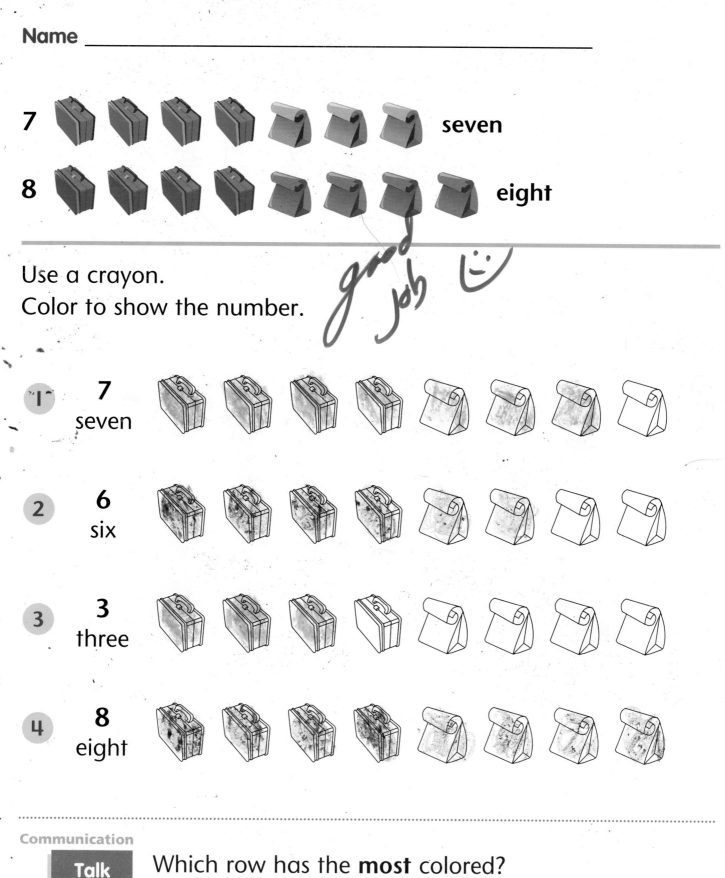

7   seven

8   eight

Use a crayon.
Color to show the number.

good job :)

1   **7** seven

2   **6** six

3   **3** three

4   **8** eight

Communication

Talk about it

Which row has the **most** colored?
Which row has the **fewest** colored?

Write the number.

7 7 7 7 7 7 7

8 8 8 8 8 8 8

Use a spinner.
Which number will you spin most?
Tell why.

Write your guess. _____

Write the number you spin.

 1 _____ | 2 _____ | 3 _____ | 4 _____ 5 _____

Dear Family: Make groups of 7 and 8 objects with your child.
Use macaroni, buttons, or toothpicks. Let your child write
number cards for 7 and 8 and place them with the objects.

Name _____

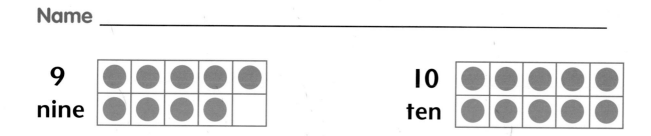

9 nine

10 ten

Use a ten frame.

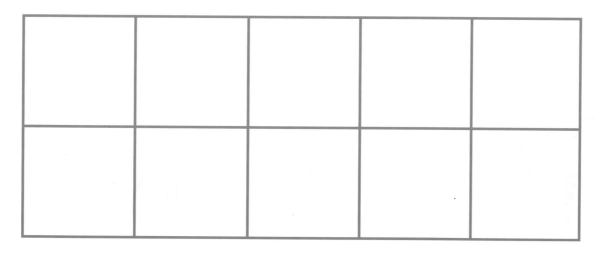

Look at the number.
Place counters on the large ten frame.
Draw the counters on the small ten frame.

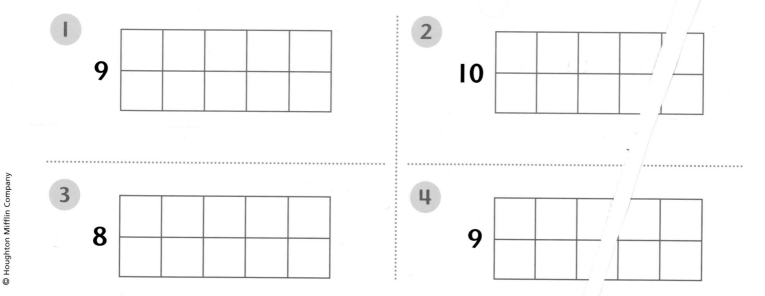

1   9

2   10

3   8

4   9

Write the number.

9 9 9 9 9 9 9

10 10 10 10 10 10 10

Write how many.

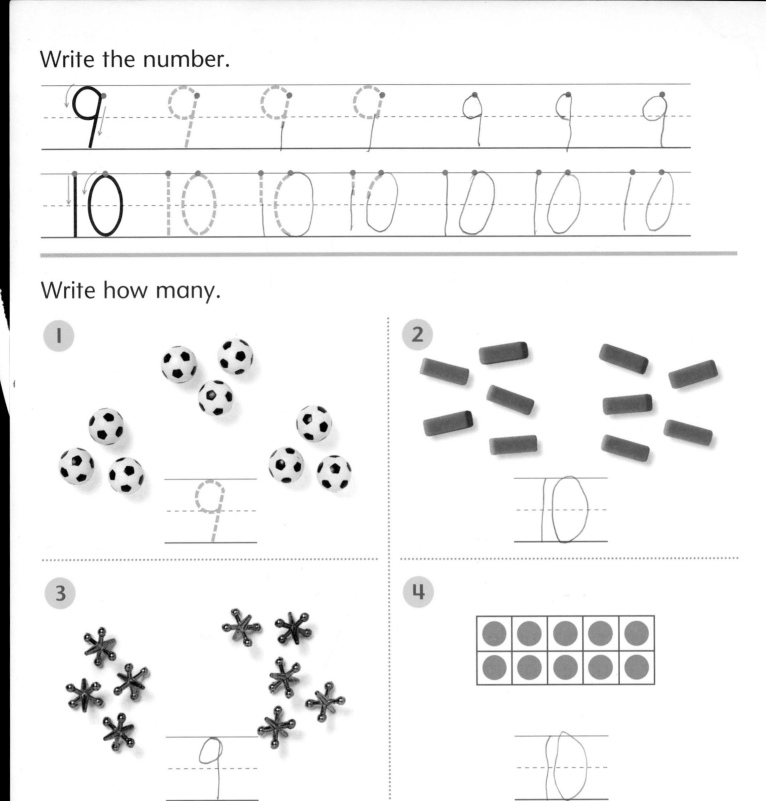

1 9

2 10

3 9

4 10

Draw a ten frame. Show **1** counter missing.
Write the number.

Dear Family: Help your child make a ten frame like
those pictured. Let your child put various objects in
the sections of the ten frame and count the objects.

▶ **More Practice, page 390**

Name _____

Use blocks.

A	B

① Sort. Tell how you sorted.
How many are in each box?   A _ _ _ _ _ _   B _ _ _ _ _ _

② Sort again. Tell how you sorted.
How many are in each box?   A _ _ _ _ _ _   B _ _ _ _ _ _

Communication

Talk about it   What other ways can you think of to sort objects?

Dear Family: Help your child become aware of things you sort at home – laundry, groceries, flatware. Involve your child in sorting – making groups of things that are alike in some way.

Draw a line to match.
Circle which has <u>more</u>. mai s

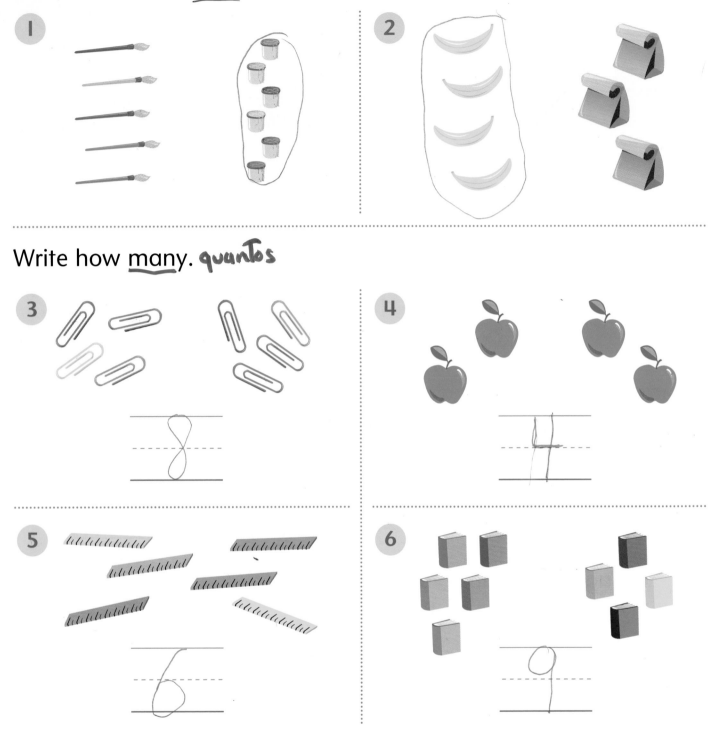

1

2

Write how <u>many</u>. quanTos

3 8

4 4

5 6

6 9

Color to show the number.

7 **5**
five

Name _____

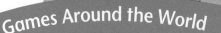

Math World

Children around the world play hopscotch games.

Children in Nigeria play this hopscotch game called **Ta Galagala**. They draw circles called **kurtus** on the ground. They throw a stone or stick called a **kwalo** into one of the circles.

Hopscotch games have many names. In Poland they call hopscotch **Klassa**. Children say **Jumby** in Trinidad.

Internet

Explore Houghton Mifflin's **Education Place Math Center.** http://www.eduplace.com

© Houghton Mifflin Company

▶ **Turn the page for directions.**

You need:
- chalk
- a stone

Try this!

Make your own Ta Galagala pattern.
Draw eight circles on the ground.
Use the pattern in the picture as a guide.

 Dear Family: As you play "Ta Galagala" (TAH GAH LAH GAH LAH) at home, encourage children to say the numbers of the circles as they jump into them.

How to Play

1. Throw the "kwalo" (KWEHL loh) into circle 1.

2. Hop over circle 1 into circle 2 and then into circle 3. Jump into circles 4 and 5 with one foot in each. Hop into circle 6 and then jump, with one foot landing in circle 7 and one foot landing in circle 8.

3. Clap your hands and then turn, jumping to face the other way.

4. Hop back. Hop over circle 1. Turn around and pick up the kwalo.

5. Throw the kwalo into circle 2 and hop through again, this time hopping over circle 2.

6. Continue this way until you've gone through the whole pattern. If you miss a circle, or hop inside a circle with the kwalo, your turn ends, and another player begins.

Cooperative Learning

Name _____

Use a crayon. Work in groups.
Are you wearing shoes that strap, tie, or slip on?

Color **1** box for each child's shoes.

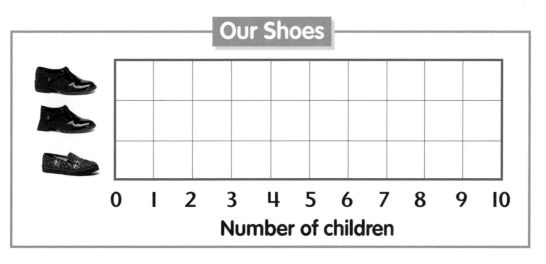

Our Shoes

| | 0 | 1 | 2 | 3 | 4 | 5 | 6 | 7 | 8 | 9 | 10 |

Number of children

Circle the answer.

Which row has the most?   Which row has the fewest?

Communication

Share How can you tell which kind of shoes the most children are wearing? the fewest?

Work in groups.
Look at the **graph**.
How many are in your classroom?
Color a box for each one you find.

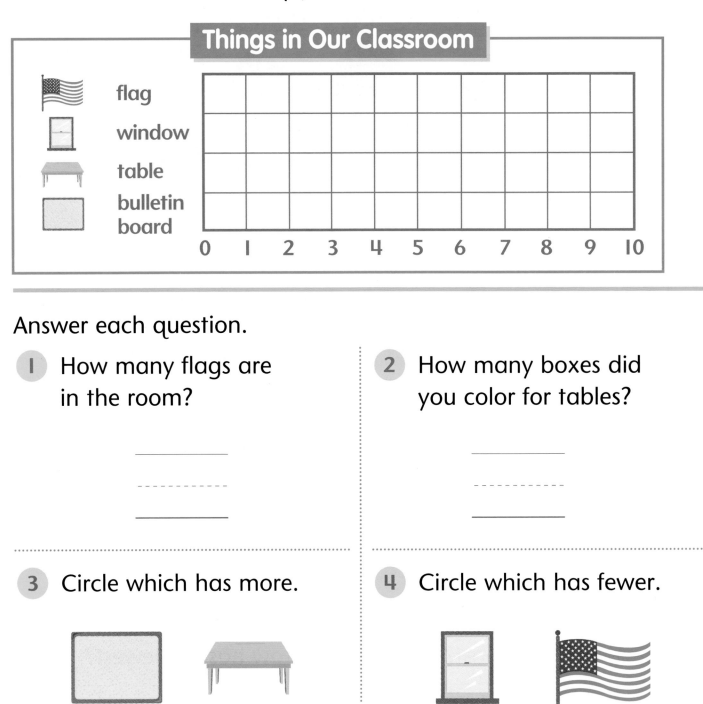

Things in Our Classroom

| | flag |
| window |
| table |
| bulletin board |

0 1 2 3 4 5 6 7 8 9 10

Answer each question.

1 How many flags are in the room?

_____

2 How many boxes did you color for tables?

_____

3 Circle which has more.

4 Circle which has fewer.

Dear Family: Help your child count numbers of objects in your home – doors, sinks, wastebaskets, or tables. Encourage your child to draw a graph of the results.

Name _____

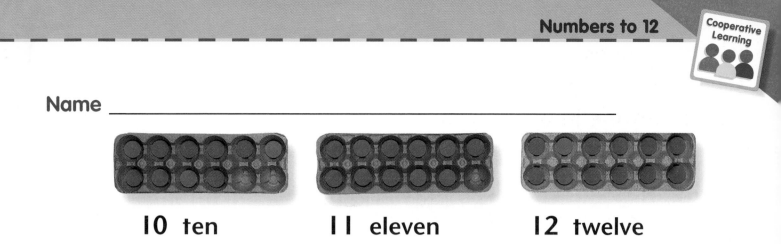

10 ten   **11** eleven   **12** twelve

Work with a partner.
Put counters on the egg carton.
Write how many.

1 _____   2 _____   3 _____   4 _____

Draw dots. Write how many.

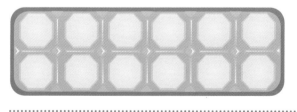   _____

© Houghton Mifflin Company

Communication

Talk about it   Show your partner how you counted.

Circle the egg carton that shows the number.
Write how many.

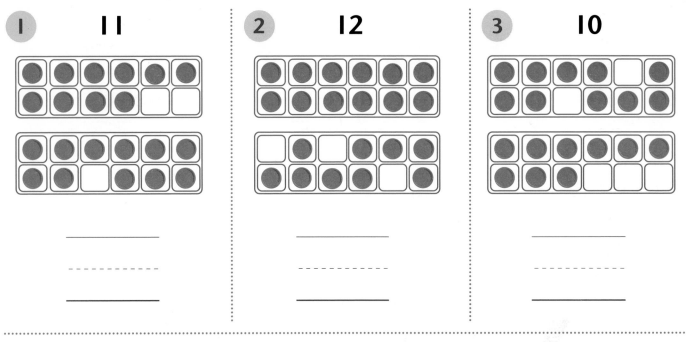

1   11

2   12

3   10

_____

_____

_____

Mixed Review

Write how many.

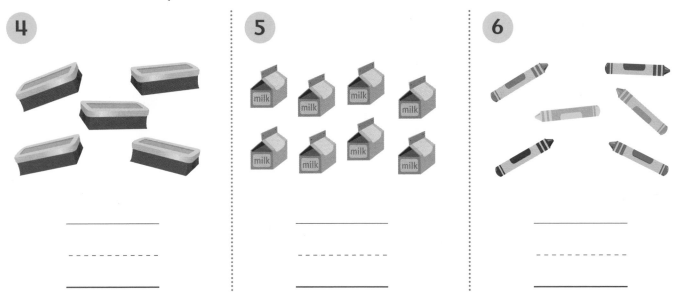

4

5

6

_____

_____

_____

Name _____

Listen to the story. 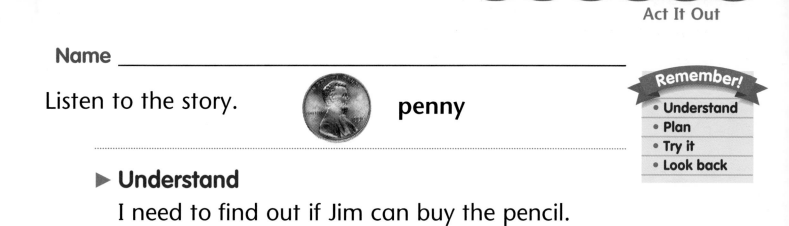 **penny**

▶ **Understand**

I need to find out if Jim can buy the pencil.

▶ **Plan**

I can act it out with pennies.

▶ **Try it**

6 is more than **4**.

▶ **Look back**

Jim can buy the pencil.
My answer makes sense.

Listen to the story. Act it out with pennies.

I have	Notebook costs

Can you buy the notebook? Circle the answer.   Yes   No

Act it out.
Circle which item you can buy.
Circle the pennies you spend.

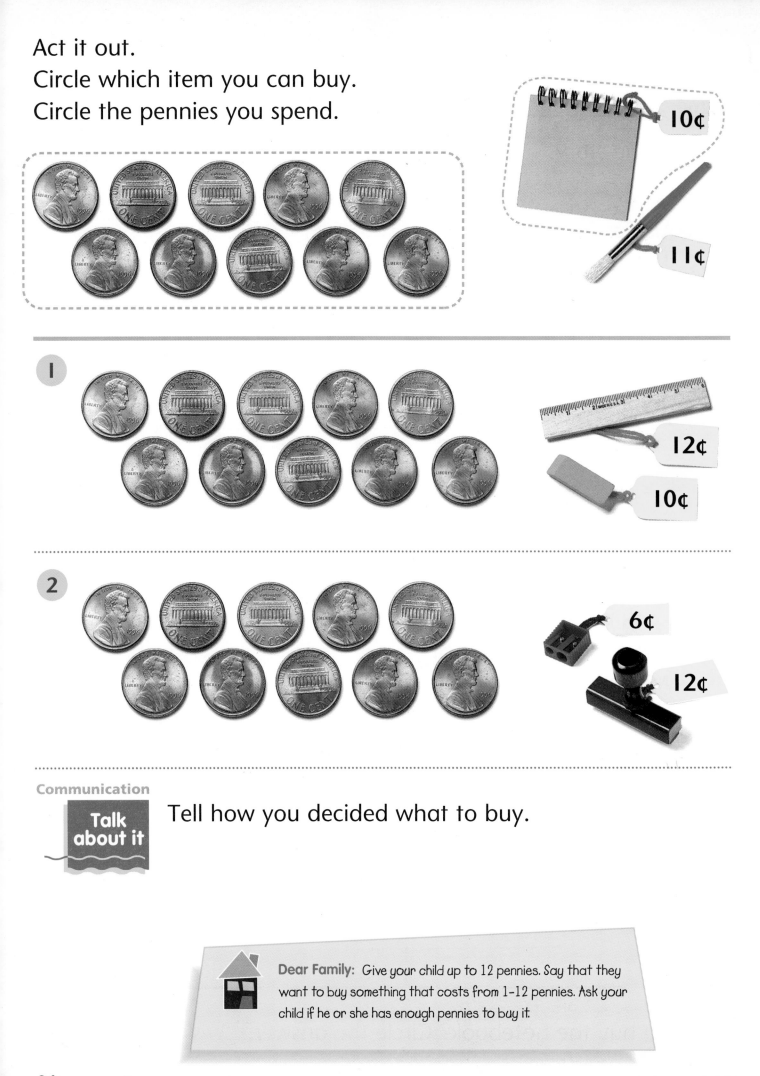

1

12¢

10¢

2

6¢

12¢

Communication

Talk about it

Tell how you decided what to buy.

Dear Family: Give your child up to 12 pennies. Say that they want to buy something that costs from 1-12 pennies. Ask your child if he or she has enough pennies to buy it.

Name _____

1 2 3 4 5 6 7 8 9 10 11 12

The number **4** is **between 3** and **5**. What number is between **9** and **11**?

Write the number.

1 Is **2** closer to **4** or **8** ? ___4___

2 Is **10** closer to **6** or **11** ? _____
perto

3 Which number is between **6** and **8** ? _____
entre

4 Which number is between **5** and **7** ? _____
entre

5 Which number comes just after **11** ? _____

6 Which number comes just before **9** ? _____

Dear Family: Make number cards from 1–10, and let your child put them in order. Turn over a few cards. Have your child tell you what the missing numbers are.

▶ **More Practice, page 391**

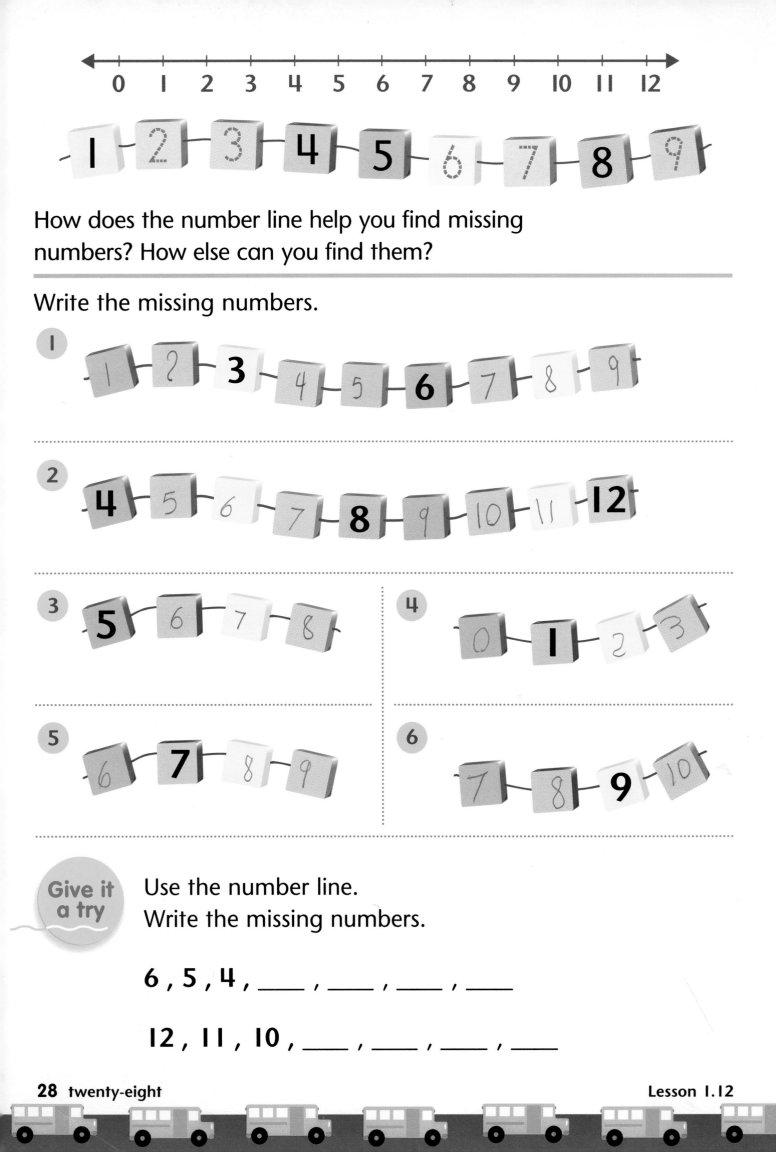

How does the number line help you find missing numbers? How else can you find them?

Write the missing numbers.

1. 1 2 3 4 5 6 7 8 9

2. 4 5 6 7 8 9 10 11 12

3. 5 6 7 8

4. 0 1 2 3

5. 6 7 8 9

6. 7 8 9 10

Give it a try

Use the number line.
Write the missing numbers.

6 , 5 , 4 , ___ , ___ , ___ , ___

12 , 11 , 10 , ___ , ___ , ___ , ___

Name _____

1 Put an X on **8**.
Circle **6**.

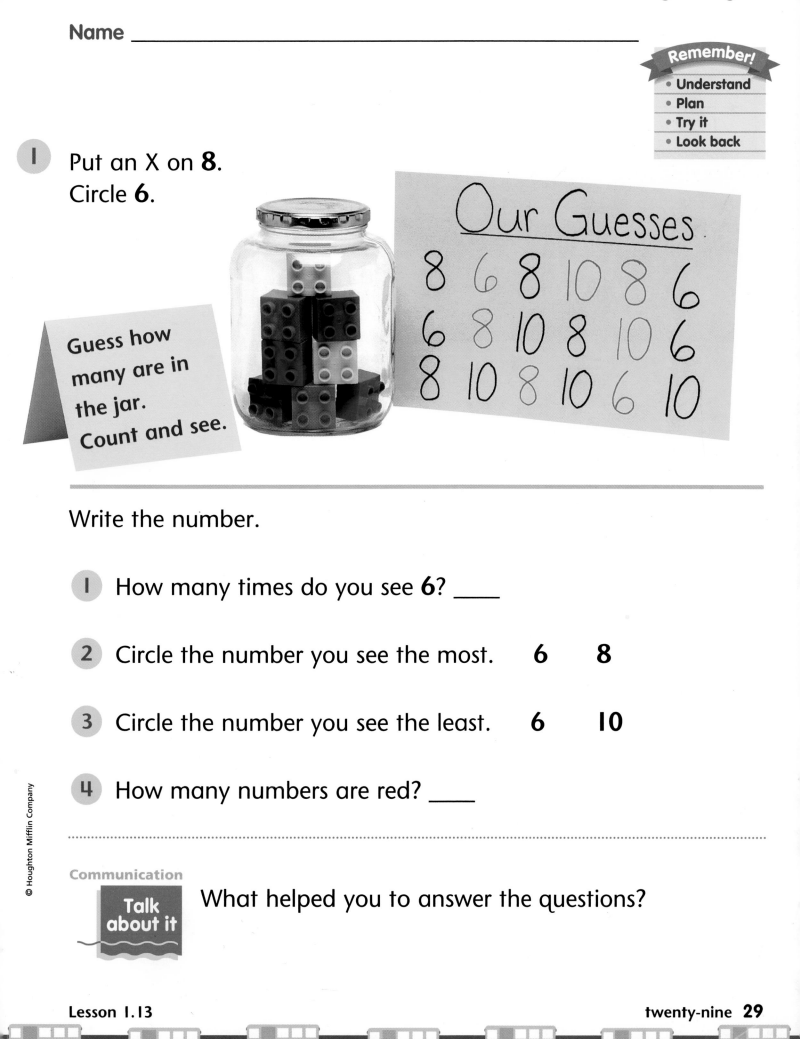

Guess how many are in the jar. Count and see.

Our Guesses
8 6 8 10 8 6
6 8 10 8 10 6
8 10 8 10 6 10

Write the number.

1 How many times do you see **6**? _____

2 Circle the number you see the most.   **6   8**

3 Circle the number you see the least.   **6   10**

4 How many numbers are red? _____

Communication

Talk about it   What helped you to answer the questions?

Look at the picture.

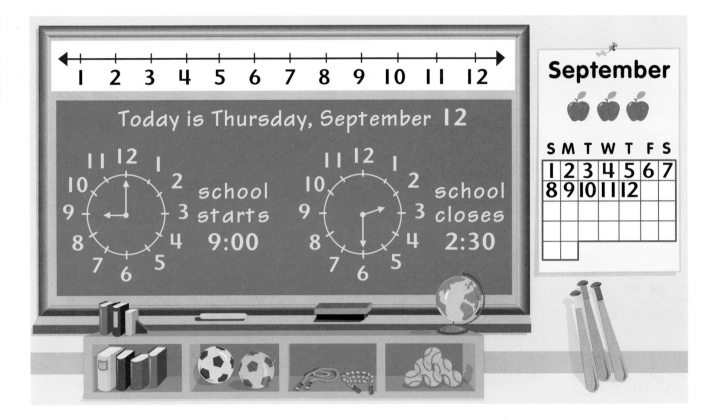

Answer the questions.

1. How many times do you see **5**? ____

2. How many times do you see **9**? ____

3. How many books do you see? ____

4. Which group has more?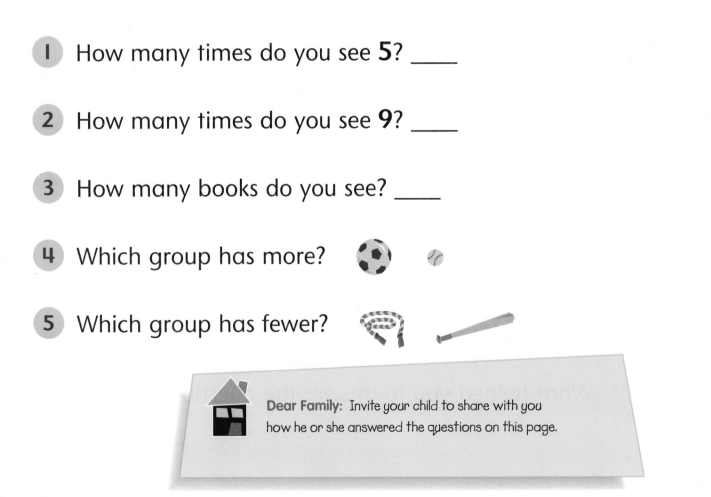

5. Which group has fewer?

Dear Family: Invite your child to share with you
how he or she answered the questions on this page.

Name _____

Write how many.

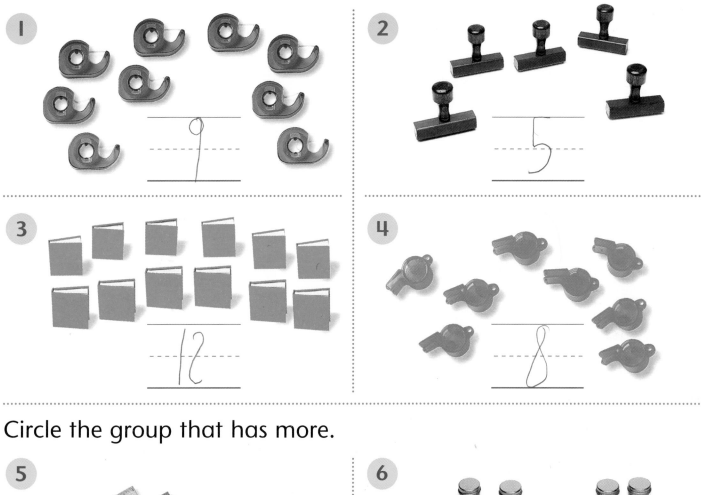

1 9	2 5
3 12	4 8

Circle the group that has more.

5 14	6 14

Circle the group that has fewer.

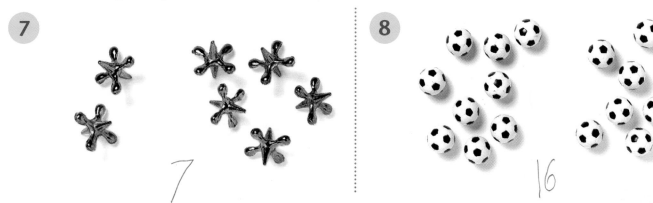

7 7	8 16

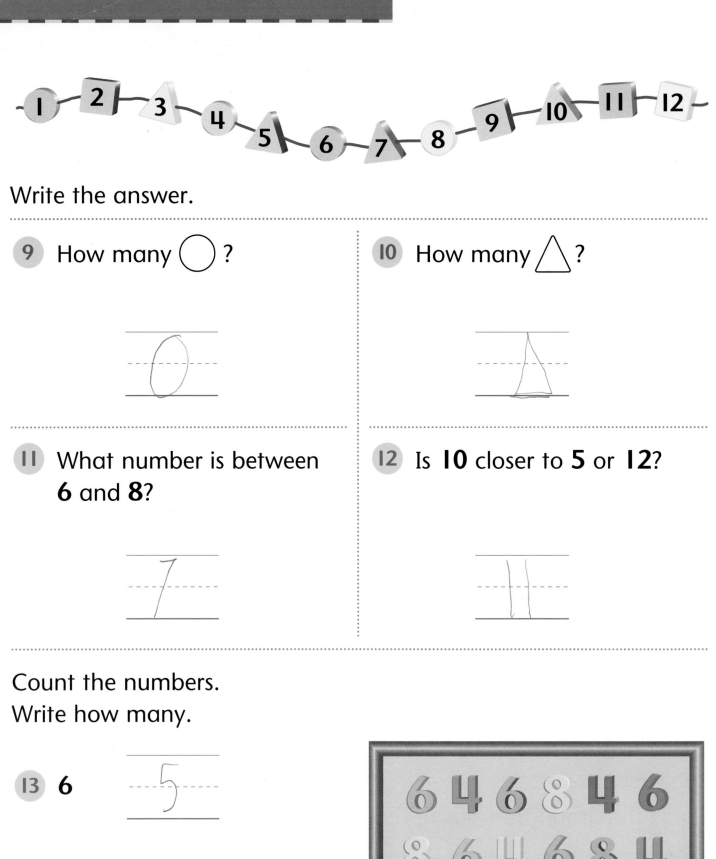

Write the answer.

9 How many ◯ ?

0

10 How many △ ?

△

11 What number is between 6 and 8?

7

12 Is 10 closer to 5 or 12?

11

Count the numbers.
Write how many.

13 6   5

14 4   5

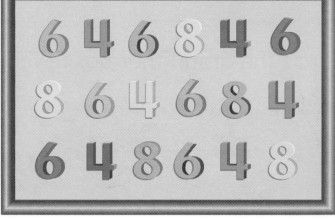

6 4 6 8 4 6
8 6 4 6 8 4
6 4 8 6 4 8

Our Names

Name _____

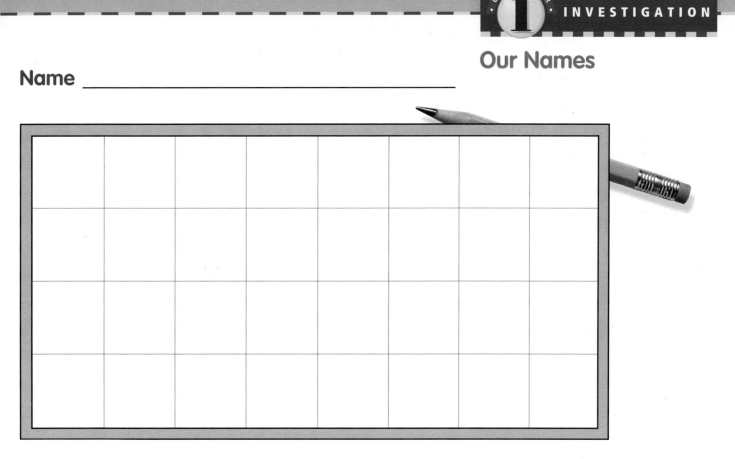

Write these names in the grid above.

Carmen   Azi
Tadashi   Alicia

Compare the names.

1 Which name is longest? _____

2 Which name is shortest? _____

3 Which names have the same number of letters?

_____

_____

4 Which names begin with the same letter?

_____

Internet
Visit Houghton Mifflin's
Education Place Math Center.
http://www.eduplace.com

Write your name in the grid.
How many letters
does your name have? _____

Write names of classmates
that have the same number
of letters in the grid.

Chapter 1

Addition Facts Through 6

Literature

The Very Nicest Place
Anonymous

Read Aloud Anthology p. 24
Theme Connection
Places We Know

My Family

See what I can do by the end of this chapter.

Use What You Know

How many adults are in the family?
How many children are in the family?
How can you find out the number
of people in all?

Listen for the different places to live.
Use cubes to act out the poem.

Dear Family: Practice adding and subtracting by discussing how many people and animals live in your home. Use the workmat to illustrate your discussion.

Name _____

Use counters and crayons.
Plan your picture with counters.

1 Show **3**. Draw its parts.

2 Show **6**. Draw its parts.

1 Show **4**. Draw its parts.

2 Show **5**. Draw its parts.

Talk about it

Look at a friend's page. How did your friend show the parts of the numbers?

 **Dear Family:** Today we learned about the parts that make a whole. Find examples around your home, such as four sticks in a whole package of butter.

Name _____

Use counters.
Listen to the story.
Act it out.
Write how many in all.

1 ____   2 ____   3 ____

Communication

How do you find how many there are in all?

Use counters.
Listen to the story.
Act it out.
Write how many in all.

1 ____ 2 ____ 3 ____ 4 ____

Give it a try   Make up your own story. Draw people in the picture. Write how many in all.

Dear Family: Encourage your child to use this page to tell you addition stories.

Name _____

Use red cubes and blue cubes.

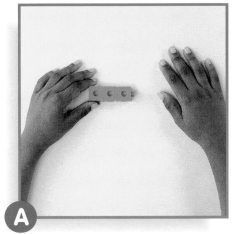

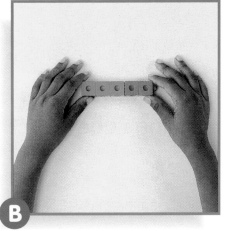

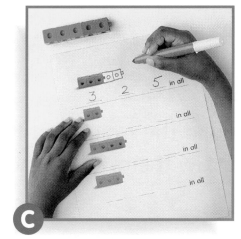

A Make one part with cubes.

B **Add** cubes for the other part.

C Draw them. Write how many in all.

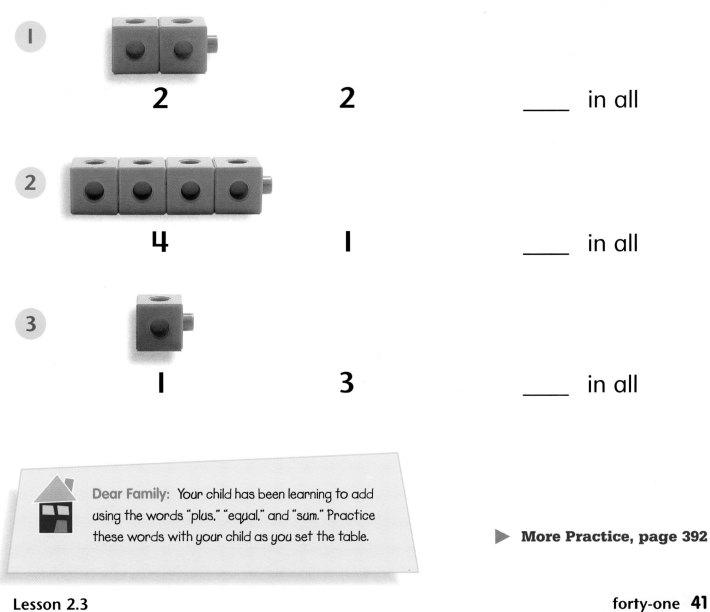

1. **2**   **2**   ____ in all

2. **4**   **1**   ____ in all

3. **1**   **3**   ____ in all

🏠 **Dear Family:** Your child has been learning to add using the words "plus," "equal," and "sum." Practice these words with your child as you set the table.

▶ **More Practice, page 392**

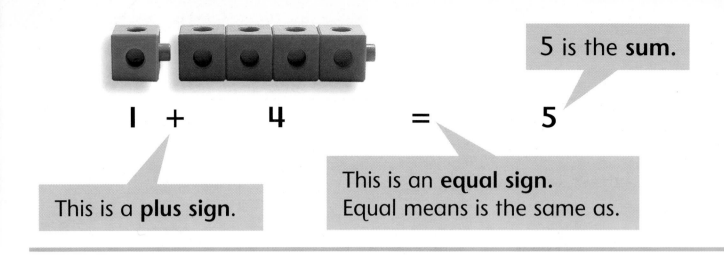

I + 4 = 5

5 is the **sum**.

This is a **plus sign**.

This is an **equal sign**.
Equal means is the same as.

Build the train. Add the missing cubes.
Draw them. Write the sum.

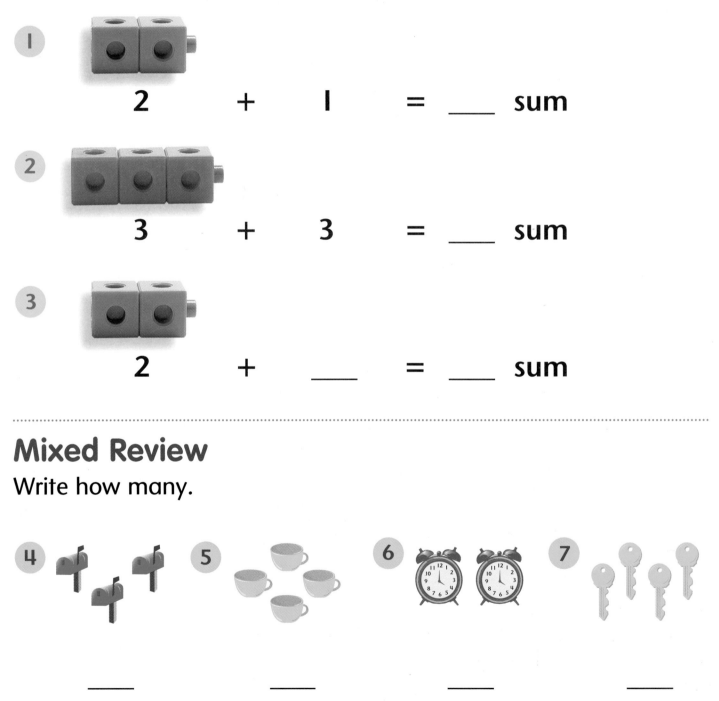

1   2   +   1   =   ___ sum

2   3   +   3   =   ___ sum

3   2   +   ___   =   ___ sum

Mixed Review

Write how many.

4   ____

5   ____

6   ____

7   ____

Name _____

José and Sheri are downstairs.

Maria is upstairs.

How many people are in the house?

▶ **Understand**

I need to find the number of people in the house.

▶ **Plan**

I could act it out with counters.

▶ **Try it**

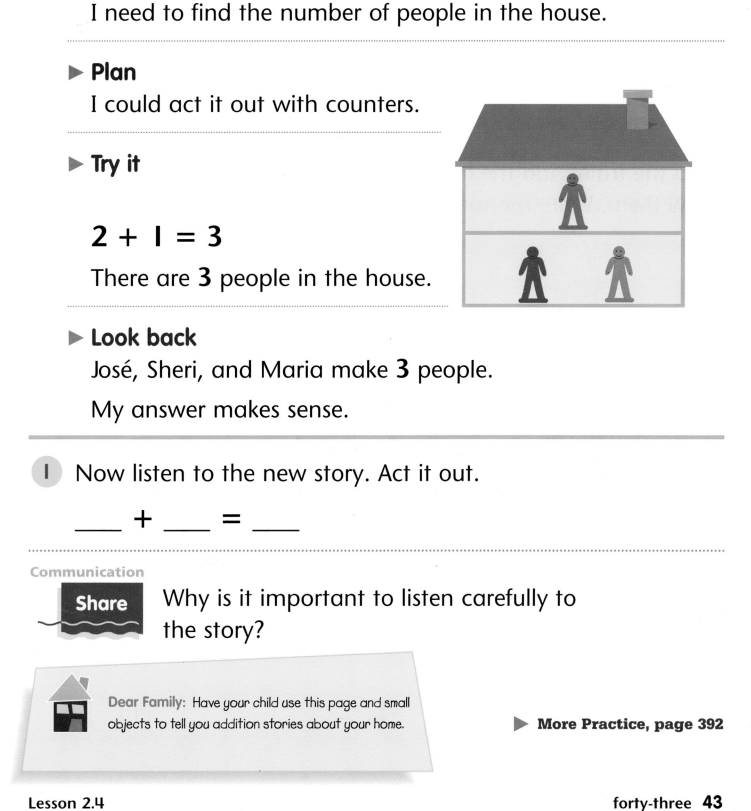

$2 + 1 = 3$

There are **3** people in the house.

▶ **Look back**

José, Sheri, and Maria make **3** people.

My answer makes sense.

1 Now listen to the new story. Act it out.

___ + ___ = ___

Communication

Share Why is it important to listen carefully to the story?

Dear Family: Have your child use this page and small objects to tell you addition stories about your home.

▶ **More Practice, page 392**

Use people counters.

1 Show **5**. Draw its parts.

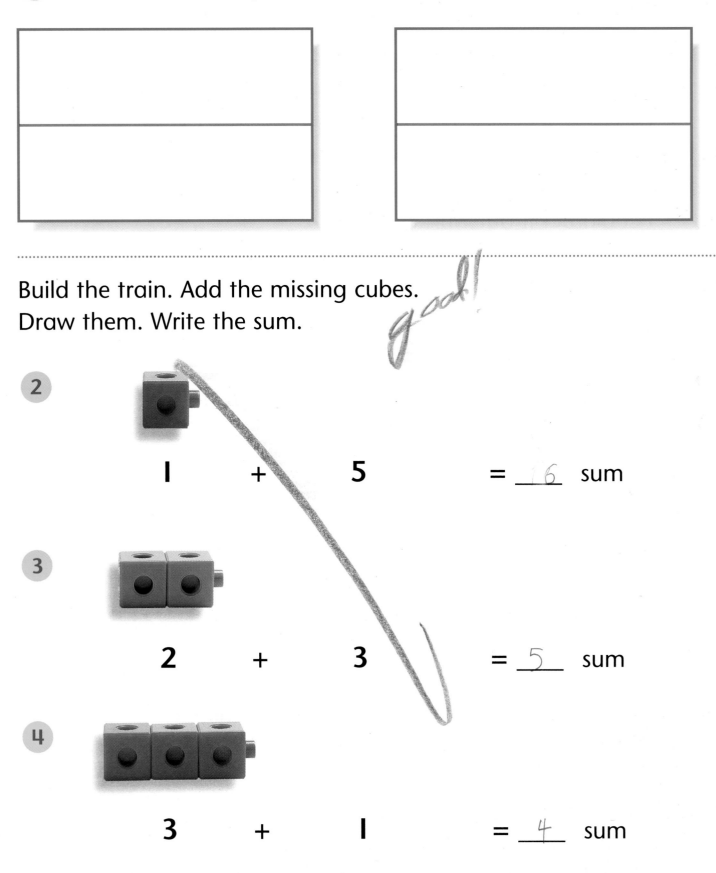

Build the train. Add the missing cubes.
Draw them. Write the sum.

good!

2

1 + 5 = _6_ sum

3

2 + 3 = _5_ sum

4

3 + 1 = _4_ sum

Name _____

Math World

Children around the world play all kinds of marble games.

Children all over the world collect marbles. In **Australia** children play a marble game called **Bounce Eye**.

Children use one of their marbles to try and knock another player's marbles out of a circle.

Internet

Explore Houghton Mifflin's
Education Place Math Center.
http://www.eduplace.com

▶ **Turn the page for directions.**

Did you know?

Marbles can be made from stones, glass, clay, wood, plastic and nuts.

Try this!

Set up your own marbles game.

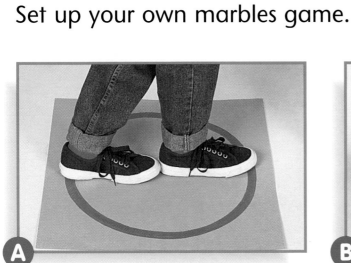

A Draw a circle on a piece of paper. Two shoes should fit across the center of the circle.

B Place the paper on a rug. Give each player **5** marbles.

Dear Family: Follow the directions to play "Bounce Eye." As you play, you can make up simple addition stories for your child to solve. For example: "You have 2 marbles in your pile, and there are 3 inside the circle. How many marbles are there in all?"

How to Play:

1. Each player puts 2–3 marbles inside the circle. Players sit around the circle.

2. Take turns. One at a time, drop a marble onto the pile of marbles.

3. If a player knocks a marble out of the circle, he or she gets to keep it and go again. If a player does not knock a marble out of the circle, that player's turn is over.

4. Play until all the marbles are knocked out of the circle. The player with the most marbles starts the next game.

Name _____

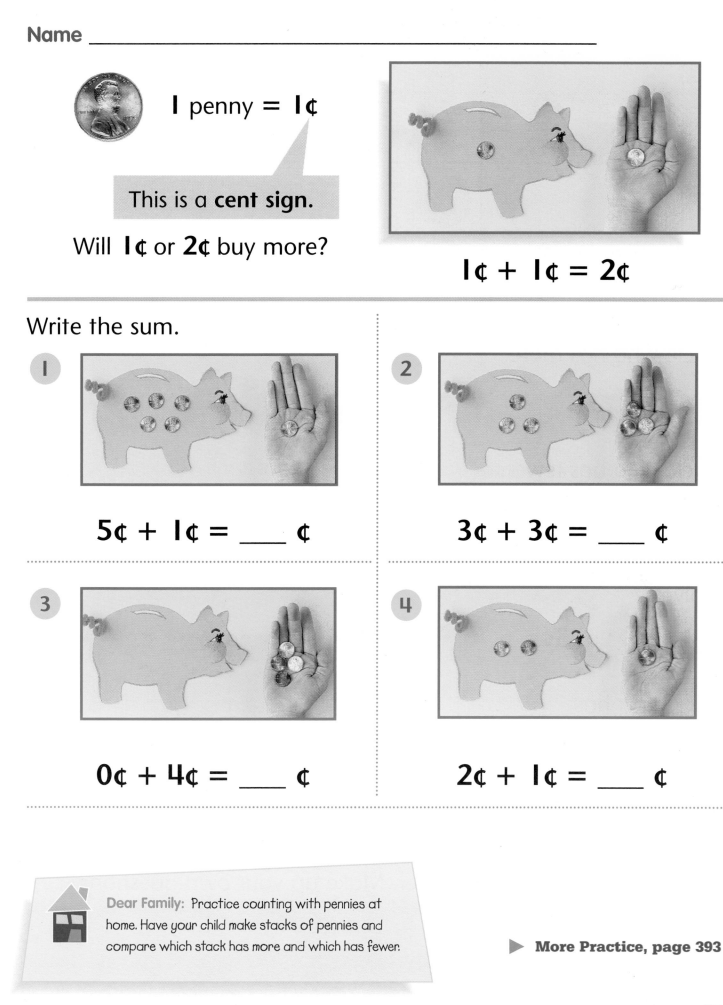

1 penny = 1¢

This is a **cent sign**.

Will **1¢** or **2¢** buy more?

1¢ + 1¢ = 2¢

Write the sum.

1   5¢ + 1¢ = ___ ¢

2   3¢ + 3¢ = ___ ¢

3   0¢ + 4¢ = ___ ¢

4   2¢ + 1¢ = ___ ¢

Dear Family: Practice counting with pennies at home. Have your child make stacks of pennies and compare which stack has more and which has fewer.

▶ **More Practice, page 393**

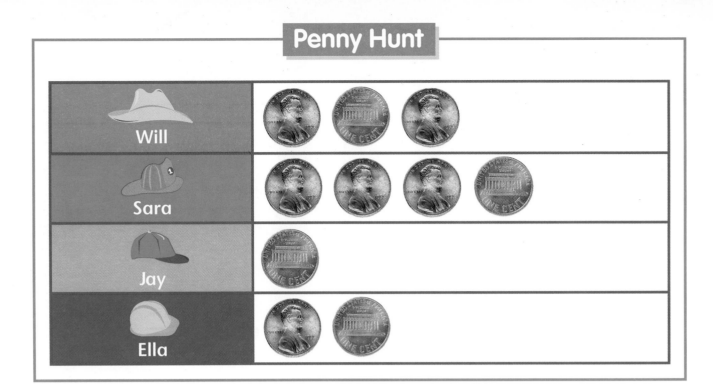

Penny Hunt

Will	
Sara	
Jay	
Ella	

Circle who has more.

1 Will or Jay

2 Sara or Jay

Circle who has fewer.

3 Ella or Will

4 Jay or Ella

Solve.

5 Will has **3¢**.

Ella has ____ ¢.

How many pennies do

they have in all? ____

6 Jay has ____ ¢.

Will has ____ ¢.

How many pennies do

they have in all? ____

Give it a try Work with a partner. Make up your own questions using the graph.

Name _____

Use a calculator.

Press [+] to add.

Write the sum.

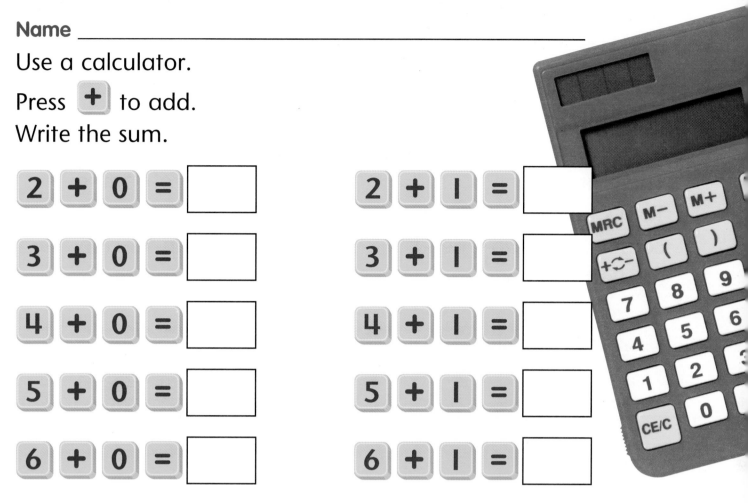

2 + 0 = ☐   2 + 1 = ☐

3 + 0 = ☐   3 + 1 = ☐

4 + 0 = ☐   4 + 1 = ☐

5 + 0 = ☐   5 + 1 = ☐

6 + 0 = ☐   6 + 1 = ☐

Talk about the patterns you see.

Continue the patterns.

Write the next **3** addition sentences.

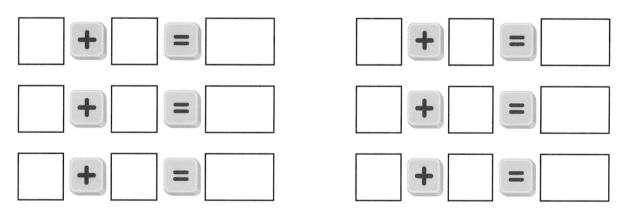

☐ + ☐ = ☐   ☐ + ☐ = ☐

☐ + ☐ = ☐   ☐ + ☐ = ☐

☐ + ☐ = ☐   ☐ + ☐ = ☐

Give it a try   Make a pattern by adding **2**. Talk about the pattern you see.

You may use people counters.
Read and listen.
Write a number sentence.

Remember!
- Understand
- Plan
- Try it
- Look back

1 There are **2** friends at Tom's house. Now **3** more come. How many friends are visiting Tom?

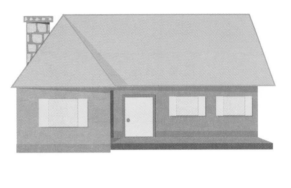

___ + ___ = ___

2 Ming and Scott are in the pool. Now **2** more children jump in. How many children are in the pool?

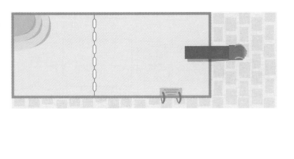

___ + ___ = ___

Draw a story for the number sentence.

5 + 1 = 6

Dear Family: Solve everyday addition problems with your child. For example, I have four apples in my bag. I buy two more. How many does that make?

▶ **More Practice, page 393**

Name _____

Use the map.
Start at the gate each time.
Count each rock as one step.

Write the answer.

1 You take _____ steps to pet the 🐶 .

2 You take _____ steps to visit the 🐝 .

3 Pick a 💐 . Then feed the 🦆 .

Write the number sentence. _____ + _____ = _____ steps

Give it a try Visit two things on the map.
Write the number sentence.
Talk about what you visit.

Lee wants to find all the cats.
Use the picture. Follow the pawprint paths.
Write how many cats you find.

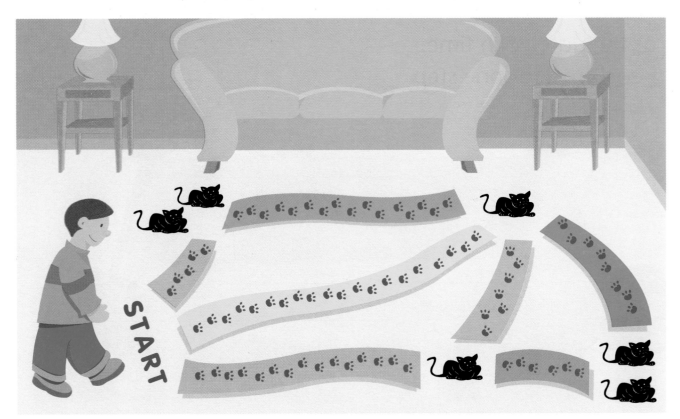

	Paths				Cats
1	🐾	🐾	🐾		3
2	🐾	🐾	🐾	🐾	
3	🐾	🐾	🐾	🐾	

How can Lee find all of the cats?

Draw the path on the map.

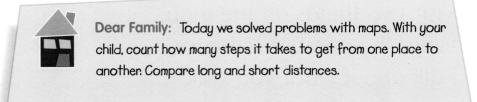

Dear Family: Today we solved problems with maps. With your child, count how many steps it takes to get from one place to another. Compare long and short distances.

Name _____

Write the sum.

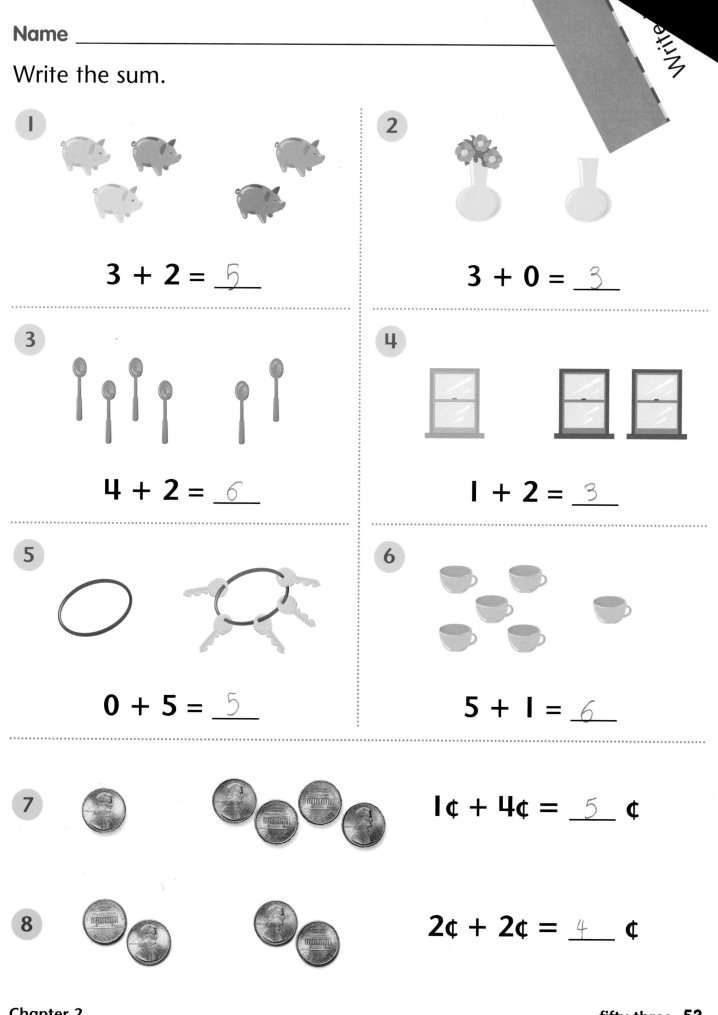

1

$3 + 2 =$ _5_

2

$3 + 0 =$ _3_

3

$4 + 2 =$ _6_

4

$1 + 2 =$ _3_

5

$0 + 5 =$ _5_

6

$5 + 1 =$ _6_

7

$1¢ + 4¢ =$ _5_ ¢

8

$2¢ + 2¢ =$ _4_ ¢

the sum.

9 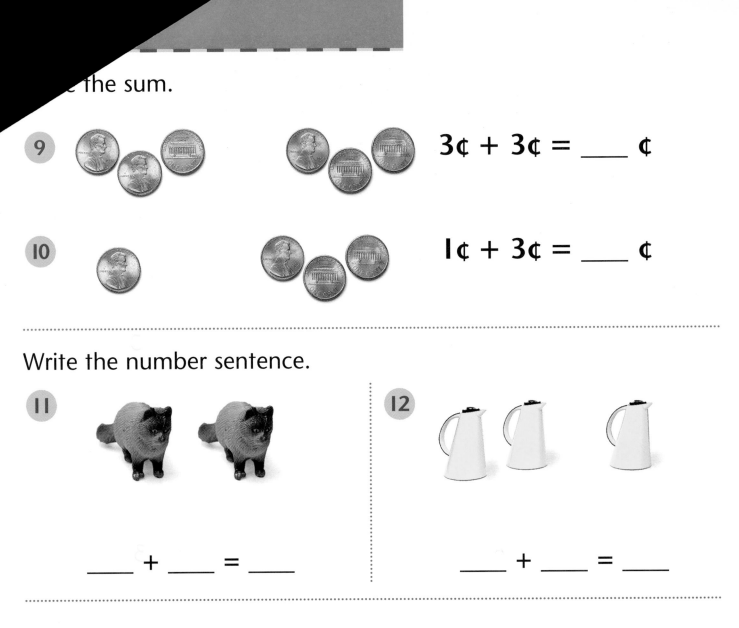 $3¢ + 3¢ =$ _____ ¢

10 $1¢ + 3¢ =$ _____ ¢

Write the number sentence.

11

_____ + _____ = _____

12

_____ + _____ = _____

Write the number sentence.

13 Anita has **3¢** in her pocket. Her mother gives her **2¢**. How much does Anita have in all?

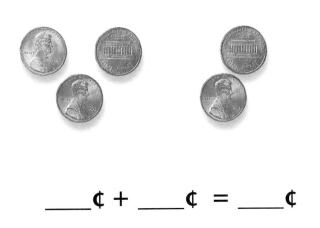

_____ ¢ + _____ ¢ = _____ ¢

14 Lisa has **4** crayons in a box. Another box has **0**. How many crayons are there in all?

_____ + _____ = _____

Name _____

$$1 + 3 = 4$$

What other addition sentences can you write about this family?

___ + ___ = ___

___ + ___ = ___

© Houghton Mifflin Company

Internet

Visit Houghton Mifflin's
Education Place Math Center.
http://www.eduplace.com

Draw a picture of your family.

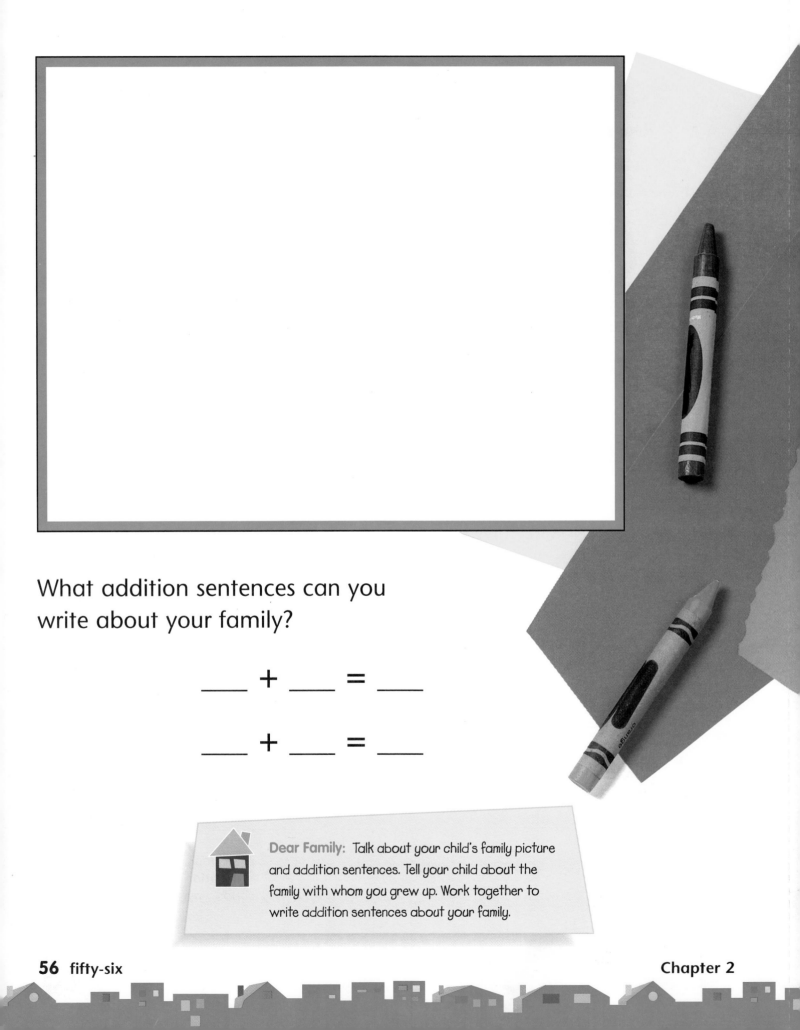

What addition sentences can you
write about your family?

___ + ___ = ___

___ + ___ = ___

Dear Family: Talk about your child's family picture
and addition sentences. Tell your child about the
family with whom you grew up. Work together to
write addition sentences about your family.

Subtraction Facts Through 6

Literature

Every Time 1 Climb a Tree
By David McCord

Read Aloud Anthology p. 26
Theme Connection
Outdoor Fun

See what I can do by the end of this chapter.

Use What You Know

How many berries did the mouse collect?

How many nuts did it collect?

How can you tell which pile has more?

Listen to what happens in the tree.
Use people counters to act it out.

Dear Family: Talk about the different outdoor activities you and your child can do near your home. In what season do you do the most outdoor activities?

Name _____

Listen to the story.
Act it out with counters.
Write how many.

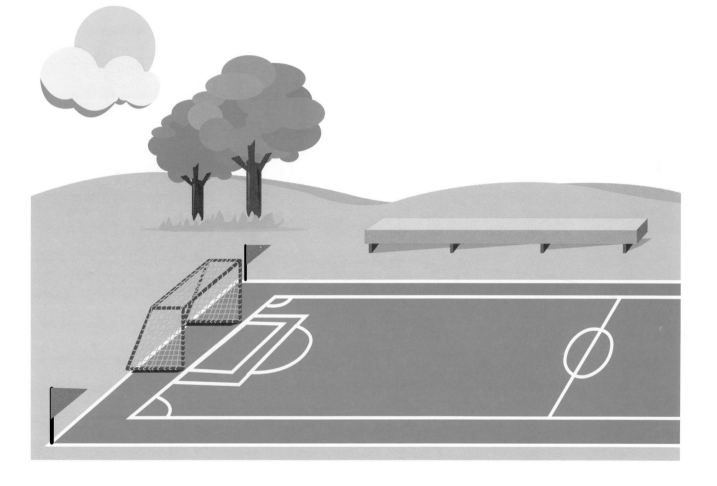

1 _____

2 _____

3 _____

Communication

Draw

Make up your own story. Draw a picture.
Write how many.

Lesson 3.1

fifty-nine **59**

Listen to the story.
Act it out with counters.
Write how many.

1 ____   **2** ____   **3** ____   **4** ____

Name _____

Listen to the story.

▶ **Understand**

I need to know how many children are left.

▶ **Plan**

I can draw a picture.

▶ **Try it**

I draw **3** children.

I cross out one.

2 children are left.

▶ **Look back**

$3 - 1 = 2$

My answer makes sense.

Listen to the story.
Draw a picture to solve.

_____ children

Communication

 **Share**   How does drawing a picture help you solve
the exercise?

▶ **More Practice, page 394**

Make the whole with cubes.
Take part away. Cross out.
Write the difference.

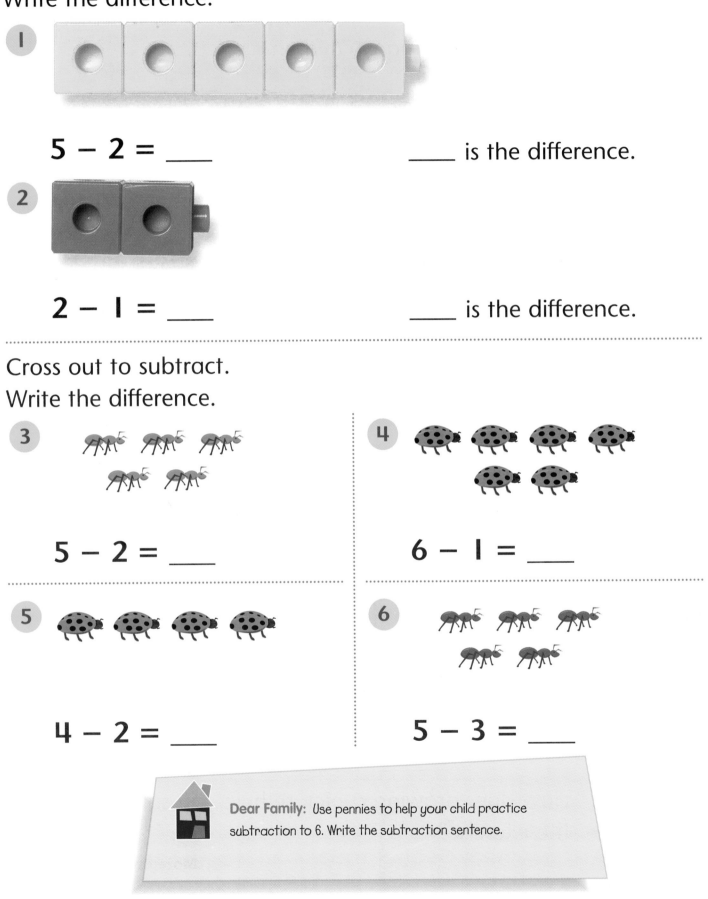

1

5 – 2 = ___   ___ is the difference.

2

2 – 1 = ___   ___ is the difference.

Cross out to subtract.
Write the difference.

3

5 – 2 = ___

4

6 – 1 = ___

5

4 – 2 = ___

6

5 – 3 = ___

Dear Family: Use pennies to help your child practice
subtraction to 6. Write the subtraction sentence.

Name _____

Math World

Children play jacks games in many places around the world.

Most jacks in the United States today are star-shaped pieces of metal. Children in **Brazil** use five small stones to play a jacks game called **Cinco Marias**.

Children play by subtracting stones from their piles while they toss and catch another stone.

Internet

Explore Houghton Mifflin's **Education Place Math Center.** http://www.eduplace.com

▶ **Turn the page for directions.**

Did you know?

Japanese children use tiny bags of rice, sand, or beans to play jacks.

Try this!

Play the game with **1** or **2** friends.

A Collect **5** stones to use as jacks. Lay **4** of the stones on the floor.

B Toss the fifth stone into the air. Try to pick up one of the stones from the floor.

Dear Family: Use these directions to play "Cinco Marias" (SEENG koh muh REE uhs). To help develop subtraction skills, children can make up subtraction stories as they play.

How to Play:

1. Place 4 stones on the floor and hold 1 stone in your hand.

2. Take turns tossing the stone into the air, picking up 1 stone from the floor, then catching the tossed stone before it hits the ground.

3. Tell how many stones are left. Play the following rounds the same way, but pick up 2, 3, or 4 stones at a time, until all of the stones have been picked up.

4. If the player misses the tossed stone, or picks up the wrong number of stones, the next player begins. When your turn begins, start over with 1. The first player to complete the rounds and pick up all 4 stones begins the next game.

Name _____

Cross out pennies to buy each item.
Write the subtraction sentence.

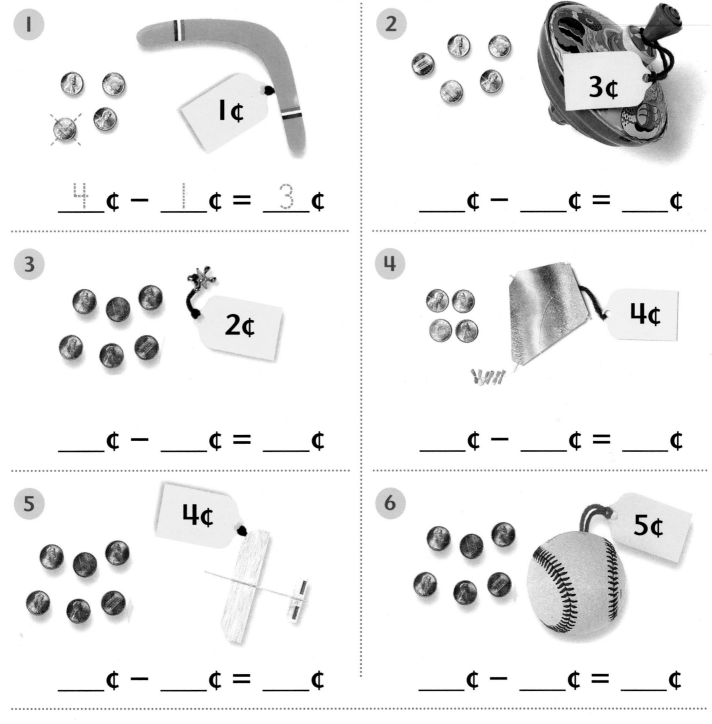

1
___4___ ¢ − ___1___ ¢ = ___3___ ¢

2
_____ ¢ − _____ ¢ = _____ ¢

3
_____ ¢ − _____ ¢ = _____ ¢

4
_____ ¢ − _____ ¢ = _____ ¢

5
_____ ¢ − _____ ¢ = _____ ¢

6
_____ ¢ − _____ ¢ = _____ ¢

Communication

Talk about it

Which costs the most?
Which costs the least?

Work with a partner.
Use pennies to solve the problems.

Juan has **4¢**. He spends **2¢**.
How many pennies does
he have now?

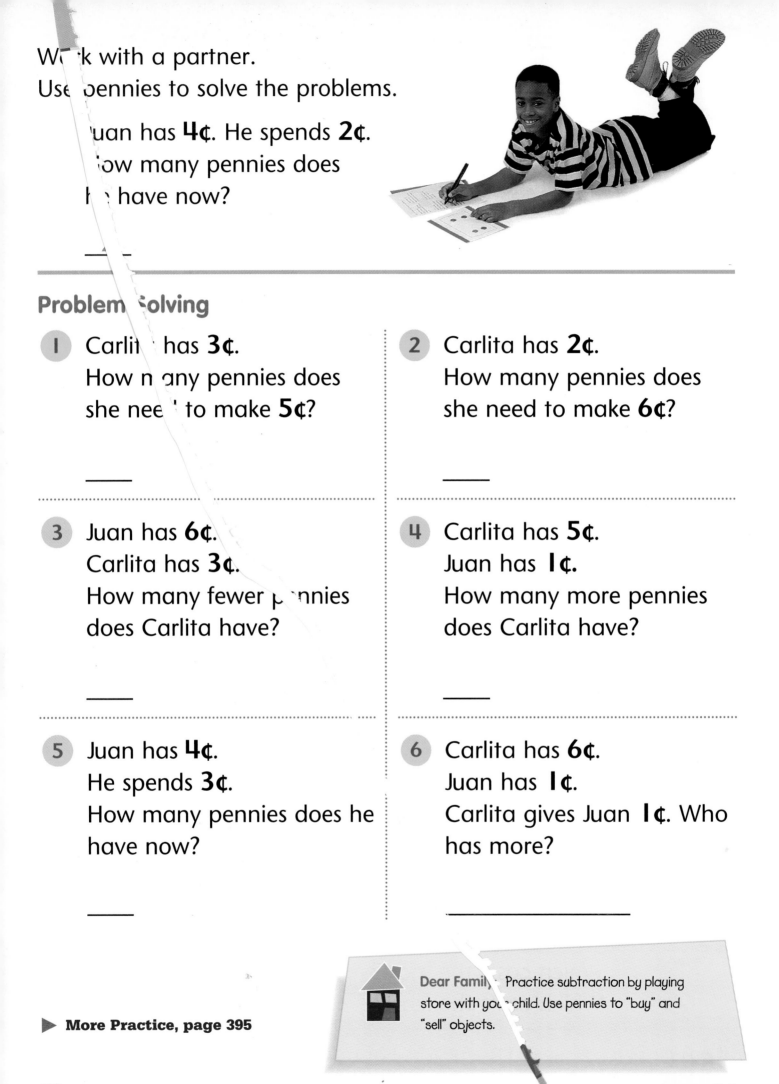

____

Problem Solving

1 Carlita has **3¢**.
How many pennies does
she need to make **5¢**?

____

2 Carlita has **2¢**.
How many pennies does
she need to make **6¢**?

____

3 Juan has **6¢**.
Carlita has **3¢**.
How many fewer pennies
does Carlita have?

____

4 Carlita has **5¢**.
Juan has **1¢**.
How many more pennies
does Carlita have?

____

5 Juan has **4¢**.
He spends **3¢**.
How many pennies does he
have now?

____

6 Carlita has **6¢**.
Juan has **1¢**.
Carlita gives Juan **1¢**. Who
has more?

____

▶ **More Practice, page 395**

Dear Family: Practice subtraction by playing
store with your child. Use pennies to "buy" and
"sell" objects.

Name _____

Work with a partner.
Use a calculator.

Press **−** to subtract.
Write the difference.

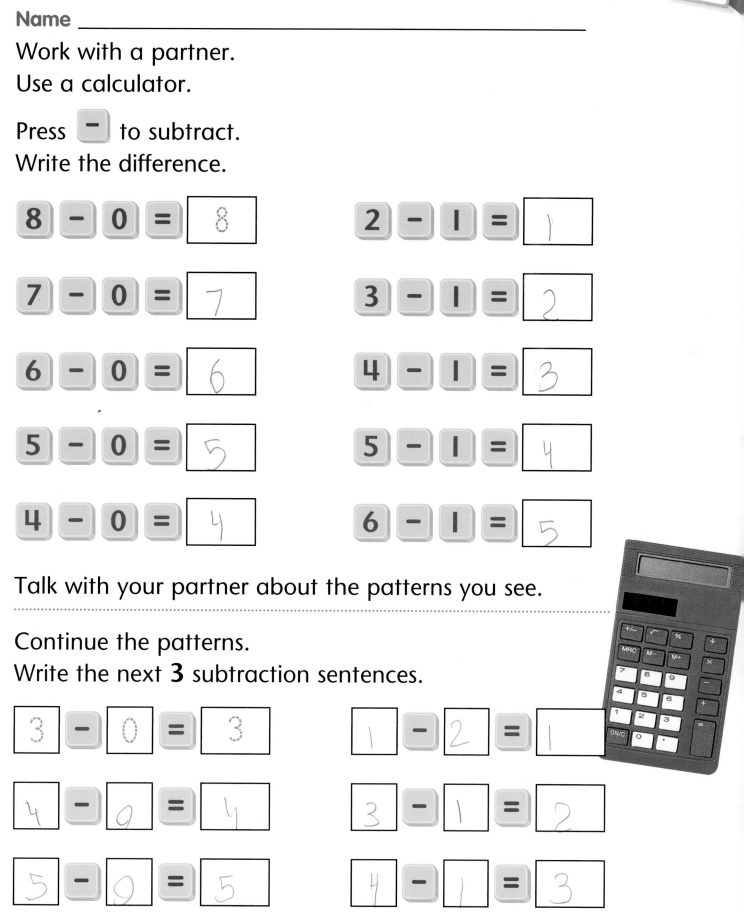

8 − 0 = 8

2 − 1 = 1

7 − 0 = 7

3 − 1 = 2

6 − 0 = 6

4 − 1 = 3

5 − 0 = 5

5 − 1 = 4

4 − 0 = 4

6 − 1 = 5

Talk with your partner about the patterns you see.

Continue the patterns.
Write the next **3** subtraction sentences.

3 − 0 = 3

1 − 2 = 1

4 − 0 = 4

3 − 1 = 2

5 − 0 = 5

4 − 1 = 3

Listen. Solve.
Write the subtraction sentence.

Remember!
- Understand
- Plan
- Try it
- Look back

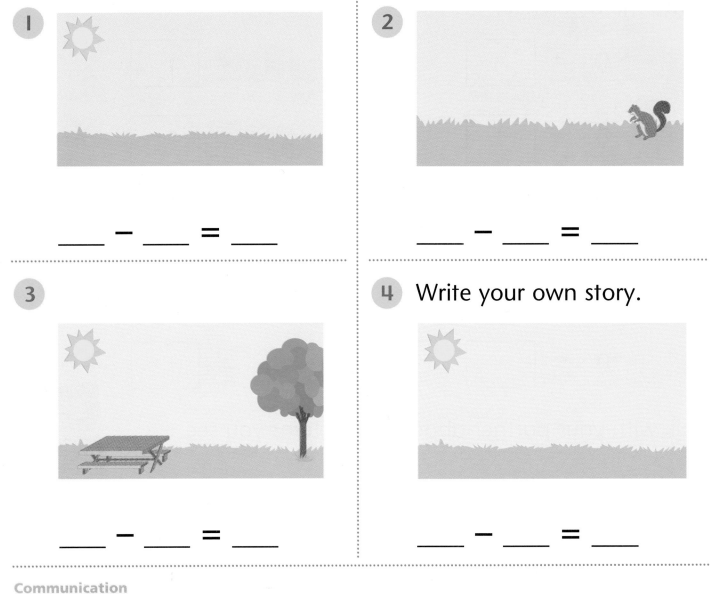

1   ____ − ____ = ____

2   ____ − ____ = ____

3   ____ − ____ = ____

4   Write your own story.

    ____ − ____ = ____

Communication

Share   Share your subtraction story with a partner.

Dear Family: Ask your child to tell you about the subtraction stories from the lesson.

Name _____

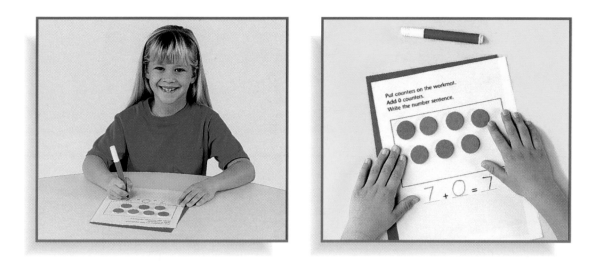

Put counters on the workmat.
Add **0** counters.
Write the number sentence.

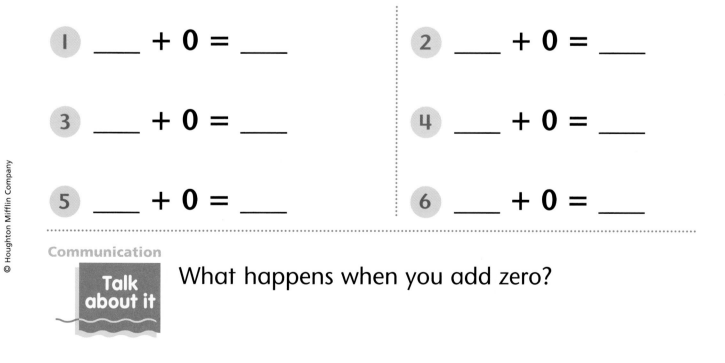

1 ___ + 0 = ___   2 ___ + 0 = ___

3 ___ + 0 = ___   4 ___ + 0 = ___

5 ___ + 0 = ___   6 ___ + 0 = ___

Communication

Talk about it   What happens when you add zero?

Put counters on the workmat.

| Take away **0** counters. Write the number sentence. | Take away all of the counters. Write the number sentence. |

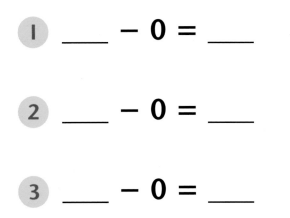

1. ___ − 0 = ___

2. ___ − 0 = ___

3. ___ − 0 = ___

4. ___ − ___ = 0

5. ___ − ___ = 0

6. ___ − ___ = 0

Name _____

Look for a pattern.
Draw. Write the numbers.

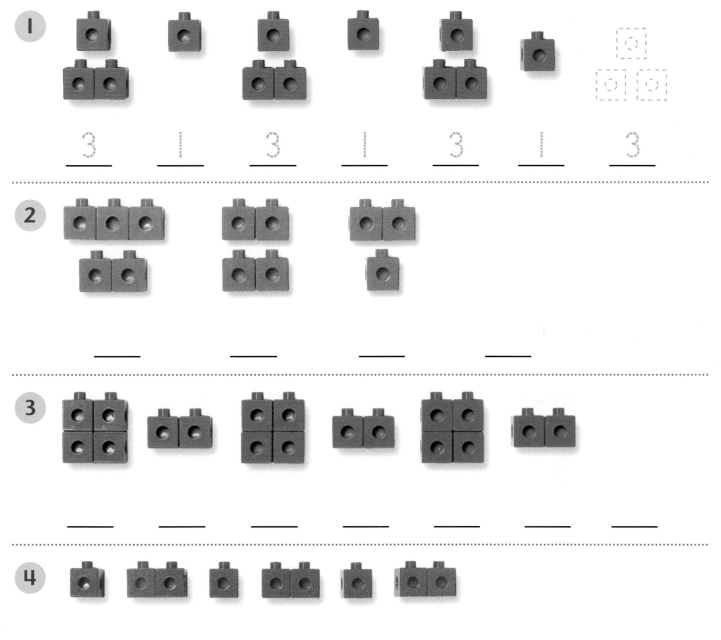

1 3   1   3   1   3   1   3

2 ____   ____   ____   ____

3 ____   ____   ____   ____   ____   ____

4 ____   ____   ____   ____   ____   ____

Communication

Talk about it   What are the patterns?
How would you continue them?

Lesson 3.9   seventy-five **75**

Cross out one cube to make the letter.
Write how many are left.

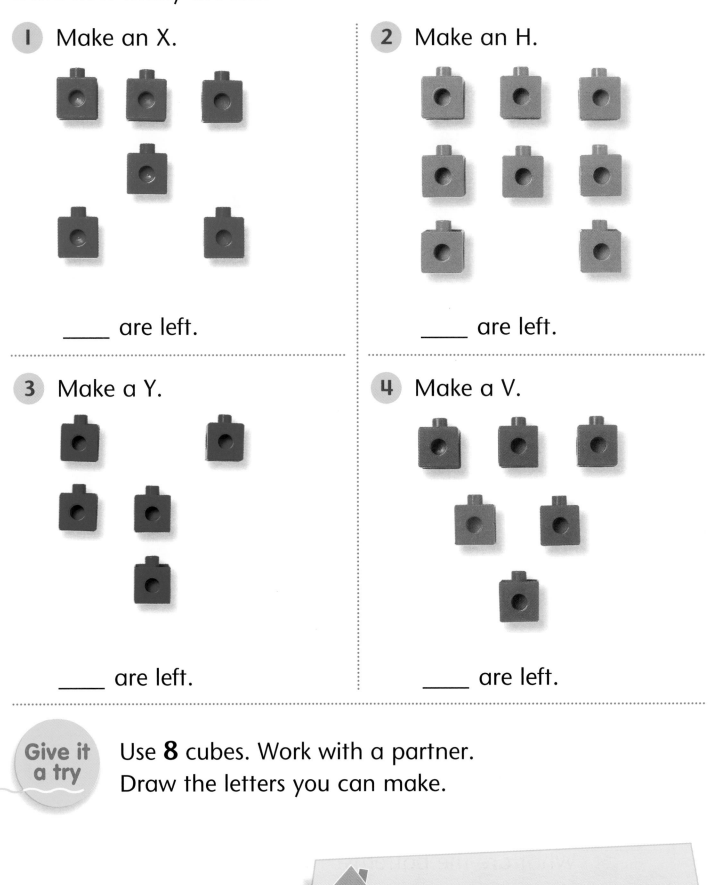

1 Make an X.

_____ are left.

2 Make an H.

_____ are left.

3 Make a Y.

_____ are left.

4 Make a V.

_____ are left.

Give it a try Use **8** cubes. Work with a partner.
Draw the letters you can make.

▶ **More Practice, page 396**

Dear Family: Have your child make patterns with small objects, such as bottle tops, buttons, or coins.

Name _____

Make the whole with cubes. Take part away.
Cross out. Write the difference.

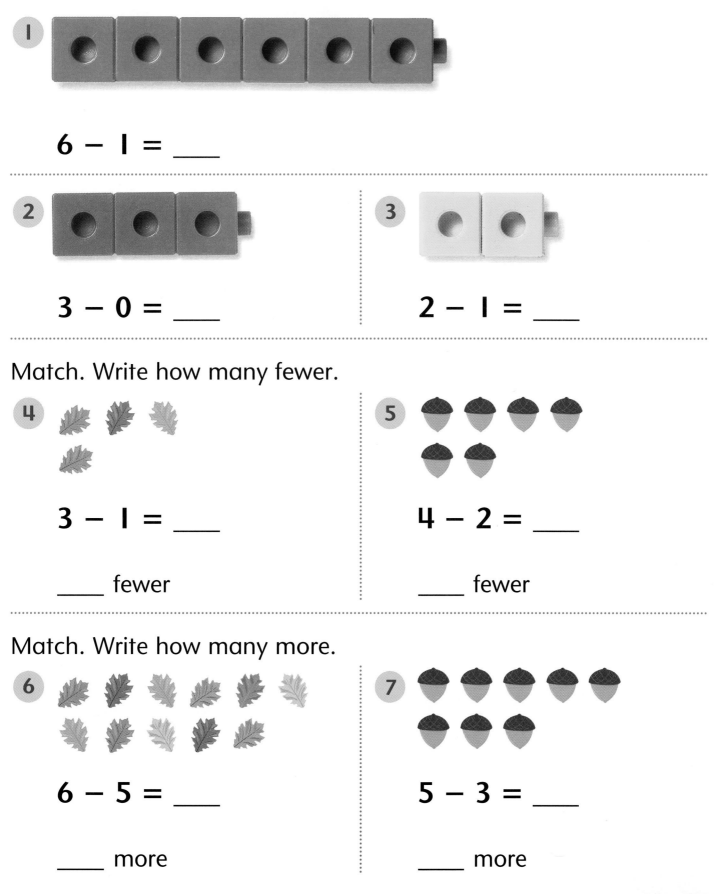

1

$6 - 1 = \underline{\quad}$

2

$3 - 0 = \underline{\quad}$

3

$2 - 1 = \underline{\quad}$

Match. Write how many fewer.

4

$3 - 1 = \underline{\quad}$

___ fewer

5

$4 - 2 = \underline{\quad}$

___ fewer

Match. Write how many more.

6

$6 - 5 = \underline{\quad}$

___ more

7

$5 - 3 = \underline{\quad}$

___ more

Cross out pennies to buy each item.
Write the subtraction sentence.

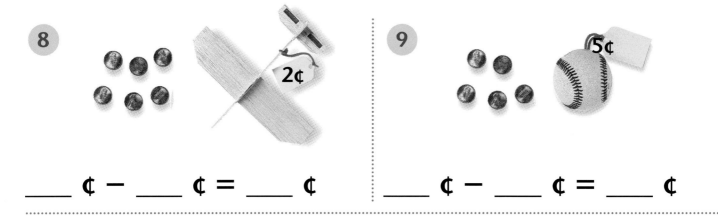

8   ___ ¢ − ___ ¢ = ___ ¢

9   ___ ¢ − ___ ¢ = ___ ¢

Listen. Draw the picture. Write the subtraction sentence.

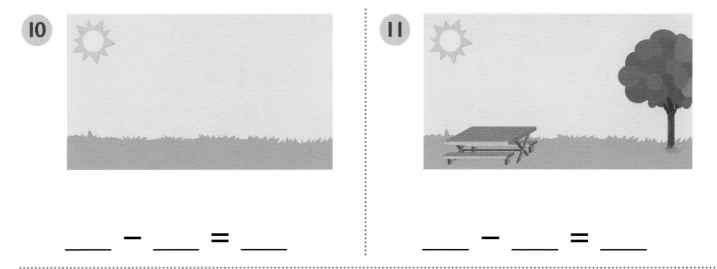

10   ___ − ___ = ___

11   ___ − ___ = ___

Look for a pattern. Draw. Write the numbers.

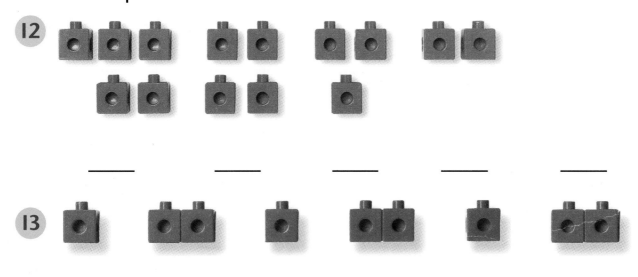

12   ___   ___   ___   ___   ___

13   ___   ___   ___   ___   ___   ___

Gathering Nuts And Berries

Name _____

Use cubes to act out the story.

1 How many more berries than nuts did the gray mouse collect?

____

2 How did you find your answer?

_____

_____

Internet

Visit Houghton Mifflin's
Education Place Math Center.
http://www.eduplace.com

Use cubes to act out the story.

1   How many red berries does the gray mouse have?

    ____

2   How many berries does the gray
    mouse have after he eats **2** berries?

    ____

3   What helped you solve the problems?

    _____

 **Dear Family:** Today we solved subtraction story problems. Encourage your child to use the workmat and small objects such as pennies to tell subtraction stories.

Addition and Subtraction Facts Through 10

Literature

Fishes' Evening Song

By Dahlov Ipcar

Read Aloud Anthology p. 28

Theme Connection

Sea Creatures

clownfish
5 + 4 =

catfish
3 + 4 =

See what I can do by the end of this chapter.

Use What You Know

Count the letters in clownfish.
Count the letters in catfish.
Which fish name has more letters?

Listen to the fish stories.
Use cubes to act out each story.

Dear Family: Practice adding and subtracting numbers through ten by telling your own fish stories. Use small objects on the workmat to act them out.

Cooperative Learning

Name _____

Work with a partner.
Play Cube Toss.

Use **10** cubes and yarn. Toss the cubes one by one.

Draw where the cubes land. Write the numbers.

A

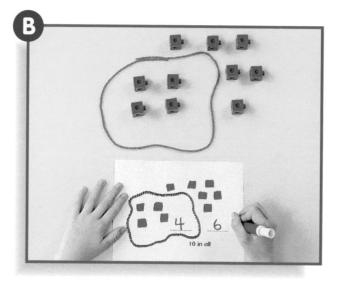

B

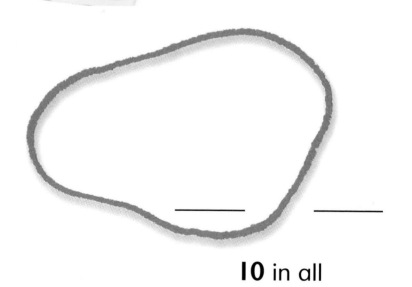

_____   _____

10 in all

Give it a try Keep playing Cube Toss.
How many different names for **10** did you find?

Play Cube Toss.
Write the numbers.

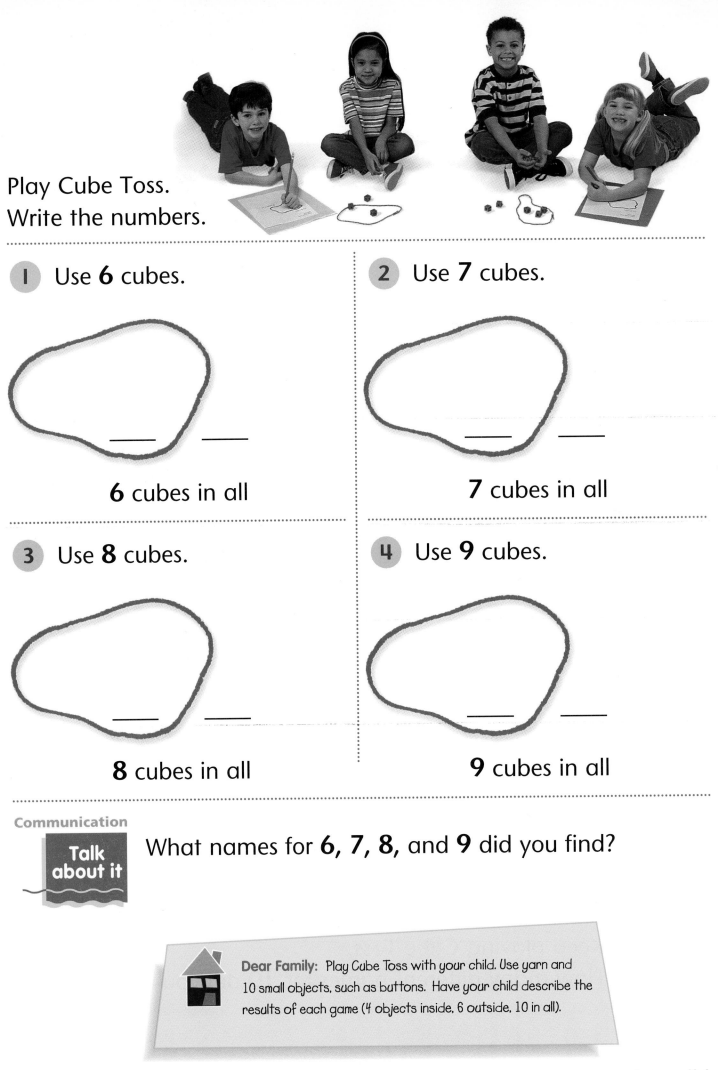

1 Use **6** cubes.

____ ____

6 cubes in all

2 Use **7** cubes.

____ ____

7 cubes in all

3 Use **8** cubes.

____ ____

8 cubes in all

4 Use **9** cubes.

____ ____

9 cubes in all

Communication

Talk
about it

What names for **6, 7, 8,** and **9** did you find?

Dear Family: Play Cube Toss with your child. Use yarn and 10 small objects, such as buttons. Have your child describe the results of each game (4 objects inside, 6 outside, 10 in all).

Cooperative Learning

Name _____

Work with a partner. Take turns.
Use a spinner and cubes in two colors.

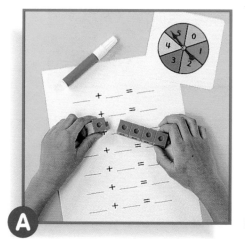

A

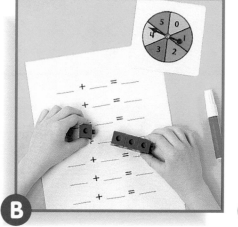

B

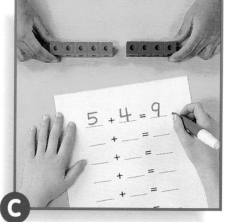

C

Spin.
Build a train in
one color.

Spin.
Build a train in
another color.

Join the trains.
Write the number
sentence.

How does joining trains of different colors help you?

1 ___ + ___ = ___

2 ___ + ___ = ___

3 ___ + ___ = ___

4 ___ + ___ = ___

5 ___ + ___ = ___

6 ___ + ___ = ___

7 ___ + ___ = ___

8 ___ + ___ = ___

Dear Family: To explore sums through 10 with your child, play Hide and Show. On the word "Go," each person shows 1 to 5 fingers. Ask your child to name the sum of the fingers.

Build each train.
Join them.
Write the number sentence.

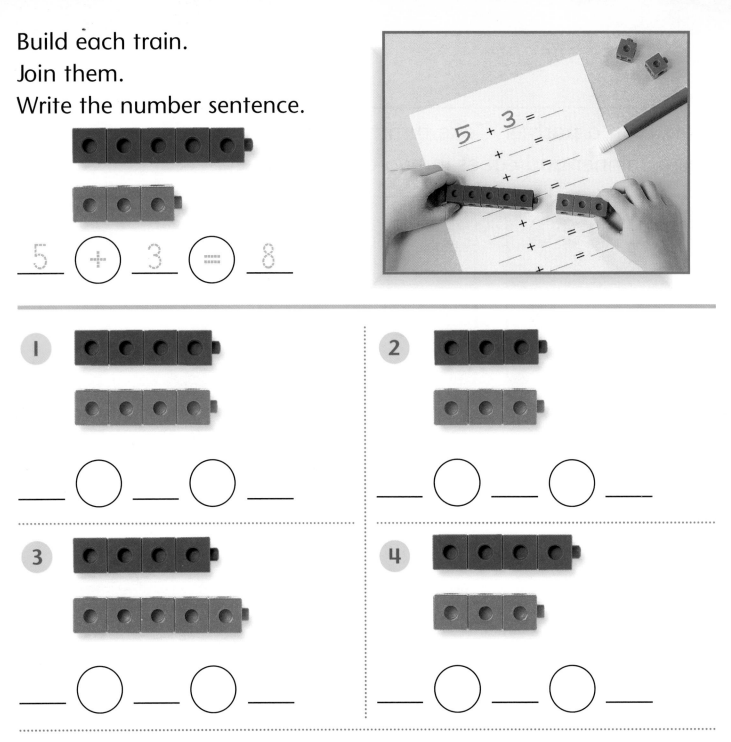

5 $\bigcirc$ (+) 3 $\bigcirc$ (=) 8

1

___ $\bigcirc$ ___ $\bigcirc$ ___

2

___ $\bigcirc$ ___ $\bigcirc$ ___

3

___ $\bigcirc$ ___ $\bigcirc$ ___

4

___ $\bigcirc$ ___ $\bigcirc$ ___

Mixed Review

Solve the problem. Write the number sentence.

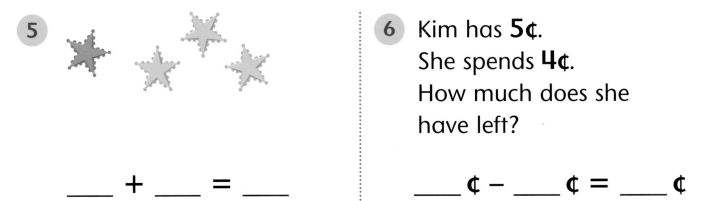

5

___ + ___ = ___

6 Kim has **5¢**.
She spends **4¢**.
How much does she
have left?

___ ¢ − ___ ¢ = ___ ¢

Name _____

Anna has **9** pennies. She can buy fish food and a plant.

Remember!
- Understand
- Plan
- Try it
- Look back

Solve the problem.

1 You have **10** pennies.
You want to buy a net, a fish, and a plant.
Draw how many pennies you need.

Do you have enough money? _____

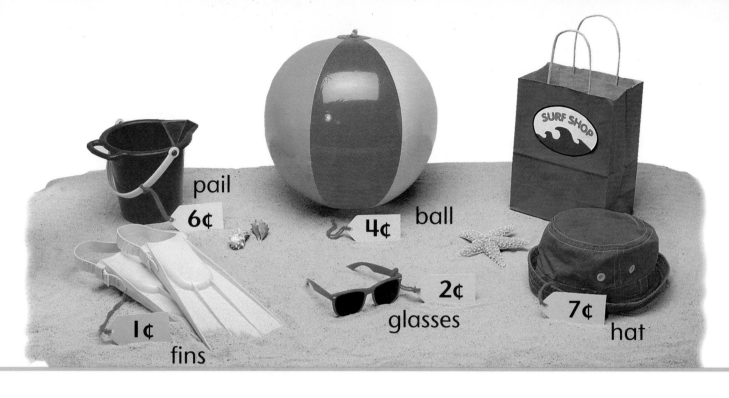

pail
6¢
ball
4¢
2¢
glasses
7¢
hat
1¢
fins

Use **10** pennies.

1 Nora has **4** pennies. Bill has **6** pennies.
Can they buy a ball, a pail, and fins? _____

2 Seth buys glasses, a hat, and fins.
How many pennies does he spend? _____

3 You have **8** pennies.
What two items can you buy? _____

_____

Give it a try   Look at the picture. Use **10** pennies.
Make up some penny stories of your own.

Name _____

Math World

Children everywhere play Mancala games.

Mancala games are played in many places and have many names. Here are a few:

Flag			
Country	Philippines	United States	Tanzania
Name	Sungka	Kalah	Bao

Players add and count the game pieces. Children play to see who gets the most pieces in his or her **kahala**.

Internet

Explore Houghton Mifflin's
Education Place Math Center.
http://www.eduplace.com

© Houghton Mifflin Company

▶ **Turn the page for directions.**

Did you know?

Mancala gameboards can be carved in stone or wood, or dug in the dirt.

Try this!

Make your own gameboard.

A Cut off the top of an egg carton.

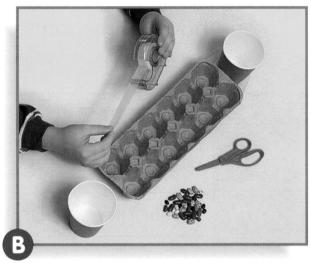

B Tape one cup to each end. Find **36** game pieces.

Dear Family: Practice adding and counting by playing Mancala (man KAH luh).

How to Play:

- Place three game pieces in each compartment of the egg carton.

- Players take turns picking up all the pieces from one of the compartments on their side of the egg carton. Moving counterclockwise, add one piece to each compartment.

- If your last piece lands in your paper cup, or kahala (KAH HAH LUH), play again.

- If your last piece lands in an empty compartment on your side of the egg carton, take all the pieces from the opposite compartment. Add them to your kahala.

- When one player's compartments are all empty, the game is over. That player takes the remaining pieces in the other player's compartments and adds them to his or her kahala. After counting their pieces, the player with the highest score starts the next game.

Name _____

Listen to the story.

▶ **Understand**

I need to know how many crabs are

on the beach now.

▶ **Plan**

I can draw a picture.

▶ **Try it**

My picture shows **4** crabs on the beach.

▶ **Look back**

$6 - 2 = 4$ My answer makes sense.

Listen to the story. Draw a picture.
Write the number sentence.

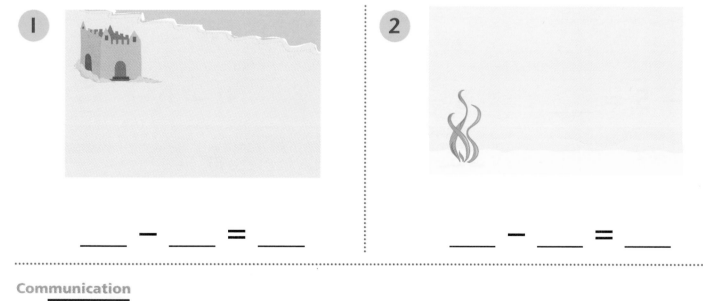

1		2	

____ – ____ = ____   ____ – ____ = ____

© Houghton Mifflin Company

Communication

Look at the number sentences.
Make up a new story to tell a friend.

Lesson 4.8

ninety-nine **99**

Listen. Draw a picture.
Write the number sentence.

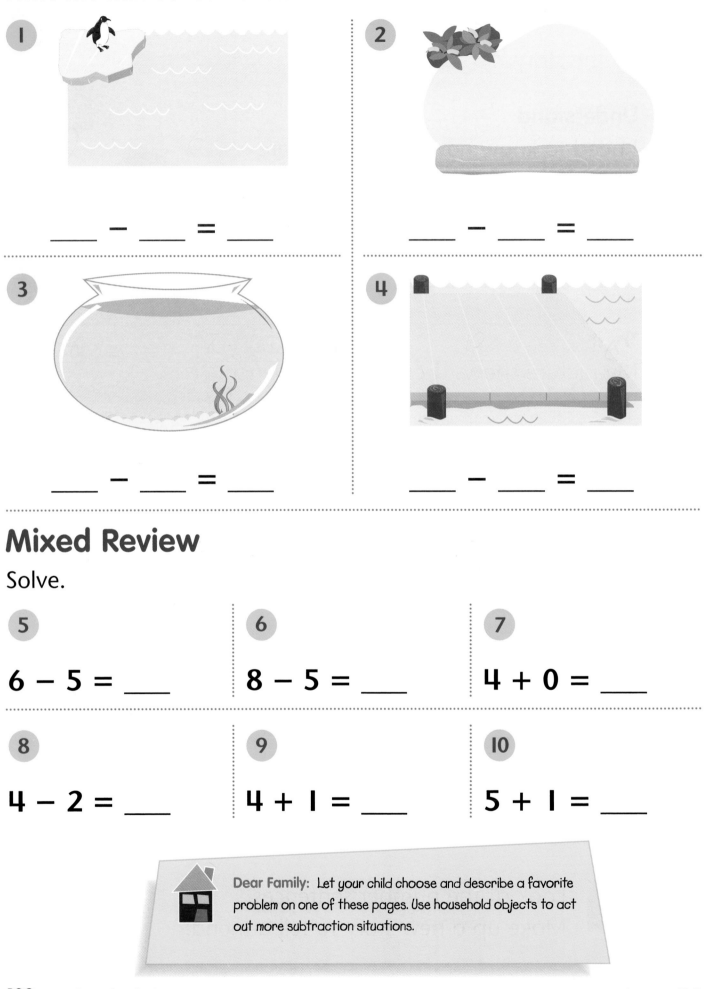

1

___ – ___ = ___

2

___ – ___ = ___

3

___ – ___ = ___

4

___ – ___ = ___

Mixed Review

Solve.

5

6 – 5 = ___

6

8 – 5 = ___

7

4 + 0 = ___

8

4 – 2 = ___

9

4 + 1 = ___

10

5 + 1 = ___

Dear Family: Let your child choose and describe a favorite problem on one of these pages. Use household objects to act out more subtraction situations.

Name _____

These are both number sentences.

$$5 - 4 = 1 \qquad 3 + 4 = 7$$

What is different about them?

Listen to the story.
Act it out with counters.
Then write a number sentence to go with it.

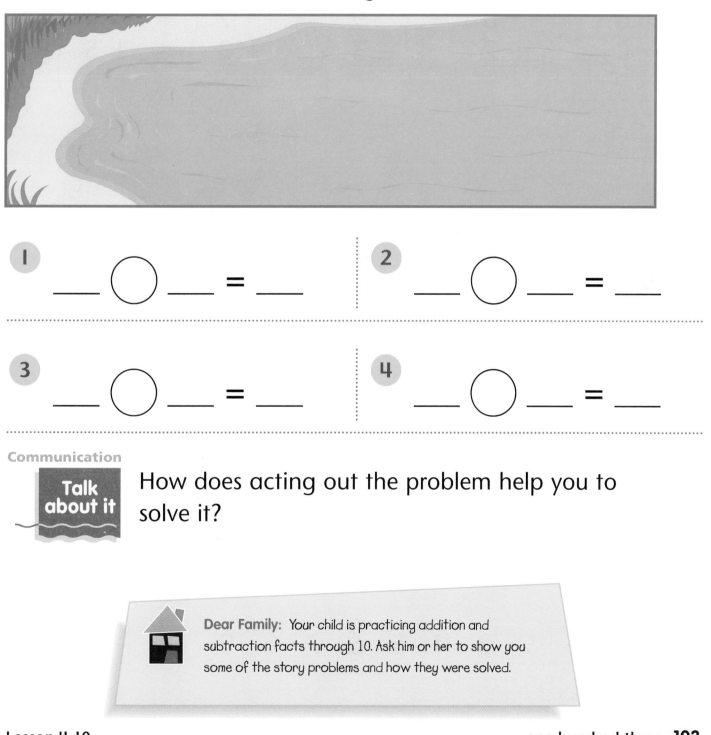

1 ___ ◯ ___ = ___

2 ___ ◯ ___ = ___

3 ___ ◯ ___ = ___

4 ___ ◯ ___ = ___

Communication

Talk about it How does acting out the problem help you to solve it?

Dear Family: Your child is practicing addition and subtraction facts through 10. Ask him or her to show you some of the story problems and how they were solved.

Solve. Color each sea horse that has the answer **6** in it.

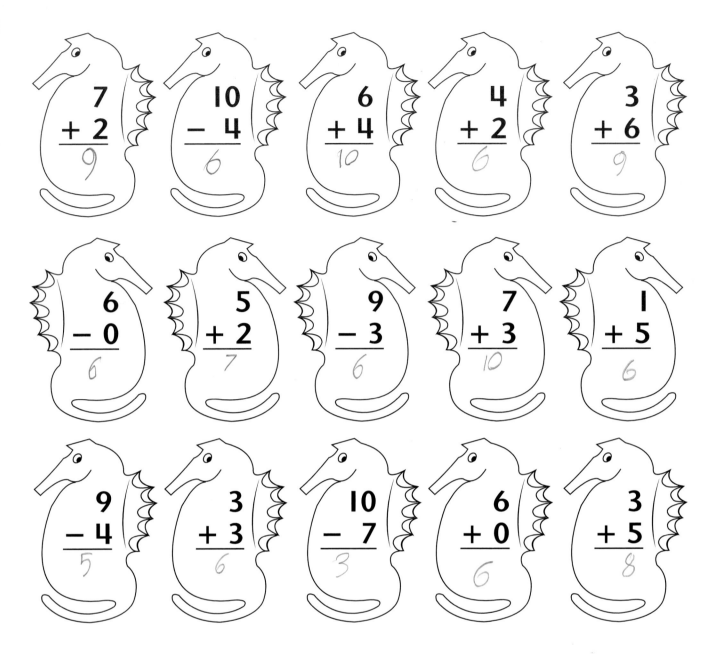

$$7 + 2 = 9$$

$$10 - 4 = 6$$

$$6 + 4 = 10$$

$$4 + 2 = 6$$

$$3 + 6 = 9$$

$$6 - 0 = 6$$

$$5 + 2 = 7$$

$$9 - 3 = 6$$

$$7 + 3 = 10$$

$$1 + 5 = 6$$

$$9 - 4 = 5$$

$$3 + 3 = 6$$

$$10 - 7 = 3$$

$$6 + 0 = 6$$

$$3 + 5 = 8$$

What do you notice about the sea horses you colored?

Give it a try

Ken sees **4** red fish and **5** blue fish. How many more blue fish than red fish does he see?
Use a calculator to solve the problem.
Circle the keys you use.

0 1 2 3 4 5 6 7 8 9 + − =

Cooperative Learning

Name _____

Work with a partner. Use counters.
Place the counters to make a **fact family**.

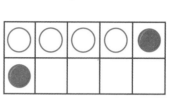

Toss **6** counters.
Sort red and white counters in
your ten frame.

$$4 + 2 = 6$$

Write **2** addition sentences.
$$2 + 4 = 6$$

$$6 - 4 = 2$$

Write **2** subtraction sentences.
$$6 - 2 = 4$$

How can knowing about fact families help you?

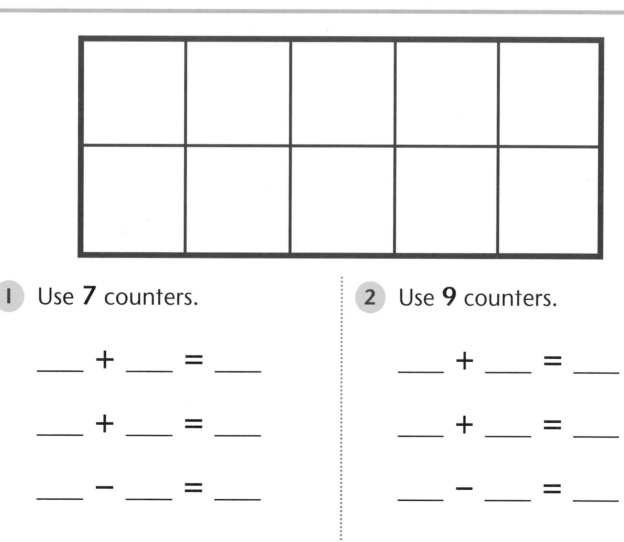

1 Use **7** counters.

___ + ___ = ___

___ + ___ = ___

___ − ___ = ___

___ − ___ = ___

2 Use **9** counters.

___ + ___ = ___

___ + ___ = ___

___ − ___ = ___

___ − ___ = ___

Lesson 4.11

Look at the counters in each ten frame.
Write the fact family.

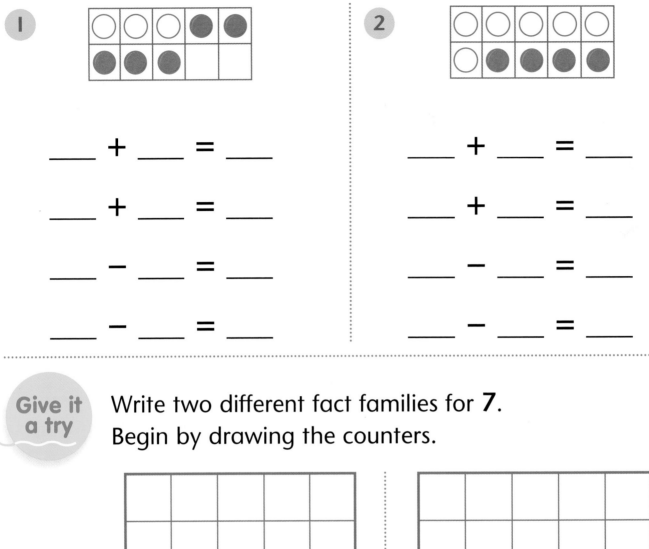

1

___ + ___ = ___

___ + ___ = ___

___ − ___ = ___

___ − ___ = ___

2

___ + ___ = ___

___ + ___ = ___

___ − ___ = ___

___ − ___ = ___

Give it a try

Write two different fact families for **7**.
Begin by drawing the counters.

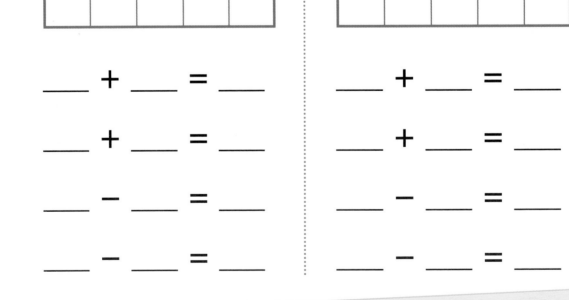

___ + ___ = ___

___ + ___ = ___

___ − ___ = ___

___ − ___ = ___

___ + ___ = ___

___ + ___ = ___

___ − ___ = ___

___ − ___ = ___

▶ **More Practice, page 399**

Dear Family: Have your child toss 5 to 10 pennies and sort them into heads and tails. Ask him or her to use the two groups to write a fact family.

Lesson 4.11

Name _____

Problem Solving

Listen and read.
Will you add or subtract?
Circle the answer.
Use your calculator.
Write the number sentence.

---

1 Vicki has **2** seashells. Mom gives her **7** more. How many seashells does Vicki have now?

$\boxed{+}$ $\boxed{-}$

_2_ $\bigcirc\!\!\!\!+$ _7_ = _9_

2 There are **8** birds on the shore. **5** of the birds are seagulls. How many are not seagulls?

$\boxed{+}$ $\boxed{-}$

___ ◯ ___ = ___

---

3 **9** frogs sit on a rock. They all jump into the pond. How many frogs are on the rock now?

$\boxed{+}$ $\boxed{-}$

___ ◯ ___ = ___

4 Joshua put **4** fish into the tank. LaToya put in **3** fish. How many fish did they put in altogether?

$\boxed{+}$ $\boxed{-}$

___ ◯ ___ = ___

Communication

Draw   Choose a number sentence.
Draw a different story.

Solve.

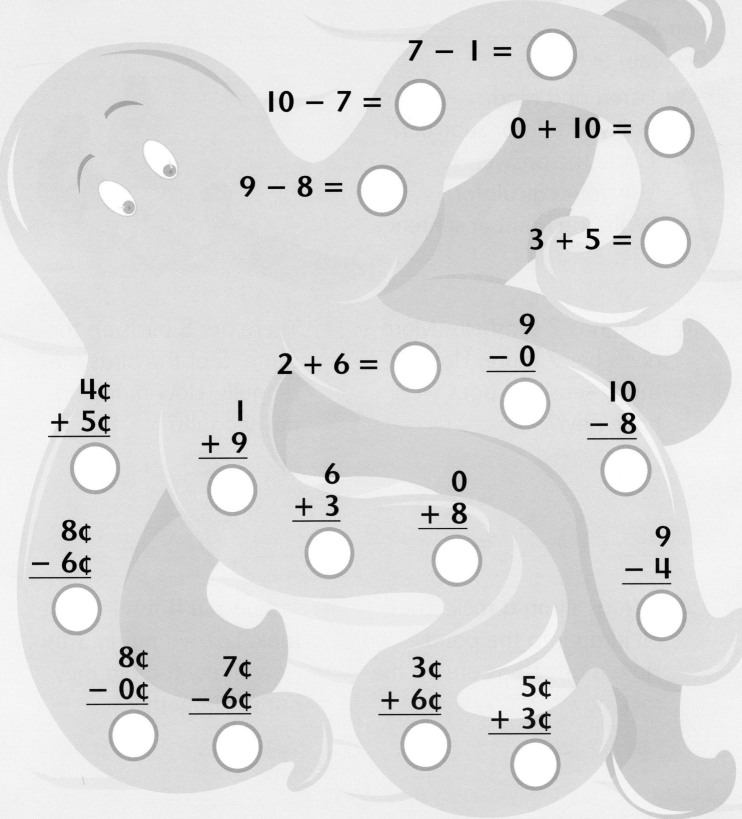

$7 - 1 =$ ◯

$10 - 7 =$ ◯

$0 + 10 =$ ◯

$9 - 8 =$ ◯

$3 + 5 =$ ◯

$2 + 6 =$ ◯

$$\begin{array}{r} 9 \\ -\ 0 \\ \hline \end{array}$$ ◯

$$\begin{array}{r} 4¢ \\ +\ 5¢ \\ \hline \end{array}$$ ◯

$$\begin{array}{r} 1 \\ +\ 9 \\ \hline \end{array}$$ ◯

$$\begin{array}{r} 6 \\ +\ 3 \\ \hline \end{array}$$ ◯

$$\begin{array}{r} 0 \\ +\ 8 \\ \hline \end{array}$$ ◯

$$\begin{array}{r} 10 \\ -\ 8 \\ \hline \end{array}$$ ◯

$$\begin{array}{r} 8¢ \\ -\ 6¢ \\ \hline \end{array}$$ ◯

$$\begin{array}{r} 9 \\ -\ 4 \\ \hline \end{array}$$ ◯

$$\begin{array}{r} 8¢ \\ -\ 0¢ \\ \hline \end{array}$$ ◯

$$\begin{array}{r} 7¢ \\ -\ 6¢ \\ \hline \end{array}$$ ◯

$$\begin{array}{r} 3¢ \\ +\ 6¢ \\ \hline \end{array}$$ ◯

$$\begin{array}{r} 5¢ \\ +\ 3¢ \\ \hline \end{array}$$ ◯

▶ **More Practice, page 399**

 Dear Family: Have your child tell you about one or more of the word problems on page 107 and why the answer makes sense.

Lesson 4.12

Name _____

Pick the shell color you like best.
Color a box to show the color you pick.
Color one box for the color each child
in your class picks.

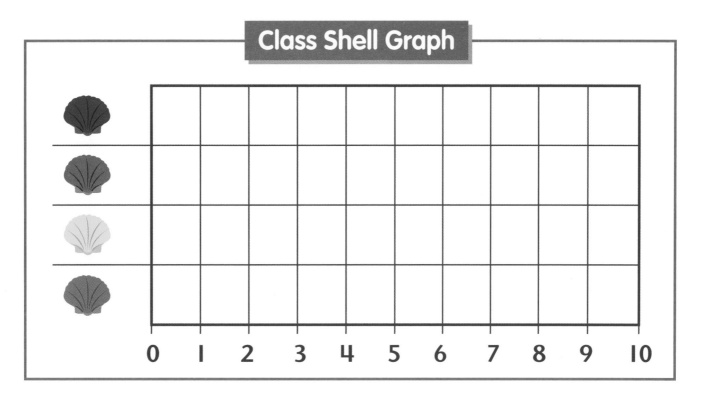

Class Shell Graph

0   1   2   3   4   5   6   7   8   9   10

Write the answer.

1   How many children like green best? _____

2   How many children like red best? _____

3   How many children in all like blue or green best? _____

Communication

Write about it   Write what else you can tell about the graph.

Lesson 4.13   one hundred nine **109**

Our Favorite Fish

	catfish	clownfish	tetra	angelfish
10				
9				
8				
7				
6				
5				
4				
3				
2				
1				
0				

catfish   clownfish   tetra   angelfish

Look at the graph. Answer the question.

1 How many children choose a catfish?

_____ children

2 What fish did only two children choose?

_____

3 How many children in all choose a tetra or a catfish?

_____ children

4 How many more children choose a clownfish than a tetra?

_____ children

Dear Family: Have your child find out each family member's favorite color. Record the information on a bar graph.

Name _____

Look at the picture. Write the addition fact.

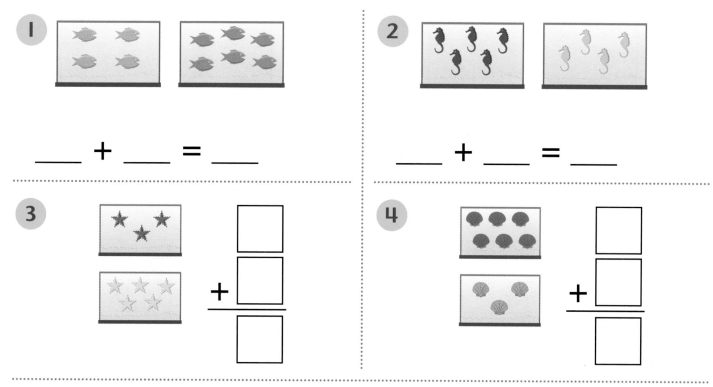

1   ___ + ___ = ___

2   ___ + ___ = ___

3   +

4   +

Match. Finish the number sentence.
Write how many more or fewer.

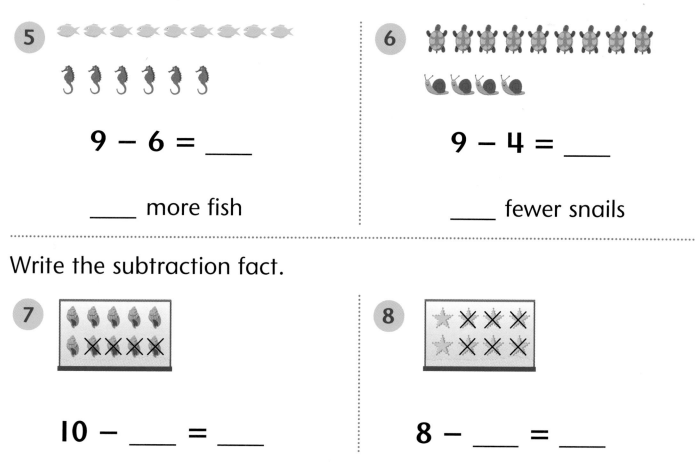

5   9 – 6 = ___

     ____ more fish

6   9 – 4 = ___

     ____ fewer snails

Write the subtraction fact.

7   10 – ___ = ___

8   8 – ___ = ___

Write the subtraction fact.

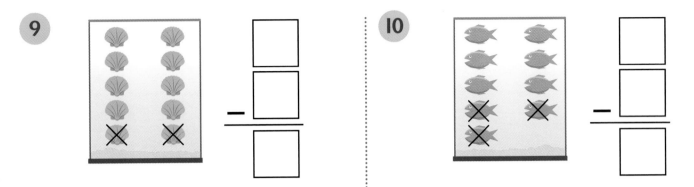

9 [image: shell ten frame with 8 shells, 2 marked with X] ☐ − ☐ / ☐

10 [image: fish ten frame with 6 fish, 3 marked with X] ☐ − ☐ / ☐

Look at each ten frame. Write the fact family.

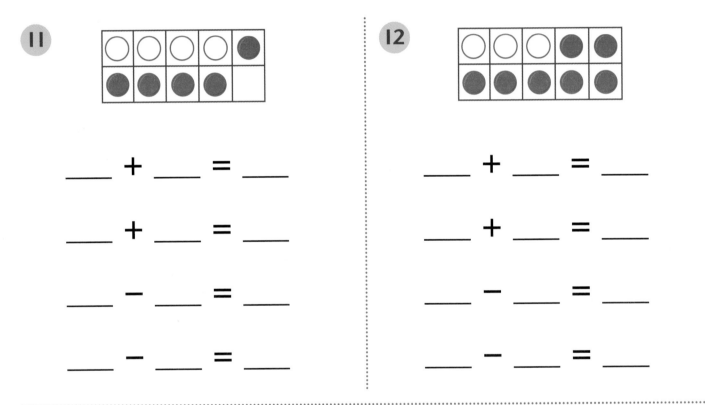

11

___ + ___ = ___

___ + ___ = ___

___ − ___ = ___

___ − ___ = ___

12

___ + ___ = ___

___ + ___ = ___

___ − ___ = ___

___ − ___ = ___

Read the story. Write the number sentence.

13 There are **10** fish. **6** fish swim away. How many fish are left?

___ ◯ ___ = ___

14 There are **7** small shells and **2** large shells. How many shells are there in all?

___ ◯ ___ = ___

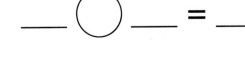

Name _____

Some real fish have funny names.

<u>cat</u> and <u>fish</u> equal <u>catfish</u>

<u>3</u> letters and <u>4</u> letters equal <u>7</u> letters

$$\underline{3} + \underline{4} = \underline{7}$$

<u>clown</u> and <u>fish</u> equal <u>clownfish</u>

$$\underline{5} + \underline{4} = \underline{9}$$

Count the letters and write the number sentence.

1. <u>angel</u> and <u>fish</u> equal <u>angelfish</u>

   _____ + _____ = _____

2. <u>dog</u> and <u>fish</u> equal <u>dogfish</u>

   _____ + _____ = _____

3. <u>parrot</u> and <u>fish</u> equal <u>parrotfish</u>

   _____ + _____ = _____

Internet

Visit Houghton Mifflin's
Education Place Math Center.
http://www.eduplace.com

Write your own funny fish name.

Count the letters and write the number sentence.

_____ and fish equal _____

_____ + _____ = _____

Draw your funny fish.

Dear Family: Ask about your child's funny fish. Help your child think of other funny fish names with two parts that can be counted and added together.

Place Value Through 100

Literature

My Teddy Bear
By Margaret Hillert

Read Aloud Anthology p. 60
Theme Connection
Our Favorite Things

90 **10**

25

See what I can do by the end of this chapter.

Use What You Know

What numbers do you see?
How many items do the collections have in all?
How can you find out?

Listen to the story.
Use counters to count teddy bears.

Name _____

Compare the tens. The tens are the same.
Then compare the ones.

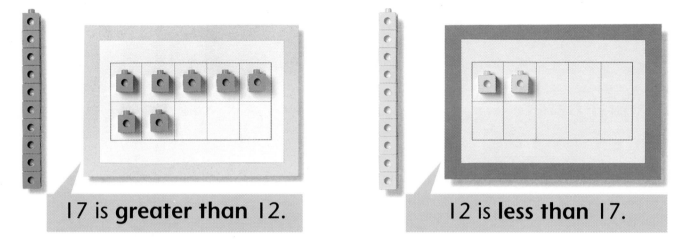

17 is **greater than** 12.

12 is **less than** 17.

How does comparing tens and ones help you
find the greater number?

Work in pairs. Use cubes.
Circle the number that is greater. *mayor*

1. (10 7) (4 11) (13 12) (15 19)

Circle the number that is less. *pequend*

2. (18 12) (5 10) (13 14) (11 16)

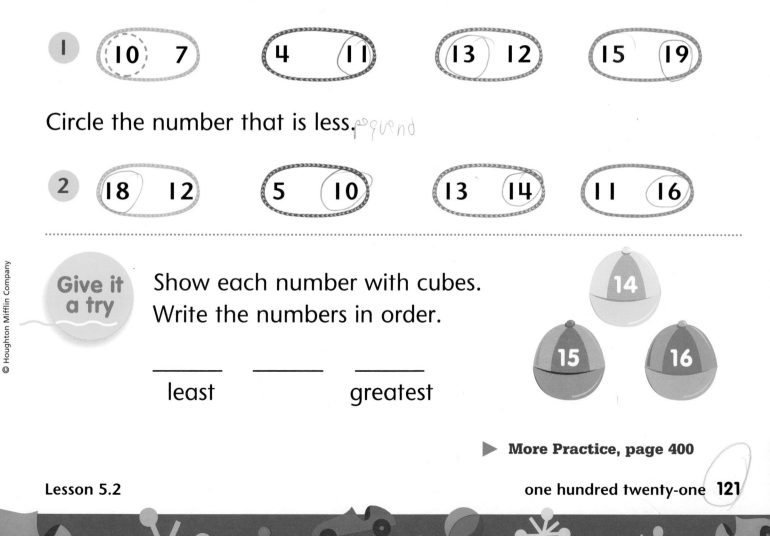

Give it a try Show each number with cubes.
Write the numbers in order.

14

15 16

_____ _____ _____
least   greatest

▶ **More Practice, page 400**

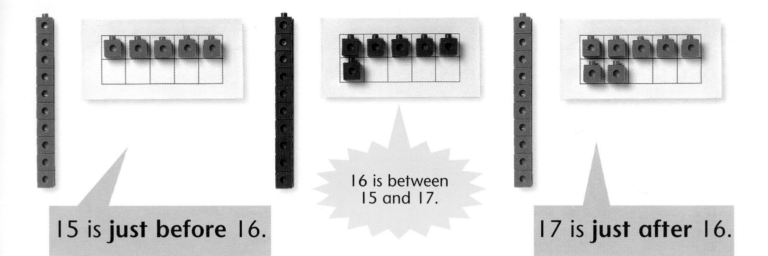

15 is **just before** 16.

16 is between 15 and 17.

17 is **just after** 16.

Why is comparing numbers helpful?

Use cubes.
Write the missing number.

1 13, _____, 15

2 7, _____, 9

3 2, _____, 4

4 10, _____, 12

5 | 10 | | 12 | | | | 16 | | 18 | |

Give it a try

Write three numbers that are after **15**.

_____, _____, _____

Write two numbers that are between **2** and **11**.

_____, _____

▶ **More Practice, page 400**

Dear Family: Write two numbers from 0 through 19. Ask your child to tell which is greater. Ask which numbers come just before and just after each one.

Name _____

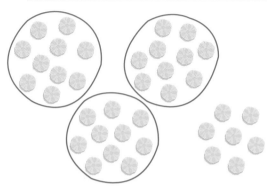

Tens	Ones
3	7

_37_

How are **24** and **42** different?

How are they alike?

Circle groups of ten. Write the numbers.

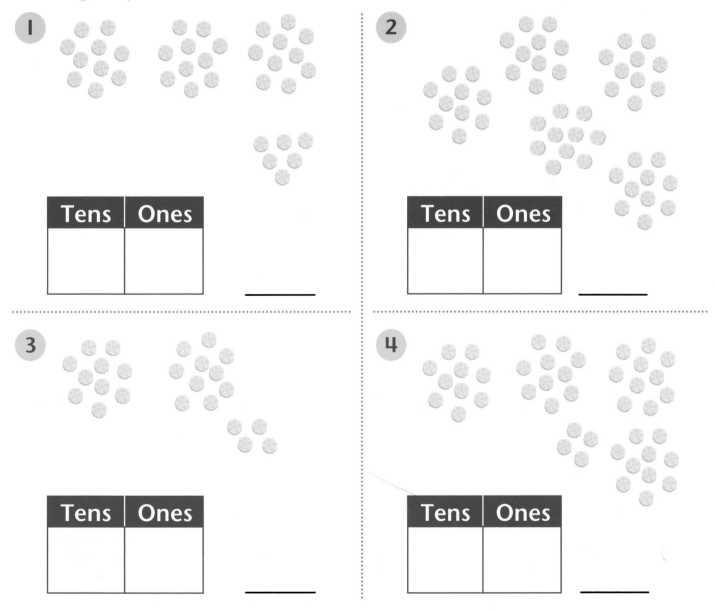

1

Tens	Ones

_____

2

Tens	Ones

_____

3

Tens	Ones

_____

4

Tens	Ones

_____

Lesson 5.5

Color the number of balls.

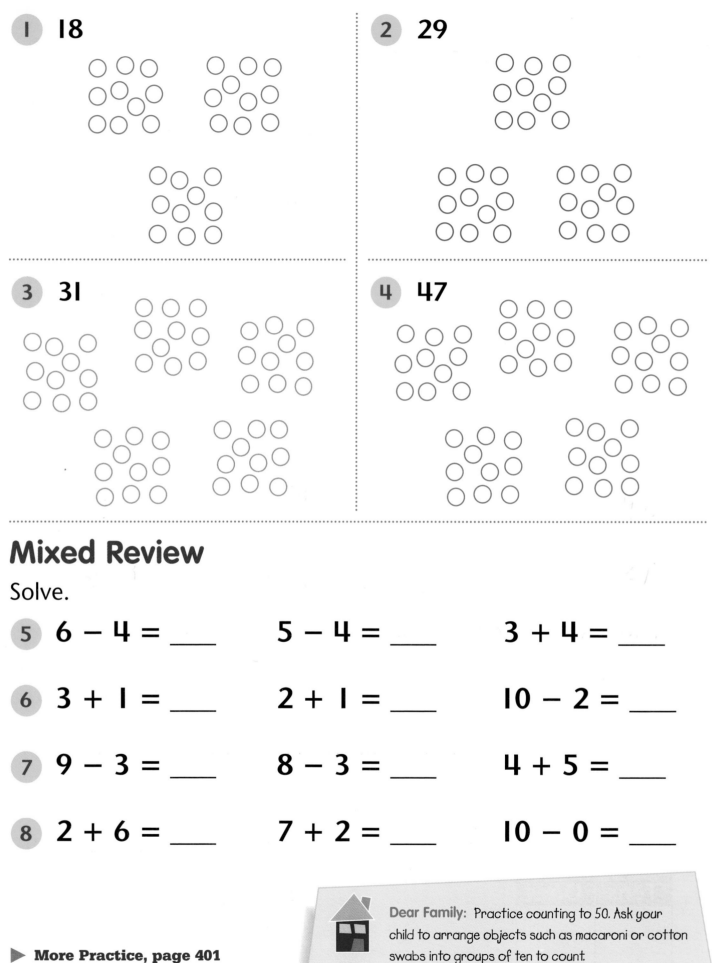

1 18

2 29

3 31

4 47

Mixed Review

Solve.

5 6 − 4 = ___   5 − 4 = ___   3 + 4 = ___

6 3 + 1 = ___   2 + 1 = ___   10 − 2 = ___

7 9 − 3 = ___   8 − 3 = ___   4 + 5 = ___

8 2 + 6 = ___   7 + 2 = ___   10 − 0 = ___

▶ **More Practice, page 401**

Dear Family: Practice counting to 50. Ask your child to arrange objects such as macaroni or cotton swabs into groups of ten to count.

Lesson 5.5

Name _____

2 tens are less than **4** tens.
24 is less than **41**.
41 is greater than **24**.

Is **41** less than **47**?
How can you tell?

Work in groups of four. Use cubes.
Circle the number that is greater.

1	(37) 10	(40) 4	(14) 7	16 (25)
2	(38) 8	(21) 12	(23) 13	2 (6)
3	(17) 11	(27) 15	18 (19)	(34) 9

Circle the number that is less.

4	42 (6)	(23) 24	9 (8)	(8) 29
5	(10) 29	35 (13)	(3) 19	46 (13)
6	30 (16)	(4) 13	25 (24)	19 (16)

Communication

| Talk about it | How do cubes help you tell which number is greater? |

▶ **More Practice, page 402**

Lesson 5.6

one hundred twenty-seven **127**

© Houghton Mifflin Company

Cooperative Learning

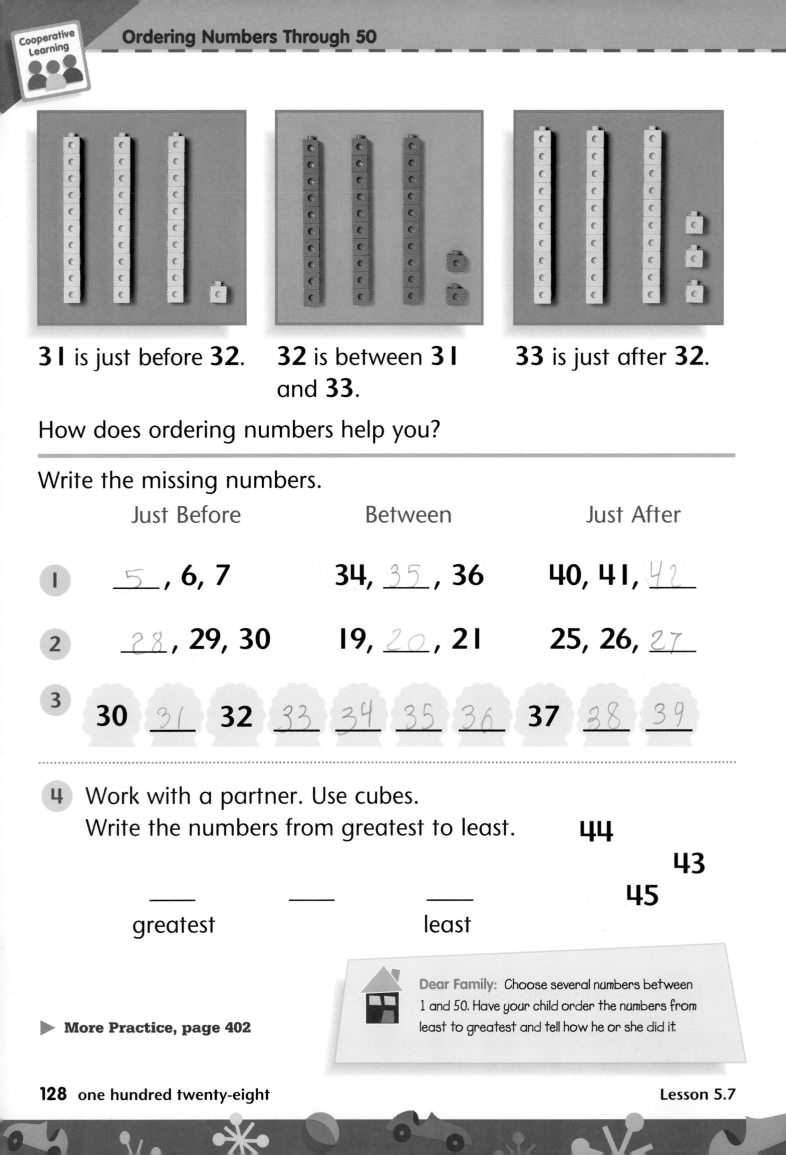

31 is just before **32**.

32 is between **31** and **33**.

33 is just after **32**.

How does ordering numbers help you?

Write the missing numbers.

	Just Before	Between	Just After
1	_5_ , 6, 7	34, _35_ , 36	40, 41, _42_
2	_28_ , 29, 30	19, _20_ , 21	25, 26, _27_

3   30 _31_ 32 _33_ _34_ _35_ _36_ 37 _38_ _39_

4 Work with a partner. Use cubes.
   Write the numbers from greatest to least.   **44**

                                                        43

___   ___   ___   **45**

greatest   least

▶ **More Practice, page 402**

Dear Family: Choose several numbers between 1 and 50. Have your child order the numbers from least to greatest and tell how he or she did it.

Lesson 5.7

Name _____

Marta has **4** cat stickers and **3** monkey stickers. How many stickers does she have?

▶ **Understand**

I need to find the number of stickers.

▶ **Plan**

I can act it out.

▶ **Try it**

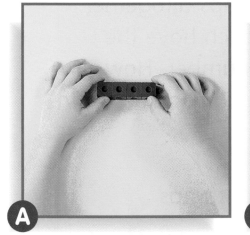

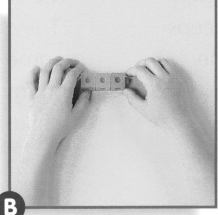

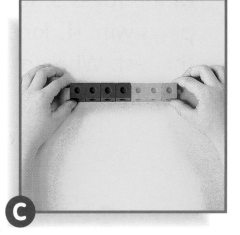

A I use blue cubes for the cat stickers.

B I use orange cubes for the monkey stickers.

C I count **7** cubes. Marta has **7** stickers.

▶ **Look back**

$$4 + 3 = 7$$

My answer makes sense.

Solve. Use cubes.

1 José has **10** balloons. He gives **2** to Ming and **3** to Keri. How many does he have left?

_____ balloons

2 Phillipo puts **5** shells in a box. He puts **3** on a shelf. He has **1** left. How many shells did Phillipo start with?

_____ shells

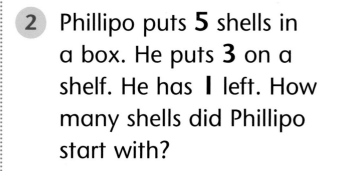

3 There are **12** toy cars. Mario takes **3**. Katrina plays with **4**. Jane keeps the rest. Who has the most?

_____

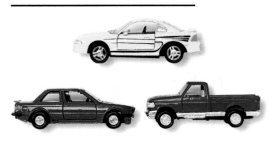

4 Eric and Tamela have **10** stamps altogether. They each have the same number. How many stamps does each child have?

_____ stamps

Communication

 Tell a partner how you solved one of the problems.

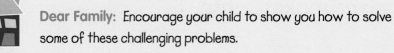

Dear Family: Encourage your child to show you how to solve some of these challenging problems.

Name _____

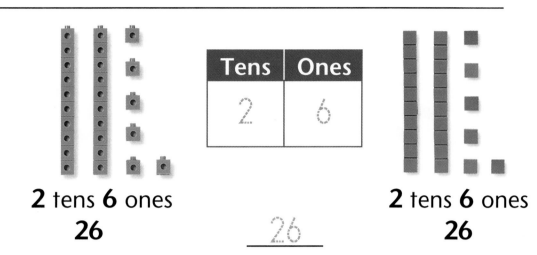

2 tens **6** ones
26

_26_

2 tens **6** ones
26

How are blocks different from cubes?

Write how many tens and ones.
Write the number.

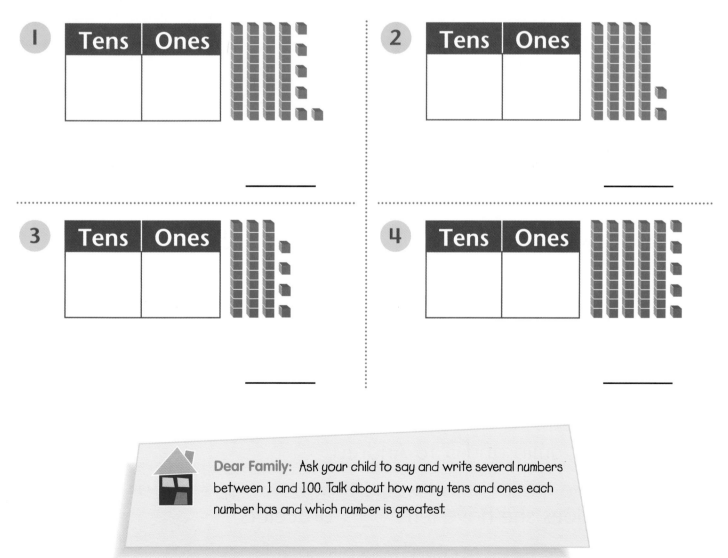

1	Tens	Ones

_____

2	Tens	Ones

_____

3	Tens	Ones

_____

4	Tens	Ones

_____

Dear Family: Ask your child to say and write several numbers between 1 and 100. Talk about how many tens and ones each number has and which number is greatest.

Write how many tens and ones.
Write the number.

1

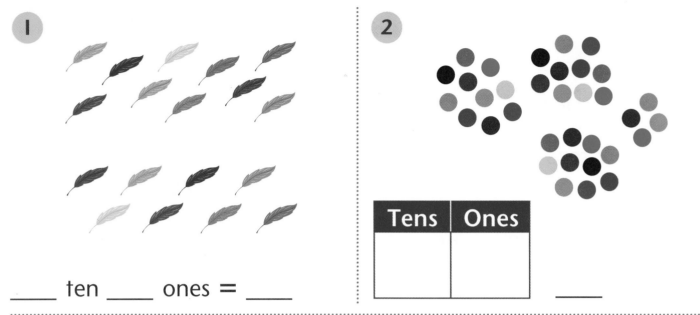

____ ten ____ ones = ____

2

Tens	Ones

____

Write the missing numbers.

3

10 ____ 12 ____ ____ 15 ____ ____ 18 ____

4

____ 34 ____ ____ 37 ____ ____ 40 ____ ____

Problem Solving

5 Write the answer. You may use cubes.

Maria has **8** bracelets.
She gives **1** to Julia and **3** to Andrea.

How many does she have left? ____ bracelets

Name _____

Math World

For thousands of years people have used numbers.

 Long ago great cities were built by the **Mayan** people. The **Mayas** lived in the areas we now call **Central America** and **Mexico**.

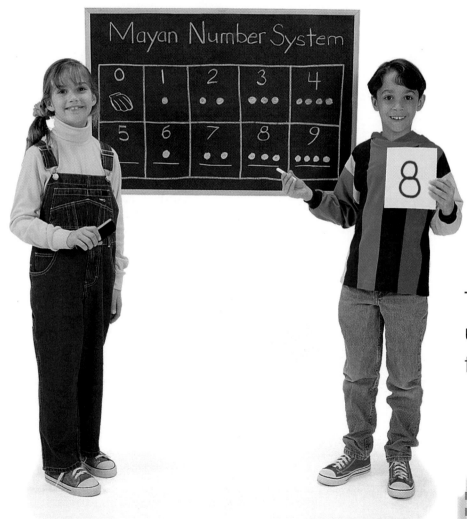

The Mayan people used dots and lines to show numbers.

Internet

Explore Houghton Mifflin's **Education Place Math Center.** http://www.eduplace.com

▶ **Turn the page for directions.**

Did you know?

Mayan people were some of the first to use a symbol for zero.

Try this!

Use ancient Mayan numbers.

A Draw each Mayan symbol on an index card. Write the number for the symbol on the back.

B Mix your cards up. Look at the Mayan symbols. Put your cards in order from the greatest number to the least number.

Dear Family: Ask your child to show you the symbols from the Mayan number system.
- Have your child teach you how the Mayan number system works.
- Think of a fun number, such as your child's age.
- Show how a Mayan child would have written that number using the symbols.

Name ___3/11/99___ Perfect

Write the missing numbers.

1	2	3	4	5	6	7	8	9	10
11	12	13	14	15	16	17	18	19	20
21	22	23	24	25	26	27	28	29	30
31	32	33	34	35	36	37	38	39	40
41	42	43	44	45	46	47	48	49	50
51	52	53	54	55	56	57	58	59	60
61	62	63	64	65	66	67	68	69	70
71	72	73	74	75	76	77	78	79	80
81	82	83	84	85	86	87	88	89	99
91	92	93	94	95	96	97	98	99	100

What number is just before 1? __2__

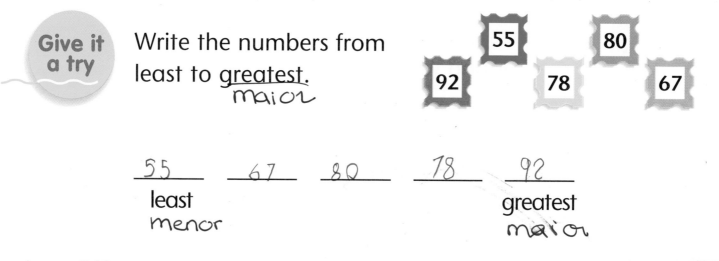

Give it a try

Write the numbers from least to greatest.
maior

55   80
92   78   67

__55__   __67__   __80__   __78__   __92__
least   greatest
menor   maior

Listen to the game rules.
Use blocks.

Write the numbers.
Circle the number that is greater.

1 ____ ____   2 ____ ____   3 ____ ____

4 ____ ____   5 ____ ____   6 ____ ____

Circle the number that is less.

7 ____ ____   8 ____ ____   9 ____ ____

10 ____ ____   11 ____ ____   12 ____ ____

Communication

Talk about it How can you tell which number is greater and which is less?

▶ **More Practice, page 403**

Dear Family: Fill two different-size containers with small objects. Let your child count the objects, write the numbers, and tell which number is greater.

Lesson 5.10

Name _____

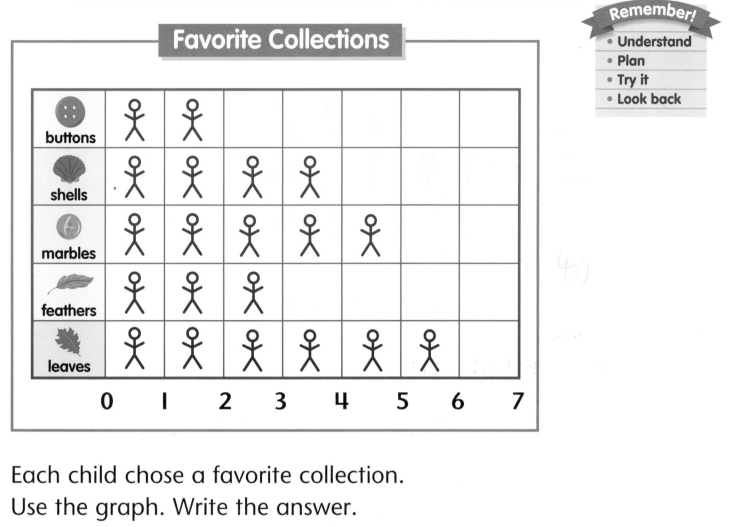

Favorite Collections

Each child chose a favorite collection.
Use the graph. Write the answer.

1 How many children chose shells? ____ children

2 Did more children pick marbles or leaves? _____

3 What collection did most children choose? _____

4 How many children did not pick feathers? ____ children

Communication

Share Look back. Tell a partner how you used the
graph to answer the questions.

6 is an **even number**.
You can make it into pairs.

7 is an **odd number**.
There is one left.

Which is easier for you and a friend to share, an odd number of shells or an even number of shells?

Work with a partner. Use cubes.
Circle odd or even.

1	**24**		2	**9**		3	**12**	
	odd	(even)		odd	even		odd	even

4	**18**		5	**23**		6	**15**	
	odd	even		odd	even		odd	even

▶ **More Practice, page 403**

Dear Family: We've been learning about even numbers. Help your child find some even numbers of things in your home.

Name _____

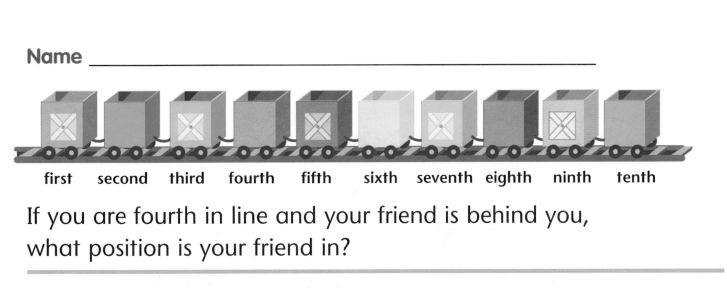

first   second   third   fourth   fifth   sixth   seventh   eighth   ninth   tenth

If you are fourth in line and your friend is behind you, what position is your friend in?

Use crayons. Listen to the directions.

first

1 Color the seventh car green.
Color the eighth car red.
Color the fourth car purple.
Color the tenth car orange.

first

2 Color the second car brown.
Color the fifth car yellow.
Color the sixth car blue.
Color the ninth car black.

Communication

 Name a color. Ask a partner to find the car and tell its ordinal name.

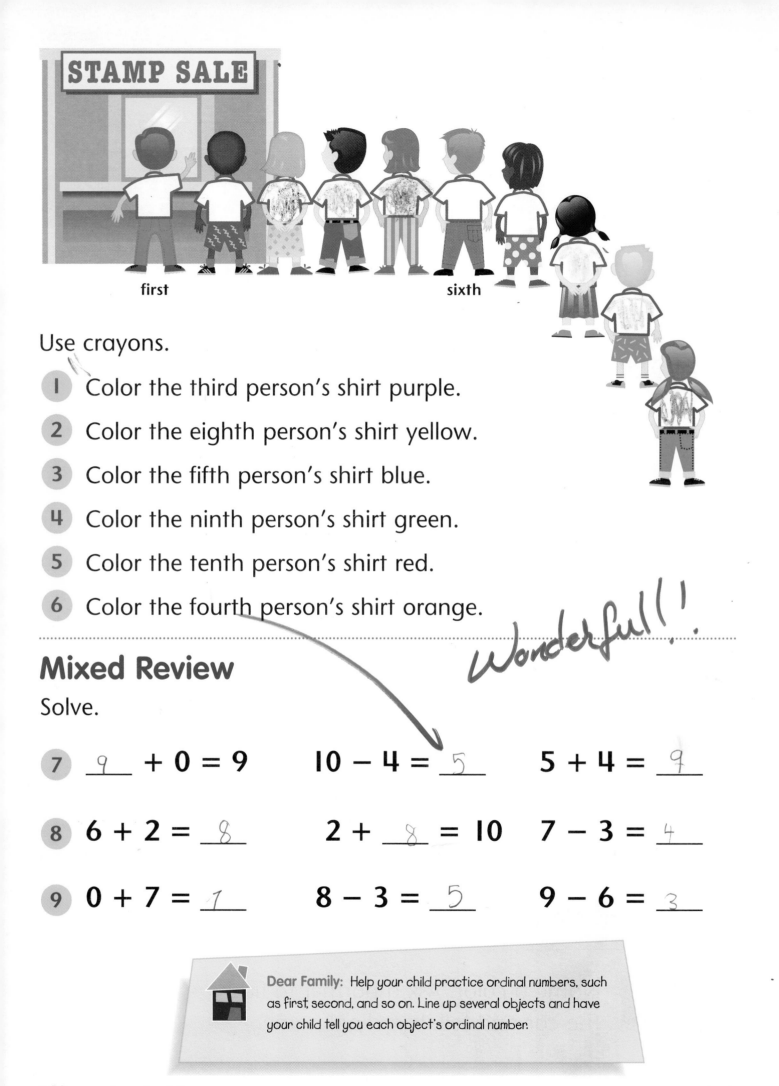

first   sixth

Use crayons.

① Color the third person's shirt purple.

② Color the eighth person's shirt yellow.

③ Color the fifth person's shirt blue.

④ Color the ninth person's shirt green.

⑤ Color the tenth person's shirt red.

⑥ Color the fourth person's shirt orange.

Wonderful!

Mixed Review

Solve.

⑦ _9_ + 0 = 9   10 − 4 = _5_   5 + 4 = _9_

⑧ 6 + 2 = _8_   2 + _8_ = 10   7 − 3 = _4_

⑨ 0 + 7 = _7_   8 − 3 = _5_   9 − 6 = _3_

Dear Family: Help your child practice ordinal numbers, such as first, second, and so on. Line up several objects and have your child tell you each object's ordinal number.

Name _____

Count by twos. Write the number.

1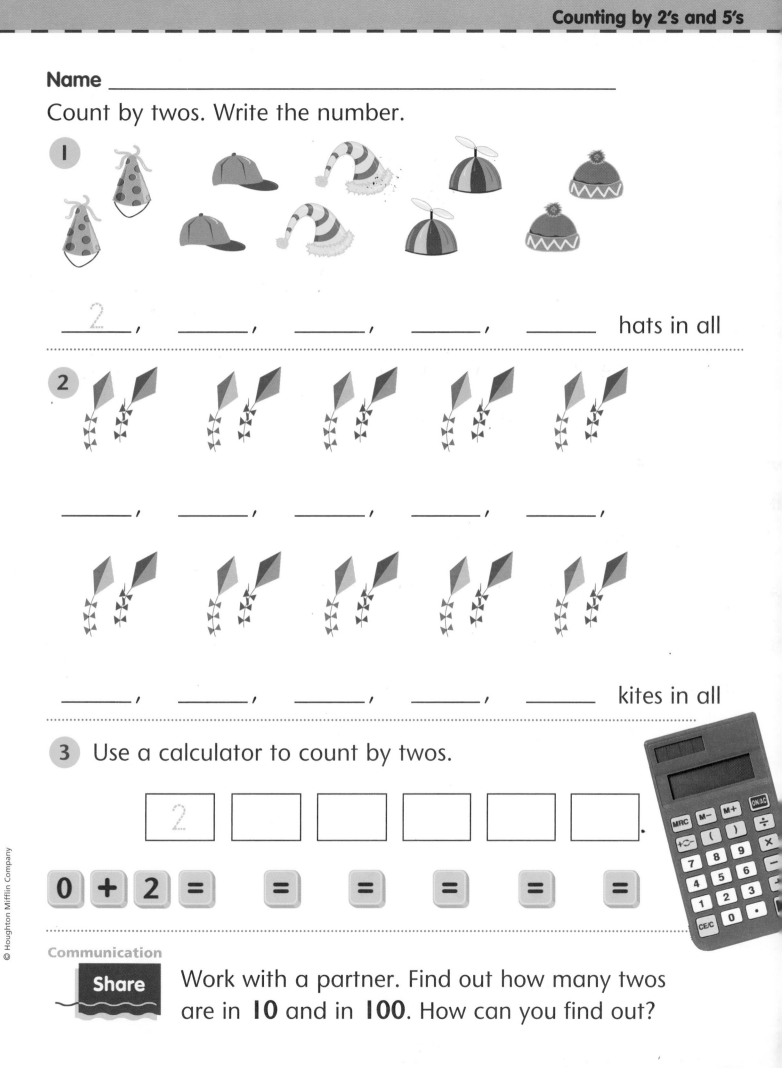

_____2_____, _____, _____, _____, _____ hats in all

2

_____, _____, _____, _____, _____,

_____, _____, _____, _____, _____ kites in all

3 Use a calculator to count by twos.

| 2 | | | | | |

`0` `+` `2` `=` `=` `=` `=` `=` `=`

Communication

Share Work with a partner. Find out how many twos are in **10** and in **100**. How can you find out?

Circle groups of **5**.
Count by fives. Write the number.

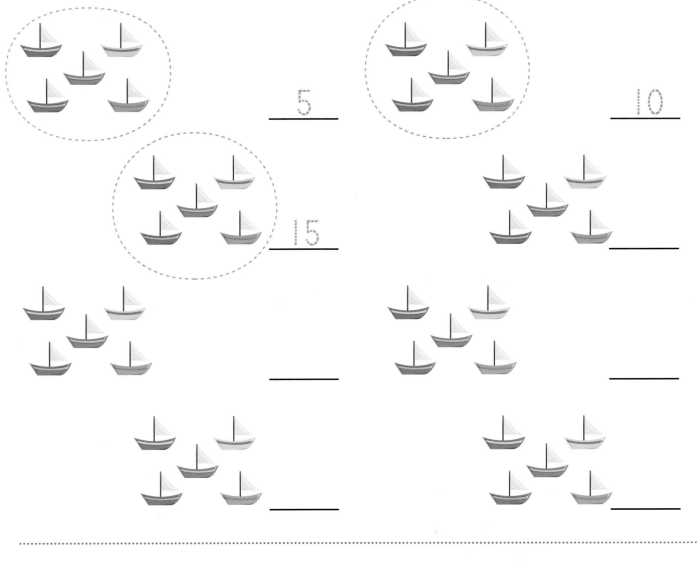

5

10

15

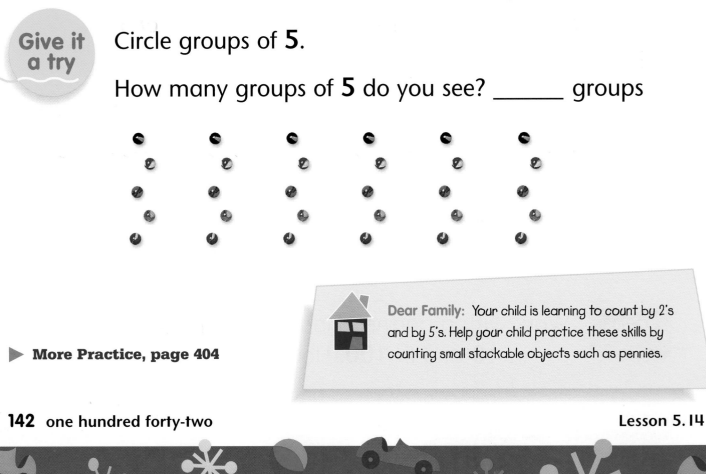

▶ **More Practice, page 404**

Give it a try

Circle groups of **5**.

How many groups of **5** do you see? _____ groups

Dear Family: Your child is learning to count by 2's and by 5's. Help your child practice these skills by counting small stackable objects such as pennies.

Name _____

Tally marks help you count.

There are **19** children in the class.
Use the table to answer each question.

1 How many children picked buttons? _____ children

2 How many children picked leaves? _____ children

3 How many tallies are there in all? _____ tallies

4 Did all the children pick a collection? _____

Communication

Talk about it

How can you tell if all the children picked a collection?

Would you like to collect shells or feathers?
Which one do you think more children will pick?
Ask each child in your class.
Use one tally mark for each child.

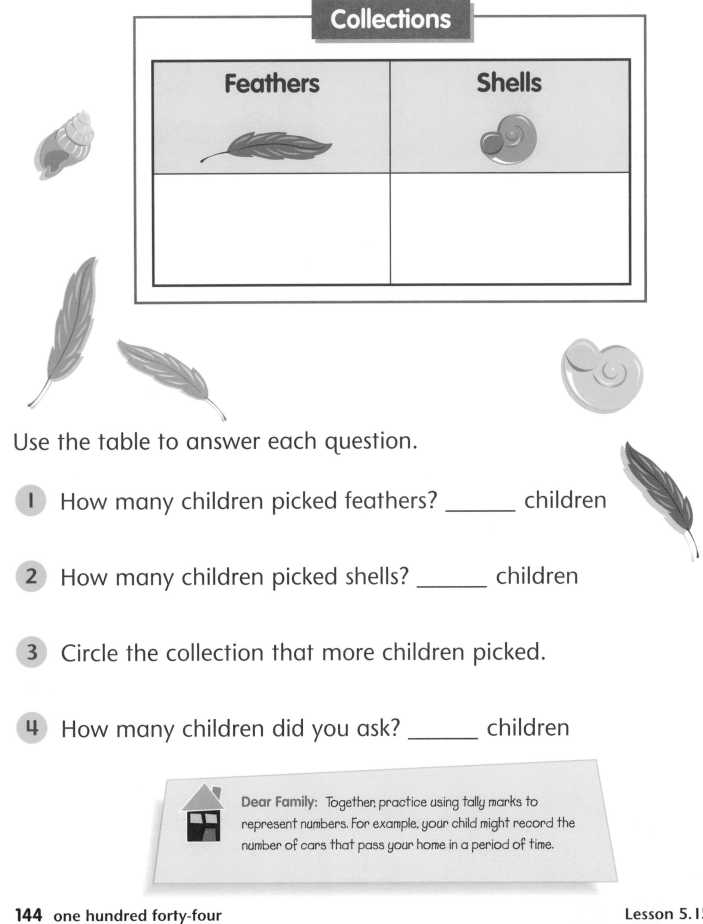

Collections

Feathers	Shells

Use the table to answer each question.

1 How many children picked feathers? _____ children

2 How many children picked shells? _____ children

3 Circle the collection that more children picked.

4 How many children did you ask? _____ children

Dear Family: Together, practice using tally marks to represent numbers. For example, your child might record the number of cars that pass your home in a period of time.

Name _____

Write how many tens and ones.
Write the number.

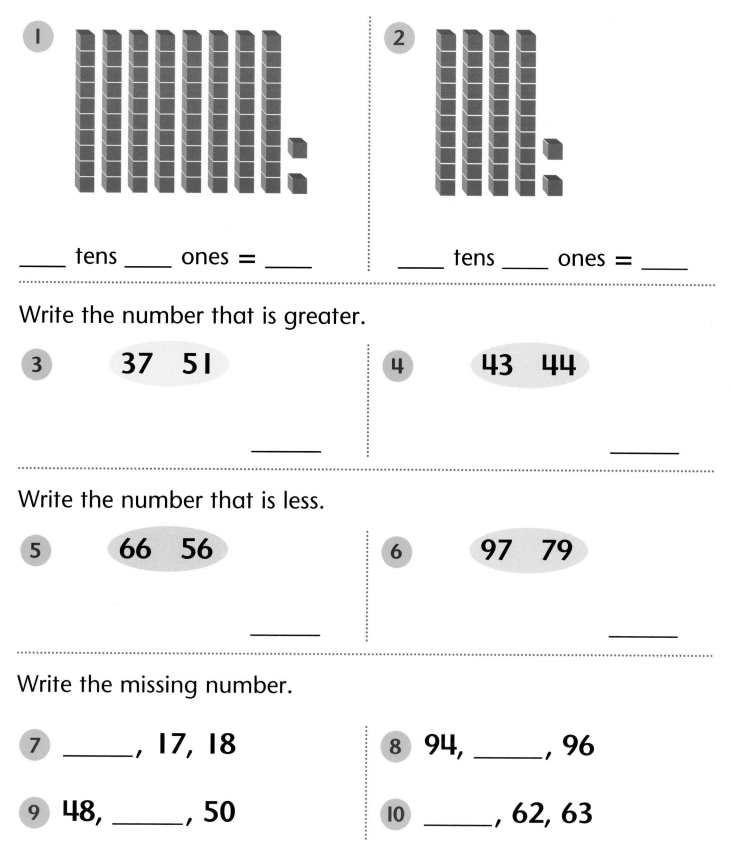

1

____ tens ____ ones = ____

2

____ tens ____ ones = ____

Write the number that is greater.

3   37   51

_____

4   43   44

_____

Write the number that is less.

5   66   56

_____

6   97   79

_____

Write the missing number.

7 _____, 17, 18

8 94, _____, 96

9 48, _____, 50

10 _____, 62, 63

Count by twos.

11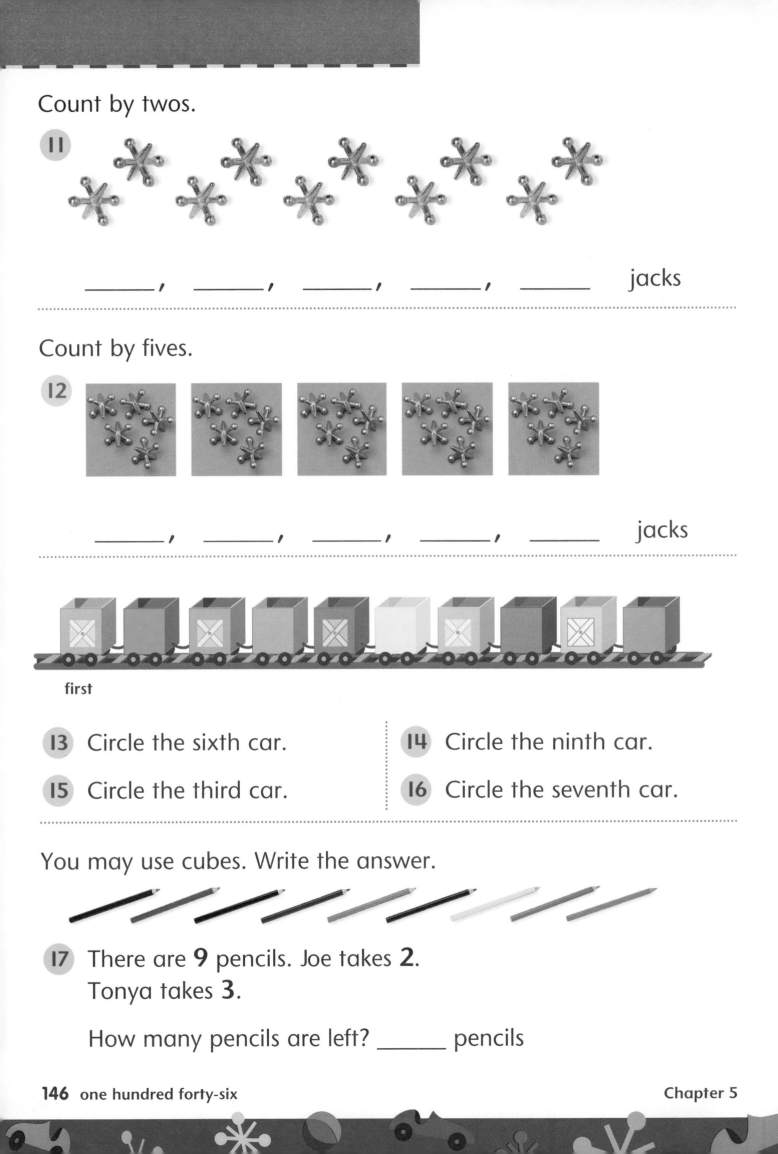

_____ , _____ , _____ , _____ , _____ jacks

Count by fives.

12

_____ , _____ , _____ , _____ , _____ jacks

first

13 Circle the sixth car.

14 Circle the ninth car.

15 Circle the third car.

16 Circle the seventh car.

You may use cubes. Write the answer.

17 There are **9** pencils. Joe takes **2**.
Tonya takes **3**.

How many pencils are left? _____ pencils

Name _____

1 Write your number. _____

2 What number did you use to make **100**? _____

3 How many tens are in your number? _____

4 How many tens are in your partner's number? _____

5 How many tens in all? _____

Internet
Visit Houghton Mifflin's
Education Place Math Center.
http://www.eduplace.com

© Houghton Mifflin Company

Write or draw your answers in the chart.

1 What are there about
  100 of in your school?

2 What are there more
  than **100** of in your school?

3 What are there fewer
  than **100** of in your school?

About 100	
More than 100	
Fewer than 100	

Dear Family: Your child has been learning about the number 100. Help your child think of things that there are 100 of, or more or fewer than 100 of, around your house or neighborhood.

Time and Money

4¢

Class Store

10¢

5¢

Literature

Charley Needs a Haircut
By Ruth I. Dowell

Read Aloud Anthology p. 76
Theme Connection
Stores and Jobs

See what I can do by
the end of this chapter.

Use What You Know

When do you use money?
Can you use money to buy
the items on this page?
How much do they cost?

Listen to the barber shop stories.
Use pennies to act out each story.

Barber Shop

Name _____

Use the calendar. Answer the question.

1. What month is after July? _____

2. How many months are in a year? _____

3. Circle your birthday month.

4. Which is your favorite month? _____

Communication

Draw something you do during your favorite month.

Lesson 6.1

one hundred fifty-one **151**

Complete the calendar.

DECEMBER

Sunday	Monday	Tuesday	Wednesday	Thursday	Friday	Saturday
	1	2				
7						
				25		
			31			

Look at the calendar. Circle the answer.

1 How many Tuesdays are in this month?

     4   5   6

2 What day is after Friday?

     Thursday   Saturday   Sunday

3 How many days are in a week?

     5   6   7

4 What day of the week is between December 17 and December 19?

     Wednesday   Thursday   Friday

Dear Family: Review the days of the week and months of the year with your child.

Lesson 6.1

Name _____

The **minute hand** is on the 12.

The **hour hand** is on the 4.

_4:00_

It is __4__ o'clock.

How can you tell the minute hand from the hour hand?

Use red and blue crayons. Color the hour hand red.
Color the minute hand blue. Say and write the time.

1   _6:00_

__6__ o'clock

2   _9:00_

__9__ o'clock

3   _11:00_

__11__ o'clock

Communication

Talk about it Which number does the minute hand point to on each clock?

Lesson 6.2

Listen to the story. Write the time.

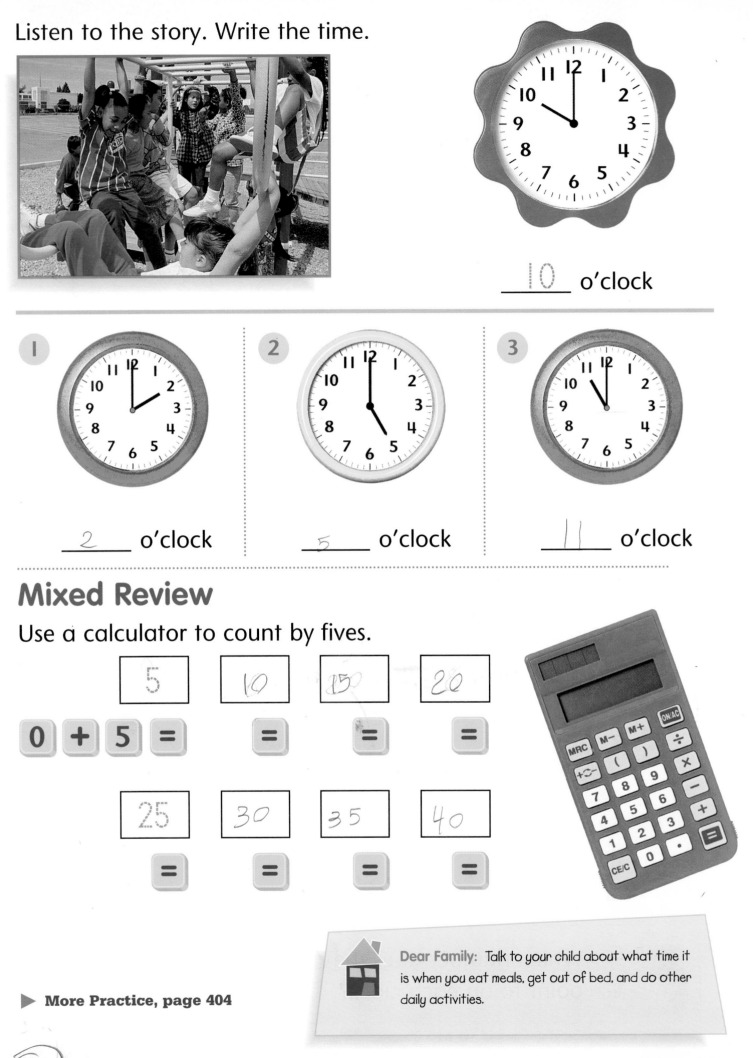

_____10 o'clock

1 ___2___ o'clock

2 ___5___ o'clock

3 ___11___ o'clock

Mixed Review

Use a calculator to count by fives.

5	10	15	20

0 + 5 =   =   =   =

25	30	35	40

=   =   =   =

▶ **More Practice, page 404**

Dear Family: Talk to your child about what time it is when you eat meals, get out of bed, and do other daily activities.

Name _____

These clocks both show 8 o'clock.

8:00

How would your life be different without clocks?

Write the time.

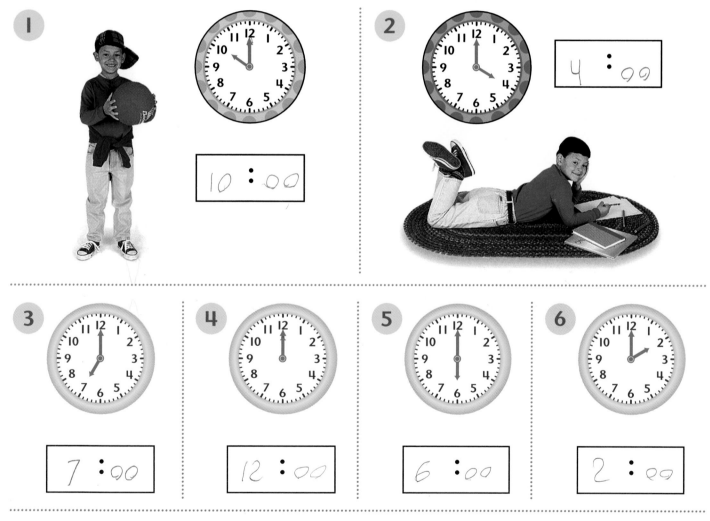

1   10 : 00

2   4 : 00

3   7 : 00

4   12 : 00

5   6 : 00

6   2 : 00

Communication

Draw   Draw what you do at **4:00** in the afternoon.

Lesson 6.3

one hundred fifty-five **155**

Work with a partner.
Look at the clock.
Show the time on your clock.
Draw the time.

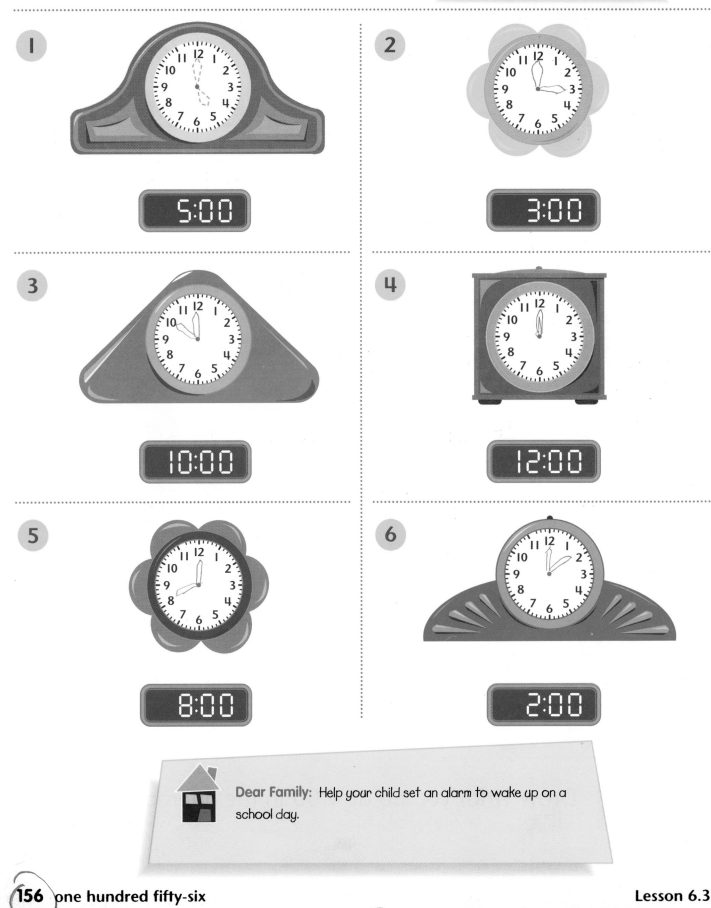

1. 5:00

2. 3:00

3. 10:00

4. 12:00

5. 8:00

6. 2:00

Dear Family: Help your child set an alarm to wake up on a school day.

Name _____

60 minutes are in an **hour**.

_____5_____ o'clock

| 5:00 |

Count by fives to tell the time.

____30____ minutes after ____5____

| 5:30 |

Say and write the time.

1 ____30____ minutes after ____11____

____11____ : ____30____

2 ____15____ minutes after ____6____

____6____ : ____15____

3 ____30____ minutes after ____1____

____1____ : ____30____

4 ____30____ minutes after ____8____

____8____ : ____30____

Communication

Share Tell a partner what you can do in **30** minutes.

Lesson 6.4

one hundred fifty-seven **157**

© Houghton Mifflin Company

Write the time.

1

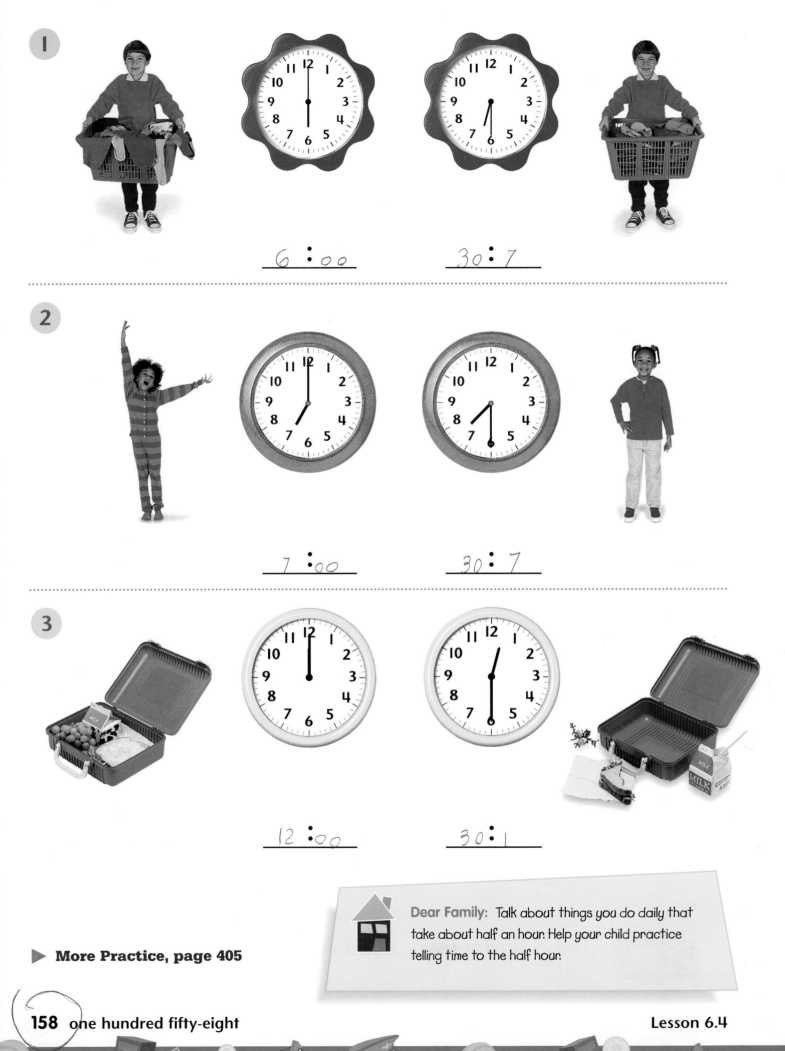

6 : oo   30 : 7

2

7 : oo   30 : 7

3

12 : oo   30 : 1

▶ **More Practice, page 405**

Dear Family: Talk about things you do daily that take about half an hour. Help your child practice telling time to the half hour.

Lesson 6.4

Name _____

Write the time.

1

3 : 00   30 : 6   4 : 00

2

10 : 00   30 : 10   11 : 00

How much time does it take? Match.

3 a few minutes

4 about half an hour

5 about an hour

Sunday	Monday	Tuesday	Wednesday	Thursday	Friday	Saturday
1	2	3	4	5	6	7

1 What day is between Tuesday and Thursday?

_____

2 What day is just before Friday? _____

Draw and write the time.

3

3 o'clock

┌─────────┐
│   :   │
└─────────┘

Write the time.

4

____ minutes after ____

┌─────────┐
│   :   │
└─────────┘

Draw the time.

5

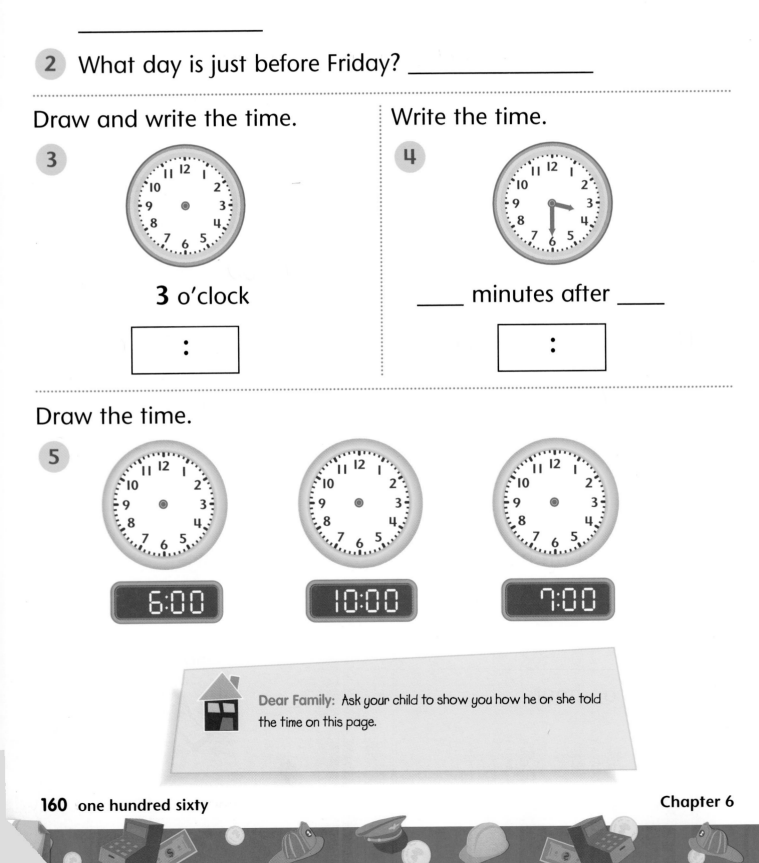

6:00   10:00   7:00

Dear Family: Ask your child to show you how he or she told the time on this page.

Name _____

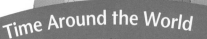

Math World

In many places, people use calendars to measure time.

People use many different measures and symbols for time in **China**. This round Chinese symbol calendar shows 12 years.

The animals stand for different years.

Internet

Explore Houghton Mifflin's
Education Place Math Center.
http://www.eduplace.com

▶ **Turn the page for directions.**

Did you know?

The Chinese use a calendar based on the moon for daily events.

Try this!

Make your own round calendar.
Use what you know about your calendar.
Create a symbol for each of the 12 months.

A Cut out a large circle. Write the name of one month in each of the 12 sections.

B Draw your symbols for each month on small pieces of paper. Glue the symbols to the months.

Dear Family: Help your child practice the months of the year.

- Ask your child to tell you about the Chinese 12 year calendar. Look at the animal symbols for the years.

- Talk about how the Chinese way of showing time is different from or similar to the calendars in your home.

- Look at your child's round calendar. Ask family members to choose a favorite month, such as a month when you have a family celebration.

Name _____

Jess has **4** chains.
He wants a chain **10** links long.
Which chains can he put together?

▶ **Understand**

I need to find out which chains will make
a **10** link chain.

▶ **Plan**

I can guess and check.

▶ **Try it**

I look at the chains. I
guess these make **10**.

I will put them together
to check. I count **10**.

▶ **Look back**

$3 + 7 = 10$ My guess was correct.

Give it a try   Use the chains Jess used. Which two make the
longest chain?

Make these chains.

Guess and Check.

1. Which two chains make a chain **6** links long?
Write the colors.

_____ and _____

2. Which two chains make a chain **8** links long?
Write the colors.

_____ and _____

3. Which two chains make a chain **7** links long?
Write the colors.

_____ and _____

4. Which two chains make a chain **9** links long?
Write the colors.

_____ and _____

Dear Family: Ask your child why someone might need to guess and check to solve some problems.

Name _____

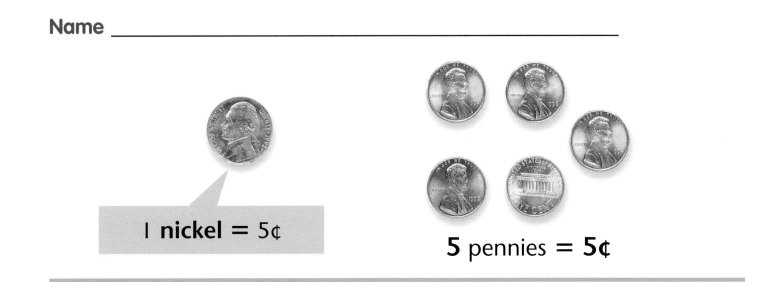

I **nickel** = 5¢

5 pennies = **5¢**

Use nickels. Count by fives. Write the amount.

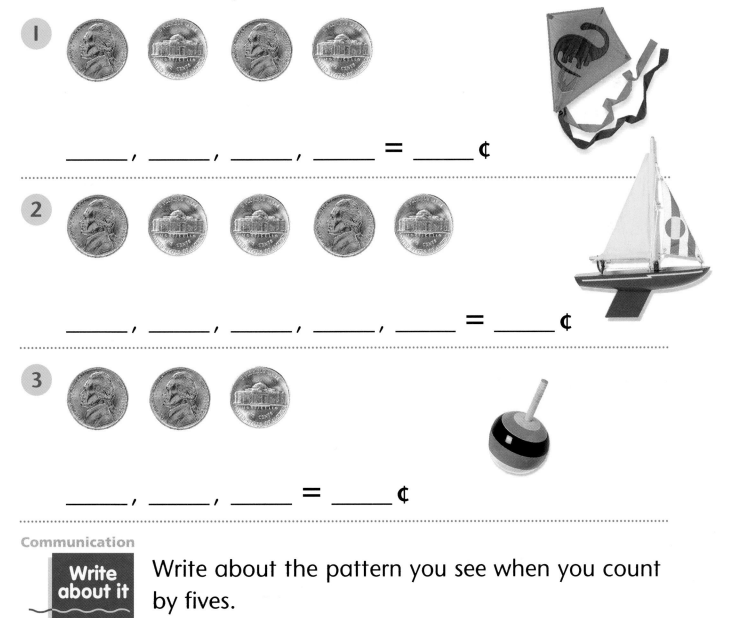

1 _____, _____, _____, _____ = _____ ¢

2 _____, _____, _____, _____, _____ = _____ ¢

3 _____, _____, _____ = _____ ¢

Communication

Write about it Write about the pattern you see when you count by fives.

© Houghton Mifflin Company

Use coins. Count the money. Write the amount.

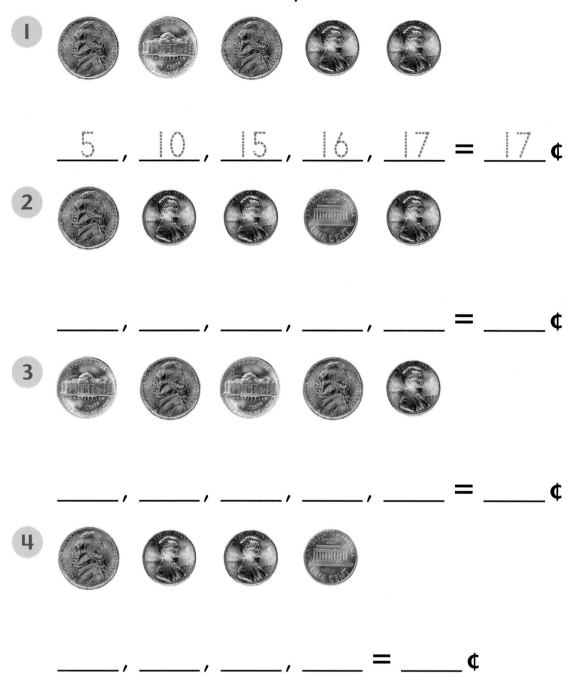

1. _5_ , _10_ , _15_ , _16_ , _17_ = _17_ ¢

2. _____ , _____ , _____ , _____ , _____ = _____ ¢

3. _____ , _____ , _____ , _____ , _____ = _____ ¢

4. _____ , _____ , _____ , _____ = _____ ¢

Communication

Talk about it

Use nickels and pennies.
How many of each do you need to make **32¢**?
Talk with your classmates. Which coins did they use?

▶ **More Practice, page 405**

Dear Family: Give your child some pennies and nickels to practice counting. Ask your child to show you how to count by fives.

Lesson 6.7

Name _____

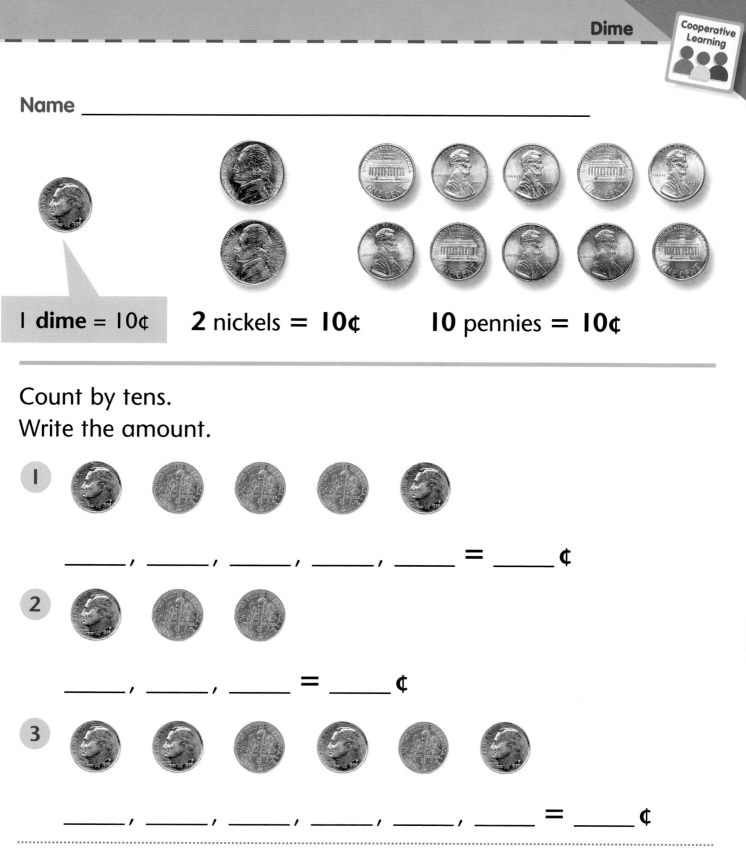

1 dime = 10¢   **2** nickels = **10¢**   **10** pennies = **10¢**

Count by tens.
Write the amount.

1 _____ , _____ , _____ , _____ , _____ = _____ ¢

2 _____ , _____ , _____ = _____ ¢

3 _____ , _____ , _____ , _____ , _____ , _____ = _____ ¢

Give it a try Use dimes, nickels, and pennies.
Cid has **8** pennies. Lisa has **2** nickels.
Greg has **3** dimes. Who has the most money?

_____

Lesson 6.8

Work with a group.
Count the money.
Write the amount.

1

= _____ ¢

2

= _____ ¢

3

= _____ ¢

4

= _____ ¢

▶ **More Practice, page 406**

Dear Family: Have your child count your change when shopping. Include only pennies, nickels, and dimes.

Lesson 6.8

Name _____

Work with a partner.
Count the money.
Write the amount.

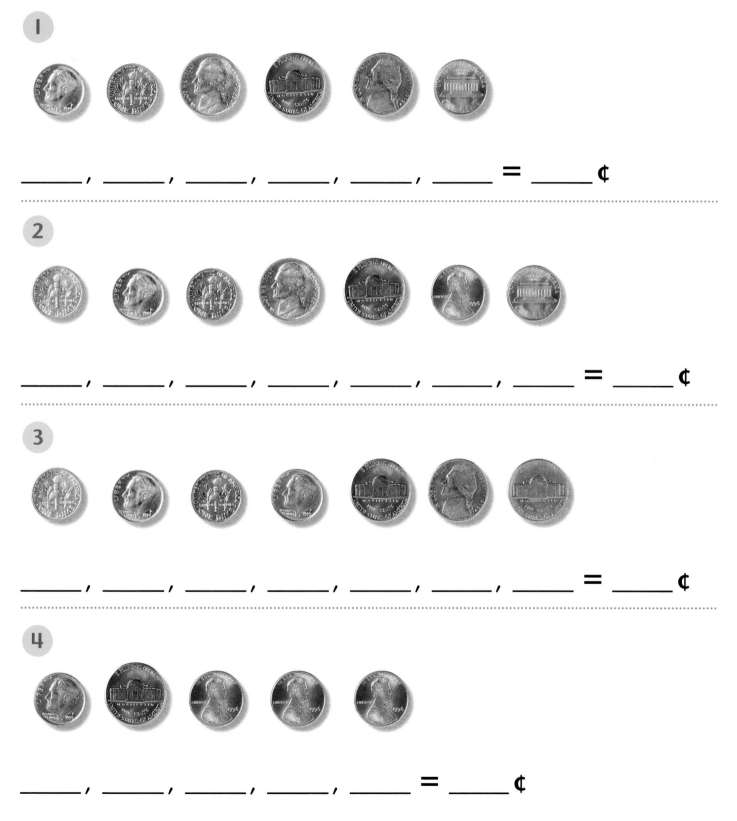

1

_____ , _____ , _____ , _____ , _____ , _____ = _____ ¢

2

_____ , _____ , _____ , _____ , _____ , _____ , _____ = _____ ¢

3

_____ , _____ , _____ , _____ , _____ , _____ , _____ = _____ ¢

4

_____ , _____ , _____ , _____ , _____ = _____ ¢

Use dimes, nickels, and pennies.
Write how many you need of each coin.

1. 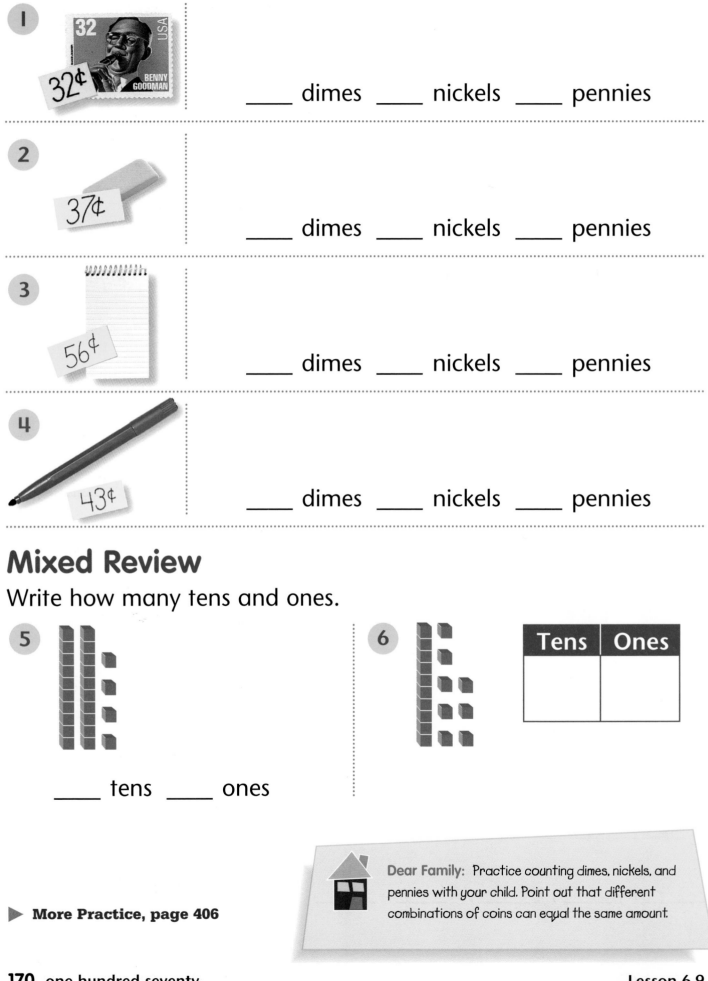 32¢

   ____ dimes ____ nickels ____ pennies

2. 37¢

   ____ dimes ____ nickels ____ pennies

3. 56¢

   ____ dimes ____ nickels ____ pennies

4. 43¢

   ____ dimes ____ nickels ____ pennies

Mixed Review

Write how many tens and ones.

5. ____ tens ____ ones

6.
Tens	Ones

▶ **More Practice, page 406**

Dear Family: Practice counting dimes, nickels, and pennies with your child. Point out that different combinations of coins can equal the same amount.

Name _____

A Guess the amount.
Write your guess.

B Check by counting.
Write the amount.

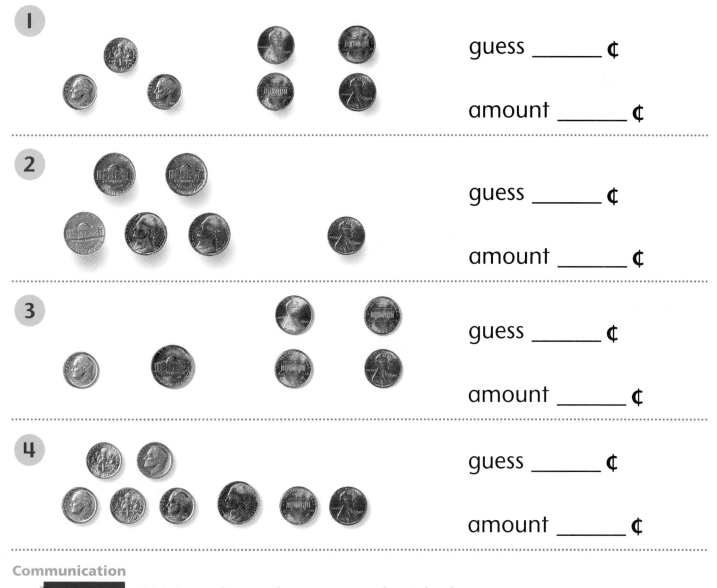

1 guess _____ ¢

amount _____ ¢

2 guess _____ ¢

amount _____ ¢

3 guess _____ ¢

amount _____ ¢

4 guess _____ ¢

amount _____ ¢

Communication

Write about how you decided on your guesses.

Look at the price.
Guess if you have enough money to buy the item.
Circle your answer.
Count the money. Was your guess correct?

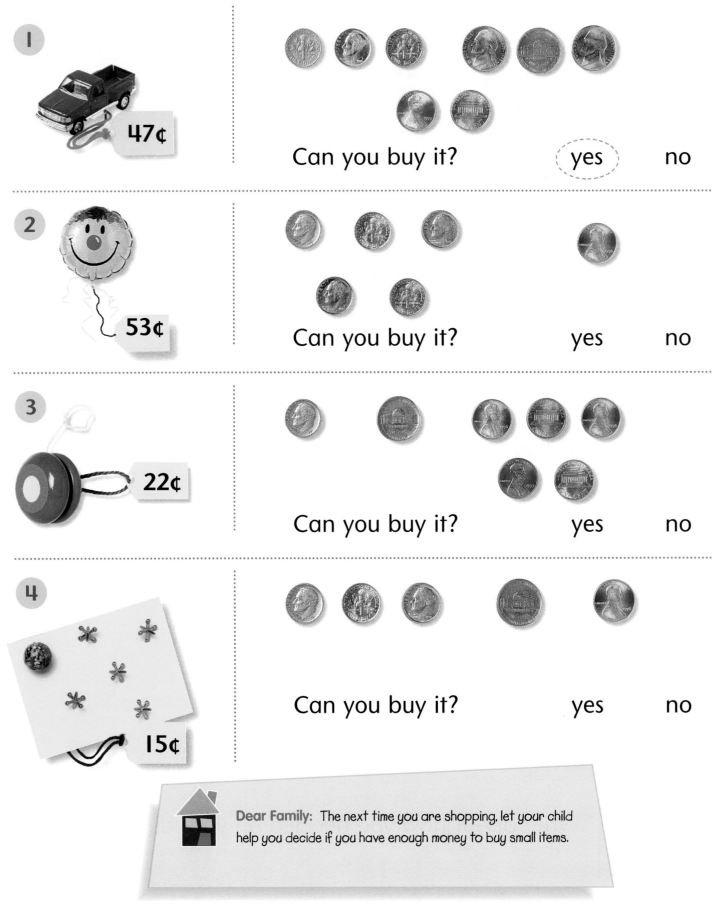

1

47¢

Can you buy it?   yes   no

2

53¢

Can you buy it?   yes   no

3

22¢

Can you buy it?   yes   no

4

15¢

Can you buy it?   yes   no

Dear Family: The next time you are shopping, let your child help you decide if you have enough money to buy small items.

Cooperative Learning

Name _____

A **quarter** equals 25¢.

Work with a partner.
Use dimes, nickels, and pennies.
How many of each coin make **25¢**?
Write your answer on the chart.

Communication

Talk with other pairs.
Compare how you made **25¢**.

Work with a partner.
Count the money.
Write the amount.

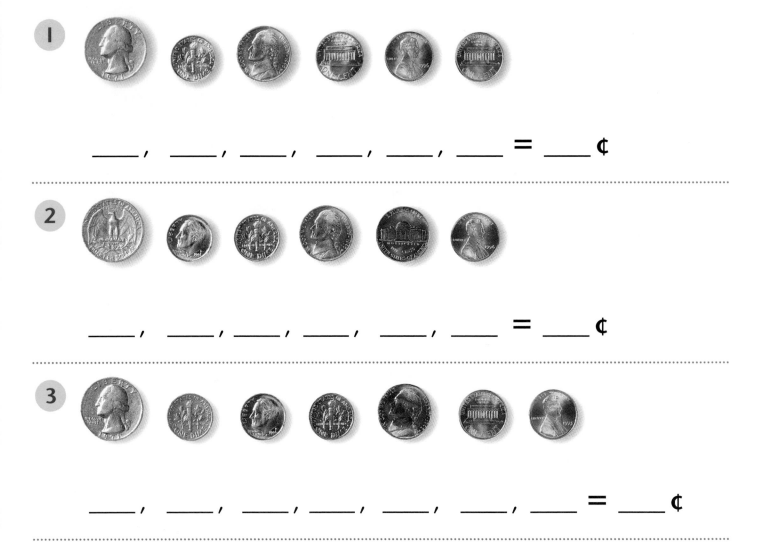

1 ____ , ____ , ____ , ____ , ____ , ____ = ____ ¢

2 ____ , ____ , ____ , ____ , ____ , ____ = ____ ¢

3 ____ , ____ , ____ , ____ , ____ , ____ , ____ = ____ ¢

Use coins.

4 Andy has **2** nickels. Trinh has **6** pennies.
Divide the money between them.
Write the coins each child will get.

____ nickel ____ pennies

▶ **More Practice, page 407**

Dear Family: Practice counting pennies, nickels, dimes, and quarters with your child.

Lesson 6.11

Name _____

Use **2** quarters, **5** dimes, **6** nickels, and **6** pennies.
Buy **3** items.
Circle the items you buy.

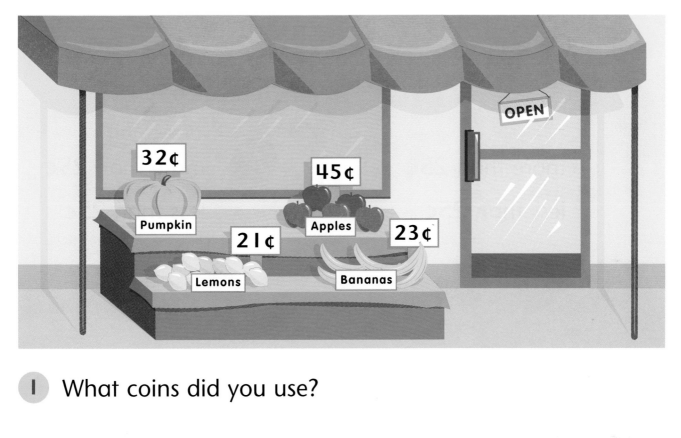

1. What coins did you use?

_____ quarters _____ dimes _____ nickels _____ pennies

2. What coins are left?

_____ quarters _____ dimes _____ nickels _____ pennies

3. Can you buy one more item? _____

How much does it cost? _____ ¢

Communication

 Talk with a friend.
Who has more money left?

How much money do you see?
Guess. Circle your guess.

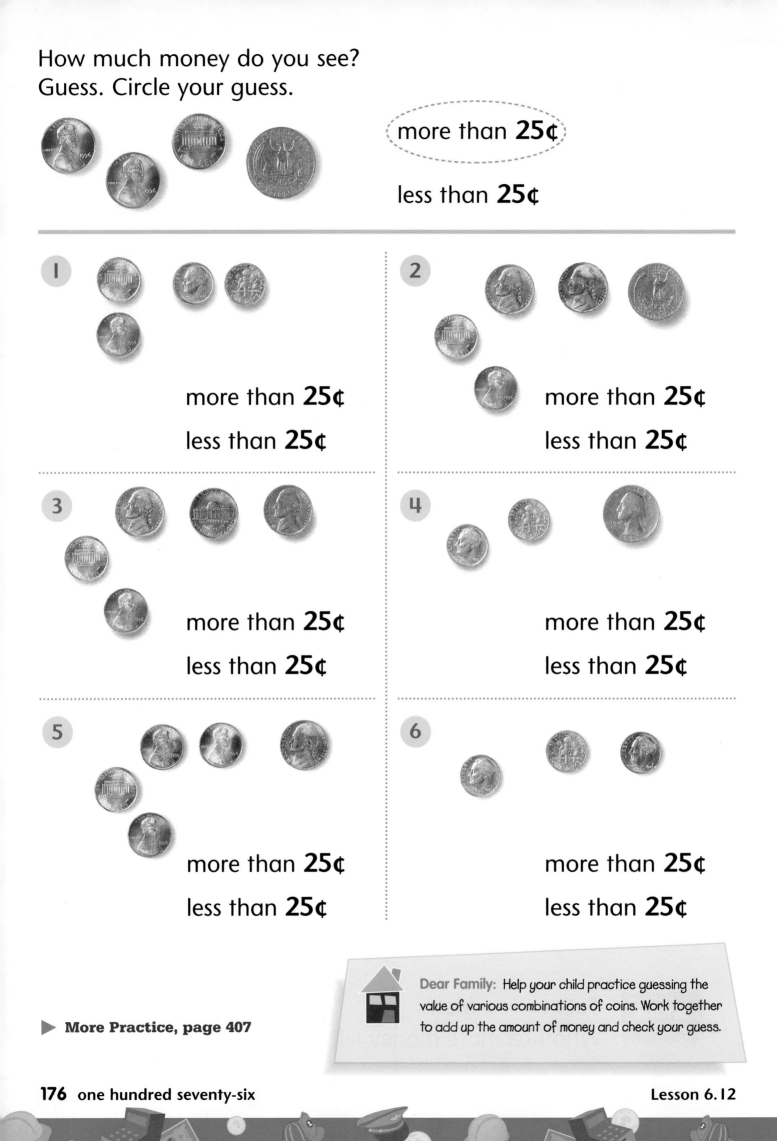

more than 25¢

less than 25¢

1

more than 25¢

less than 25¢

2

more than 25¢

less than 25¢

3

more than 25¢

less than 25¢

4

more than 25¢

less than 25¢

5

more than 25¢

less than 25¢

6

more than 25¢

less than 25¢

▶ **More Practice, page 407**

Dear Family: Help your child practice guessing the value of various combinations of coins. Work together to add up the amount of money and check your guess.

Name _____

Andrew and Paula went to a store.
Look at the table.
It tells how much things cost at the store.

Supply Sale

	1	2	3	4	5
envelope	5¢	10¢	15¢	20¢	25¢
pen	10¢	20¢	30¢	40¢	50¢

Use the table to solve each problem.

1 How much does **1** envelope cost? _____ ¢

2 How much do **2** pens cost? _____ ¢

3 How much do **4** envelopes cost? _____ ¢

4 How much do **3** pens and **2** envelopes cost? _____ ¢

5 Andrew and Paula have **40¢** in all. What can they buy?

_____ pens _____ envelopes

6 Andrew and Paula have **35¢** in all. What can they buy?

_____ pens _____ envelopes

Communication

Share   Tell a partner how you found your answers.

Lesson 6.13   one hundred seventy-seven **177**

The bar graph shows how much each child saved.

Money We Have Saved

	Dwayne	Ken	Lori	Miranda	James
11 ¢					
10 ¢	■				
9 ¢	■				
8 ¢	■			■	
7 ¢	■		■	■	
6 ¢	■	■	■	■	
5 ¢	■	■	■	■	
4 ¢	■	■	■	■	■
3 ¢	■	■	■	■	■
2 ¢	■	■	■	■	■
1 ¢	■	■	■	■	■
0 ¢					

Use the graph to answer each question.

1 How many children saved at least **7¢**? _____

2 Who saved **8¢**? _____

3 Who saved the most money? _____

4 Who saved the least money? _____

5 How much did Ken save? _____

6 One child saved only a nickel and two pennies.

   Who was it? _____

Dear Family: Help your child save money in a piggy bank.
Keep track of the money saved by making a graph.

Name _____

Sunday	Monday	Tuesday	Wednesday	Thursday	Friday	Saturday
1	2	3	4	5	6	7

1 What is the fourth day of the week? _____

Write the time.

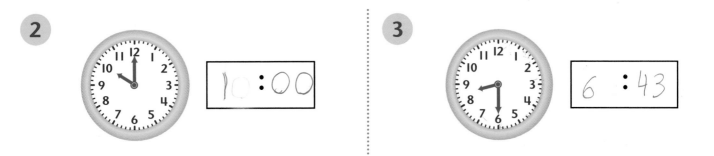

2 10 : 00

3 6 : 43

Draw or write the time.

4 12:00

5 6 : 10

6 9:00

7 6 : 4

Write the amount.

8  _____ ¢

9 _____ ¢

10 _____ ¢

Look at the price.
Guess if you have enough money.
Count the money. Circle your answer.

11  **36¢**

Can you buy it?   yes   no

12 **27¢**

Can you buy it?   yes   no

Name _____

1 Write or draw something you
can buy at the class store.

2 How much does it cost? _____

3 Draw the coins you use to pay for it.

4 What other coins can you use to buy it?

Internet
Visit Houghton Mifflin's
Education Place Math Center.
http://www.eduplace.com

1 Draw what you can buy if you have
2 dimes and **5** pennies.

2 Draw the coins you will use.

3 Do you have money left over?   yes   no

4 How can you tell?

_____

_____

Dear Family: Today your child practiced using coins to buy and sell things. Help your child think of other things that can be bought with dimes and pennies.

Addition and Subtraction Facts Through 12

Literature

Mr. Finney's Turnip

Anonymous

Read Aloud Anthology pp. 30
Theme Connection
Good Things to Eat

See what I can do by
the end of this chapter.

Use What You Know

Count the cherries.
Count the oranges.
How many pieces of fruit
are there in all?

Listen to the vegetable stories.
Use cubes to act out each story.

 Dear Family: Think about the foods you eat. Keep a record of how many fruits and vegetables you eat in a week. Do you eat more vegetables or fruits? Hint: Some vegetables are really fruits in disguise.

Name _____

Problem Solving

Act out the problems.
Use cubes and a workmat.

1. Juan has **7** apples. He gives away **4** apples. How many apples does Juan have now?

_____ apples

2. Maria eats **5** red grapes. Then she eats **4** white grapes. How many grapes does Maria eat?

_____ grapes

3. There are **5** girls at the table. There are **5** boys at the table. How many children are at the table?

_____ children

4. Jerome has **10** raisins. He eats **6** raisins. How many raisins does Jerome have left?

_____ raisins

Dear Family: Take turns counting out 2 groups of objects (totaling no more than 10) and telling an addition or a subtraction sentence to match.

▶ **More Practice, page 408**

Lesson 7.1

Add or subtract.

$$\begin{array}{r} 8 \\ -0 \\ \hline 8 \end{array}$$

$$\begin{array}{r} 3 \\ +6 \\ \hline 9 \end{array}$$

$$\begin{array}{r} 9 \\ -5 \\ \hline 4 \end{array}$$

$$\begin{array}{r} 7 \\ +2 \\ \hline 9 \end{array}$$

$$\begin{array}{r} 1 \\ +8 \\ \hline 9 \end{array}$$

$$\begin{array}{r} 8 \\ -3 \\ \hline 5 \end{array}$$

$$8 - 5 = 3$$

$$\begin{array}{r} 6 \\ +4 \\ \hline 0 \end{array}$$

$$0 + 4 = 4$$

$$6 - 3 = 3$$

$$4 + 5 = 9$$

$$4 + 2 = 6$$

$$7 \\ -6 \\ \hline 1$$

$$9 - 3 = 6$$

$$3 + 7 = 4$$

$$5 - 5 = 0$$

Give it a try

Circle the answer.

Are there more beets or tomatoes?

Are there more carrots or peppers?

Are there fewer tomatoes or carrots?

Are there fewer peppers or beets?

Name _____

A Make the train.
Write the addition sentence.

B Flip the train over.
Write the addition sentence.

Does the order of the numbers change their sum?

Use cubes. Write the addition sentence two ways.

1. **8** red cubes and **3** blue cubes

    _8_ + _3_ = _11_   _3_ + _8_ = _11_

2. **5** red cubes and **7** blue cubes

    _5_ + _7_ = _11_   _7_ + _5_ = _11_

3. **9** red cubes and **3** blue cubes

    _9_ + _3_ = _12_   _3_ + _9_ = _12_

Organize 2 groups of objects with sums up to 12 (fruits, vegetables, nuts). Ask your child to tell you two ways to say the addition sentence.

Use the picture.
Write **2** addition sentences.

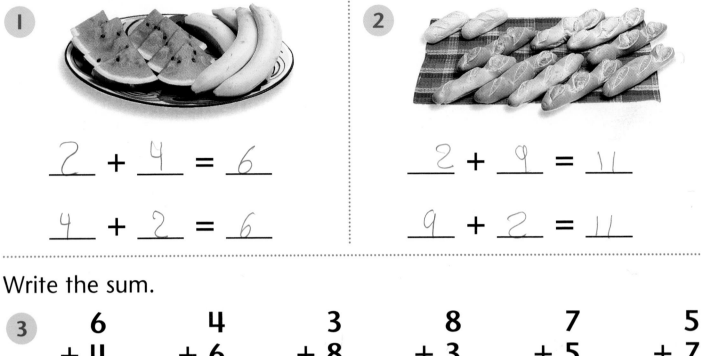

1

$2 + 4 = 6$

$4 + 2 = 6$

2

$2 + 9 = 11$

$9 + 2 = 11$

Write the sum.

3

6	4	3	8	7	5
+ 4	+ 6	+ 8	+ 3	+ 5	+ 7
10	10	11	11	12	12

4

6	5	2	4	2	8
+ 3	+ 2	+ 7	+ 3	+ 6	+ 0
9	7	9	7	8	8

5

5	1	7	6	3	2
+ 4	+ 9	+ 0	+ 4	+ 5	+ 8
9	10	7	10	8	10

6

4	9	0	4	5	8
+ 5	+ 1	+ 7	+ 6	+ 3	+ 2
9	10	7	10	8	10

Communication

Talk about it

Look carefully at rows **5** and **6**.
What do you see?

Name _____

How many apples are there?

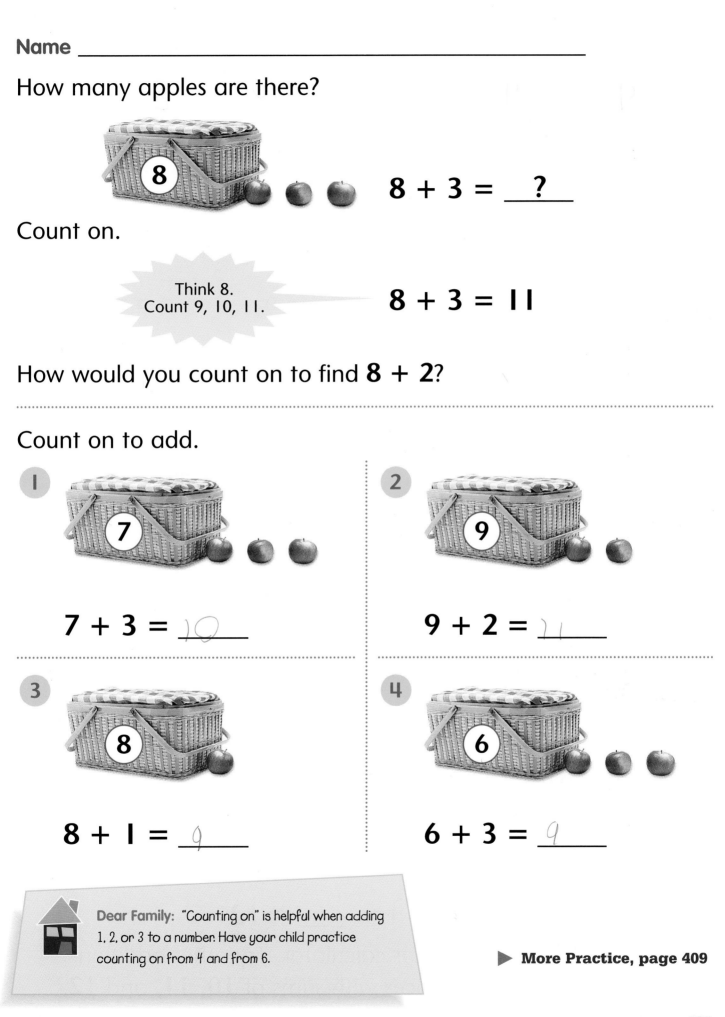

8 + 3 = ___?___

Count on.

Think 8.
Count 9, 10, 11.

8 + 3 = 11

How would you count on to find **8 + 2**?

Count on to add.

1.

7 + 3 = _10_

2.

9 + 2 = _11_

3.

8 + 1 = _9_

4.

6 + 3 = _9_

Dear Family: "Counting on" is helpful when adding 1, 2, or 3 to a number. Have your child practice counting on from 4 and from 6.

▶ **More Practice, page 409**

© Houghton Mifflin Company

Lesson 7.4

Count on to add.

1

$$7 + 2 = 9$$ $$8 + 1 = 9$$ $$5 + 3 = 8$$ $$8 + 2 = 10$$ $$7 + 1 = 8$$ $$6 + 3 = 9$$

2

$$4 + 2 = 6$$ $$8 + 3 = 11$$ $$9 + 1 = 10$$ $$6 + 2 = 8$$ $$9 + 3 = 12$$ $$5 + 2 = 7$$

3

$$4 + 3 = 7$$ $$6 + 1 = 7$$ $$10 + 1 = 11$$ $$5 + 2 = 7$$ $$7 + 1 = 8$$ $$10 + 2 = 12$$

4 $8 + 2 = \underline{10}$ $9 + 3 = \underline{12}$ $6 + 1 = \underline{7}$

5 $7 + 3 = \underline{10}$ $8 + 1 = \underline{9}$ $9 + 2 = \underline{11}$

Give it a try

Write **3** addition sentences.
Use each number once.

3 4 5 6 7 8

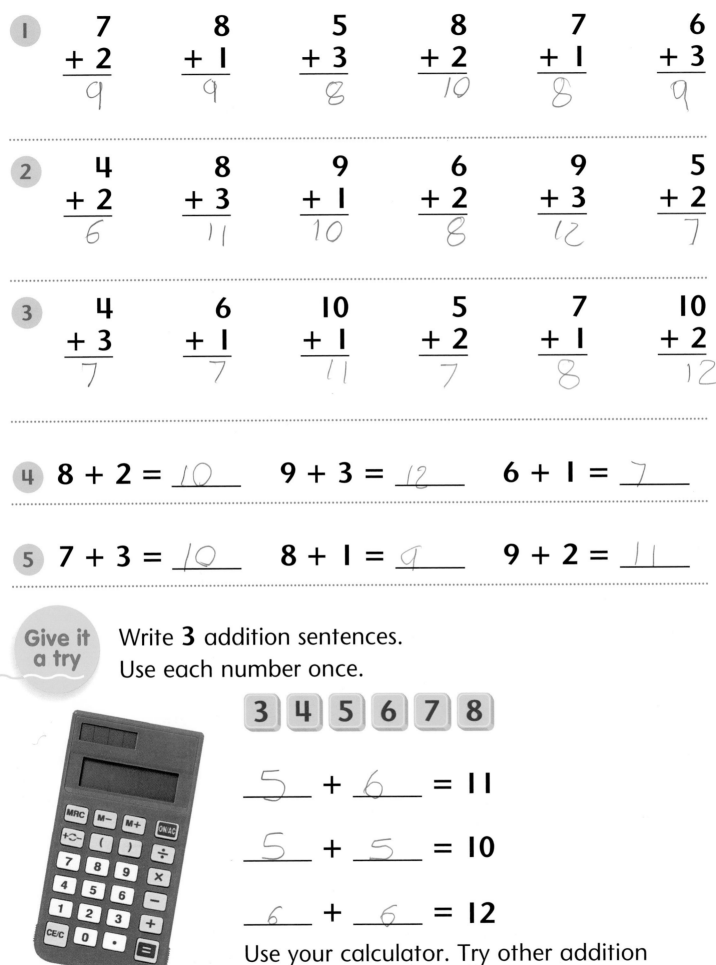

$$\underline{5} + \underline{6} = 11$$

$$\underline{5} + \underline{5} = 10$$

$$\underline{6} + \underline{6} = 12$$

Use your calculator. Try other addition
sentences with sums of **10, 11,** and **12.**

Name _____

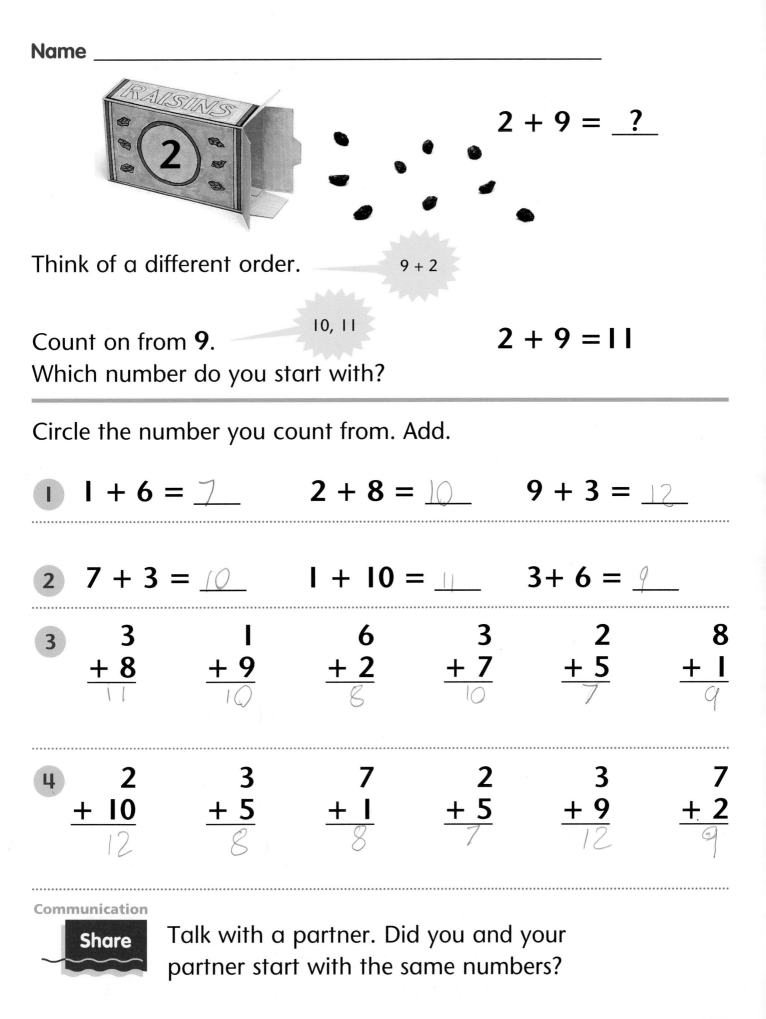

$2 + 9 = \underline{\ ?\ }$

Think of a different order.

9 + 2

Count on from **9**.
Which number do you start with?

10, 11

$2 + 9 = 11$

Circle the number you count from. Add.

1 $1 + 6 = \underline{7}$ $2 + 8 = \underline{10}$ $9 + 3 = \underline{12}$

2 $7 + 3 = \underline{10}$ $1 + 10 = \underline{11}$ $3 + 6 = \underline{9}$

3
$$\begin{array}{r} 3 \\ +\ 8 \\ \hline 11 \end{array} \qquad \begin{array}{r} 1 \\ +\ 9 \\ \hline 10 \end{array} \qquad \begin{array}{r} 6 \\ +\ 2 \\ \hline 8 \end{array} \qquad \begin{array}{r} 3 \\ +\ 7 \\ \hline 10 \end{array} \qquad \begin{array}{r} 2 \\ +\ 5 \\ \hline 7 \end{array} \qquad \begin{array}{r} 8 \\ +\ 1 \\ \hline 9 \end{array}$$

4
$$\begin{array}{r} 2 \\ +\ 10 \\ \hline 12 \end{array} \qquad \begin{array}{r} 3 \\ +\ 5 \\ \hline 8 \end{array} \qquad \begin{array}{r} 7 \\ +\ 1 \\ \hline 8 \end{array} \qquad \begin{array}{r} 2 \\ +\ 5 \\ \hline 7 \end{array} \qquad \begin{array}{r} 3 \\ +\ 9 \\ \hline 12 \end{array} \qquad \begin{array}{r} 7 \\ +\ 2 \\ \hline 9 \end{array}$$

Communication

Share   Talk with a partner. Did you and your partner start with the same numbers?

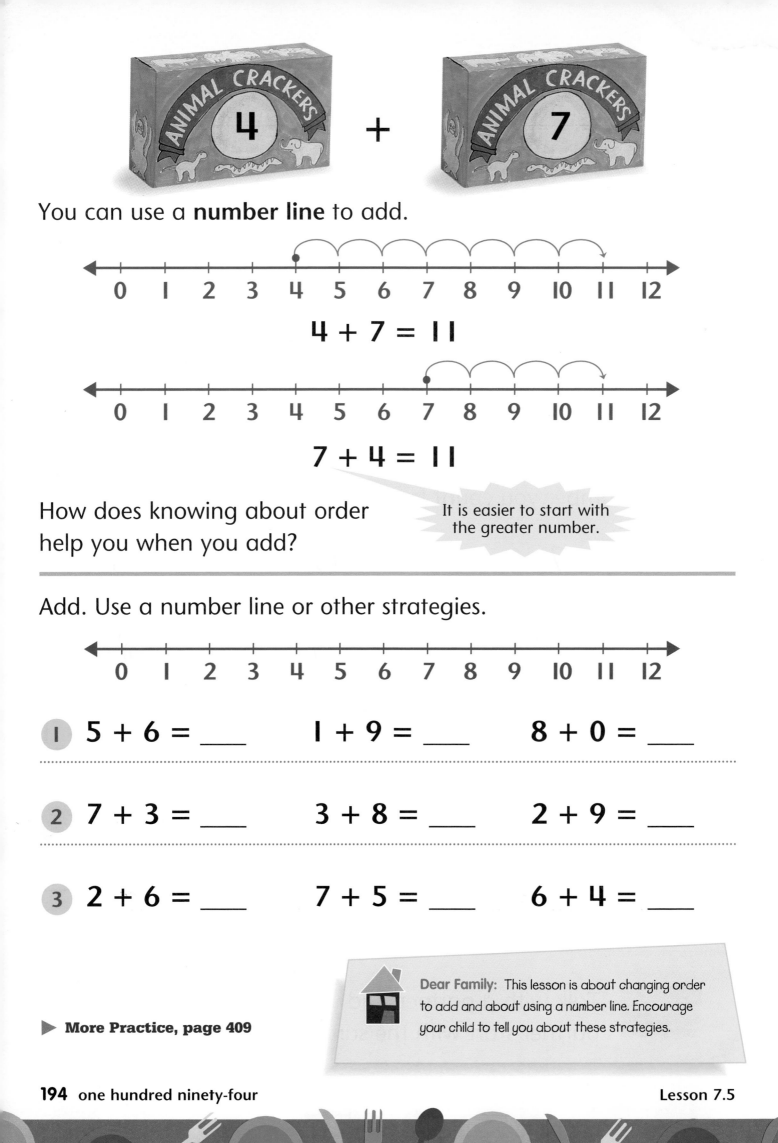

You can use a **number line** to add.

$$4 + 7 = 11$$

$$7 + 4 = 11$$

How does knowing about order help you when you add?

It is easier to start with the greater number.

Add. Use a number line or other strategies.

1. $5 + 6 = \underline{}$ $1 + 9 = \underline{}$ $8 + 0 = \underline{}$

2. $7 + 3 = \underline{}$ $3 + 8 = \underline{}$ $2 + 9 = \underline{}$

3. $2 + 6 = \underline{}$ $7 + 5 = \underline{}$ $6 + 4 = \underline{}$

Dear Family: This lesson is about changing order to add and about using a number line. Encourage your child to tell you about these strategies.

▶ **More Practice, page 409**

Lesson 7.5

Name _____

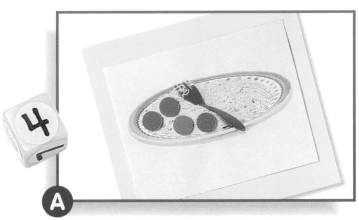

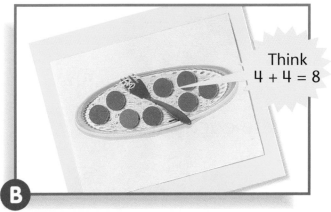

Think
4 + 4 = 8

A Work with a partner. Roll a number cube. Show the number with counters.

B Make **doubles**. Write the number sentence.

What things come in doubles?

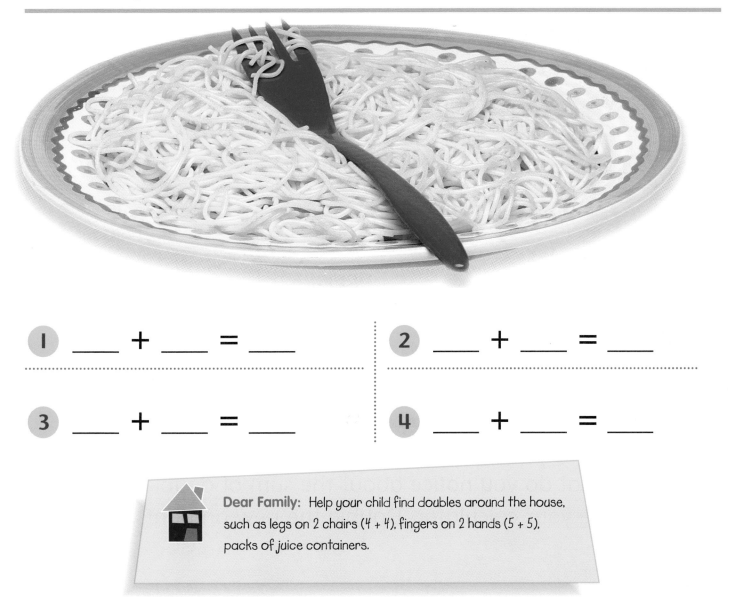

1 ___ + ___ = ___

2 ___ + ___ = ___

3 ___ + ___ = ___

4 ___ + ___ = ___

Dear Family: Help your child find doubles around the house, such as legs on 2 chairs (4 + 4), fingers on 2 hands (5 + 5), packs of juice containers.

© Houghton Mifflin Company

Lesson 7.6

Write the sum. You may use counters.

1

3	1	5	2	4	6
+ 3	+ 1	+ 5	+ 2	+ 4	+ 6

Complete each double.

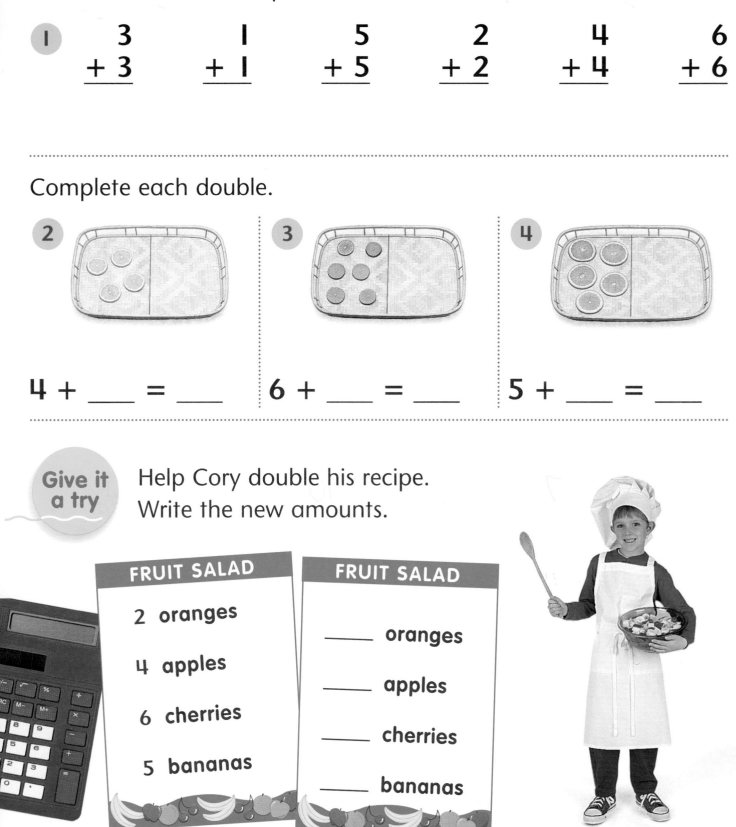

2

4 + ___ = ___

3

6 + ___ = ___

4

5 + ___ = ___

Give it a try

Help Cory double his recipe.
Write the new amounts.

FRUIT SALAD

2 oranges

4 apples

6 cherries

5 bananas

FRUIT SALAD

____ oranges

____ apples

____ cherries

____ bananas

What do you notice about the sum of doubles?
Use your calculator. Double the new amounts.

Cooperative Learning

Name _____

Work with a partner.

Take some cubes. Sort them in the gardens.

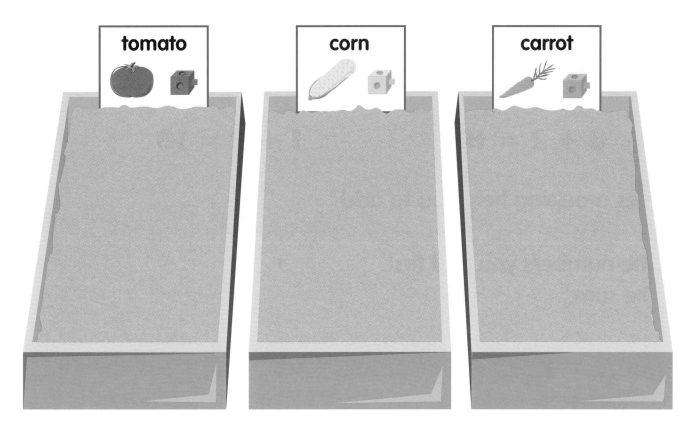

tomato   corn   carrot

Write the number sentence.

1 _____ + _____ + _____ = _____

2 _____ + _____ + _____ = _____

3 _____ + _____ + _____ = _____

4 _____ + _____ + _____ = _____

Dear Family: Show 3 groups of objects (no more than 12 in all). Ask how many. Ask if the sum changes when the numbers are added in a different order.

▶ **More Practice, page 410**

Lesson 7.7

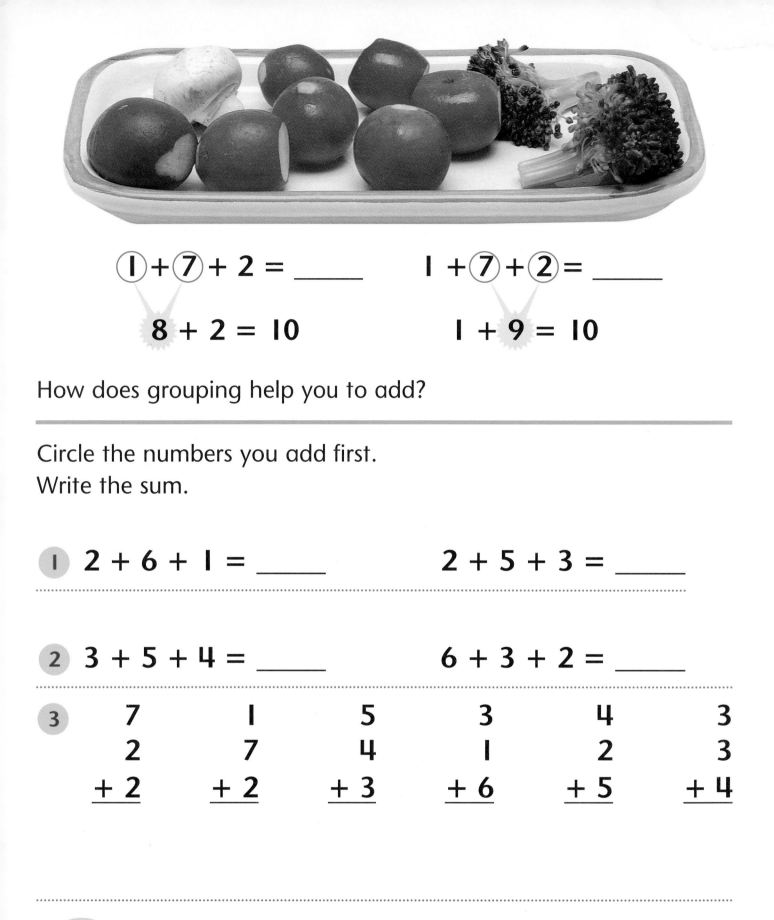

$①+⑦+2 = \rule{1cm}{0.1mm}$ $1 +⑦+② = \rule{1cm}{0.1mm}$

$8 + 2 = 10$ $1 + 9 = 10$

How does grouping help you to add?

Circle the numbers you add first.
Write the sum.

1. $2 + 6 + 1 = \rule{1cm}{0.1mm}$ $2 + 5 + 3 = \rule{1cm}{0.1mm}$

2. $3 + 5 + 4 = \rule{1cm}{0.1mm}$ $6 + 3 + 2 = \rule{1cm}{0.1mm}$

3.

7	1	5	3	4	3
2	7	4	1	2	3
+ 2	+ 2	+ 3	+ 6	+ 5	+ 4

Give it a try   Write addition sentences.
Use **2**, **5**, and **4**. The sum is **11**.
How many different sentences can you write?

Name _____

Lucy wants to know what is in the bags.

Add. Use the code to find the message.
Write a letter to match each sum.

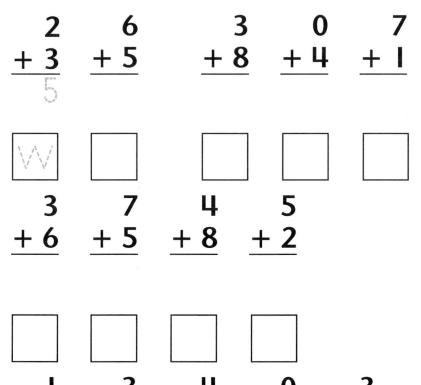

$$2 \atop +3$$ $$6 \atop +5$$ $$3 \atop +8$$ $$0 \atop +4$$ $$7 \atop +1$$

□ □ □ □ □

$$3 \atop +6$$ $$7 \atop +5$$ $$4 \atop +8$$ $$5 \atop +2$$

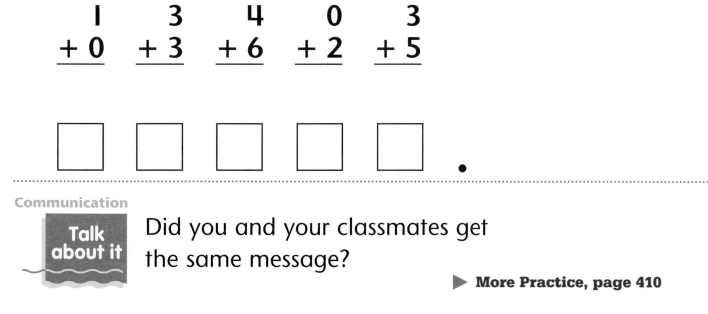

□ □ □ □

$$1 \atop +0$$ $$3 \atop +3$$ $$4 \atop +6$$ $$0 \atop +2$$ $$3 \atop +5$$

□ □ □ □ □ .

Communication

Talk about it Did you and your classmates get the same message?

▶ **More Practice, page 410**

Lesson 7.8

Write the sum.

1.
$$\begin{array}{r} 4 \\ +\ 3 \\ \hline \end{array}$$

2.
$$\begin{array}{r} 2 \\ +\ 9 \\ \hline \end{array}$$

3.
$$\begin{array}{r} 1 \\ +\ 7 \\ \hline \end{array}$$

4.
$$\begin{array}{r} 6 \\ +\ 0 \\ \hline \end{array}$$

5.
$$\begin{array}{r} 7 \\ +\ 5 \\ \hline \end{array}$$

6.
$$\begin{array}{r} 3 \\ +\ 8 \\ \hline \end{array}$$

7.
$$\begin{array}{r} 4 \\ +\ 4 \\ \hline \end{array}$$

8.
$$\begin{array}{r} 0 \\ +\ 9 \\ \hline \end{array}$$

9.
$$\begin{array}{r} 2 \\ +\ 5 \\ \hline \end{array}$$

10.
$$\begin{array}{r} 3 \\ +\ 3 \\ \hline \end{array}$$

Add. Use the number line or other strategies.

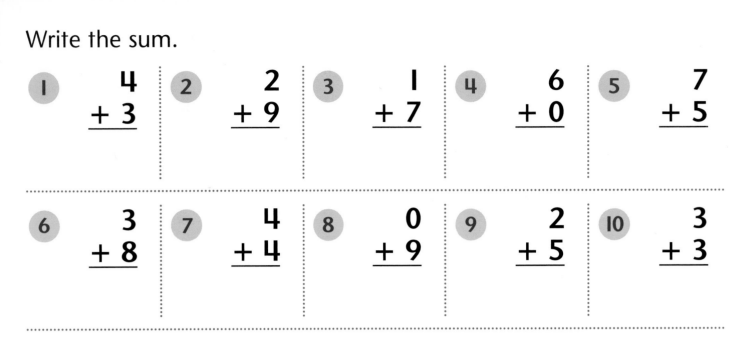

0 1 2 3 4 5 6 7 8 9 10 11 12

11.
$$\begin{array}{r} 4 \\ +\ 6 \\ \hline \end{array}$$

12.
$$\begin{array}{r} 3 \\ +\ 8 \\ \hline \end{array}$$

13.
$$\begin{array}{r} 5 \\ +\ 7 \\ \hline \end{array}$$

14.
$$\begin{array}{r} 6 \\ +\ 2 \\ \hline \end{array}$$

15.
$$\begin{array}{r} 5 \\ +\ 6 \\ \hline \end{array}$$

Add. Circle the numbers you add first.

16.
$$\begin{array}{r} 3 \\ 5 \\ +\ 2 \\ \hline \end{array}$$

17.
$$\begin{array}{r} 1 \\ 3 \\ +\ 6 \\ \hline \end{array}$$

18.
$$\begin{array}{r} 2 \\ 5 \\ +\ 4 \\ \hline \end{array}$$

19.
$$\begin{array}{r} 6 \\ 3 \\ +\ 3 \\ \hline \end{array}$$

20.
$$\begin{array}{r} 1 \\ 5 \\ +\ 5 \\ \hline \end{array}$$

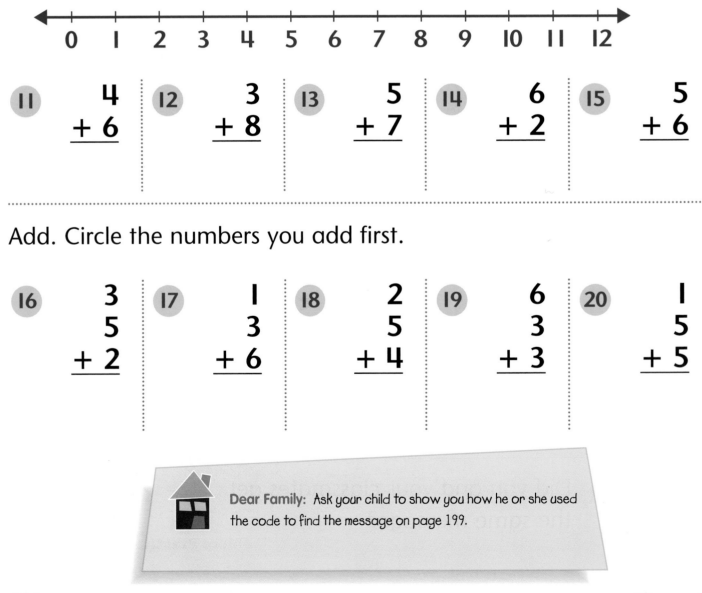

Dear Family: Ask your child to show you how he or she used the code to find the message on page 199.

Name _____

Math World

Children in West Africa play a tossing game called Haba Gaba.

There are many places where children play tossing games. West African children play **Haba Gaba** by tossing **3** beanbags into **3** different size holes.

Native American Zuni children toss a small ring inside of a large ring in a game called **Tsi-ko-na**.

Internet

Explore Houghton Mifflin's
Education Place Math Center.
http://www.eduplace.com

© Houghton Mifflin Company

▶ **Turn the page for directions.**

You need:
- 3 beanbags per player
- sturdy cardboard
- markers

Try this!

Make your own **Haba Gaba** game.

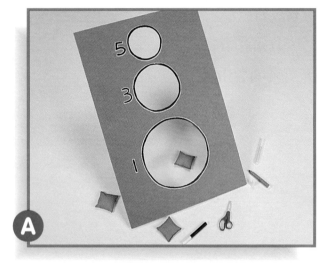

A

B

Have your teacher or another grown-up help you cut **3** holes in the cardboard.

Label the largest hole **1**, the middle hole **3**, and the smallest hole **5**.

Dear Family: Play Haba Gaba (HAH BAH GAH BAH) at home to give your child practice with his or her math facts.

How to Play:

- Stand several feet from the board and toss each beanbag. If a beanbag goes through one of the holes, count the number of points shown.
- Add the number of points for each beanbag toss.
- The first player to reach 12 points starts again.

Note: Try subtraction. Each player starts with 12 points. Subtract each toss from the player's total. When you reach zero, start again.

Name _____

Nina waits in the milk line.
2 children are in front of her.
6 children are behind her.
How many children are in line?

▶ **Understand**

I need to find the number of children.

▶ **Plan**

I will draw a picture.

▶ **Try it**

My picture shows **9** children.

▶ **Look back**

2 + 1 + 6 = 9

My answer makes sense.

Read and listen. Draw a picture to solve the problem.

1 There are **9** red beans on the plate. Kim takes **4** beans. Sam takes **2** beans. How many red beans are left on the plate?

_____ red beans

2 Tony's group sits at a square table. He puts **2** small paper plates on each side for snacks. How many plates does Tony put on the table?

_____ plates

3 There are **5** carrot sticks on the tray. Paula has **9** on her plate. She eats **3** of them. Are there more carrot sticks on Paula's plate or on the tray?

_____

Communication

Talk about it How did drawing a picture help you to solve a problem?

Dear Family: Imagine you needed to place 10 chairs around the table for dinner. Help your child draw a picture to solve the problem.

Lesson 7.9

Name _____

Listen to the story.
Write the subtraction sentence.

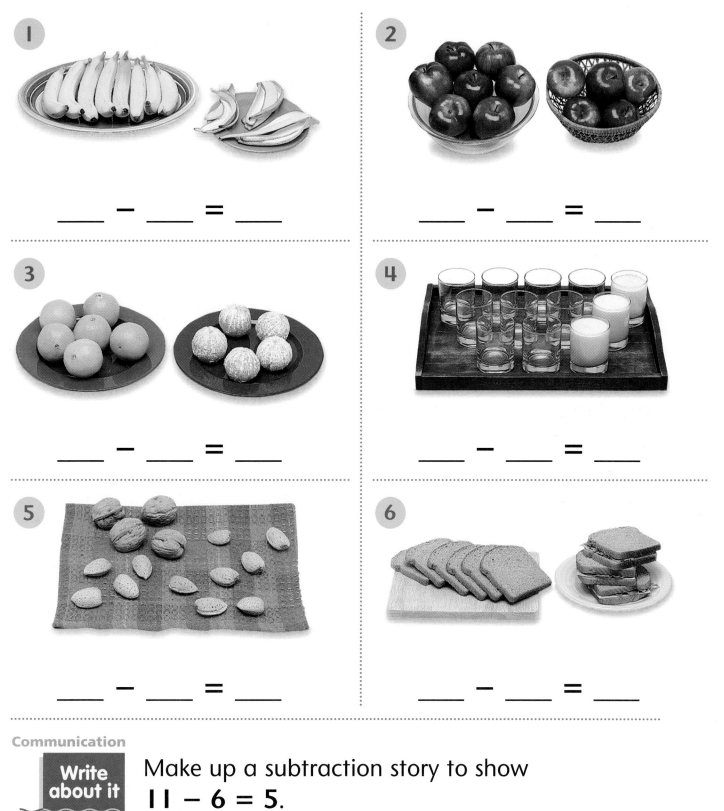

1

_____ − _____ = _____

2

_____ − _____ = _____

3

_____ − _____ = _____

4

_____ − _____ = _____

5

_____ − _____ = _____

6

_____ − _____ = _____

Communication

Write about it Make up a subtraction story to show
11 − 6 = 5.

Listen to the story.
Write the subtraction sentence.

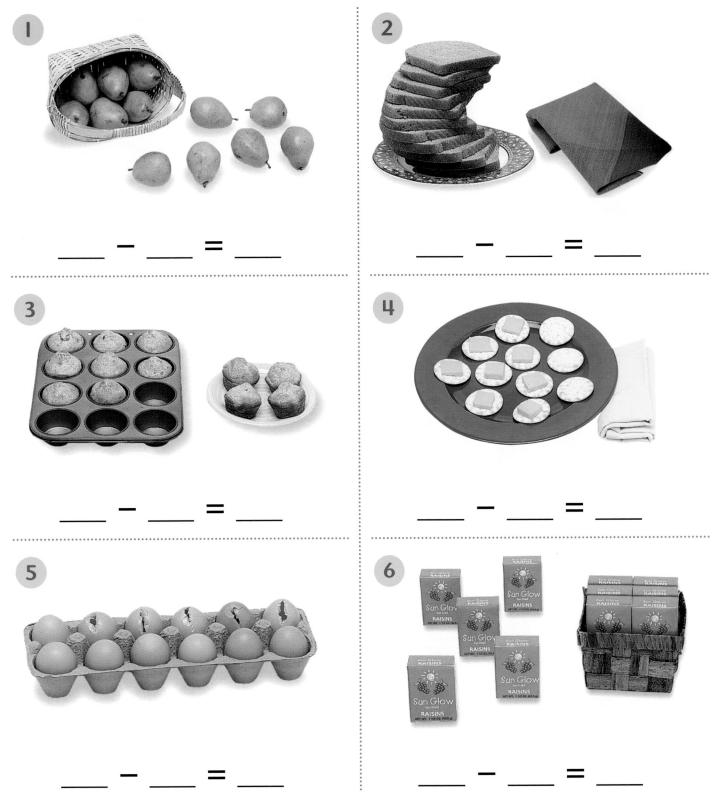

1

___ − ___ = ___

2

___ − ___ = ___

3

___ − ___ = ___

4

___ − ___ = ___

5

___ − ___ = ___

6

___ − ___ = ___

Dear Family: Use buttons or other small objects to make up some subtraction stories such as the ones on these pages. Ask your child to tell you a subtraction sentence for each one.

Lesson 7.10

Name _____

How many shells are left?

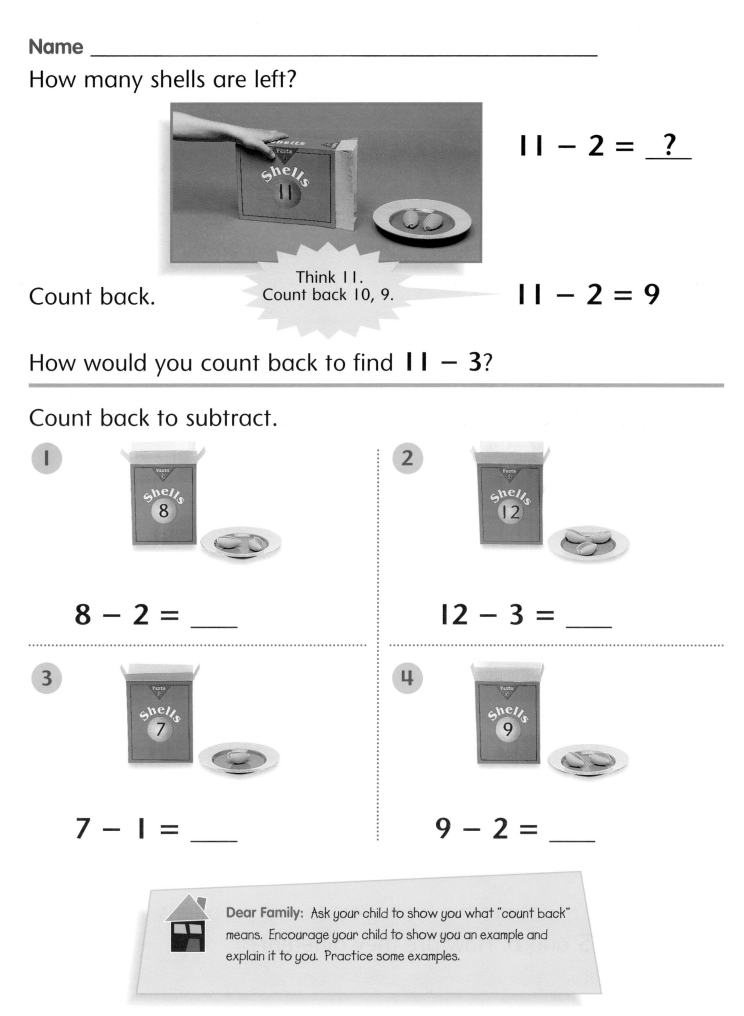

$11 - 2 = \underline{\ ?\ }$

Count back.

Think 11.
Count back 10, 9.

$11 - 2 = 9$

How would you count back to find $11 - 3$?

Count back to subtract.

1.

$8 - 2 = \underline{\ \ \ }$

2.

$12 - 3 = \underline{\ \ \ }$

3.

$7 - 1 = \underline{\ \ \ }$

4.

$9 - 2 = \underline{\ \ \ }$

Dear Family: Ask your child to show you what "count back" means. Encourage your child to show you an example and explain it to you. Practice some examples.

© Houghton Mifflin Company

Lesson 7.11

Count back to subtract.

1.
$$\begin{array}{r} 8 \\ -\ 1 \\ \hline \end{array}$$
$$\begin{array}{r} 12 \\ -\ 3 \\ \hline \end{array}$$
$$\begin{array}{r} 9¢ \\ -\ 2¢ \\ \hline \end{array}$$
$$\begin{array}{r} 7 \\ -\ 1 \\ \hline \end{array}$$
$$\begin{array}{r} 10 \\ -\ 3 \\ \hline \end{array}$$
$$\begin{array}{r} 8 \\ -\ 3 \\ \hline \end{array}$$

2.
$$\begin{array}{r} 10 \\ -\ 2 \\ \hline \end{array}$$
$$\begin{array}{r} 11 \\ -\ 3 \\ \hline \end{array}$$
$$\begin{array}{r} 8 \\ -\ 2 \\ \hline \end{array}$$
$$\begin{array}{r} 7 \\ -\ 3 \\ \hline \end{array}$$
$$\begin{array}{r} 4¢ \\ -\ 2¢ \\ \hline \end{array}$$
$$\begin{array}{r} 9 \\ -\ 1 \\ \hline \end{array}$$

3. $11 - 2 = \underline{\quad}$ $9 - 3 = \underline{\quad}$ $12 - 2 = \underline{\quad}$

4. $9 - 2 = \underline{\quad}$ $10 - 1 = \underline{\quad}$ $7 - 3 = \underline{\quad}$

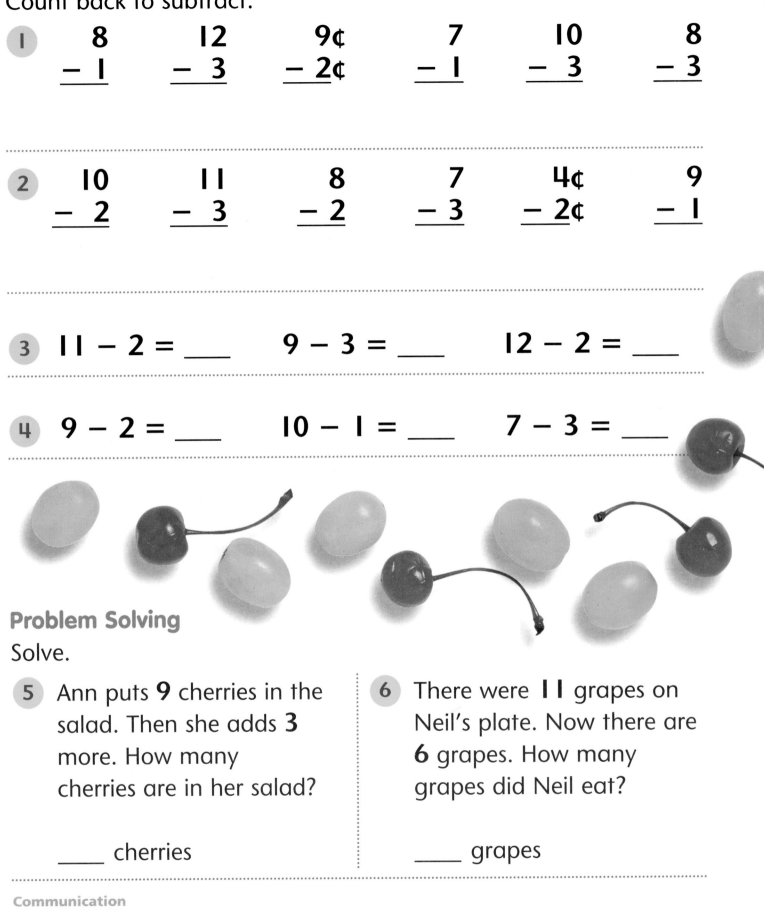

Problem Solving
Solve.

5. Ann puts **9** cherries in the salad. Then she adds **3** more. How many cherries are in her salad?

____ cherries

6. There were **11** grapes on Neil's plate. Now there are **6** grapes. How many grapes did Neil eat?

____ grapes

Communication

Talk about it Talk about the ways you solved problems **5** and **6**. How are they different?

Name _____

Jerry uses **9** chili peppers and
7 olives in tacos. How many more
peppers are there than olives?

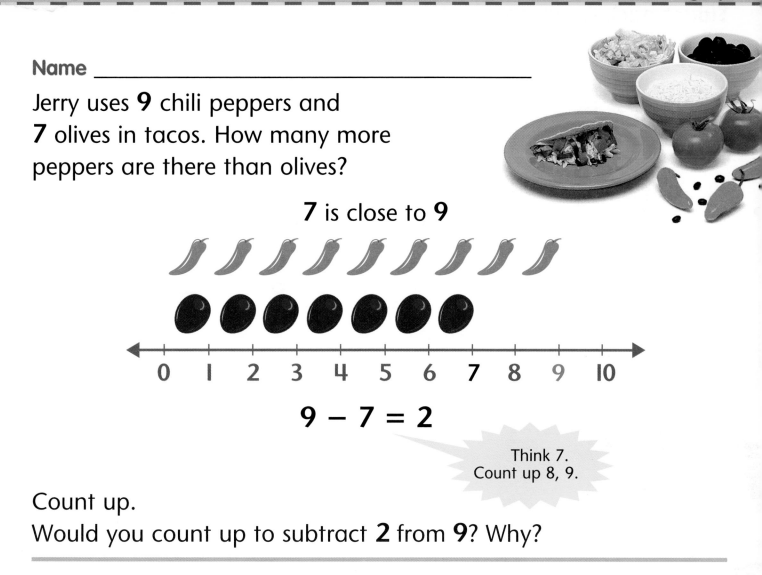

7 is close to **9**

$$9 - 7 = 2$$

Think 7.
Count up 8, 9.

Count up.
Would you count up to subtract **2** from **9**? Why?

Count up. Write the difference.

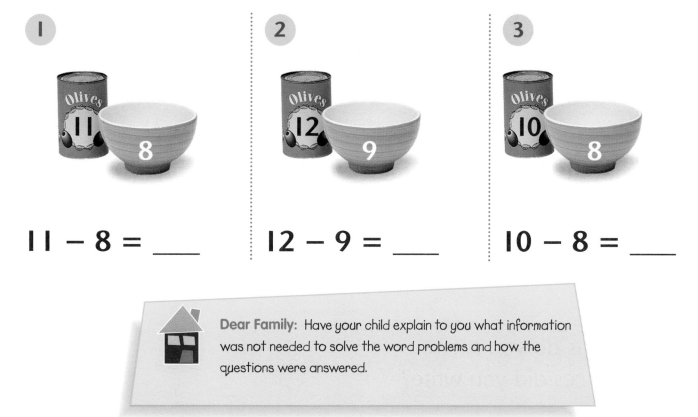

1

$11 - 8 = $ _____

2

$12 - 9 = $ _____

3

$10 - 8 = $ _____

Dear Family: Have your child explain to you what information
was not needed to solve the word problems and how the
questions were answered.

Subtract.
Circle the facts you count up.

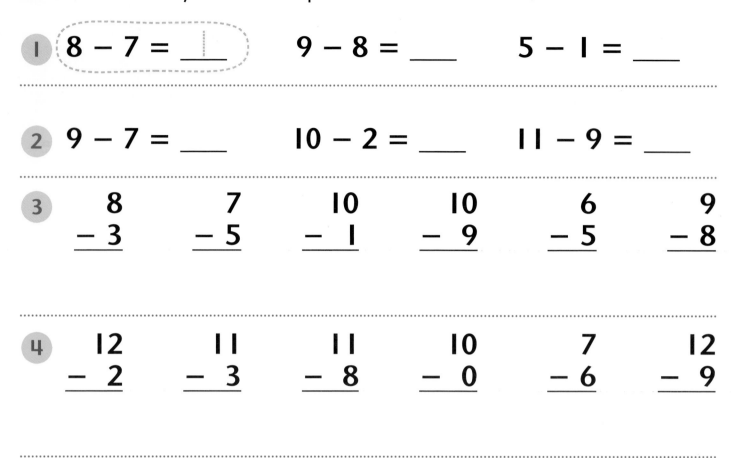

1. (8 − 7 = __1__)   9 − 8 = ___   5 − 1 = ___

2. 9 − 7 = ___   10 − 2 = ___   11 − 9 = ___

3.
8	7	10	10	6	9
− 3	− 5	− 1	− 9	− 5	− 8

4.
12	11	11	10	7	12
− 2	− 3	− 8	− 0	− 6	− 9

Give it a try

Look for a pattern.
Write the next number sentences.

10 − 9 = 1   4 − 2 = 2
9 − 8 = 1   5 − 3 = 2
8 − 7 = 1   6 − 4 = 2

_7_ − ___ = 1   ___ − ___ = 2

___ − ___ = 1   ___ − ___ = 2

What patterns do you see?
What sentences did you write?

Name _____

Use the number line to subtract.
Start at **11**. Go back **4**.
You finish at **7**.

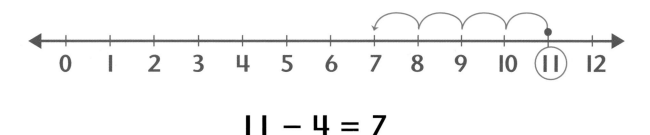

$$11 - 4 = 7$$

Can you use this number line to subtract any facts
through **12**?

Use the number line to subtract.

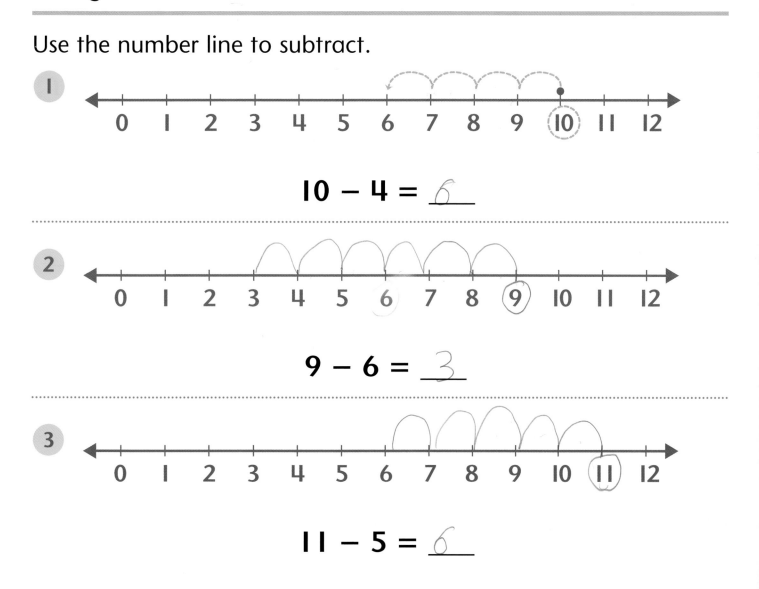

1

$$10 - 4 = \underline{6}$$

2

$$9 - 6 = \underline{3}$$

3

$$11 - 5 = \underline{6}$$

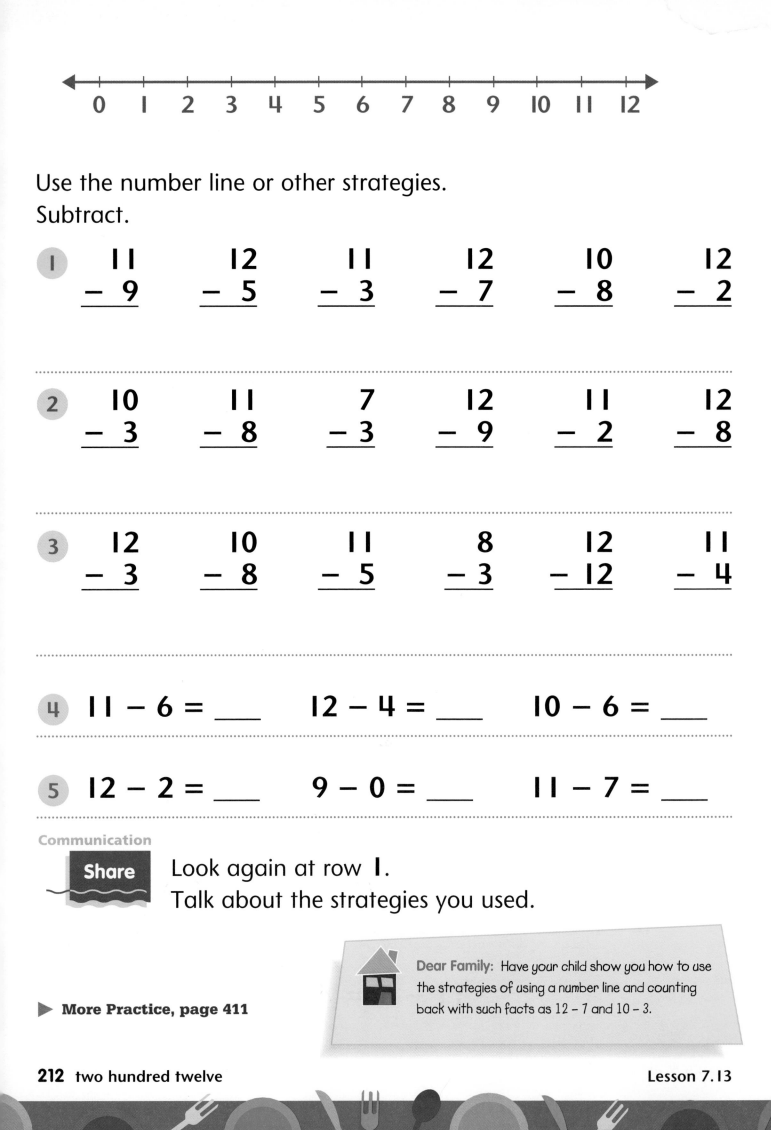

Use the number line or other strategies.
Subtract.

1

11	12	11	12	10	12
− 9	− 5	− 3	− 7	− 8	− 2

2

10	11	7	12	11	12
− 3	− 8	− 3	− 9	− 2	− 8

3

12	10	11	8	12	11
− 3	− 8	− 5	− 3	− 12	− 4

4 $11 - 6 =$ ___ $12 - 4 =$ ___ $10 - 6 =$ ___

5 $12 - 2 =$ ___ $9 - 0 =$ ___ $11 - 7 =$ ___

Communication

Share   Look again at row **1**.
Talk about the strategies you used.

Dear Family: Have your child show you how to use the strategies of using a number line and counting back with such facts as 12 − 7 and 10 − 3.

▶ **More Practice, page 411**

Name _____

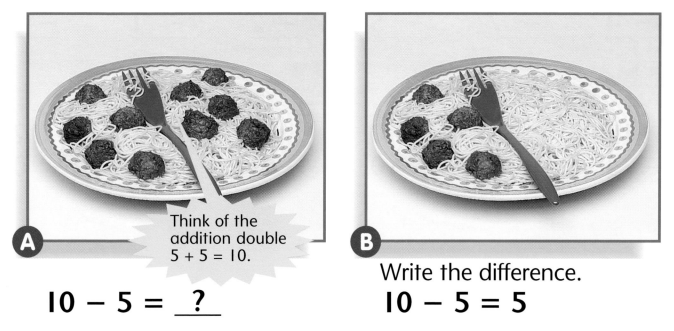

A

Think of the addition double 5 + 5 = 10.

10 − 5 = _?_

B

Write the difference.

10 − 5 = 5

How do addition doubles help you with doubles in subtraction?

Write the sum. Circle the doubles.

1 4 + 3 = ___   6 + 6 = ___   2 + 2 = ___

2 3 + 3 = ___   2 + 1 = ___   4 + 4 = ___

Write the difference. Use doubles.

3 12 − 6 = ___   6 − 3 = ___   2 − 1 = ___

4 8 − 4 = ___   10 − 5 = ___   4 − 2 = ___

Communication

Talk about it

How did knowing about doubles help you to solve the problems?

© Houghton Mifflin Company

Lesson 7.14

Circle the doubles. Subtract them first.
Then subtract the others.

1. ⊘ 8   11   10   9   12   4
    − 4   − 7   − 5   − 2   − 1   − 2
    ‾‾‾   ‾‾‾   ‾‾‾   ‾‾‾   ‾‾‾   ‾‾‾
      4

2.   12   6   10   12   12   12
    − 3   − 3   − 10   − 2   − 6   − 0
    ‾‾‾   ‾‾‾   ‾‾‾‾   ‾‾‾   ‾‾‾   ‾‾‾

Problem Solving

Draw a picture to solve each problem.

3   The server has **12** bowls of rice.
    He serves **6** bowls to people at
    one table. How many bowls of
    rice are left?

    ____ bowls

4   The chef needs **8** slices of pepper.
    She has **4** slices. How many more
    slices does she need?

    ____ slices

Dear Family: Ask your child to tell you how adding doubles
helps him or her to subtract doubles. Ask your child to show
you how to subtract 10 − 5 or 6 − 3.

Name _____

Solve. Use strategies you know.

1.
11	10	12	9	11
− 2	− 1	− 3	− 2	− 3

2.
2	8	3	2	9
+ 9	+ 3	+ 9	+ 8	+ 1

3.
12	11	9	10	11
− 9	− 8	− 7	− 8	− 9

4.
3	8	5	12	2
+ 3	− 4	+ 5	− 6	+ 2

5.
10	8	10	0	8
− 0	+ 0	− 10	+ 9	− 8

Communication

 **Share** Look again at each row. Share with a friend what helped you to add or subtract.

 Dear Family: Alert your child to everyday activities in which addition and subtraction are being used (board games, recipes, and so on).

▶ **More Practice, page 411**

© Houghton Mifflin Company

Lesson 7.15

Add.

1.

2	6	2	4	5	7
3	2	4	1	0	2
+ 5	+ 4	+ 3	+ 6	+ 4	+ 1

Problem Solving

2. There are **12** carrot sticks on the plate. Cindy eats **4**. Her sister eats **3**. How many carrot sticks are there now?

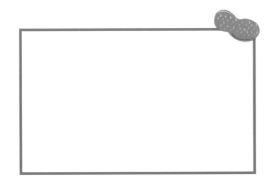

____ carrot sticks

---

3. Luis has **11** peanuts in a dish. He eats **8** peanuts. Mom puts **6** more in the dish. How many peanuts are there now?

____ peanuts

Mixed Review

4. Circle the even numbers.

1 2 3 4 5 6 7 8 9 10 11 12

5. Write the time two ways.

____ o'clock

____ : ____

Cooperative Learning

Name _____

Work with a partner. Use cubes and a workmat.
Write the missing part. Then write the fact family.

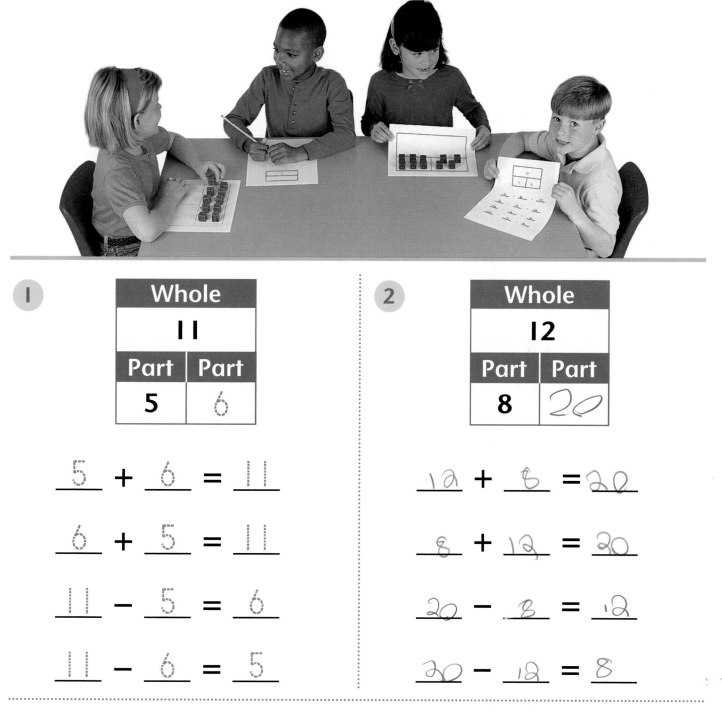

1

Whole	
11	
Part	Part
5	6

_5_ + _6_ = 11

_6_ + _5_ = 11

11 − _5_ = _6_

11 − _6_ = _5_

2

Whole	
12	
Part	Part
8	20

_12_ + _8_ = _20_

_8_ + _12_ = _20_

_20_ − _8_ = _12_

_20_ − _12_ = _8_

Give it a try

Write two different fact families that share
one number. For example: **4 + 2 = 6**;
4 + 7 = 11. Both share the number **4**.

Use cubes and a workmat.
Write the missing part.
Then write the fact family.

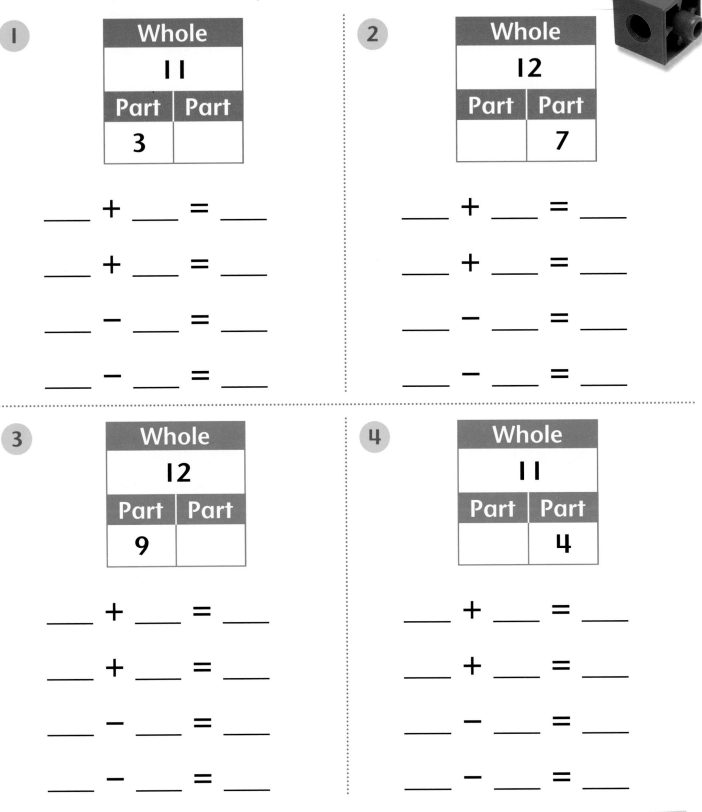

1

Whole	
11	
Part	Part
3	

___ + ___ = ___

___ + ___ = ___

___ − ___ = ___

___ − ___ = ___

2

Whole	
12	
Part	Part
	7

___ + ___ = ___

___ + ___ = ___

___ − ___ = ___

___ − ___ = ___

3

Whole	
12	
Part	Part
9	

___ + ___ = ___

___ + ___ = ___

___ − ___ = ___

___ − ___ = ___

4

Whole	
11	
Part	Part
	4

___ + ___ = ___

___ + ___ = ___

___ − ___ = ___

___ − ___ = ___

▶ **More Practice, page 412**

Dear Family: Ask your child to show you a fact family using the numbers 5 and 4 and 9. Ask your child how many number sentences can be written about it.

Lesson 7.16

Name _____

Solve each problem.

1   Peter eats **2** plums. There
    are **5** left. How many plums
    were there to begin with?

    ____ plums

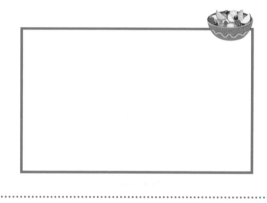

2   **9** girls and **12** boys make a
    fruit salad. How many fewer
    girls are there than boys?

    ____ fewer girls

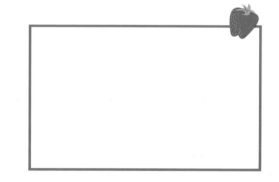

3   Kim has **9** berries. She eats **4**.
    Then she gets **5** more. How
    many berries are there now?

    ____ berries

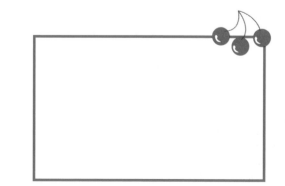

4   Seth has **11** cherries. He gives
    2 to Adam. He gives **7** to Sara.
    How many cherries are left?

    ____ cherries

Solve each problem.

1 Hannah has **11** oranges.
She uses some to make juice.
Now she has **3** oranges.
How many did she use?

____ oranges

2 Jeremy picks **4** tomatoes.
Cindy picks **3**. Luis picks **5**.
How many tomatoes did
they pick in all?

____ tomatoes

3 There are **7** children. Each
child needs a carton of milk.
There are **8** cartons of milk.
Are there enough?

_____

Mary bought some
apples. Look at the
pictures. How many
apples did Mary buy?

____ apples

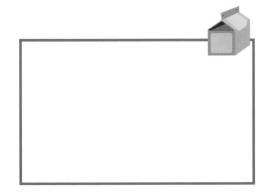

Dear Family: Invite your child to explain how he or she
solved some of the problems on these pages.

Name _____

Write the number sentence.

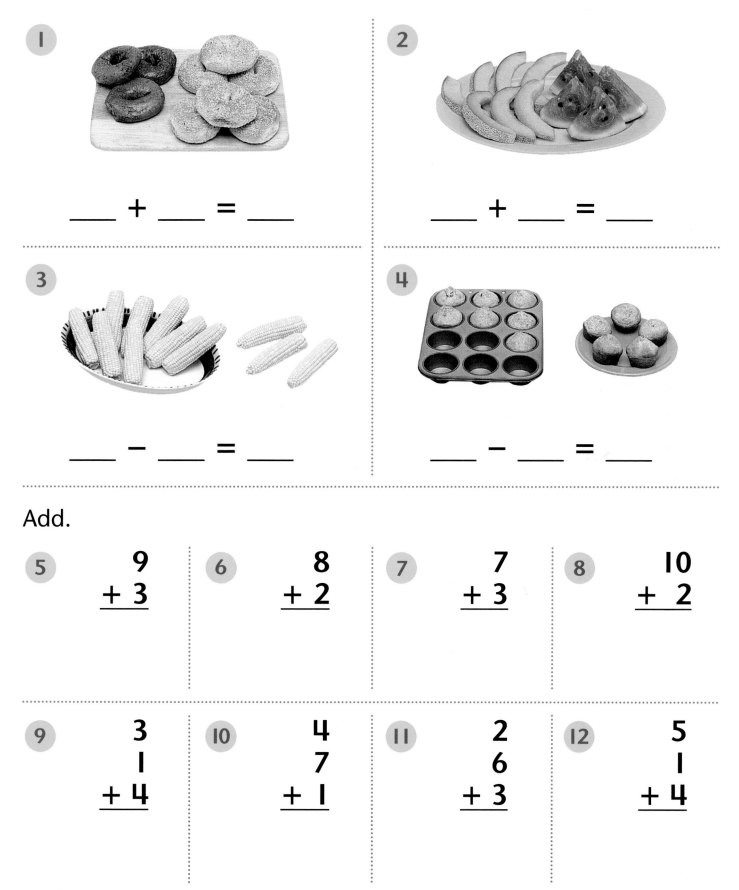

1

___ + ___ = ___

2

___ + ___ = ___

3

___ – ___ = ___

4

___ – ___ = ___

Add.

5
$$\begin{array}{r} 9 \\ + 3 \\ \hline \end{array}$$

6
$$\begin{array}{r} 8 \\ + 2 \\ \hline \end{array}$$

7
$$\begin{array}{r} 7 \\ + 3 \\ \hline \end{array}$$

8
$$\begin{array}{r} 10 \\ + 2 \\ \hline \end{array}$$

9
$$\begin{array}{r} 3 \\ 1 \\ + 4 \\ \hline \end{array}$$

10
$$\begin{array}{r} 4 \\ 7 \\ + 1 \\ \hline \end{array}$$

11
$$\begin{array}{r} 2 \\ 6 \\ + 3 \\ \hline \end{array}$$

12
$$\begin{array}{r} 5 \\ 1 \\ + 4 \\ \hline \end{array}$$

Subtract.

13

11 − 2 = ___

14

12 − 3 = ___

15

10 − 2 = ___

16

10 − 9 = ___

17

8 − 7 = ___

18

11 − 8 = ___

Use the number line to subtract.

19

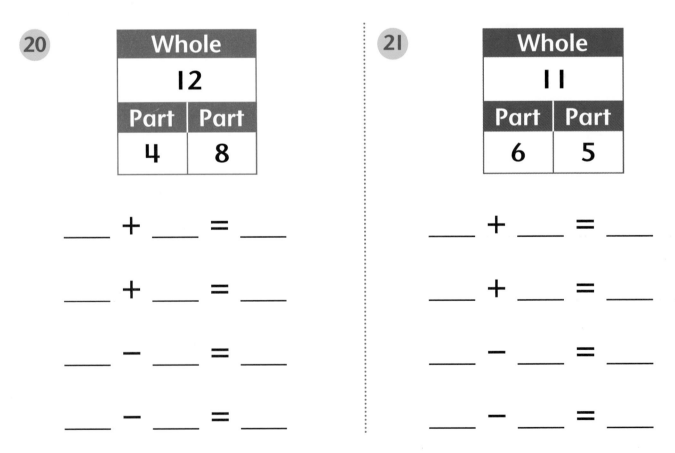

```
←──┼──┼──┼──┼──┼──┼──┼──┼──┼──┼──┼──┼──→
   0  1  2  3  4  5  6  7  8  9  10 11 12
```

12 − 4 = ___

Write the number sentences for each fact family.

20

Whole	
12	
Part	Part
4	8

___ + ___ = ___

___ + ___ = ___

___ − ___ = ___

___ − ___ = ___

21

Whole	
11	
Part	Part
6	5

___ + ___ = ___

___ + ___ = ___

___ − ___ = ___

___ − ___ = ___

Chapter 7

Name _____

Feed the baby birds!
Roll the number cube.
Say the number. Count out the spaces.
Mark the space on which you land.
Guess how many spaces are left in the row.
Check your guess.

Internet
Visit Houghton Mifflin's
Education Place Math Center.
http://www.eduplace.com

Make your own baby bird game.
Draw what the baby bird eats.
Then roll and play.
Write the number sentence.

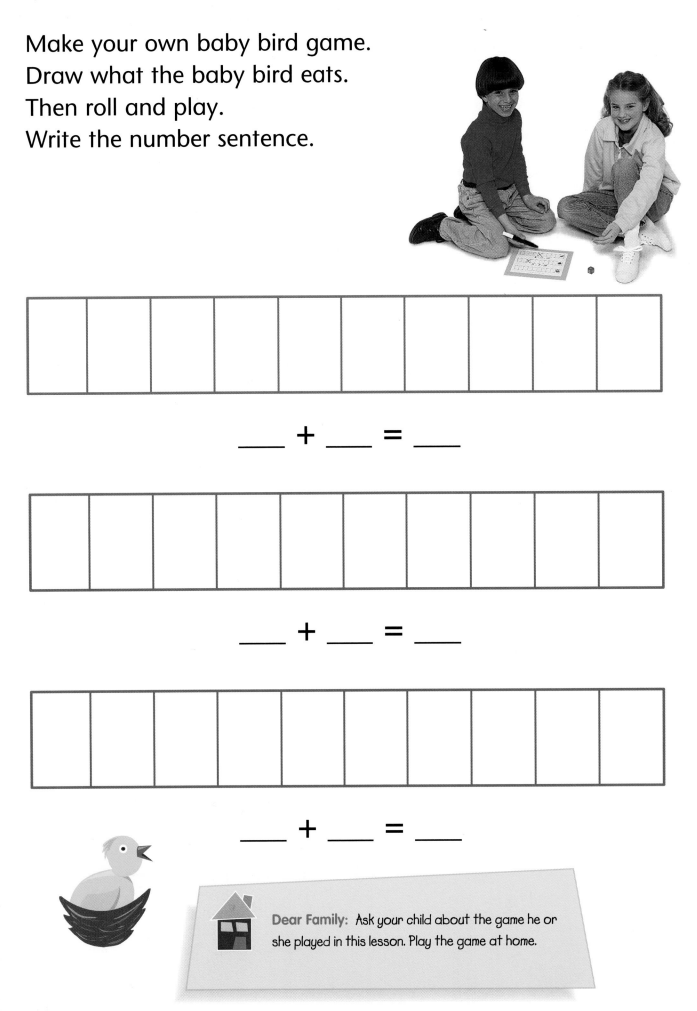

___ + ___ = ___

___ + ___ = ___

___ + ___ = ___

Dear Family: Ask your child about the game he or she played in this lesson. Play the game at home.

Chapter 7

Geometry and Fractions

CHAPTER 8

© Houghton Mifflin Company

Literature

Dangerous
By Dorothy Aldis

Read Aloud Anthology p. 90

Theme Connection

Shapes Around Us

YIELD

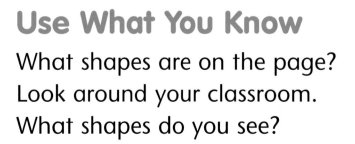

See what I can do by the end of this chapter.

Use What You Know

What shapes are on the page?
Look around your classroom.
What shapes do you see?

Use pattern blocks to design the kitchen floor.

Dear Family: Your child has been learning about geometric shapes. What kinds of shapes are in your home? Identify shapes that you see every day.

Name _____

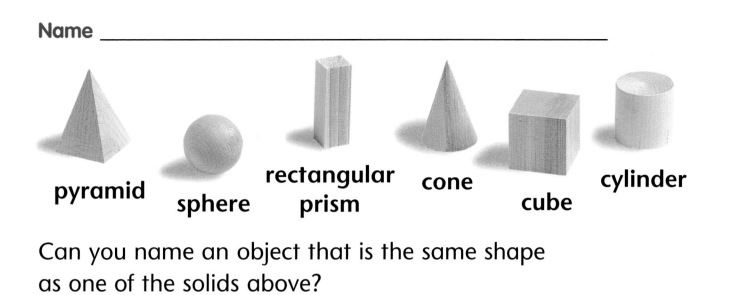

pyramid **sphere** **rectangular prism** **cone** **cube** **cylinder**

Can you name an object that is the same shape as one of the solids above?

Circle each object that has the same shape.

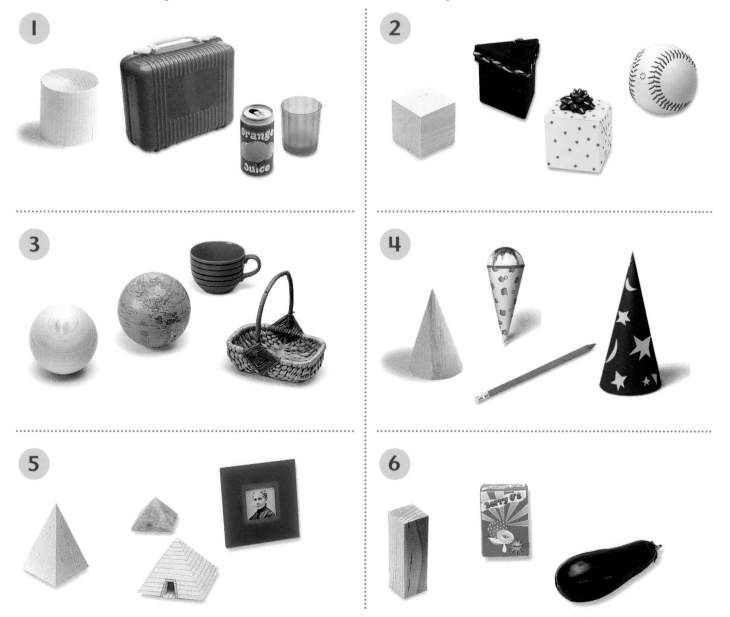

1

2

3

4

5

6

Lesson 8.1

Color the picture to match the shapes.
How will you decide which shapes to color?

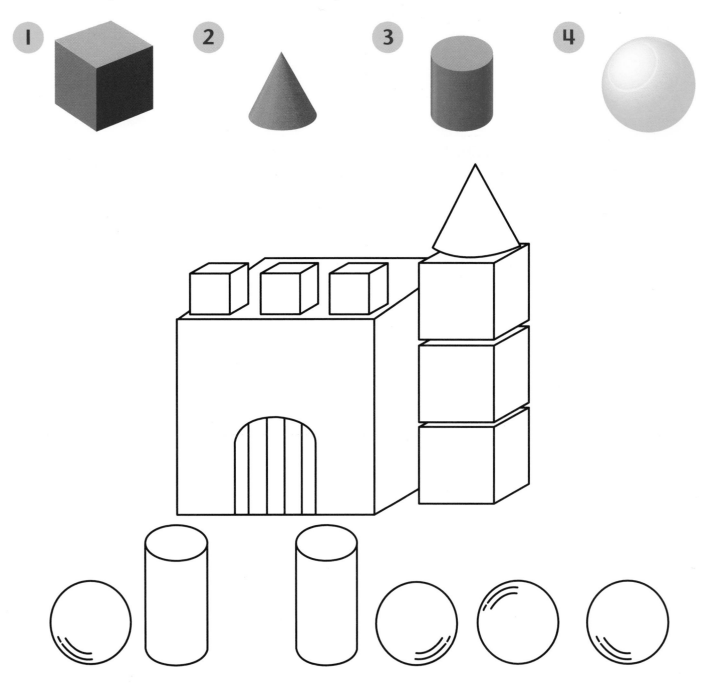

1 2 3 4

....

Communication

Draw

Trace each solid. Compare the shapes you get.
Which solid is hard to trace? Why?

Dear Family: Take a "shape walk" with your child. Look at buildings, fences, and other objects to find the shapes. Talk about how some shapes stack, some roll, and some do both.

Name _____

triangle

square

rectangle

circle

A square is a special kind of rectangle.
What makes a square special?

Use blocks.
Find and trace each shape.

1 circle

2 square

3 triangle

4 rectangle

© Houghton Mifflin Company

Communication

Share Look at a friend's shapes. Find ways that are the same as or different from yours.

Work with a partner.
Use blocks.

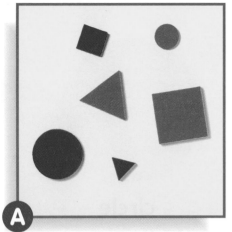

A Pick a triangle.

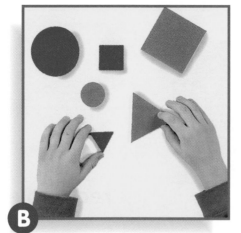

B Find a larger or smaller triangle.

C Draw each shape. Compare them.

Pick another shape.
Follow the steps **4** more times.

 Give it a try

Draw a picture with the shapes.

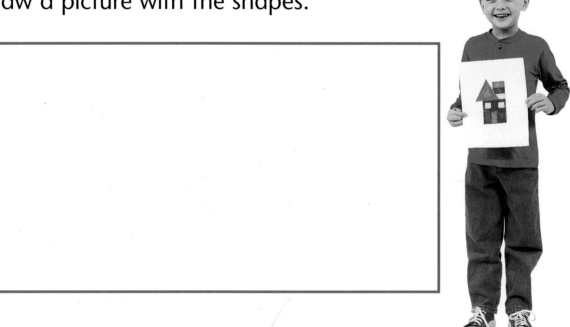

 **Dear Family:** Make a shape lunch. Slice an orange into circles or cut square sandwiches into triangles and rectangles. Ask your child to identify each shape.

Lesson 8.2

Name _____

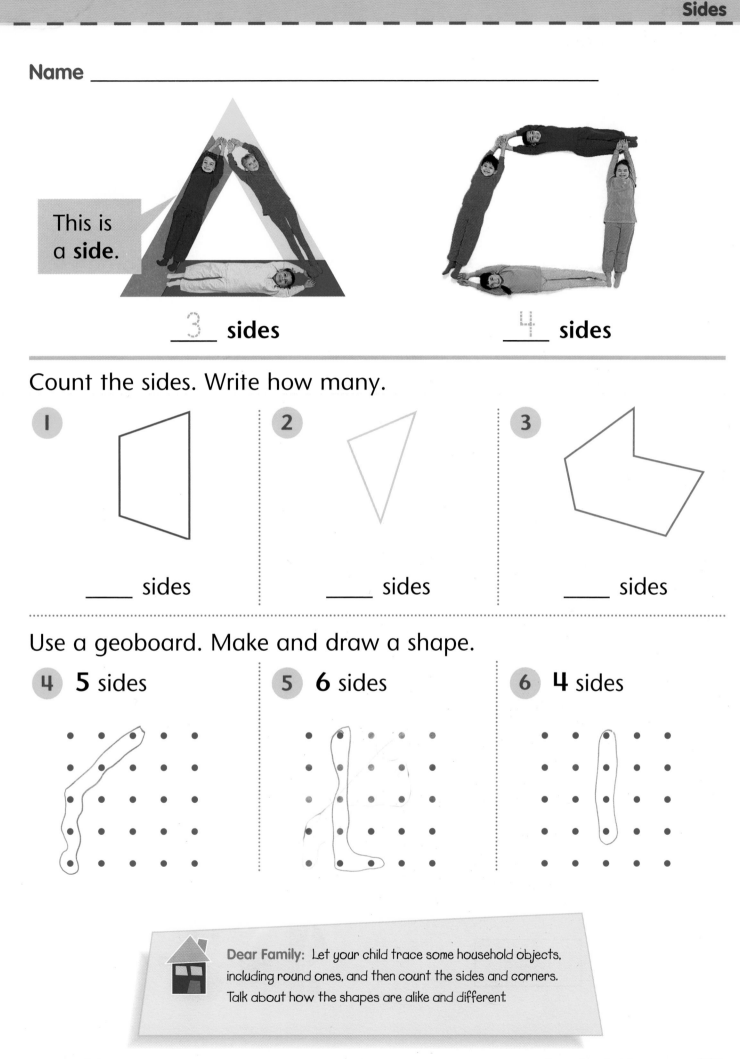

This is a **side**.

___3___ sides   ___4___ sides

Count the sides. Write how many.

1   ____ sides   **2**   ____ sides   **3**   ____ sides

Use a geoboard. Make and draw a shape.

4   **5** sides   **5**   **6** sides   **6**   **4** sides

Dear Family: Let your child trace some household objects, including round ones, and then count the sides and corners. Talk about how the shapes are alike and different.

Two sides join at a **corner**.

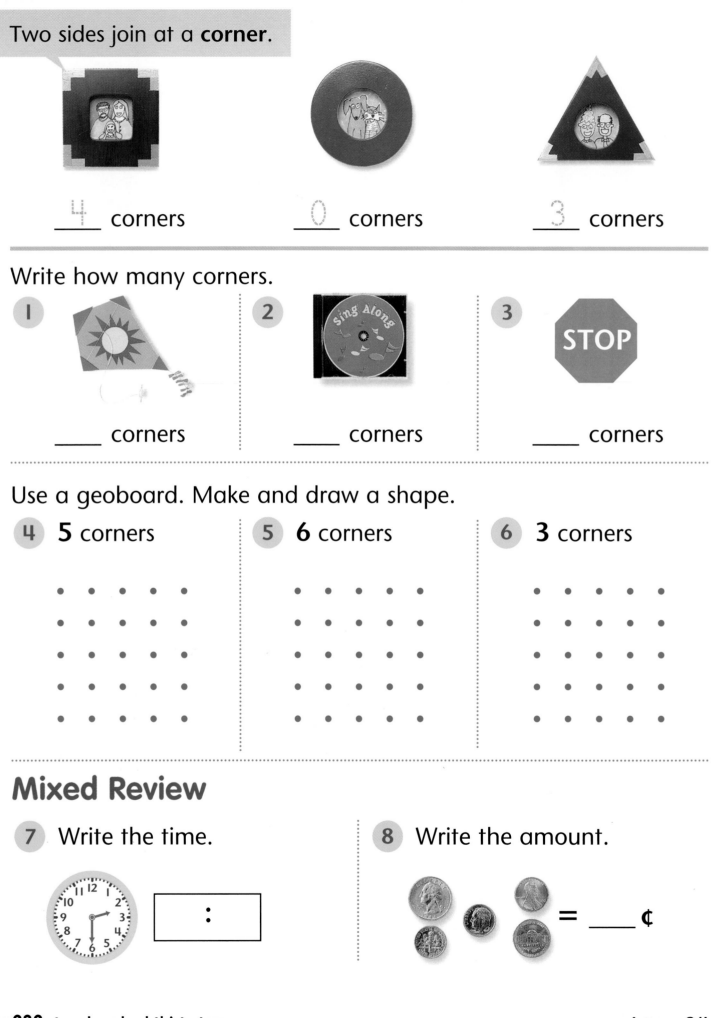

_4_ corners

_0_ corners

_3_ corners

Write how many corners.

1 ____ corners

2 ____ corners

3 ____ corners

Use a geoboard. Make and draw a shape.

4 **5** corners

5 **6** corners

6 **3** corners

Mixed Review

7 Write the time.

8 Write the amount.

= ____ ¢

Name _____

Use crayons. You may use pattern blocks.

Work with a partner. Color the shape to match.

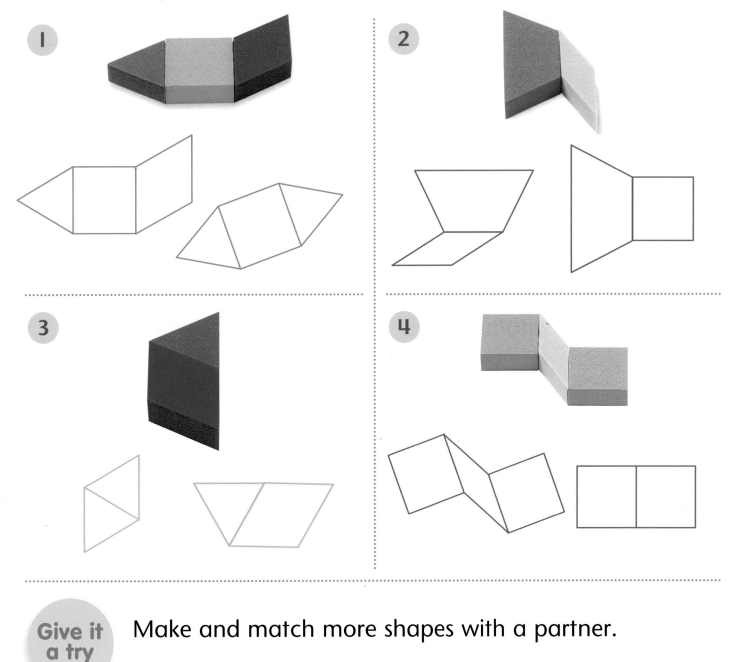

1

2

3

4

Give it a try   Make and match more shapes with a partner.

Work with a partner. Circle same size and shape.

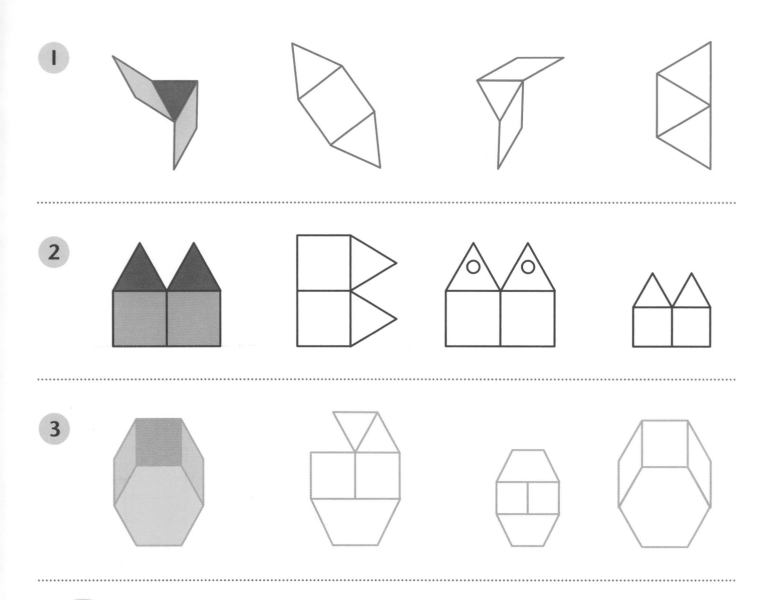

1

2

3

Give it a try

Work with a partner. Color some squares to make
a shape. Ask your partner to match your shape.

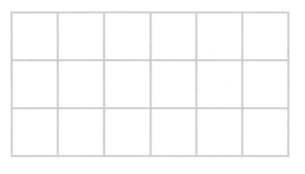

▶ **More Practice, page 412**

Dear Family: Gather objects such as envelopes,
index cards, and coins. Let your child explain which
objects match in size and shape, and which do not.

Name _____

Use squares.
Cover the shape.
How many squares
do you use?

_____6_____

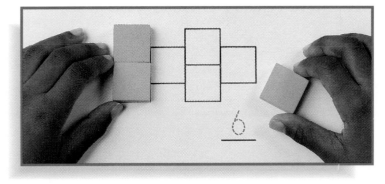

Would circles cover the shape?

Work with a partner. Cover the shapes.

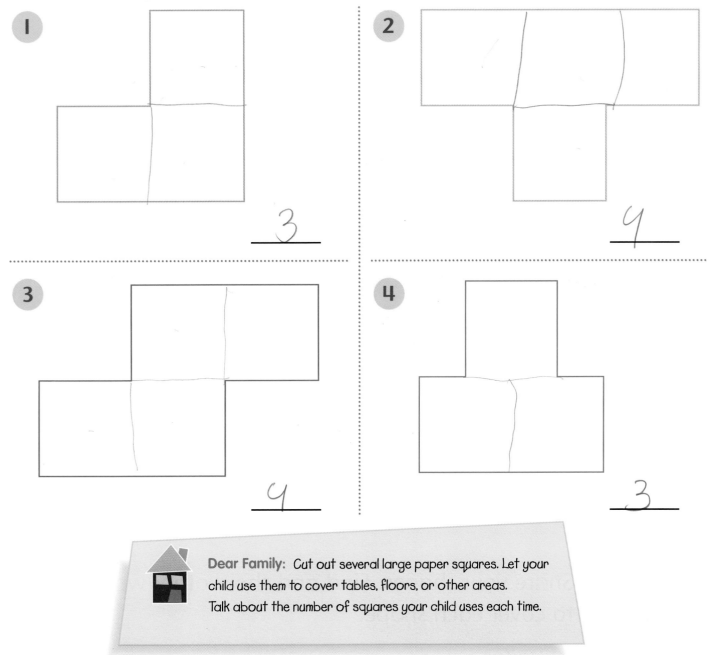

1 _____3_____

2 _____4_____

3 _____4_____

4 _____3_____

Dear Family: Cut out several large paper squares. Let your child use them to cover tables, floors, or other areas. Talk about the number of squares your child uses each time.

Work with a partner.
Use pattern blocks.
Cover each shape.
Write how many blocks you use.

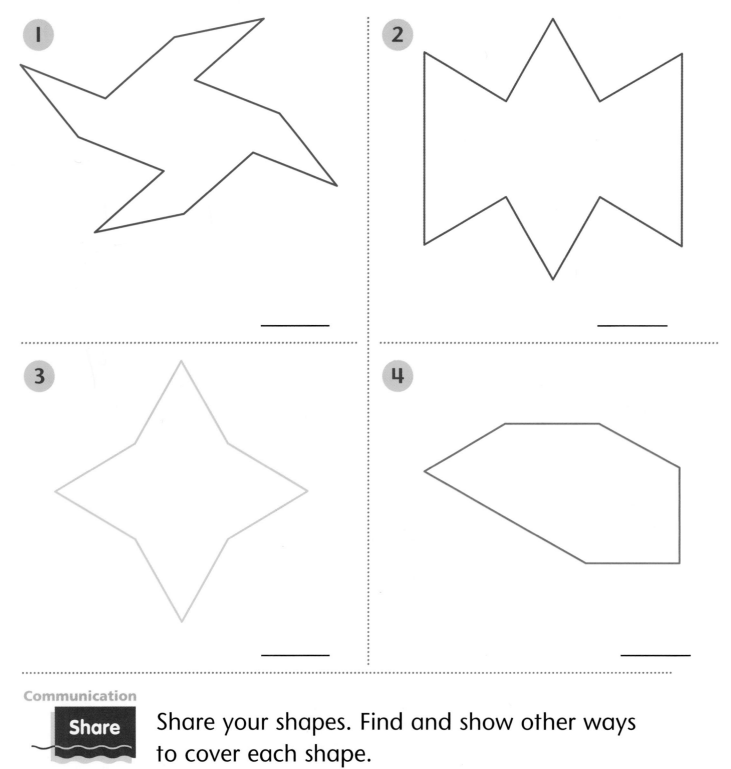

1 _____

2 _____

3 _____

4 _____

Share Share your shapes. Find and show other ways to cover each shape.

Name _____

Draw the next shape.

 ____

▶ **Understand**

I must find out which shape comes next.

▶ **Plan**

I can look for a pattern.

▶ **Try it**

Three shapes repeat.

A yellow diamond comes next.

▶ **Look back**

I can see that the pattern continues.

My answer makes sense.

Circle the group that comes next.

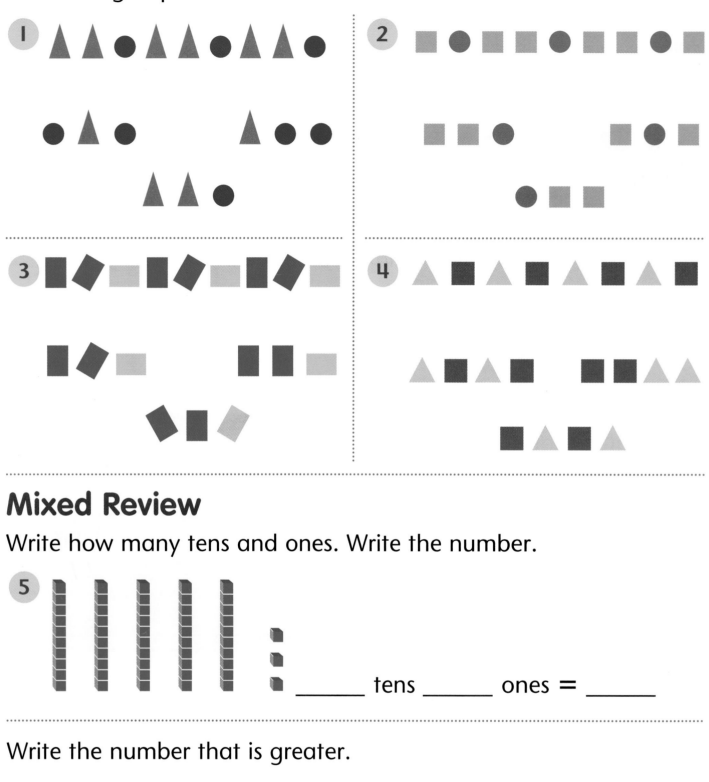

Mixed Review

Write how many tens and ones. Write the number.

5 _____ tens _____ ones = _____

Write the number that is greater.

6 **86 64** _____

7 **57 52** _____

Dear Family: Help your child find patterns in quilts, carpets, tiles, and wallpaper. Together, you might design patterns using paper cutouts or crayons.

Lesson 8.7

Name _____

Use crayons.
Color the next shape.

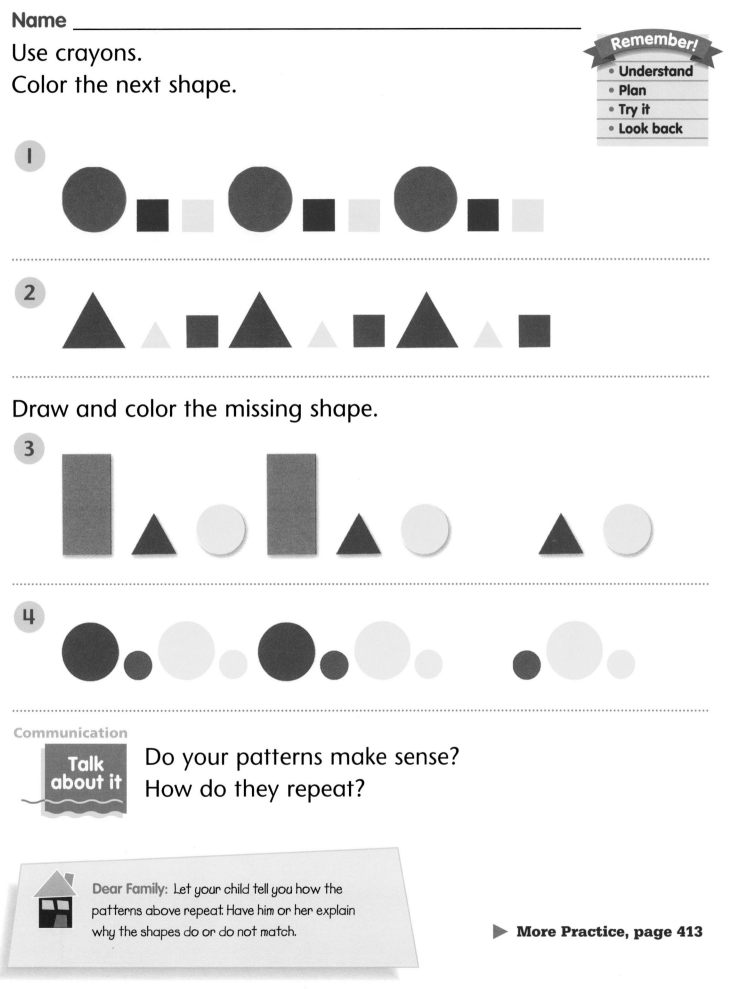

1

2

Draw and color the missing shape.

3

4

Communication

Talk about it
Do your patterns make sense?
How do they repeat?

Dear Family: Let your child tell you how the patterns above repeat. Have him or her explain why the shapes do or do not match.

▶ **More Practice, page 413**

Write how many of each shape you can see.

1 _____ rectangles

2 _____ triangles

3 _____ squares

··

Draw

Use blocks to draw your own quilt pattern.
Ask a partner to find the pattern.

Cooperative Learning

Name _____

Work in groups of three.
Make a shape.

A Fold your
paper.

B Cut out
a shape.

C Open the
shape.

What is special about the shape you made?

Draw the fold line on your shape.
Cut your shape along the line.
Make and cut **2** more shapes.
Mix up all the pieces.
Find the pieces that match.

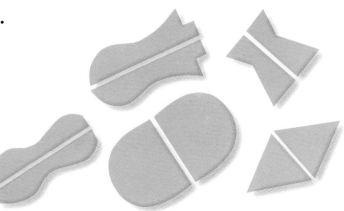

Communication

Share

Show or tell a friend how you find
the parts that match.

Dear Family: Have your child show you how to cut
symmetrical designs and match the mirrored halves.

▶ **More Practice, page 413**

Draw each shape.

1 rectangle

· · · · ·
· · · · ·
· · · · ·
· · · · ·
· · · · ·

2 triangle

· · · · ·
· · · · ·
· · · · ·
· · · · ·
· · · · ·

3 square

· · · · ·
· · · · ·
· · · · ·
· · · · ·
· · · · ·

Write how many sides or corners.

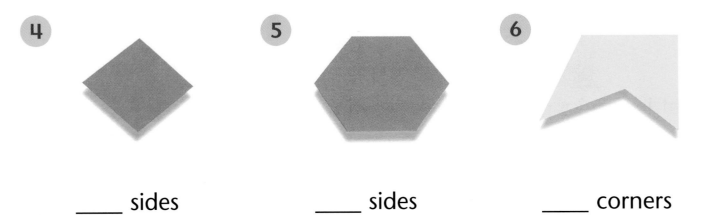

4 ____ sides

5 ____ sides

6 ____ corners

Cover each shape.
Write how many blocks you use.

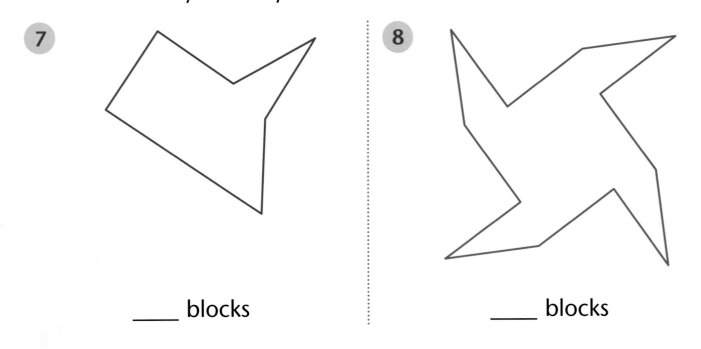

7 ____ blocks

8 ____ blocks

Name _____

Math World

Children in China use 7 shapes to play a game called tangram.

A **tangram** has **5** triangles and **1** square. The last shape has **4** sides and is called a parallelogram. Children use the shapes to make a design. Then other players guess the design.

Internet

Explore Houghton Mifflin's **Education Place Math Center.** http://www.eduplace.com

▶ **Turn the page for directions.**

two hundred forty-three **243**

You need:
- pencil
- ruler
- scissors
- heavy paper
- tangram pattern

Try this!

Make your own **tangram** puzzle.

Cut out the tangram design.

Move the pieces to make shapes like birds, animals, and flowers. Be sure you use all **7** pieces.

Dear Family: Ask your child to show you how to make shapes with tangram pieces. You may wish to play the following game to review geometric shapes.

How to Play:

- Make a shape using all **7** tangram pieces. Trace around the outline of your shape.
- Switch outlines with another player. Try to fit your tangram pieces into their shape. Can you do it?
- As you play, have your child name the geometric shapes you are using.

Name _____

These show equal parts.

Are these parts equal?
How can you tell?

Which shapes have equal parts?
Color one of the equal parts.

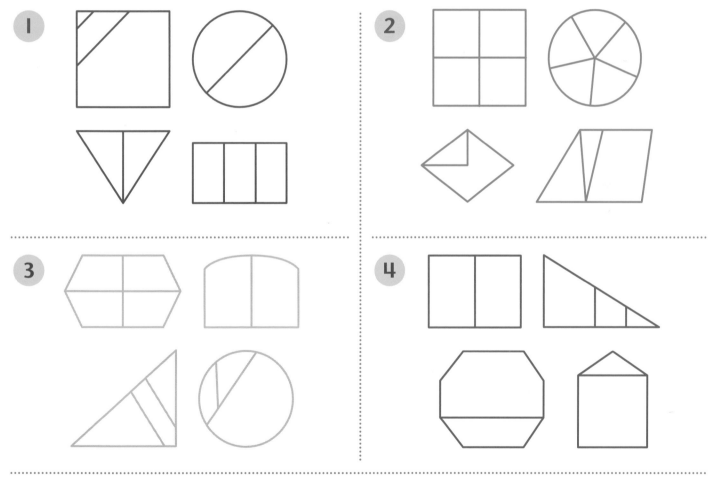

1

2

3

4

Communication

Tell your partner which shapes were harder
to figure out. Explain.

Write how many equal parts.

1

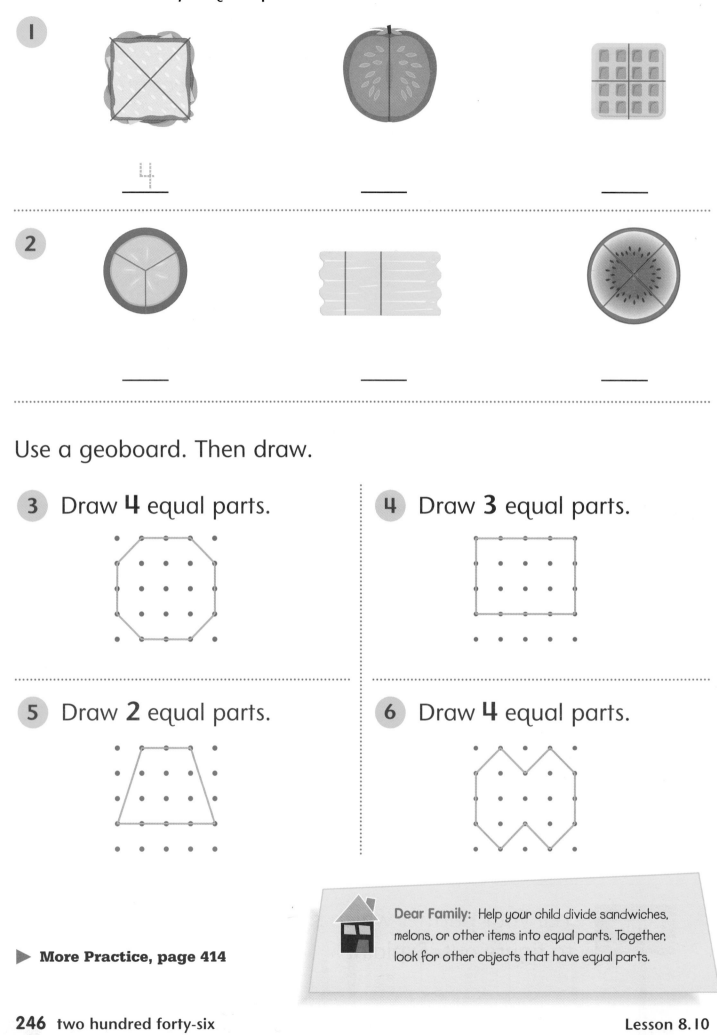

___

___

___

2

___

___

___

Use a geoboard. Then draw.

3 Draw **4** equal parts.

4 Draw **3** equal parts.

5 Draw **2** equal parts.

6 Draw **4** equal parts.

▶ **More Practice, page 414**

Dear Family: Help your child divide sandwiches, melons, or other items into equal parts. Together, look for other objects that have equal parts.

Lesson 8.10

Name _____

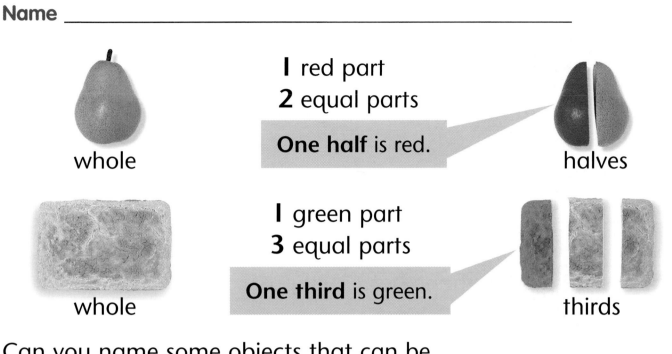

1 red part
2 equal parts

One half is red.

whole   halves

1 green part
3 equal parts

One third is green.

whole   thirds

Can you name some objects that can be
separated into halves and thirds?

Use pattern blocks. Draw and color the parts.
Show halves.

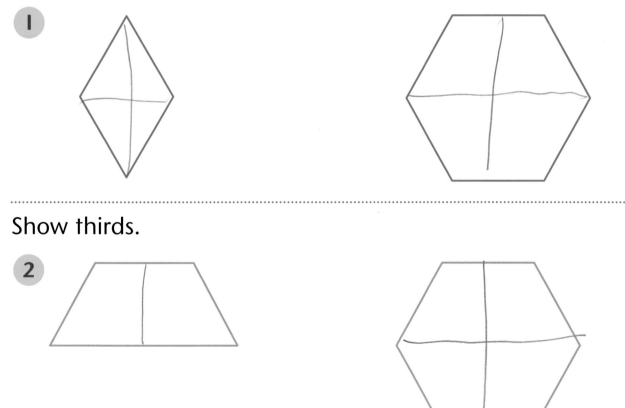

1

Show thirds.

2

Use a crayon.
Color one half if the shape has equal parts.

1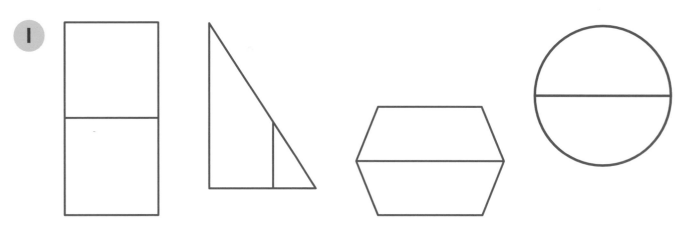

Color one third if the shape has equal parts.

2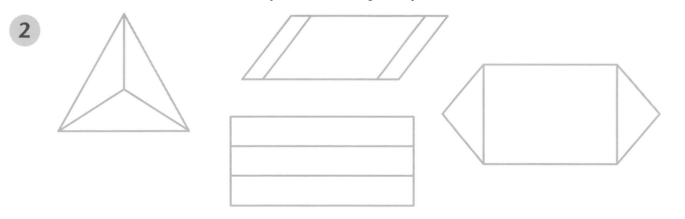

Mixed Review

3 Solve.

$12 - 9 = $ ___ $3 + 7 = $ ___ $6 + $ ___ $= 12$

4 Write the missing numbers.

 49 ▢ ▢ ▢ 53 ▢ ▢ 56 ▢ 58

▶ **More Practice, page 414**

Dear Family: Help your child find halves and thirds. Divide fruit into two or three equal pieces, or look at windows to find two or three equal parts.

Name _____

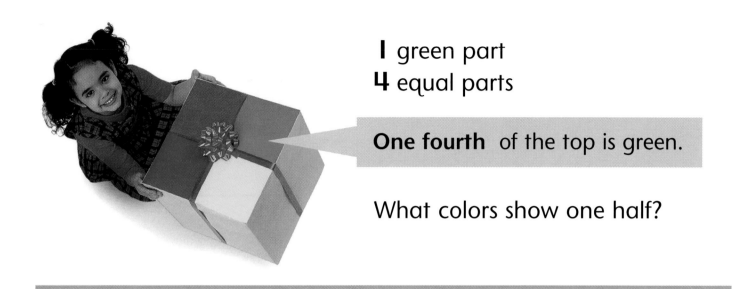

I green part
4 equal parts

One fourth of the top is green.

What colors show one half?

Use a crayon.
Color one fourth if the shape has **4** equal parts.

1

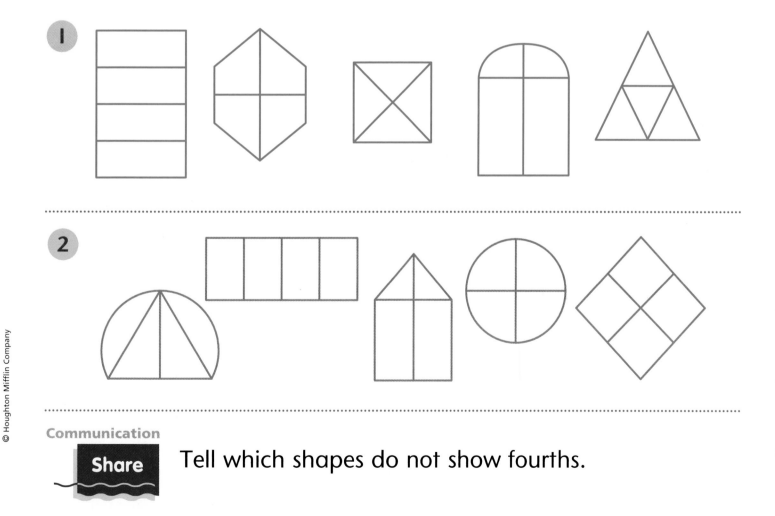

2

© Houghton Mifflin Company

Communication

Share   Tell which shapes do not show fourths.

Lesson 8.12

Use crayons.
Color one half blue.
Color one third red.
Color one fourth yellow.

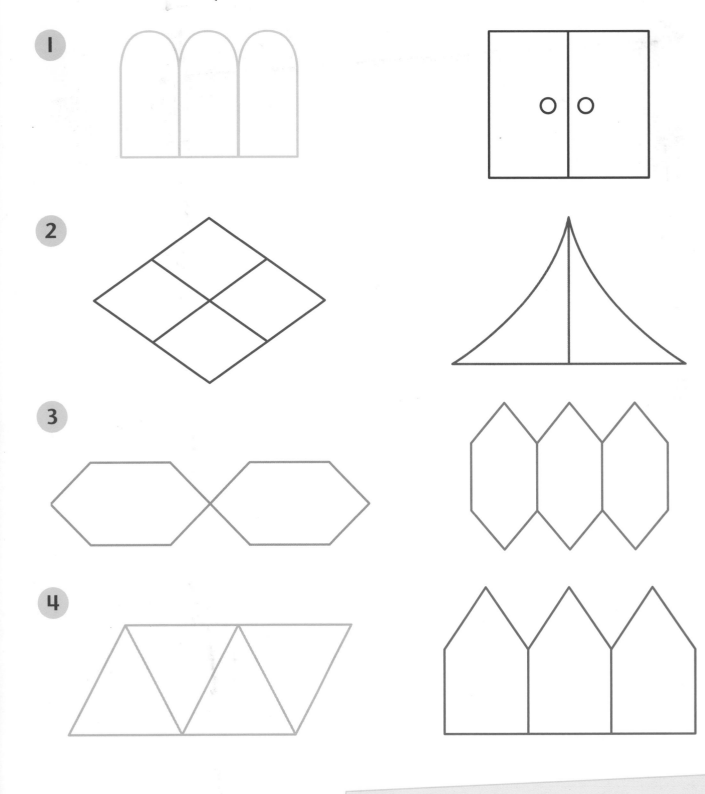

▶ **More Practice, page 415**

Dear Family: Have your child fold napkins into halves and fourths. Then try thirds. Talk about the number of equal parts.

Lesson 8.12

Name _____

Use a geoboard. Play in groups of three.

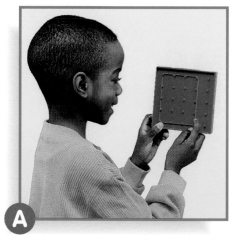

A Make the shape.
Pass it on.

B Show halves.
Pass it on.

C Show thirds
or fourths.

Take turns starting. Draw the equal parts.
Color one of the equal parts each time.

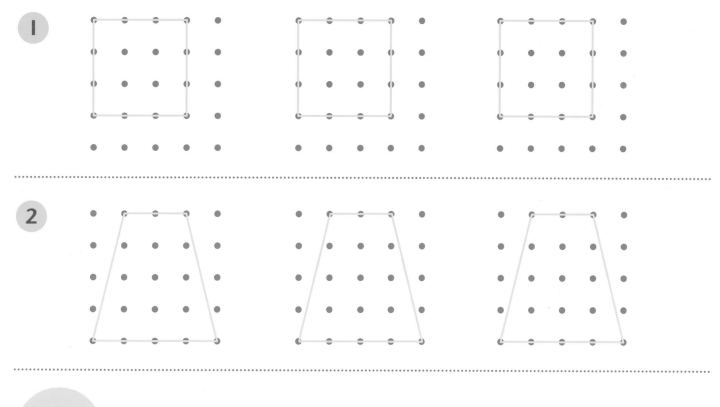

1

2

Give it a try Play again. Start with your own shape.

Draw to continue the pattern.

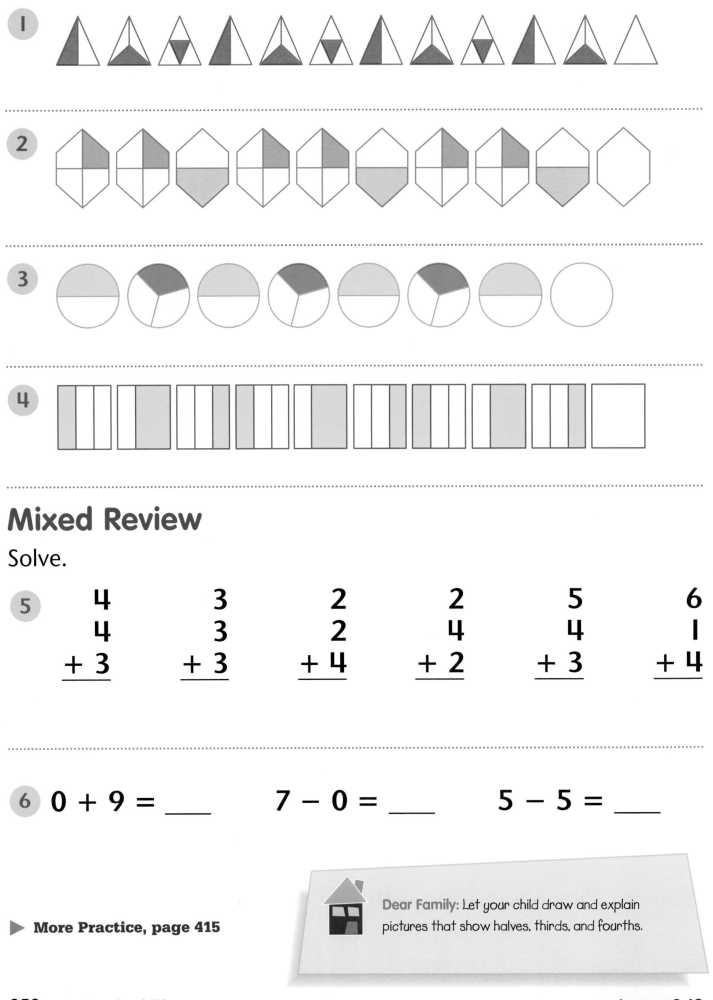

1

2

3

4

Mixed Review

Solve.

5

$$
\begin{array}{r} 4 \\ 4 \\ +\ 3 \\ \hline \end{array}
\qquad
\begin{array}{r} 3 \\ 3 \\ +\ 3 \\ \hline \end{array}
\qquad
\begin{array}{r} 2 \\ 2 \\ +\ 4 \\ \hline \end{array}
\qquad
\begin{array}{r} 2 \\ 4 \\ +\ 2 \\ \hline \end{array}
\qquad
\begin{array}{r} 5 \\ 4 \\ +\ 3 \\ \hline \end{array}
\qquad
\begin{array}{r} 6 \\ 1 \\ +\ 4 \\ \hline \end{array}
$$

6 $0 + 9 =$ ___ $7 - 0 =$ ___ $5 - 5 =$ ___

▶ **More Practice, page 415**

Dear Family: Let your child draw and explain pictures that show halves, thirds, and fourths.

Cooperative Learning

Name _____

Work in small groups.

Does the size of the half change if you color the half another way?

Color one half **3** different ways.

1

Color one third **4** different ways.

2

Communication

Share answers with another group. Tell how you decide which parts to color.

Work in small groups.

Draw triangles in one fourth of each box.

Show **8** different answers.

What patterns can you make?

Dear Family: Ask your child to show you fractions of 12, using an egg carton and macaroni. Do the same for 24, using two egg cartons. Talk about patterns you notice in the answers.

Name _____

Match the shapes.

1

Draw a shape.

2 **4** sides	3 **5** sides	4 **3** corners
· · · · ·	· · · · ·	· · · · ·
· · · · ·	· · · · ·	· · · · ·
· · · · ·	· · · · ·	· · · · ·
· · · · ·	· · · · ·	· · · · ·
· · · · ·	· · · · ·	· · · · ·

Circle the shape that matches.

5

6

Draw and color the missing shape.

7

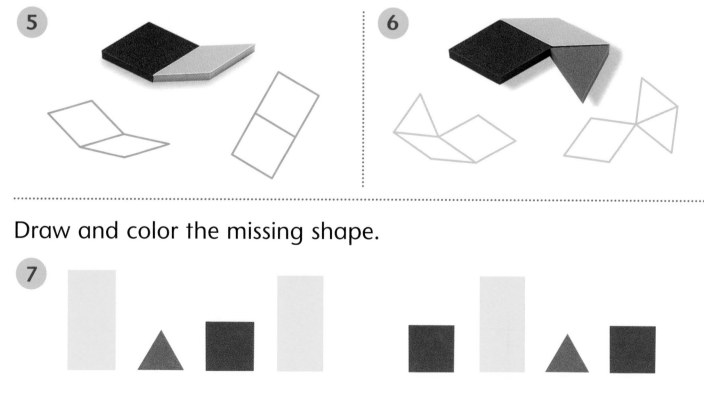

Circle each shape that has matching parts.

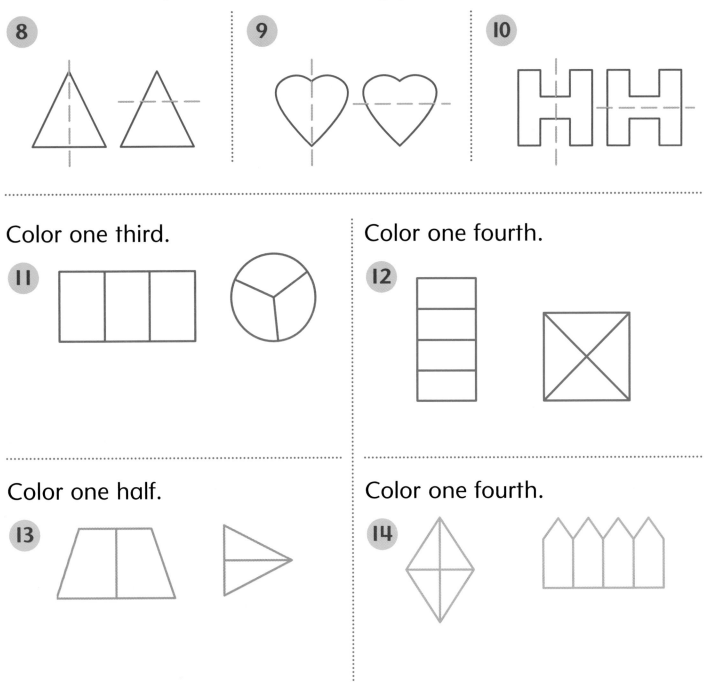

8   **9**   **10**

Color one third.   Color one fourth.

11   **12**

Color one half.   Color one fourth.

13   **14**

Color one third **4** different ways.

15

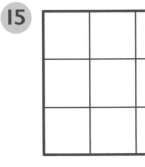
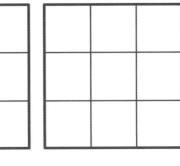
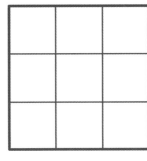
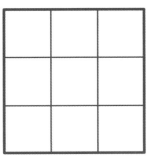

Make a Shape

Name _____

Work with a partner.
Cover each yellow block with red blocks.

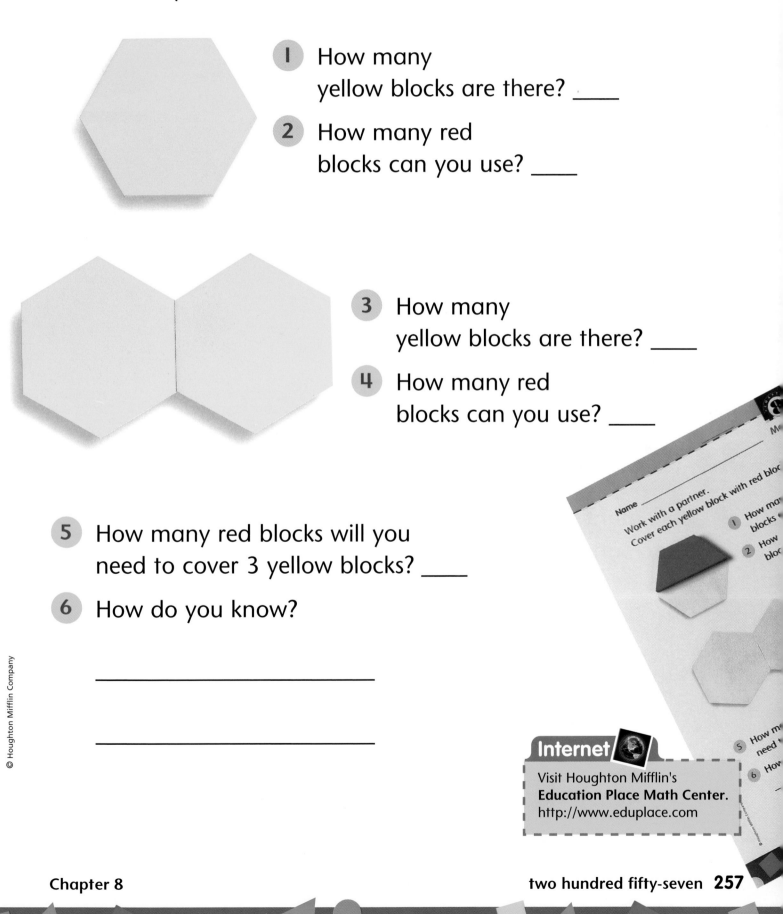

1 How many
yellow blocks are there? ____

2 How many red
blocks can you use? ____

3 How many
yellow blocks are there? ____

4 How many red
blocks can you use? ____

5 How many red blocks will you
need to cover 3 yellow blocks? ____

6 How do you know?

_____

_____

Internet

Visit Houghton Mifflin's
Education Place Math Center.
http://www.eduplace.com

Take turns with a partner.

Make a design with yellow and red blocks. Trace your design on the workmat.

Cover your partner's design with blue and green blocks.

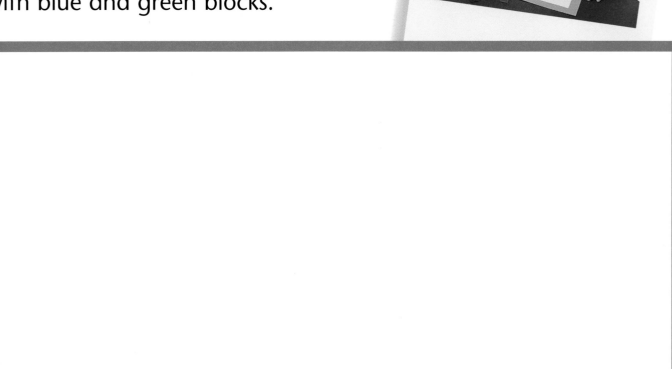

1 How many blue and green blocks did you use? _____
Switch and try again.

2 How many blocks did you use this time? _____

3 Is the number of blocks equal each time? _____

 Dear Family: Discuss with your child different ways that familiar shapes can be broken up into other shapes.

Name _____

Write the tens and ones. Write the number.

1 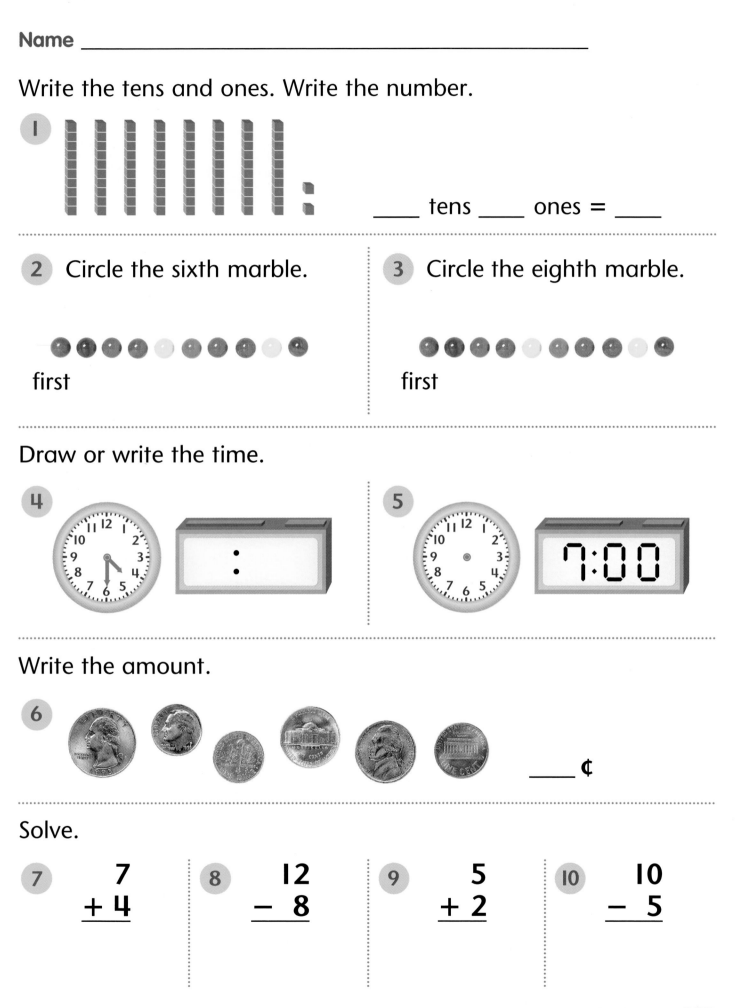   ____ tens ____ ones = ____

2 Circle the sixth marble.

first

3 Circle the eighth marble.

first

Draw or write the time.

4

5   7:00

Write the amount.

6   ____ ¢

Solve.

7   7
      + 4

8   12
      − 8

9   5
      + 2

10   10
       − 5

Write the addition or subtraction sentence.

11
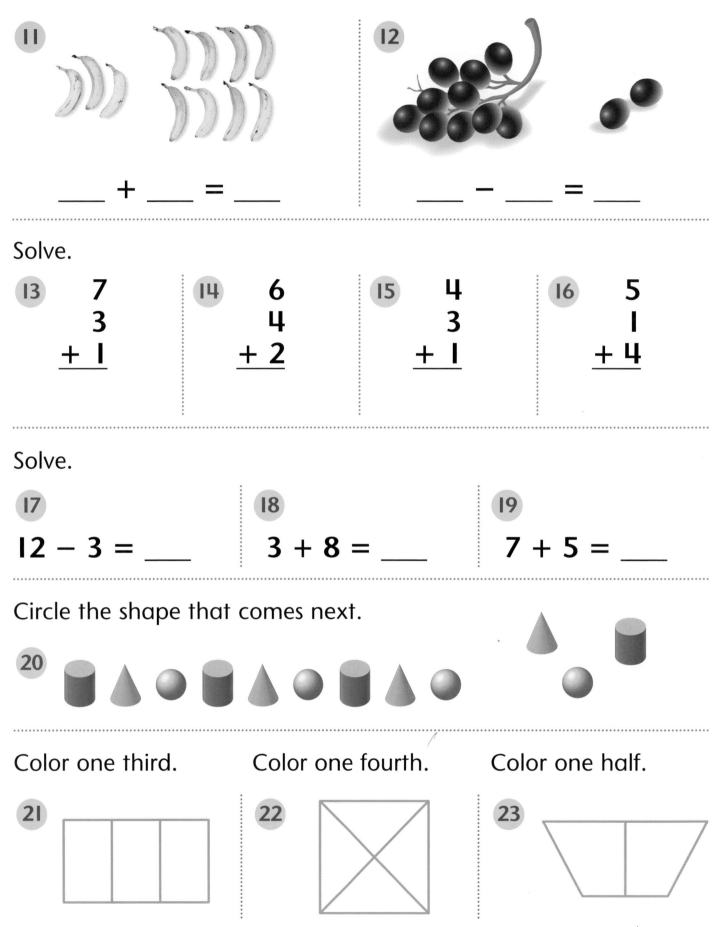
___ + ___ = ___

12
___ – ___ = ___

Solve.

13
$$\begin{array}{r} 7 \\ 3 \\ + 1 \\ \hline \end{array}$$

14
$$\begin{array}{r} 6 \\ 4 \\ + 2 \\ \hline \end{array}$$

15
$$\begin{array}{r} 4 \\ 3 \\ + 1 \\ \hline \end{array}$$

16
$$\begin{array}{r} 5 \\ 1 \\ + 4 \\ \hline \end{array}$$

Solve.

17
$12 - 3 =$ ___

18
$3 + 8 =$ ___

19
$7 + 5 =$ ___

Circle the shape that comes next.

20

Color one third.

21

Color one fourth.

22

Color one half.

23

Addition and Subtraction Facts Through 20

CHAPTER 9

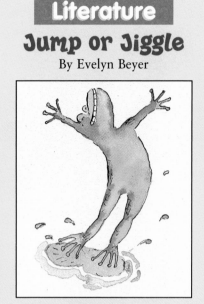

Literature

Jump or Jiggle
By Evelyn Beyer

Read Aloud Anthology p. 32
Theme Connection
Animals, Animals

See what I can do by the end of this chapter.

Use What You Know

How many ducklings do you see?
How many chicks do you see?
How can you find the number of baby birds in all?

Use a number cube and counters to play the game.

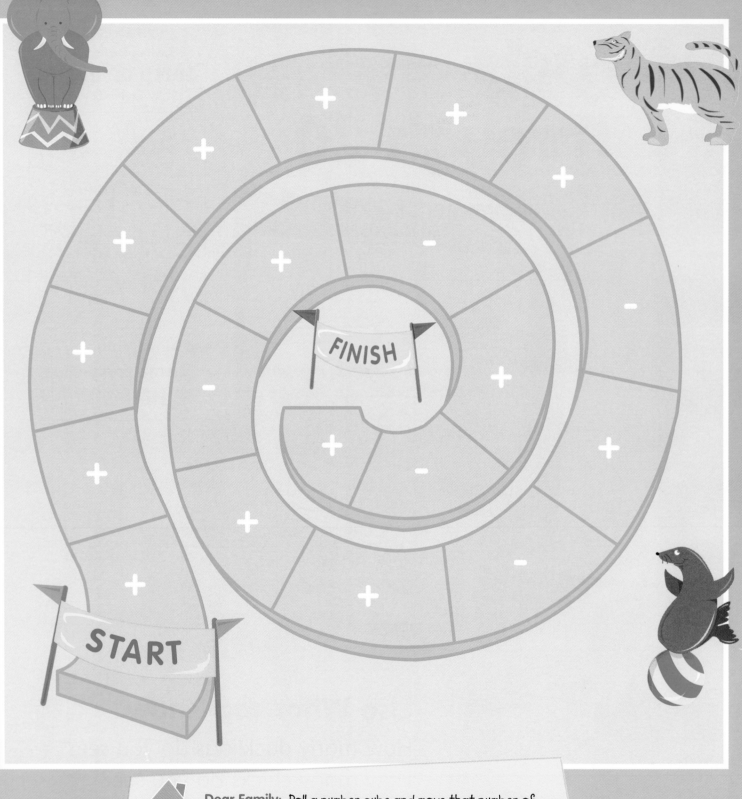

START

FINISH

Dear Family: Roll a number cube and move that number of spaces. Roll the cube again and either add or subtract (moving forward or backward) the new number. Say the number sentence aloud. Continue until one player reaches the finish.

Name _____

Problem Solving
Solve.

1 **5** penguins are in the water.
   7 more sit on the rock. How
   many are there in all?   _____ penguins

2 **8** seals are in the water.
   12 seals are on the shore. How
   many more are on the shore?   _____ seals

3 There are **5** parrots and **5**
   macaws in the exhibit. How
   many birds are in the exhibit?   _____ birds

4 There are **11** horses. There are
   9 piles of hay. How many
   more horses are there than
   piles of hay?   _____ horses

Mixed Review

Solve.

5
5	10	12	7	10	5
+ 3	+ 2	− 5	+ 1	− 4	− 5

Lesson 9.1

Problem Solving

1 There are **12** animals in a field.
3 are zebras. How many animals
are not zebras?   ____ animals

2 Bob has **12¢**. He buys food for
the animals for **7¢**. How much
money does he have left?   ____ ¢

3 **4** polar bears are in the sun.
2 polar bears are in the water.
How many polar bears are there?   ____ polar bears

4 There are **10** ducks in the pond.
Some ducks fly away. There are **4**
ducks left. How many flew away?   ____ ducks

▶ **More Practice, page 416**

Dear Family: Ask your child to read this page of
word problems to you and explain how to solve them.

Cooperative Learning

Name _____

Use crayons. Color the two groups that show **10**.
Write how many in all.

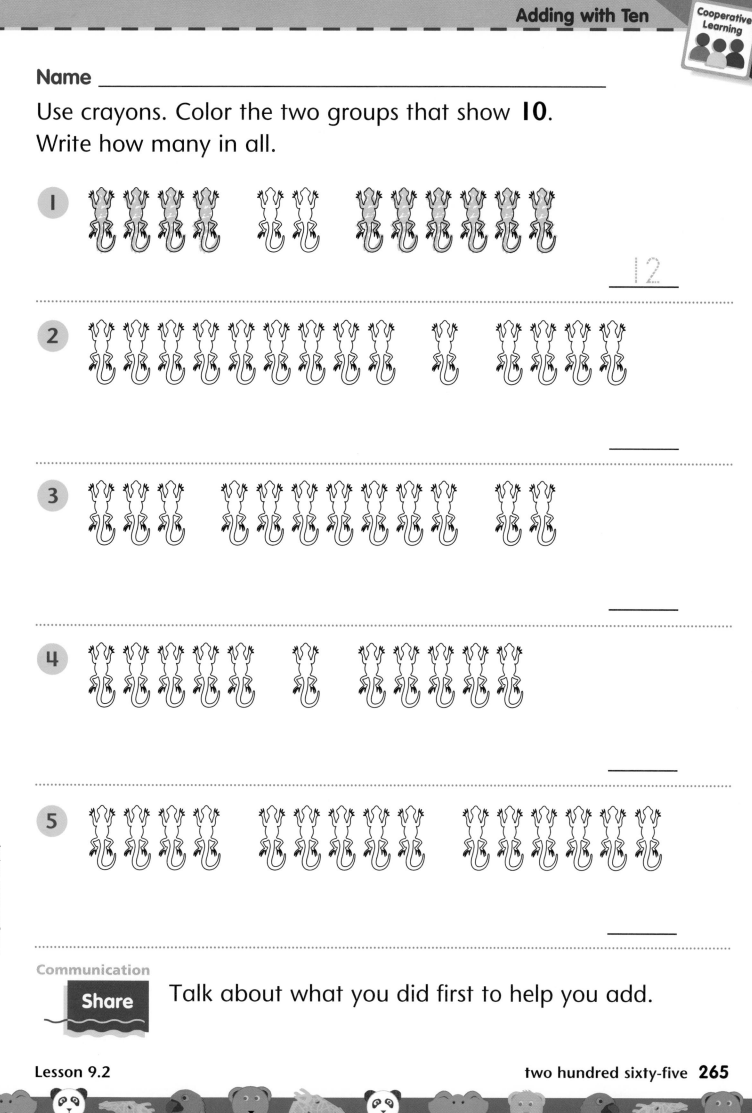

1 ____ 12

2 _____

3 _____

4 _____

5 _____

Communication

Share Talk about what you did first to help you add.

Work with a group.
You may use cubes.

Circle the two numbers that make **10**.
Write the sum.

1 1 + 9 + 4 = _____   3 + 2 + 8 = _____

2 7 + 6 + 3 = _____   6 + 8 + 4 = _____

3 4 + 5 + 5 = _____   10 + 0 + 2 = _____

4
$$
\begin{array}{cccccc}
3 & 5 & 9 & 4 & 2 & 4 \\
7 & 9 & 2 & 6 & 8 & 6 \\
+\,8 & +\,5 & +\,1 & +\,4 & +\,5 & +\,9 \\
\hline
\end{array}
$$

5
$$
\begin{array}{cccccc}
9 & 3 & 2 & 7 & 0 & 1 \\
7 & 3 & 6 & 7 & 10 & 1 \\
+\,1 & +\,7 & +\,8 & +\,3 & +\,8 & +\,9 \\
\hline
\end{array}
$$

Dear Family: Have your child tell you about these pages and the special way that finding ten helps in adding.

Cooperative Learning

Name _____

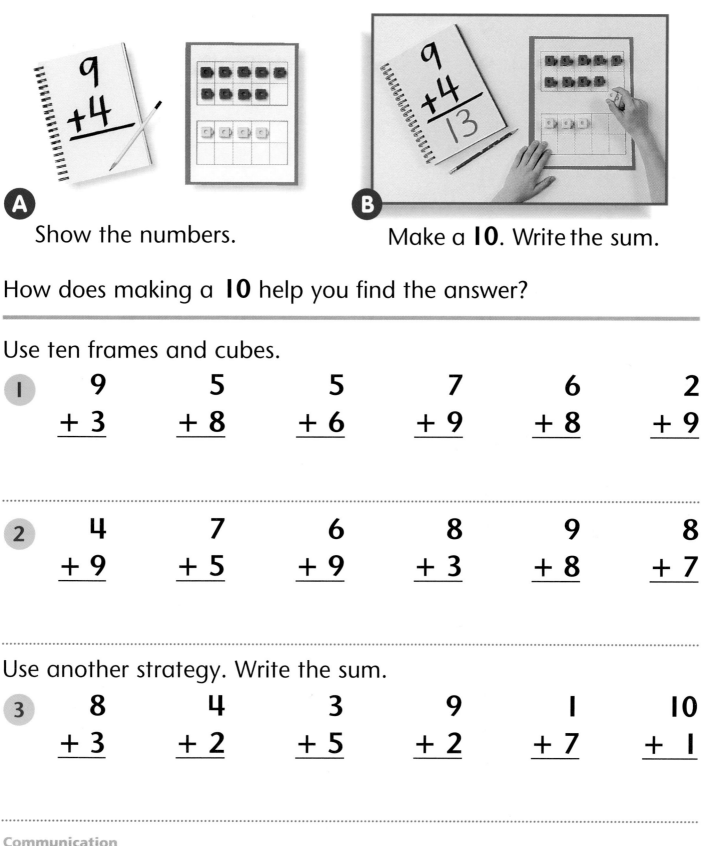

A Show the numbers.

B Make a **10**. Write the sum.

How does making a **10** help you find the answer?

Use ten frames and cubes.

1.
$$\begin{array}{r} 9 \\ + 3 \\ \hline \end{array} \qquad \begin{array}{r} 5 \\ + 8 \\ \hline \end{array} \qquad \begin{array}{r} 5 \\ + 6 \\ \hline \end{array} \qquad \begin{array}{r} 7 \\ + 9 \\ \hline \end{array} \qquad \begin{array}{r} 6 \\ + 8 \\ \hline \end{array} \qquad \begin{array}{r} 2 \\ + 9 \\ \hline \end{array}$$

2.
$$\begin{array}{r} 4 \\ + 9 \\ \hline \end{array} \qquad \begin{array}{r} 7 \\ + 5 \\ \hline \end{array} \qquad \begin{array}{r} 6 \\ + 9 \\ \hline \end{array} \qquad \begin{array}{r} 8 \\ + 3 \\ \hline \end{array} \qquad \begin{array}{r} 9 \\ + 8 \\ \hline \end{array} \qquad \begin{array}{r} 8 \\ + 7 \\ \hline \end{array}$$

Use another strategy. Write the sum.

3.
$$\begin{array}{r} 8 \\ + 3 \\ \hline \end{array} \qquad \begin{array}{r} 4 \\ + 2 \\ \hline \end{array} \qquad \begin{array}{r} 3 \\ + 5 \\ \hline \end{array} \qquad \begin{array}{r} 9 \\ + 2 \\ \hline \end{array} \qquad \begin{array}{r} 1 \\ + 7 \\ \hline \end{array} \qquad \begin{array}{r} 10 \\ + 1 \\ \hline \end{array}$$

Communication

Share Check your answers with a partner.
Tell how you made **10** for each.

Work with a partner.
Use ten frames and cubes.
Write the sum.

1.
$\begin{array}{r} 6 \\ + 8 \\ \hline \end{array}$ $\begin{array}{r} 9 \\ + 9 \\ \hline \end{array}$ $\begin{array}{r} 8 \\ + 5 \\ \hline \end{array}$ $\begin{array}{r} 3 \\ + 8 \\ \hline \end{array}$ $\begin{array}{r} 4 \\ + 9 \\ \hline \end{array}$ $\begin{array}{r} 9 \\ + 7 \\ \hline \end{array}$

2.
$\begin{array}{r} 8 \\ + 6 \\ \hline \end{array}$ $\begin{array}{r} 4 \\ + 8 \\ \hline \end{array}$ $\begin{array}{r} 5 \\ + 9 \\ \hline \end{array}$ $\begin{array}{r} 7 \\ + 8 \\ \hline \end{array}$ $\begin{array}{r} 9 \\ + 3 \\ \hline \end{array}$ $\begin{array}{r} 9 \\ + 7 \\ \hline \end{array}$

3.
$\begin{array}{r} 2 \\ + 9 \\ \hline \end{array}$ $\begin{array}{r} 8 \\ + 4 \\ \hline \end{array}$ $\begin{array}{r} 8 \\ + 8 \\ \hline \end{array}$ $\begin{array}{r} 9 \\ + 5 \\ \hline \end{array}$ $\begin{array}{r} 8 \\ + 3 \\ \hline \end{array}$ $\begin{array}{r} 4 \\ + 9 \\ \hline \end{array}$

4. $8 + 9 = \underline{\hspace{1cm}}$ $4 + 8 = \underline{\hspace{1cm}}$ $8 + 7 = \underline{\hspace{1cm}}$

5. $6 + 3 = \underline{\hspace{1cm}}$ $6 + 4 = \underline{\hspace{1cm}}$ $3 + 1 = \underline{\hspace{1cm}}$

Problem Solving

6.   Mr. Smith bought apples for his class. He put **8** in one bag. He put **10** in another bag. How many apples did Mr. Smith buy in all?

_____ apples

▶ **More Practice, page 416**

Dear Family: Help your child practice adding numbers to 20 by counting items throughout the house, such as cans in the cupboard.

Name _____

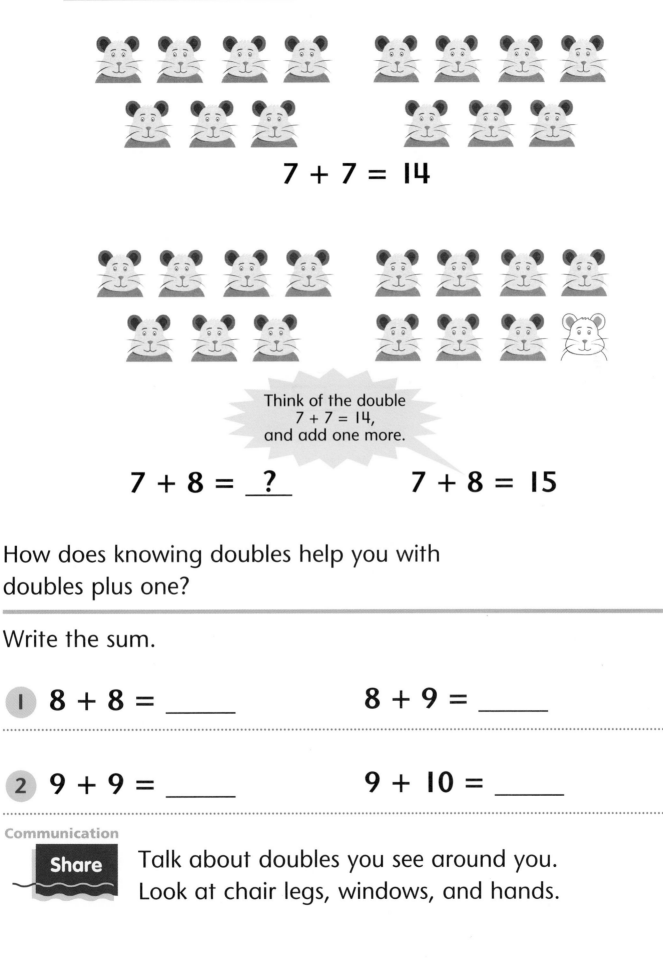

$7 + 7 = 14$

Think of the double
$7 + 7 = 14$,
and add one more.

$7 + 8 = \underline{\ ?\ }$ $7 + 8 = 15$

How does knowing doubles help you with
doubles plus one?

_____

Write the sum.

1 $8 + 8 =$ _____ $8 + 9 =$ _____

2 $9 + 9 =$ _____ $9 + 10 =$ _____

Communication

Share   Talk about doubles you see around you.
Look at chair legs, windows, and hands.

Write the sum.

1. $8 + 8 =$ _____ $10 + 9 =$ _____ $7 + 6 =$ _____

2. $9 + 8 =$ _____ $5 + 5 =$ _____ $12 + 7 =$ _____

3. $10 + 10 =$ _____ $6 + 5 =$ _____ $4 + 4 =$ _____

4.
$$\begin{array}{r} 2 \\ + 2 \\ \hline \end{array} \qquad \begin{array}{r} 11 \\ + 4 \\ \hline \end{array} \qquad \begin{array}{r} 6 \\ + 6 \\ \hline \end{array} \qquad \begin{array}{r} 8 \\ + 7 \\ \hline \end{array} \qquad \begin{array}{r} 14 \\ + 4 \\ \hline \end{array}$$

5.
$$\begin{array}{r} 12 \\ + 6 \\ \hline \end{array} \qquad \begin{array}{r} 9 \\ + 9 \\ \hline \end{array} \qquad \begin{array}{r} 3 \\ + 3 \\ \hline \end{array} \qquad \begin{array}{r} 10 \\ + 7 \\ \hline \end{array} \qquad \begin{array}{r} 1 \\ + 1 \\ \hline \end{array}$$

Use a calculator to solve.
Write your sentence.

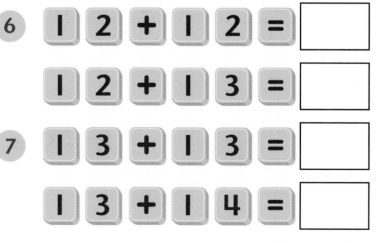

6. $12 + 12 =$ ☐

$12 + 13 =$ ☐

7. $13 + 13 =$ ☐

$13 + 14 =$ ☐

▶ **More Practice, page 417**

Dear Family: Ask your child to add some doubles, such as 5+5 and 7+7. Then try some doubles plus one, such as 6+7 and 3+4.

Lesson 9.4

Name _____

The spotted pig is third in line from the tree.
There are **5** pigs in line behind it.
How many pigs are in line?

▶ **Understand**

I need to know how many pigs are in line.

▶ **Plan**

I can draw a picture.

▶ **Try it**

My picture shows **8** pigs.

▶ **Look back**

3 + 5 = 8

My answer makes sense.

Communication

Talk about it How do pictures help you solve the question?

Problem Solving

Draw a picture to solve.

1 **6** cows are in the shed.
11 are in the pen.
How many cows are there in all?

_____ cows

2 There are **12** rabbits. **2** rabbits
are white. **4** rabbits are black.
The rest are brown.
How many rabbits are brown?

_____ rabbits

3 There are **8** hens in the coop.
5 hens have laid eggs.
How many hens have not
laid eggs?

_____ hens

4 There are **3** rows of nests.
There are **3** nests in each row.
Only **4** nests are empty.
How many nests are not empty?

_____ nests

Dear Family: Ask your child to show you the pictures he or
she used to solve the problems on this page.

Name _____

Take some blocks. Spread them out.
About how many blocks are there?
Find out without counting.

A

Estimate.
Make groups
of about **10**.

B

Count by tens.
Write your estimate.
Check your estimate.

When is estimating numbers helpful?

Take some more blocks.
Try again. Write your estimate.

1 about _____ blocks

2 about _____ blocks

3 about _____ blocks

4 about _____ blocks

Communication

Talk about it

How is estimating like counting?
How is it different?

Write the sum.

1   5 + 3 = _____   3 + 8 = _____   8 + 4 = _____

2   9 + 9 = _____   5 + 4 = _____   6 + 6 = _____

3
10	7	6	7	9	5
+ 5	+ 9	+ 3	+ 8	+ 9	+ 4

4
9	10	2	10	9	9
+ 4	+ 10	+ 1	+ 7	+ 5	+ 7

Use blocks. Show the numbers.
Make a **10**. Write the sum.

5
```
    9
  + 4
```

Problem Solving

6   **8** horses and **14** cows are in the field.
How many fewer horses are there than cows?

_____ horses

Dear Family: Help your child practice estimating by using beans, macaroni, or other small items.

Name _____

Math World

Children in Afghanistan play a game called Khana Baudakan.

In **Afghanistan**, children use a stick to draw a design on the ground. The design shows **4** rows of **5** dots.

Players make squares by drawing lines between two dots.

The player with the most boxes starts the next game.

Internet

Explore Houghton Mifflin's
Education Place Math Center.
http://www.eduplace.com

© Houghton Mifflin Company

▶ **Turn the page for directions.**

Did you know?

The Persian word **khana** means house or enclosure.

You need:
- pencil
- paper
- page with dots

Try this!

Make your own **Khana Baudakan** game.

Play the game with a friend. Take turns drawing a line between the dots. Try to make squares.

Dear Family: Use the following rules to play "Khana Baudakan" (HAH nuh BOW doo kahn). At the end of the game, have your child count the number of squares each of you made.

How to Play:

- Copy the dot design onto a sheet of paper.
- Have players take turns drawing lines between two dots. Lines should be drawn horizontally or vertically.
- When a player draws a line that completes a box, that player puts her or his initials in the box.
- Play continues until all the dots are connected to form boxes.
- The player whose initials are in the most boxes starts the next game.

276 two hundred seventy-six

Chapter 9

Name _____

Use coins.

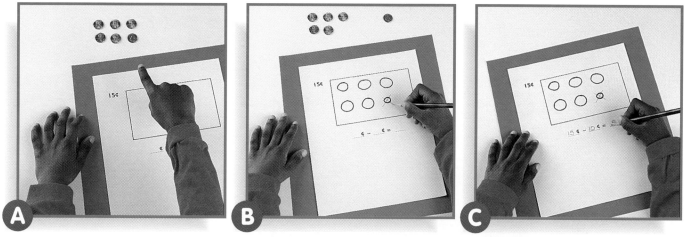

A Show the amount.

B Draw the coins. Subtract **10¢**.

C Write the number sentence.

Which coin do you use to subtract? Why?

---

1 18¢ [ ]   ____ ¢ − ____ ¢ = ____ ¢

2 11¢ [ ]   ____ ¢ − ____ ¢ = ____ ¢

3 14¢ [ ]   ____ ¢ − ____ ¢ = ____ ¢

Communication

Talk about it How is subtracting **10** different than subtracting other numbers?

Lesson 9.7

You may use coins.
Subtract **10¢**. Find the difference.

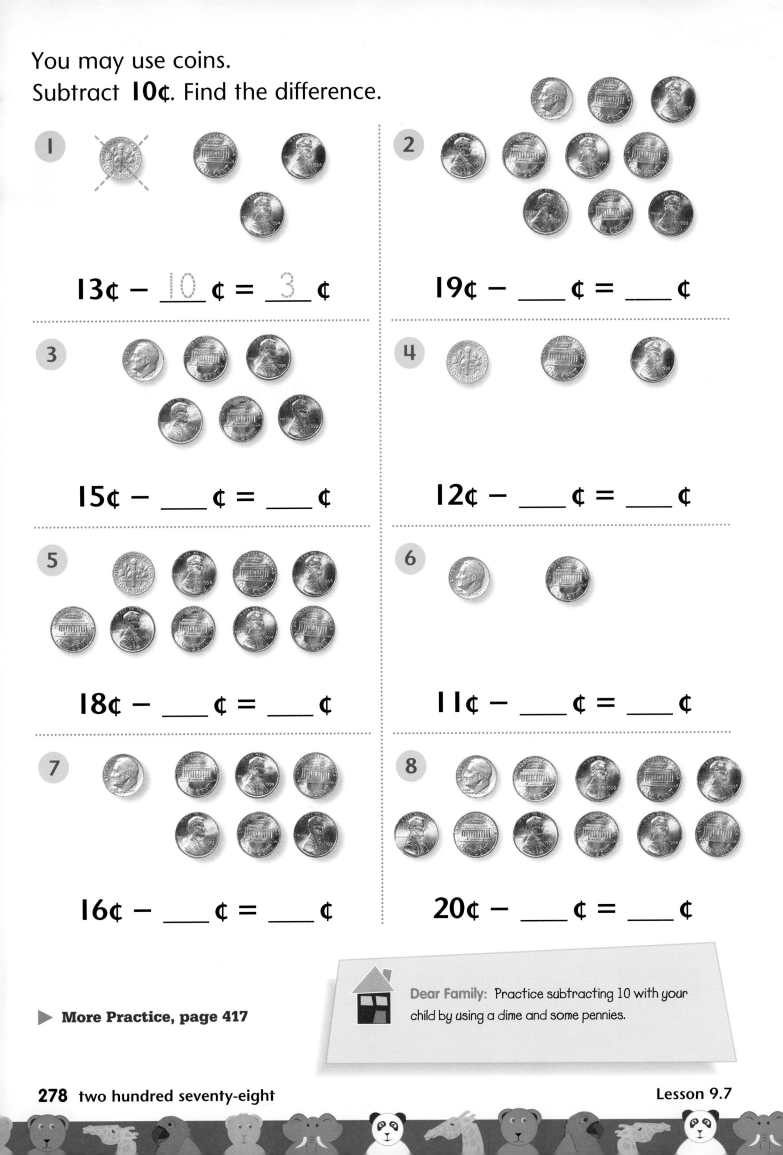

1

13¢ – __10__ ¢ = __3__ ¢

2

19¢ – ___ ¢ = ___ ¢

3

15¢ – ___ ¢ = ___ ¢

4

12¢ – ___ ¢ = ___ ¢

5

18¢ – ___ ¢ = ___ ¢

6

11¢ – ___ ¢ = ___ ¢

7

16¢ – ___ ¢ = ___ ¢

8

20¢ – ___ ¢ = ___ ¢

▶ **More Practice, page 417**

Dear Family: Practice subtracting 10 with your child by using a dime and some pennies.

Cooperative Learning

Name _____

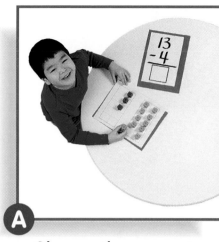

A Show the greater number.

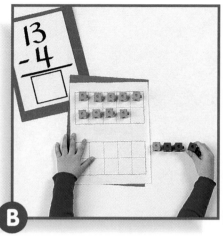

B Subtract. Remove counters from the bottom first.

C Write the difference.

Why is it important to remove counters from the bottom first?

Use counters and ten frames.

1

13	19	14	20	17	16
− 6	− 7	− 5	− 9	− 6	− 8

2

15	17	16	18	14	18
− 7	− 8	− 5	− 9	− 2	− 5

Communication

Write about it

Write a number sentence. Trade with a partner. Draw the ten frame. Draw counters to show your answer.

Work with a group.
Use ten frames and counters.
Solve.

1.

16	12	14	20	13	19
− 9	− 8	− 6	− 1	− 4	− 6

2.

15	13	17	19	17	13
− 8	− 9	− 8	− 2	− 9	− 8

3.

14	20	17	16	18	14
− 7	− 10	− 7	− 7	− 5	− 9

4.

19	20	12	18	13	16
− 8	− 6	− 5	− 9	− 1	− 6

▶ **More Practice, page 418**

🏠 **Dear Family:** Practice subtraction with your child. Use household items, such as flatware.

Lesson 9.8

Name _____

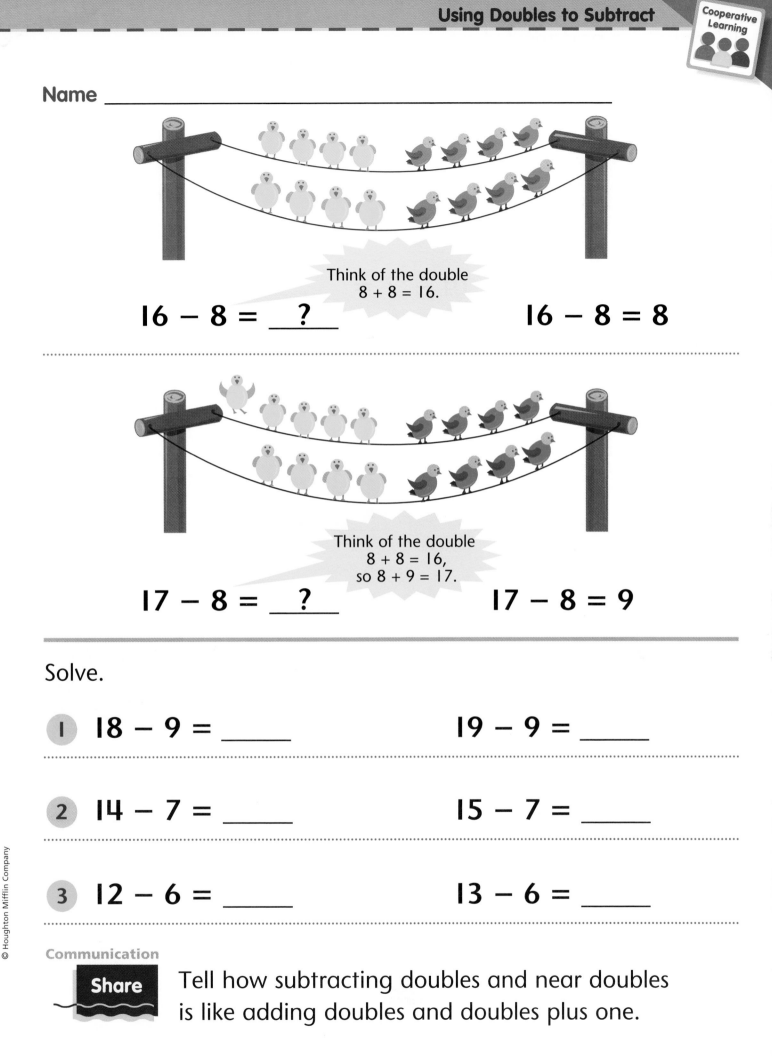

Think of the double
$8 + 8 = 16$.

$16 - 8 = $ ___?___ $16 - 8 = 8$

Think of the double
$8 + 8 = 16$,
so $8 + 9 = 17$.

$17 - 8 = $ ___?___ $17 - 8 = 9$

Solve.

1 $18 - 9 = $ _____ $19 - 9 = $ _____

2 $14 - 7 = $ _____ $15 - 7 = $ _____

3 $12 - 6 = $ _____ $13 - 6 = $ _____

Communication

Share Tell how subtracting doubles and near doubles is like adding doubles and doubles plus one.

Work with a partner. Subtract.

1   17 − 8 = ___   20 − 10 = ___   13 − 6 = ___

2   12 − 3 = ___   10 − 5 = ___   19 − 9 = ___

3   9 − 4 = ___   14 − 7 = ___   18 − 6 = ___

4   7   15   10   20   11
      − 3   − 7   − 6   − 8   − 5
     ____   ____   ____   ____   ____

5   18   12   3   5   16
      − 9   − 6   − 1   − 2   − 8
     ____   ____   ____   ____   ____

Use a calculator to solve.
Write your sentence.

6   [2] [2] [−] [1] [1] [=] [____]

    [2] [3] [−] [1] [1] [=] [____]

7   [2] [4] [−] [1] [2] [=] [____]

    [2] [5] [−] [1] [2] [=] [____]

Dear Family: Practice subtracting doubles with your child, such as 18−9 and 16−8. Then try subtracting near doubles, such as 17−8 and 15−7.

Name _____

FEED THE ANIMALS

5¢   6¢   7¢   7¢   4¢

Problem Solving

1   Sergio has **15¢**. Can he feed both
the donkey and sheep?

_____

2   Rashida has **8¢**. She wants
to feed the pig. How much money
will she have left?

_____ ¢

3   Alexander wants to feed the
horse, pig, and sheep.
How much money will he need?

_____ ¢

4   Marqui has **3** pennies. Andrea has a dime.
Will they have enough money
for each of them to feed the horse?

_____

Give it a try   Work with a partner. Use pennies and dimes.
Which animals can you feed with **20¢**?

2	4	5	7	8	9	10	11	12	14	16	17	18	20
i	a	s	c	b	h	t	r	d	n	w	g	u	f

Work with a partner. Solve.
Use the code to find the message.

$$\begin{array}{r} 12 \\ -\ 4 \\ \hline 8 \end{array} \qquad \begin{array}{r} 0 \\ +2 \\ \hline \end{array} \qquad \begin{array}{r} 6 \\ +5 \\ \hline \end{array} \qquad \begin{array}{r} 10 \\ +2 \\ \hline \end{array}$$

B ☐ ☐ ☐

$$\begin{array}{r} 8 \\ +8 \\ \hline \end{array} \quad \begin{array}{r} 9 \\ -5 \\ \hline \end{array} \quad \begin{array}{r} 10 \\ +0 \\ \hline \end{array} \quad \begin{array}{r} 12 \\ -5 \\ \hline \end{array} \quad \begin{array}{r} 5 \\ +4 \\ \hline \end{array} \quad \begin{array}{r} 9 \\ -7 \\ \hline \end{array} \quad \begin{array}{r} 7 \\ +7 \\ \hline \end{array} \quad \begin{array}{r} 8 \\ +9 \\ \hline \end{array}$$

☐ ☐ ☐ ☐ ☐ ☐ ☐ ☐

$$\begin{array}{r} 6 \\ -4 \\ \hline \end{array} \quad \begin{array}{r} 5 \\ +0 \\ \hline \end{array} \qquad \begin{array}{r} 10 \\ +10 \\ \hline \end{array} \quad \begin{array}{r} 9 \\ +9 \\ \hline \end{array} \quad \begin{array}{r} 5 \\ +9 \\ \hline \end{array}$$

☐ ☐ ☐ ☐ ☐ !

▶ **More Practice, page 418**

Dear Family: Ask your child to explain the code on this page. Make up your own problems and code to solve.

Lesson 9.10

Name _____

Draw shapes to make both sides the same.
Write how many you added.

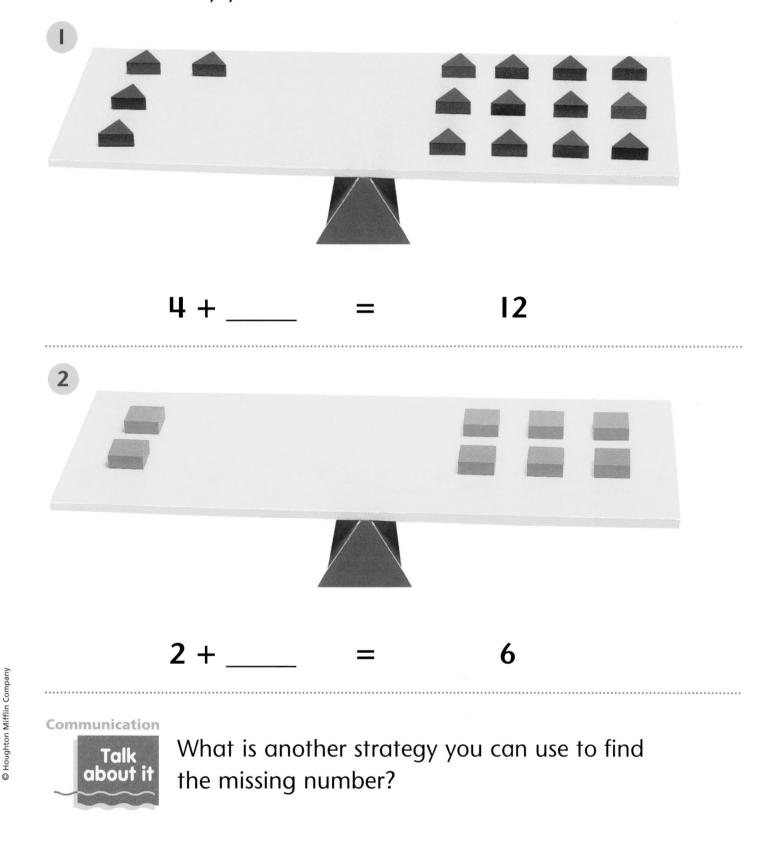

1

$$4 + \underline{\hspace{1.5em}} = 12$$

2

$$2 + \underline{\hspace{1.5em}} = 6$$

Communication

Talk about it

What is another strategy you can use to find the missing number?

Lesson 9.11

Draw shapes to make both sides the same.
Write how many you added.

1

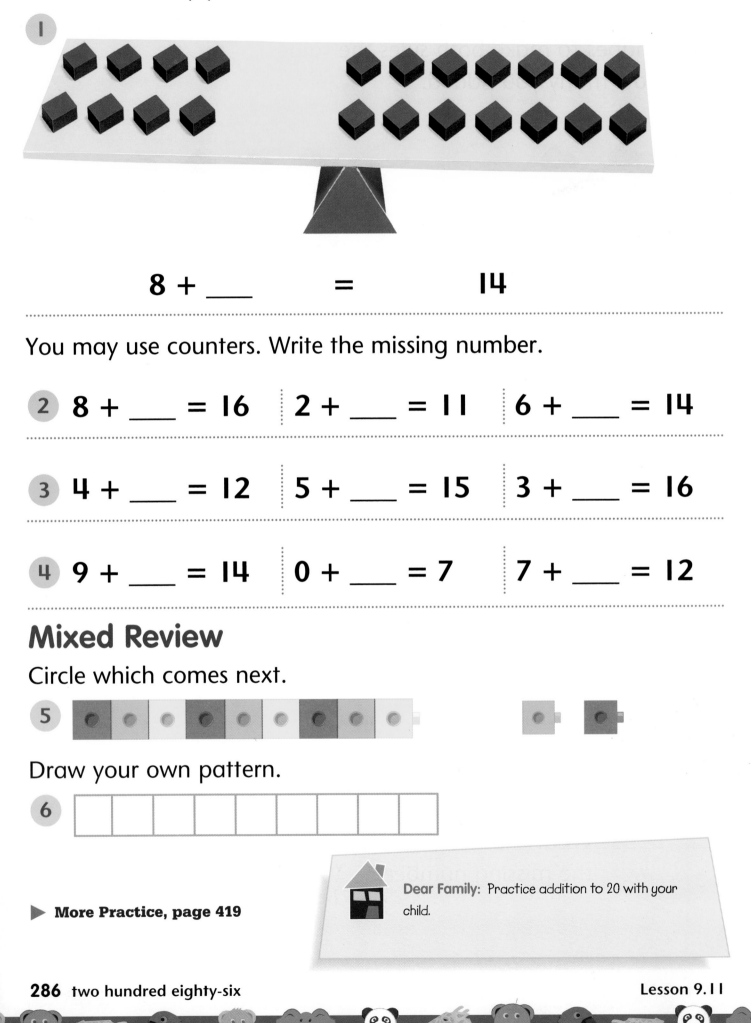

8 + ___   =   14

You may use counters. Write the missing number.

2 8 + ___ = 16   2 + ___ = 11   6 + ___ = 14

3 4 + ___ = 12   5 + ___ = 15   3 + ___ = 16

4 9 + ___ = 14   0 + ___ = 7   7 + ___ = 12

Mixed Review

Circle which comes next.

5

Draw your own pattern.

6

▶ **More Practice, page 419**

Dear Family: Practice addition to 20 with your child.

Name _____

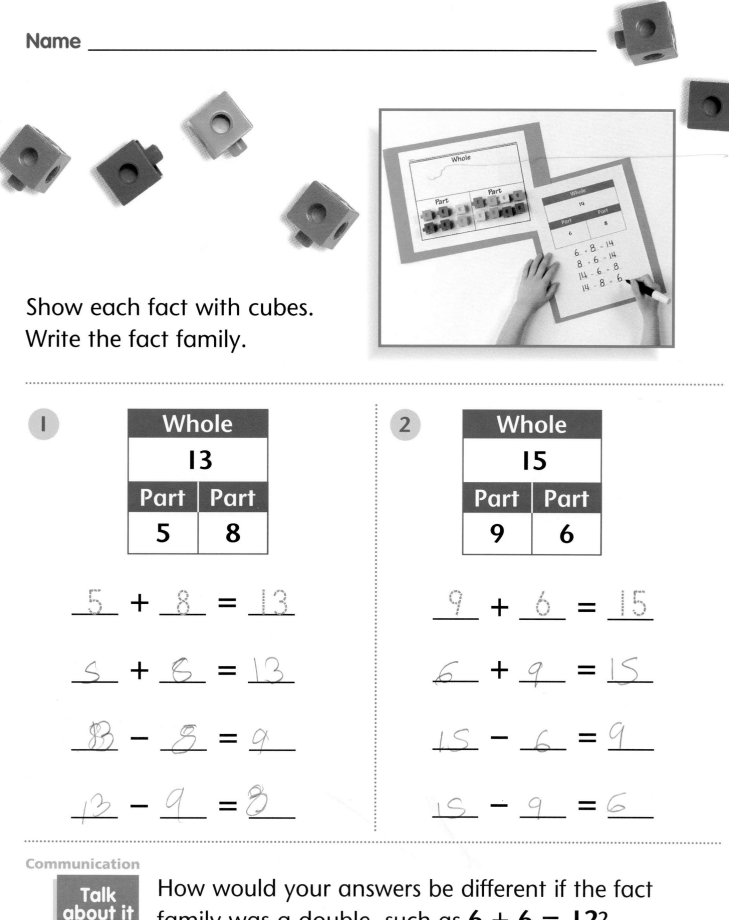

Show each fact with cubes.
Write the fact family.

1

Whole	
13	
Part	Part
5	8

_5_ + _8_ = _13_

_5_ + _8_ = _13_

_8_ – _8_ = _9_

_13_ – _9_ = _8_

2

Whole	
15	
Part	Part
9	6

_9_ + _6_ = _15_

_6_ + _9_ = _15_

_15_ – _6_ = _9_

_15_ – _9_ = _6_

Communication

Talk about it

How would your answers be different if the fact family was a double, such as **6 + 6 = 12**?

Use cubes. Show each fact.
Write the missing number.
Write the fact family.

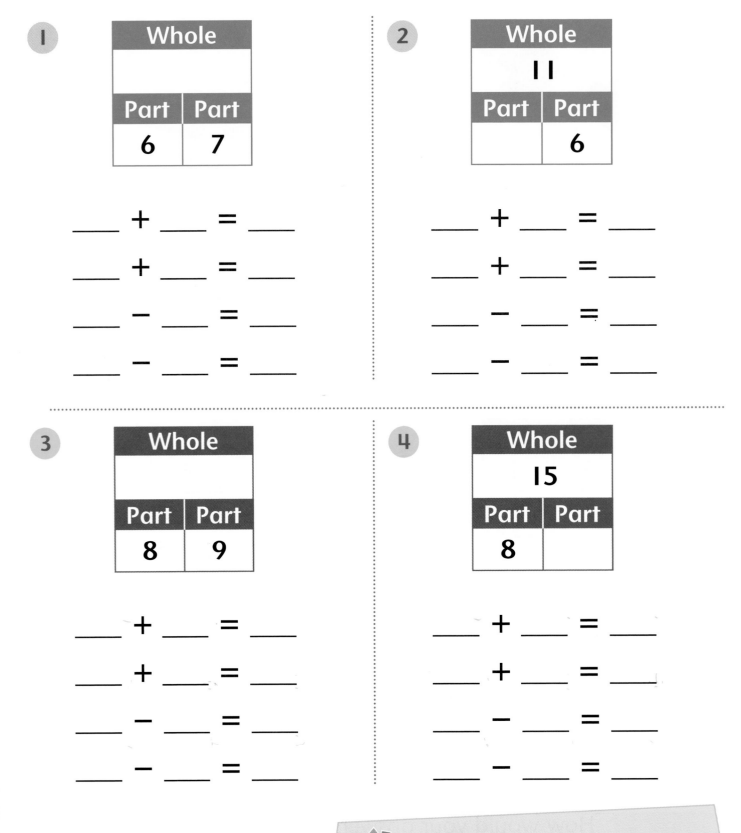

1

Whole	
Part	Part
6	7

___ + ___ = ___

___ + ___ = ___

___ − ___ = ___

___ − ___ = ___

2

Whole	
11	
Part	Part
	6

___ + ___ = ___

___ + ___ = ___

___ − ___ = ___

___ − ___ = ___

3

Whole	
Part	Part
8	9

___ + ___ = ___

___ + ___ = ___

___ − ___ = ___

___ − ___ = ___

4

Whole	
15	
Part	Part
8	

___ + ___ = ___

___ + ___ = ___

___ − ___ = ___

___ − ___ = ___

Dear Family: Ask your child about fact families. Have your child work with the numbers 6, 7, and 13 and show you how to write the fact family.

▶ **More Practice, page 419**

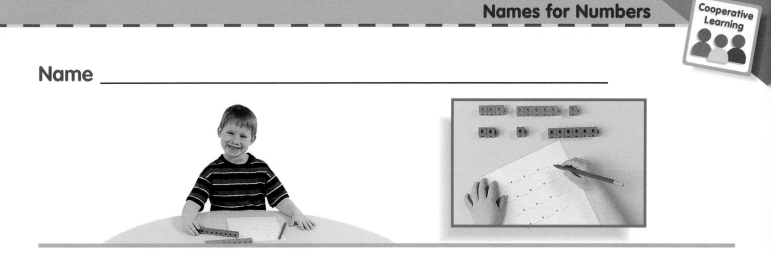

Name _____

Make a train for the number. Break the train
into three parts. Write a number sentence.
Find four names for each number.

1 **18**

_4_ + _6_ + _8_ = _18_

_3_ + _5_ + _10_ = _18_

___ + ___ + ___ = ___

___ + ___ + ___ = ___

2 **11**

___ + ___ + ___ = ___

___ + ___ + ___ = ___

___ + ___ + ___ = ___

___ + ___ + ___ = ___

3 **15**

___ + ___ + ___ = ___

___ + ___ + ___ = ___

___ + ___ + ___ = ___

___ + ___ + ___ = ___

4 **20**

___ + ___ + ___ = ___

___ + ___ + ___ = ___

___ + ___ + ___ = ___

___ + ___ + ___ = ___

Communication

Share Compare your answers with your partner's.

Play the game with a partner.

Make these cards.
Put the cards into the bag.
Pick a card.

Use a tally mark to show the
name. Put the card back. Do
this ten times.

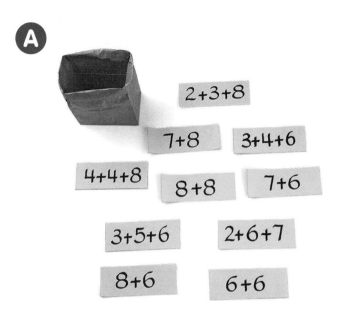

Write a tally mark on the chart for each card you pick.

Names for 12	
Names for 13	
Names for 14	
Names for 15	
Names for 16	

Write the number you picked the most. _____

Dear Family: Practice making up names for numbers with
your child, such as 8+7+4=19 and 3+6+10=19.

Lesson 9.13

Name _____

Solve.

1 **4** green birds are in one cage.
Another cage has **2** blue birds.
A third cage has **2** yellow birds.
How many birds are there in all?

_____ birds

2 There are **17** kittens. **8** are black.
3 are brown. The rest have spots.
How many kittens have spots?

_____ kittens

3 The pet store has **11** fish. **7** fish
are sold. How many fish are left?

_____ fish

4 There are **10** puppies. Each puppy
needs a bowl. There are **6** bowls.
How many more are needed?

_____ bowls

Communication

Share   Tell a partner how you solved the problems.

Solve.

Pet Store

Special Cat Food 3/$1.00

Dog Food

1 Jan has **2** nickels and **5** pennies.
A dog biscuit costs **15¢**.
Can Jan buy a biscuit?

_____

2 Marty buys **7** puppy treats.
Rob buys **2** fewer than Marty.
How many puppy treats did
Rob buy?

_____ puppy treats

3 Kelly needs **10** cans of cat food.
The store has only **7** cans.
How many more cans does
Kelly need?

_____ cans

Dear Family: Help your child practice word problems by
making up some of your own. Have your child use household
items or draw to solve the questions.

Name _____

Write the sum or difference.

1.
```
    7
  + 7
  ____
```

2.
```
   14
  − 4
  ____
```

3.
```
   11
  + 9
  ____
```

4.
```
   18
  − 9
  ____
```

5.
```
   19
  − 2
  ____
```

6.
```
    8
  + 8
  ____
```

7.
```
   12
  + 7
  ____
```

8.
```
   16
  − 3
  ____
```

9. $7 + 8 =$ _____

10. $18 − 8 =$ _____

11. $13 − 8 =$ _____

12. $5 + 8 =$ _____

Write the missing number.

13. $8 +$ _____ $= 16$

14. $4 +$ _____ $= 15$

15. $16 +$ _____ $= 19$

16. $7 +$ _____ $= 16$

17. $9 +$ _____ $= 18$

18. $7 +$ _____ $= 14$

19. $6 +$ _____ $= 15$

20. $10 +$ _____ $= 13$

Write the fact family. Show each fact with cubes.

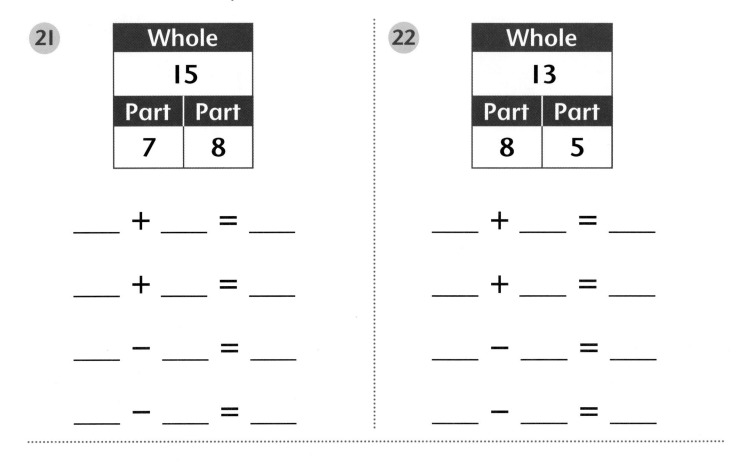

21

Whole	
15	
Part	Part
7	8

___ + ___ = ___

___ + ___ = ___

___ − ___ = ___

___ − ___ = ___

22

Whole	
13	
Part	Part
8	5

___ + ___ = ___

___ + ___ = ___

___ − ___ = ___

___ − ___ = ___

Solve.

23 Tyrone gives **10¢** to a friend. He has **7¢** left. How much money did he start with?

_____ ¢

24 There are **15** kittens in a box. **8** kittens leave to eat. How many kittens are left in the box?

_____ kittens

25 **12** birds sit on a branch. **9** birds fly away. How many birds are left?

_____ birds

26 Carmen has **18¢**. She spends **10¢**. How much money does she have left?

_____ ¢

Name _____

Use number cards and cubes.
Work with a partner.
Listen to the directions.

1   How many chicks do you have? _____

2   How many ducklings do you have? _____

3   How many baby birds are there in all? _____

4   Write the number sentence.

___ + ___ = ___

5   How many chicks does your partner have? _____

6   How many ducklings does your partner have? _____

7   How many baby birds are there in all? _____

8   Write the number sentence.

___ + ___ = ___

9   What can you write about the sums of both the number sentences?

_____

_____

Internet 🌐

Visit Houghton Mifflin's
Education Place Math Center.
http://www.eduplace.com

© Houghton Mifflin Company

Play again.
Write the number sentence
below if your sums match.

1 ___ + ___ = ___ + ___

chicks   ducklings   chicks   ducklings

2 ___ + ___ = ___ + ___

chicks   ducklings   chicks   ducklings

3 ___ + ___ = ___ + ___

chicks   ducklings   chicks   ducklings

Write your own story problem
about chicks and ducklings.

_____

_____

_____

_____

Share your story with a friend.

Dear Family: Ask your child about this lesson. How
did he or she know if two sums were equal?

Measurement

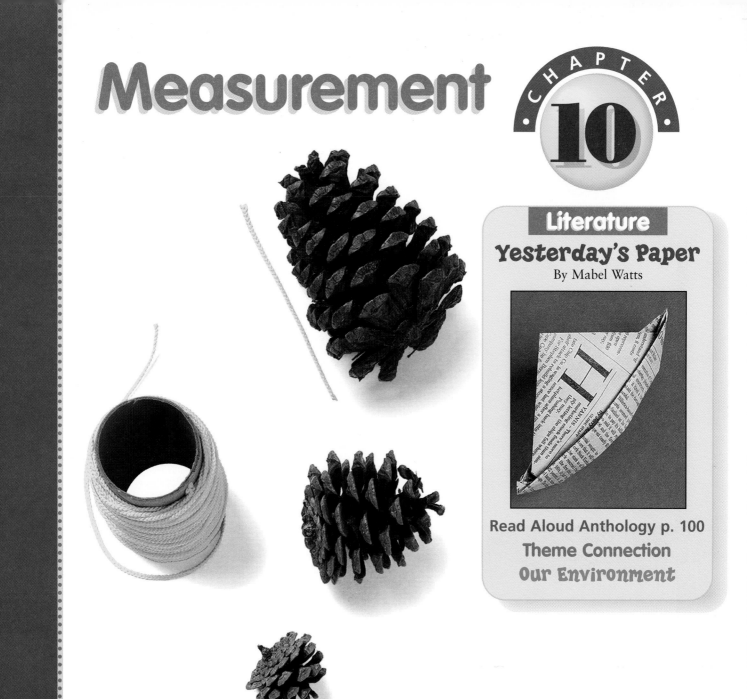

CHAPTER 10

Literature
Yesterday's Paper
By Mabel Watts

Read Aloud Anthology p. 100
Theme Connection
Our Environment

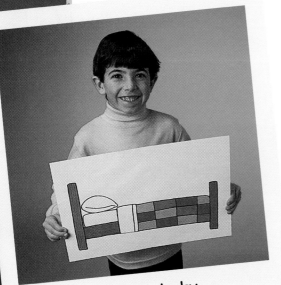

See what I can do by the end of this chapter.

Use What You Know

How can you compare the sizes of the pine cones?

Which one is the shortest?

Which one is the longest?

Find a piece of newspaper.
Use the picture to help make a hat.
Does your hat fit on your head?

Dear Family: See how many shapes you can create by folding newspaper. Compare the size and shape of your folded papers. Measure the length and width of your shapes using objects around your house.

Name _____

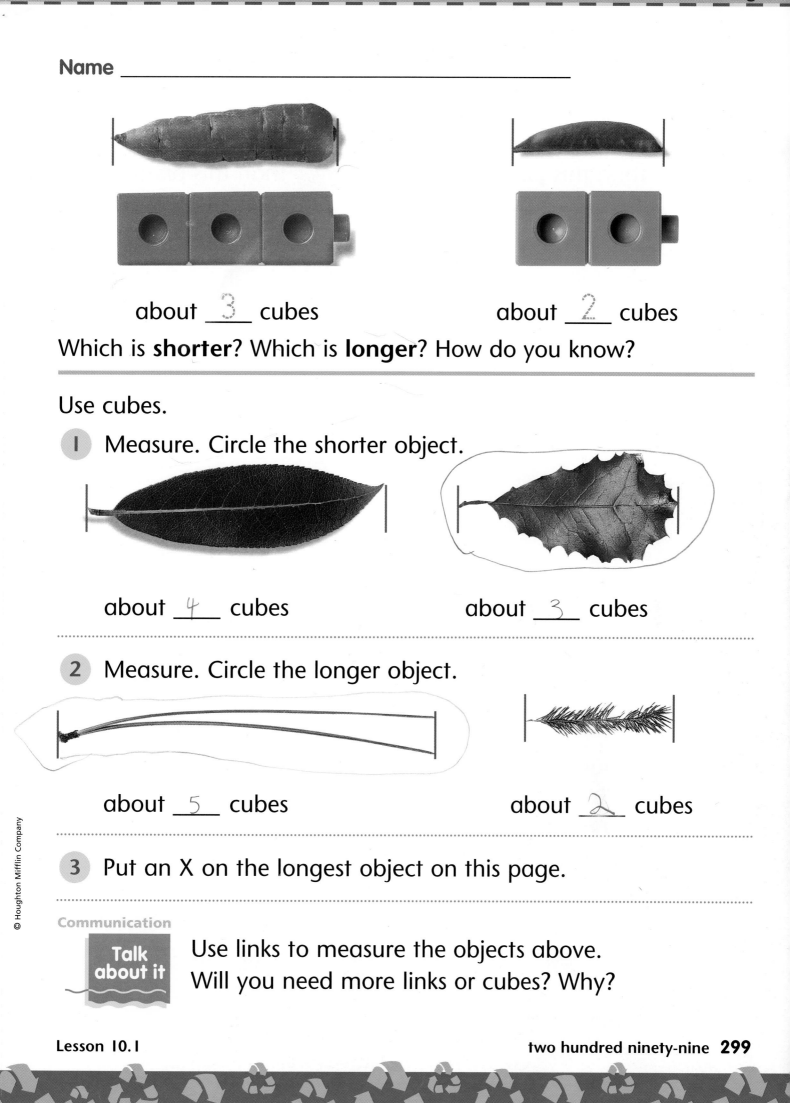

about __3__ cubes   about __2__ cubes

Which is **shorter**? Which is **longer**? How do you know?

Use cubes.

1 Measure. Circle the shorter object.

about __4__ cubes   about __3__ cubes

2 Measure. Circle the longer object.

about __5__ cubes   about __2__ cubes

3 Put an X on the longest object on this page.

Communication

Talk about it Use links to measure the objects above.
Will you need more links or cubes? Why?

The boy is **shorter** than this plant.

The boy is **taller** than this plant.

Measure. Use cubes.

1 Circle the taller object.

2 Circle the shorter object.

about __2__ cubes

about __6__ cubes

about __3__ cubes

about __3__ cubes

3 Put an X on the tallest object.
Put a ✓ on the shortest object.

Dear Family: Invite your child to choose 3–4 household objects and tell you which is tallest, which is shortest. Then measure them with blocks or cotton swabs.

Name _____

Work with a partner. Find each object.
Estimate. Then measure. Use links.

	Object	Estimate	Measure
1		about _6_ links	about _6_ links
2		about _4_ links	about _4_ links
3		about _3_ links	about _3_ links
4	Draw your choice.	about ____ links	about ____ links

Communication

Write about it   You can measure the length of other objects.
Draw and write to show some ideas.

Work with a partner.
Use links to measure.

How do you know
how many links to use?

	Object	Estimate	Measure
1	across a table	about ____ links	about ____ links
2	across a door	about ____ links	about ____ links
3	across a bookshelf	about ____ links	about ____ links
4	Draw your choice.	about ____ links	about ____ links

Communication

Talk about it

How do your estimates compare with your measurements?

Dear Family: In this lesson, your child used links to measure. Have your child use paper clips to estimate and measure the lengths of several household items.

Cooperative Learning

Name _____

$\vdash\!\!—\!\!\dashv$ = 1 inch

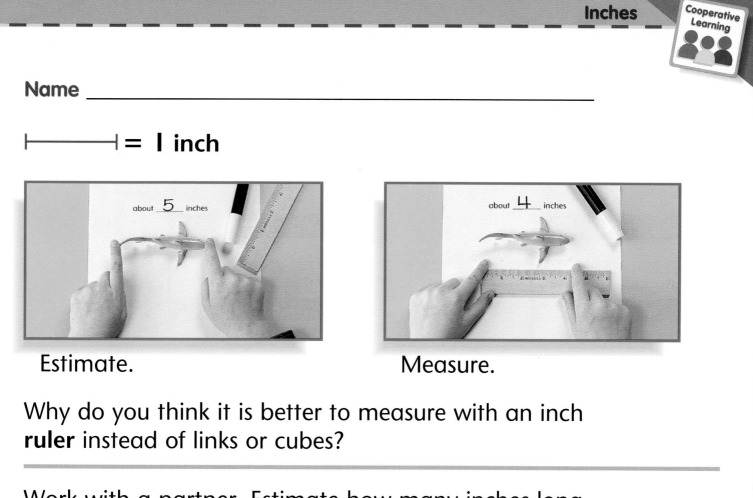

Estimate.   Measure.

Why do you think it is better to measure with an inch **ruler** instead of links or cubes?

Work with a partner. Estimate how many inches long. Then measure. Use an inch ruler.

Object	Estimate	Measure
1	about ____ inches	about __3__ inches
2	about ____ inches	about ____ inches
3	about ____ inches	about ____ inches

Estimate how many inches tall.
Then measure. Use an inch ruler.

1

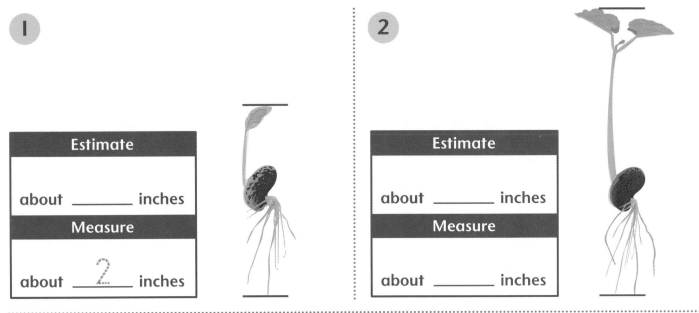

Estimate
about _____ inches
Measure
about __2__ inches

2

Estimate
about _____ inches
Measure
about _____ inches

3 Find and measure each object. Use an inch ruler.
Color the graph to show how tall each object is.

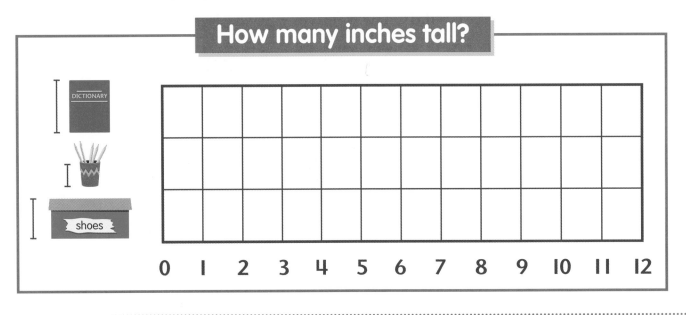

How many inches tall?

DICTIONARY

shoes

0 1 2 3 4 5 6 7 8 9 10 11 12

Communication

Talk about it

What are some things the graph shows you?

▶ **More Practice, page 420**

Dear Family: Share with your child any inch ruler
you may have in your home. Let him or her measure
some objects to the nearest inch.

Cooperative Learning

Name _____

Work with a partner to make a **tape measure**.

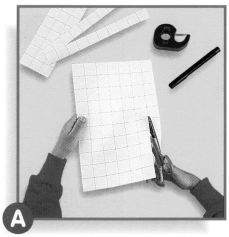
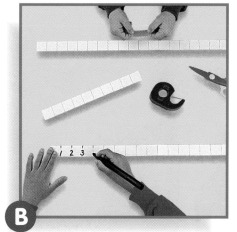

A Cut the paper into strips.

B Tape the strips together. Write the numbers.

C Measure an object.

When is a tape measure helpful?

Measure. Write about how many inches around.

1   about _____ inches around

2   about _____ inches around

3   about _____ inches around

Dear Family: Have your child tell about the experience of making and using a tape measure. Ask him or her to use a tape measure to measure around several things in your home.

Work with your partner. Measure.

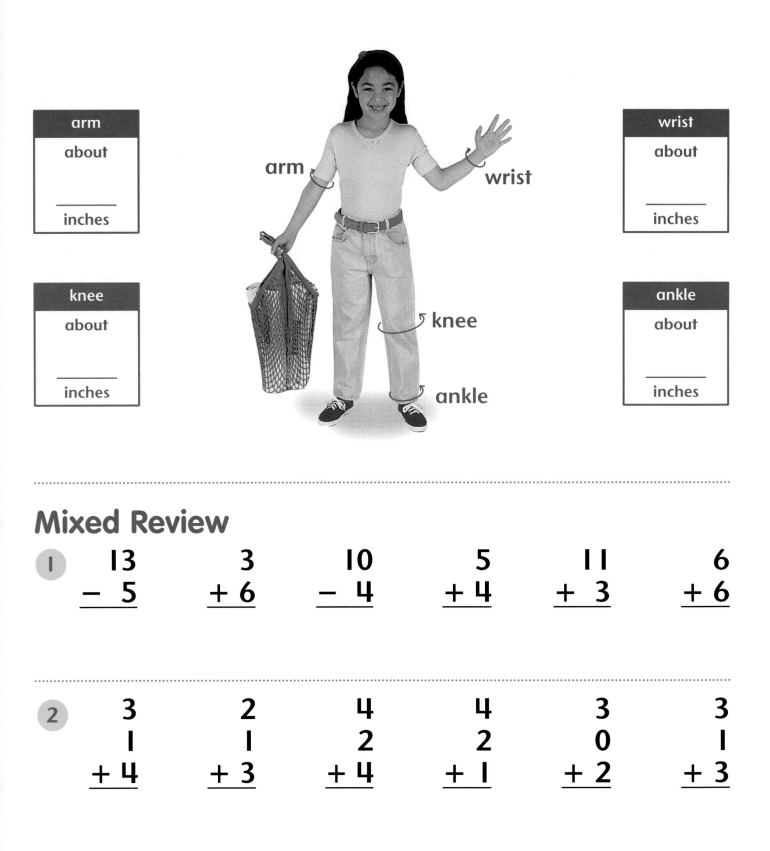

arm
about
_____
inches

wrist
about
_____
inches

knee
about
_____
inches

ankle
about
_____
inches

arm   wrist   knee   ankle

Mixed Review

1.
13	3	10	5	11	6
− 5	+ 6	− 4	+ 4	+ 3	+ 6

2.
3	2	4	4	3	3
1	1	2	2	0	1
+ 4	+ 3	+ 4	+ 1	+ 2	+ 3

Communication

Talk about it

What kinds of objects can you measure with a tape measure? With a ruler? Why?

Name _____

Lift each object.
The apple is heavier
than the marker.

How else can
you tell an
object's weight?

Find and lift each object. Circle the heavier object.

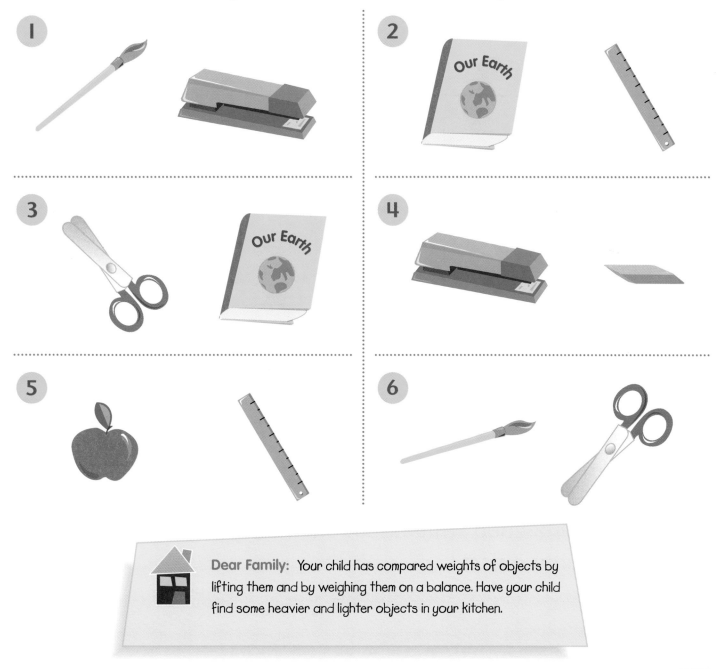

1

2

Our Earth

3

Our Earth

4

5

6

Dear Family: Your child has compared weights of objects by lifting them and by weighing them on a balance. Have your child find some heavier and lighter objects in your kitchen.

You need cubes, links, and pennies.
Use a **balance.**

Write how many cubes **weigh** the same as the object on the balance.

Then weigh the object with links.

Now weigh the object with pennies.

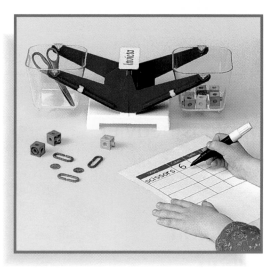

	Object	Cubes	Links	Pennies
1				
2				
3				
4	Draw your choice.			

Communication

Write about it   Draw and write about one heavy object and one light object.

Name _____

The feather is lighter than **1 pound**.

| lighter | same | heavier |

Use a balance and something that weighs **1** pound.
Weigh each object. Put an X in the matching box.

	Object	lighter	same	heavier
1	☕			
2	📖			
3	🗒			
4	Draw your choice.			

....

Communication

What other objects weigh about a pound?

Use green, red, and purple crayons.
Circle in green objects that are lighter than a pound.
Circle in red objects that weigh about a pound.
Circle in purple objects that are heavier than a pound.

1

2

 Dear Family: Have your child find some food packages that weigh about a pound. Find others that are lighter or heavier than a pound.

▶ **More Practice, page 420**

Name _____

Brent has a box that is
1 inch wide and **2** inches long.
What can he put in it?

▶ **Understand**

I need to find out what Brent can put
in the box.

▶ **Plan**

I can draw a picture.

▶ **Try it**

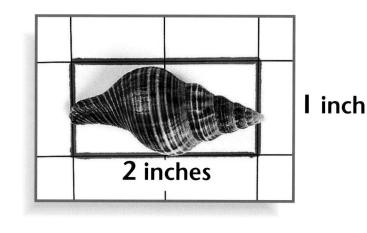

1 inch

2 inches

Brent can put a small shell in the box.

▶ **Look back**

A small shell fits in a box that is

1 inch wide and **2** inches long.

My answer makes sense.

1 Dena has a box that is **1** inch wide and **5** inches long. Draw the shape of the box. What can she put in it? Draw the object. Measure it.

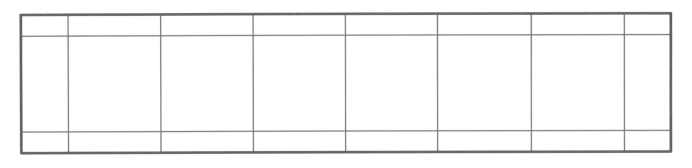

2 Chen has a box that is **2** inches wide and **6** inches long. Draw the shape of the box. What can he put in it? Draw the object. Measure it.

Communication

What other objects can you put in the boxes that you drew?

 Dear Family: Find some small boxes around your home. Ask your child to estimate something that might fit in the box. Then ask him or her to try the object in the box.

Lesson 10.7

Name _____

cold   warm   hot

Look at the picture and the **thermometer**.
Circle what you should wear.

1

2

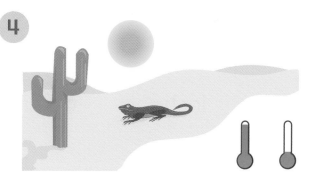

Circle the **temperature**.

3

4

Communication

Share

Tell a friend how your choice of clothes changes when the temperature changes.

Dear Family: Discuss with your child the pictures and the effects temperature has on people's activities and clothing. Talk about thermometers in your home and their purposes.

Lesson 10.8

Use cubes to measure.
Write how many cubes.

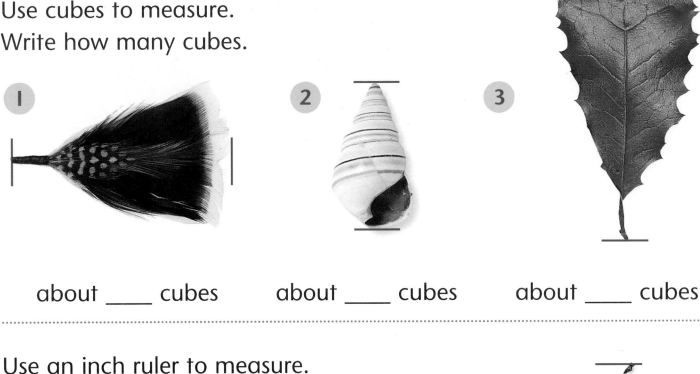

1

about ____ cubes

2

about ____ cubes

3

about ____ cubes

Use an inch ruler to measure.
Write how many inches.

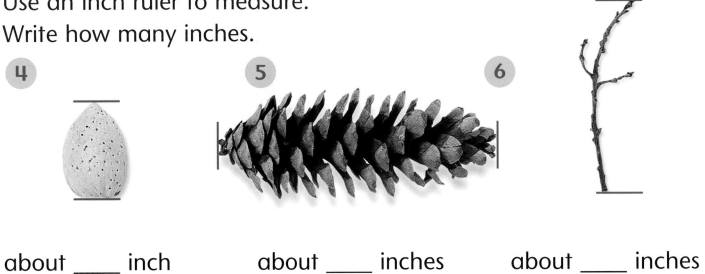

4

about ____ inch

5

about ____ inches

6

about ____ inches

Problem Solving
Solve.

7 The seedling is **11** inches tall. Three weeks ago it was **7** inches tall. How many inches did the seedling grow?

____ inches

8 One pumpkin weighs **5** pounds. Another pumpkin weighs **8** pounds. How much do they weigh in all?

____ pounds

Name _____

Math World

In this game from Spain, children measure by steps, hops, and jumps.

 Children play **Brinca**, **Da un paso**, **Salta** in **Spain**. They try to see who can reach the finish line in the fewest steps, hops, or jumps.

Start

Finish

Internet

Explore Houghton Mifflin's **Education Place Math Center.** http://www.eduplace.com

© Houghton Mifflin Company

▶ **Turn the page for directions.**

three hundred fifteen **315**

Did you know?

Brinca means hop. **Da un paso** means take a step. **Salta** means jump.

You need:
- paper
- pencil
- chalk
- tape
- classroom objects

Try this!

Play **Brinca, Da un paso, Salta**

A Use chalk or tape to mark your starting and ending place.

B Use classroom objects to measure the distance between the start and finish line.

Dear Family: Play "Brinca, Da un paso, Salta" (breen kah, dah oon pah so, sahl-tah) at home. Help your child measure the distance between the start and finish line by using objects around your home (brooms, toys, shoes, etc.).

To Play
- Choose a person to be the announcer.
- Have players line up in a row behind the starting line.
- The announcer calls out "Brinca," "Da un Paso," or "Salta."
- Players move according to the announcer's call. The player who reaches the goal in the fewest movements is the announcer for the next game.

Name _____

Work with a small group.
Use water to measure.

Which holds more? Draw your answer.

	Containers	Which holds more?	
		Estimate	Measure
1		Estimate	Measure
2		Estimate	Measure
3		Estimate	Measure
4	Draw your choice.	Estimate	Measure

© Houghton Mifflin Company

Communication

Write about it

How did measuring help you to decide which holds more?

Lesson 10.9

three hundred seventeen **317**

You need a blue crayon and a red crayon.
Color in blue what holds less.
Color in red what holds more.

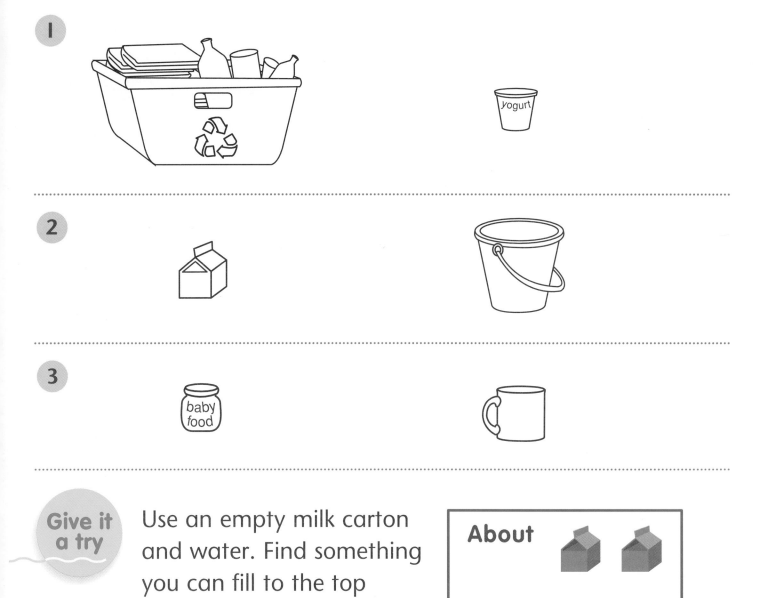

1

2

3

Give it
a try

Use an empty milk carton
and water. Find something
you can fill to the top
with about **2** milk cartons.
Draw it.

About

Name _____

Work with a partner or small group.
Use these containers.

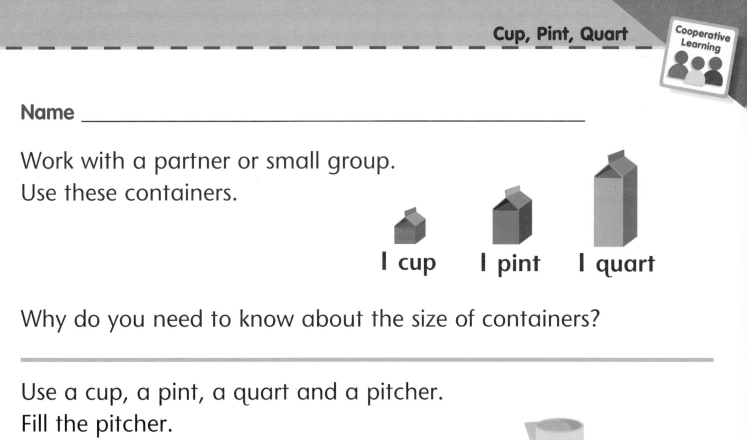

I cup   I pint   I quart

Why do you need to know about the size of containers?

Use a cup, a pint, a quart and a pitcher.
Fill the pitcher.
Color the boxes to show how many.

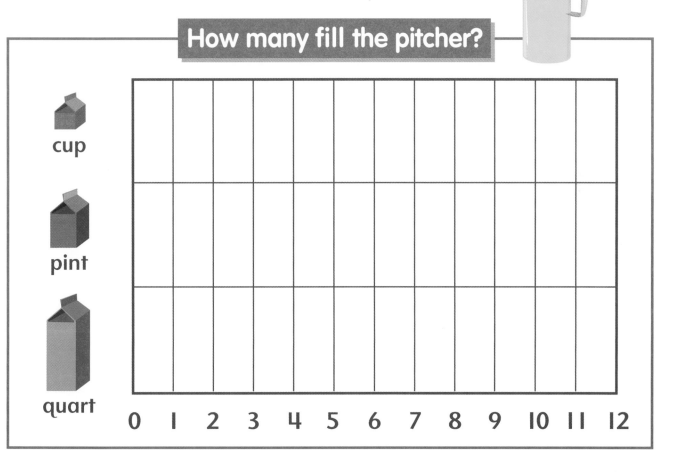

How many fill the pitcher?

cup

pint

quart

0 I 2 3 4 5 6 7 8 9 I0 II I2

Communication

Draw Draw and write about something
you can buy in a **I** cup size.

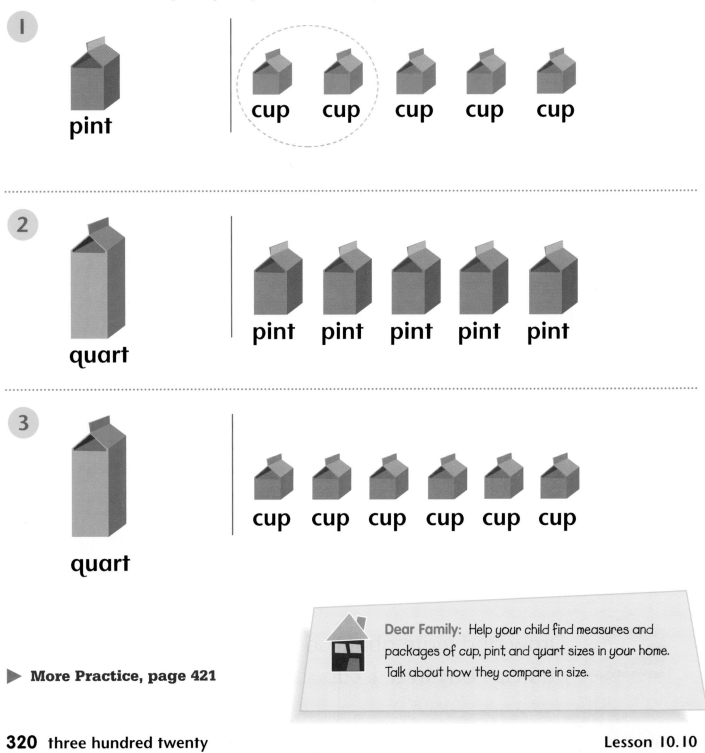

I pint equals 2 cups.

pint = cup cup

I quart equals 2 pints.

quart = pint pint

Try these with water.

Circle how many cups, pints, and quarts you can fill.

1 pint — (cup cup) cup cup cup

2 quart — pint pint pint pint pint

3 quart — cup cup cup cup cup cup

Dear Family: Help your child find measures and packages of cup, pint, and quart sizes in your home. Talk about how they compare in size.

▶ **More Practice, page 421**

Lesson 10.10

Name _____

$\vdash\!\!-\!\!\dashv$ = **1 centimeter**

How is a centimeter like an inch?

Look at each animal track.
Estimate. Then measure.
Use a centimeter ruler.

	Animal Tracks	Estimate	Measure
1		about ___ centimeters	about ___ centimeters
2		about ___ centimeters	about ___ centimeters
3		about ___ centimeters	about ___ centimeters

Estimate how many centimeters tall.
Then measure with a centimeter ruler.

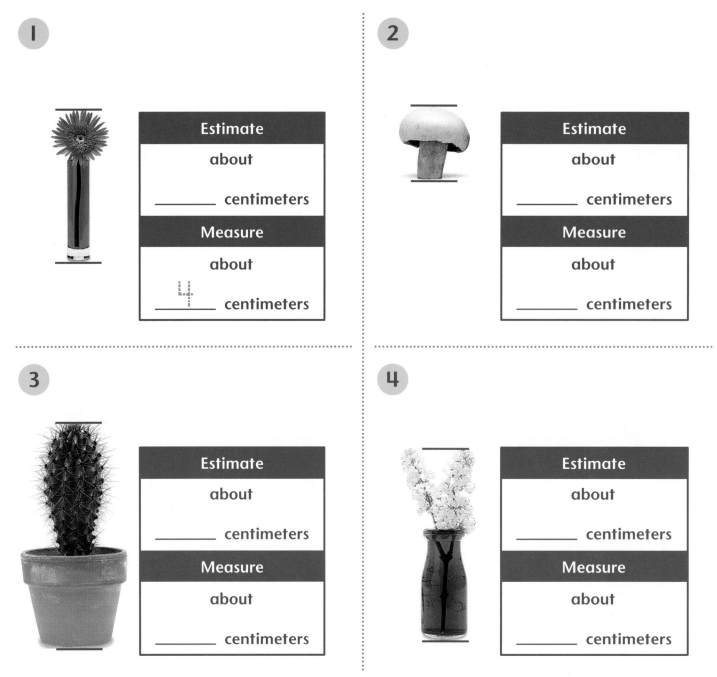

1

Estimate

about

_____ centimeters

Measure

about

___4___ centimeters

2

Estimate

about

_____ centimeters

Measure

about

_____ centimeters

3

Estimate

about

_____ centimeters

Measure

about

_____ centimeters

4

Estimate

about

_____ centimeters

Measure

about

_____ centimeters

Give it a try

Use a centimeter ruler.
Find and measure objects in your classroom.

▶ **More Practice, page 421**

Dear Family: Help your child find several things in your home that are about 1 centimeter long.

Name _____

Look at the balance.
The bananas are about **1 kilogram**.

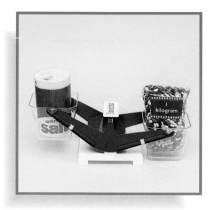      

less than   about the same   more than

What can you think of that is about **1** kilogram?

Use a balance and something that is about
1 kilogram. Measure objects in your classroom.
Put an X in the matching box.

Object	less than a kilogram	about the same as a kilogram	more than a kilogram
1			
2			
3 MATH BOOK			
4 Draw your choice.			

Look at the pictures.
Circle the objects that are about
the same as 1 kilogram.

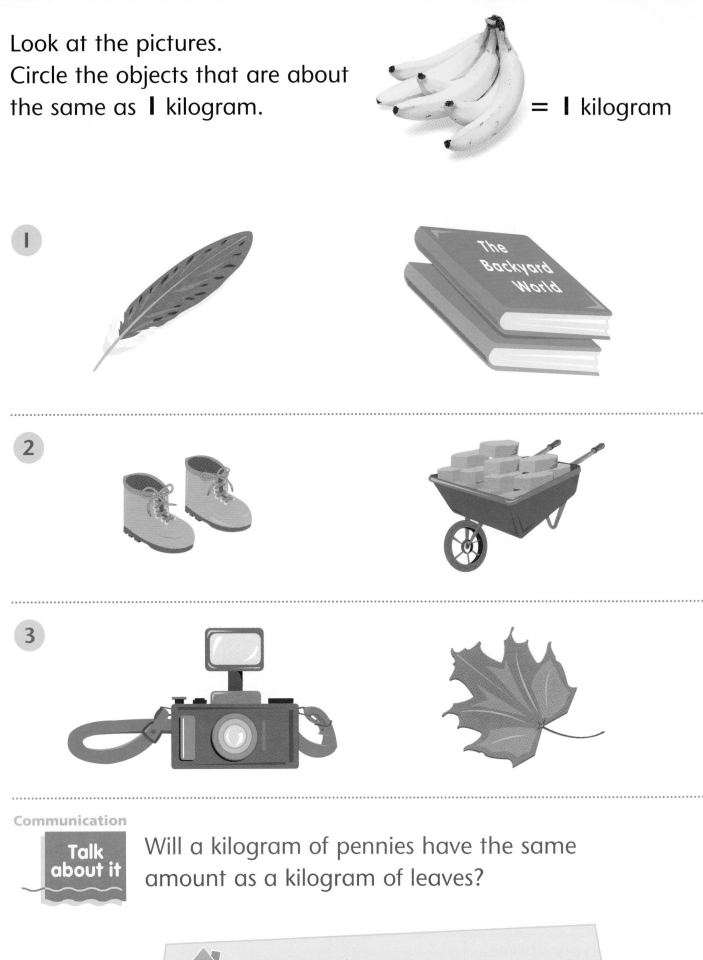

= 1 kilogram

1

2

3

Dear Family: Look over the examples on these pages with your child. Help him or her find some objects in your home that are about 1 kilogram.

Name _____

1 liter   holds less   holds about the same   holds more

What can you think of that holds about **1** liter?

Use a liter bottle and water.
Test how much water objects hold.
Draw the object.

holds less	holds about the same	holds more

Dear Family: Find bottles in your home that measure liquid in liters. Compare these bottles with containers that measure quarts or gallons.

Lesson 10.13   three hundred twenty-five **325**

Circle the **measuring tool** you use.

1 how heavy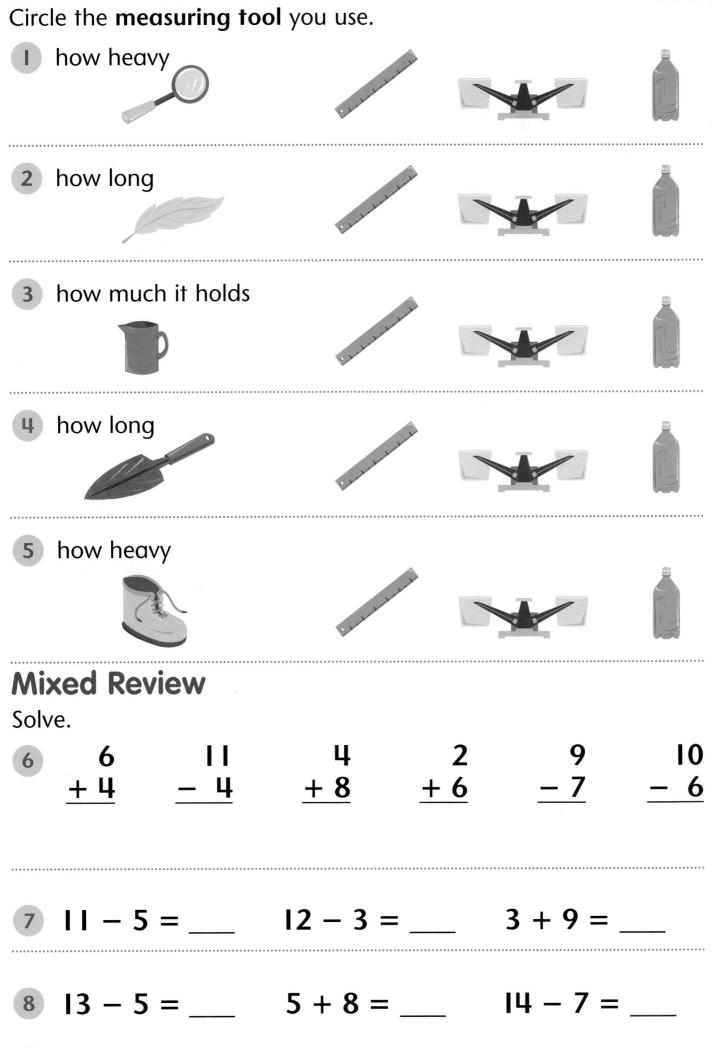

2 how long

3 how much it holds

4 how long

5 how heavy

Mixed Review

Solve.

6
$$6 + 4$$ $$11 - 4$$ $$4 + 8$$ $$2 + 6$$ $$9 - 7$$ $$10 - 6$$

7 $11 - 5 =$ ___ $12 - 3 =$ ___ $3 + 9 =$ ___

8 $13 - 5 =$ ___ $5 + 8 =$ ___ $14 - 7 =$ ___

Lesson 10.13

Name _____

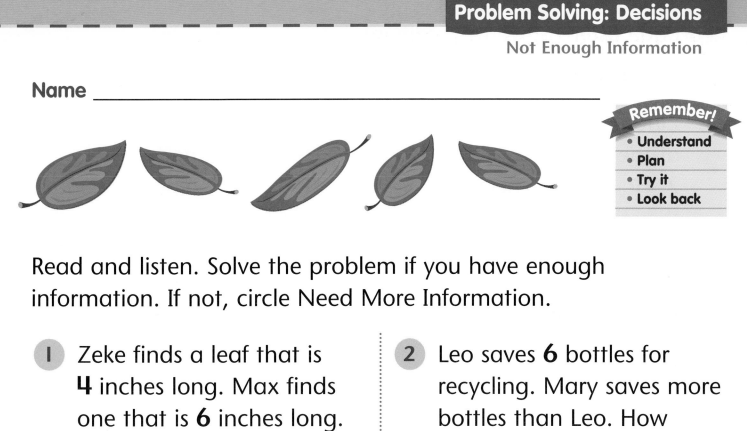

Remember!
• Understand
• Plan
• Try it
• Look back

Read and listen. Solve the problem if you have enough information. If not, circle Need More Information.

1 Zeke finds a leaf that is **4** inches long. Max finds one that is **6** inches long. How much longer is the leaf Max finds?

____ inches

Need More Information

2 Leo saves **6** bottles for recycling. Mary saves more bottles than Leo. How many bottles does Mary save?

____ bottles

Need More Information

3 Jane's plant is **12** inches tall. Manda's plant is taller. How tall is Manda's plant?

____ inches

Need More Information

4 Heather has a melon that weighs **2** pounds. She has a grapefruit that weighs **1** pound. Which weighs more?

_____

Need More Information

Give it a try Add information to one problem so there is enough to solve it. Write the answer.

Read and listen. Solve the problem if you have enough information. If not, circle Need More Information.

1 Zina finds **8** shells at the beach. Tanya finds **7**. How many shells do they find in all?

_____ shells

Need More Information

2 Arlo finds **10** pine cones. He gives some to Mosi. How many pine cones does Arlo have now?

_____ pine cones

Need More Information

3 The blue fish is **8** inches long. The striped fish is **6** inches long. How much do they weigh?

_____ pounds

Need More Information

4 Matt has a pint of milk. He needs **2** cups of milk for his recipe. Does he have enough milk?

_____

Need More Information

Mixed Review

5 Write the time.

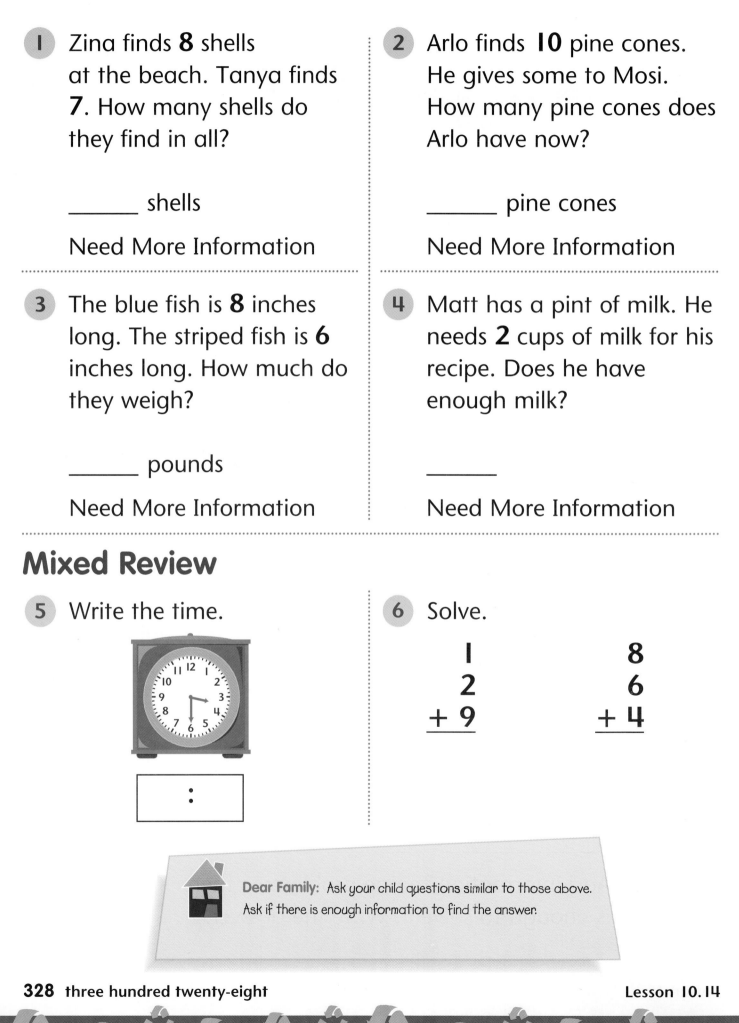

:

6 Solve.

$$\begin{array}{r} 1 \\ 2 \\ +\ 9 \\ \hline \end{array} \qquad \begin{array}{r} 8 \\ 6 \\ +\ 4 \\ \hline \end{array}$$

Dear Family: Ask your child questions similar to those above. Ask if there is enough information to find the answer.

Name _____

Measure. Use an inch ruler.

1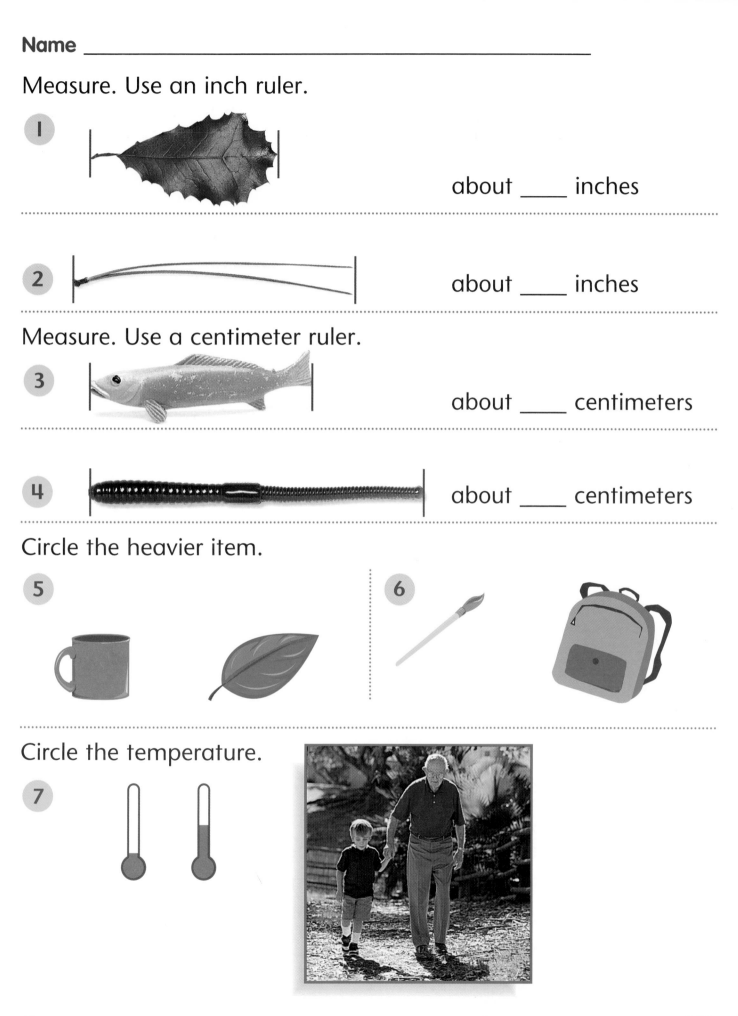

about ____ inches

2

about ____ inches

Measure. Use a centimeter ruler.

3

about ____ centimeters

4

about ____ centimeters

Circle the heavier item.

5

6

Circle the temperature.

7

8 Look at the picture and the thermometer.
Circle the right clothing.

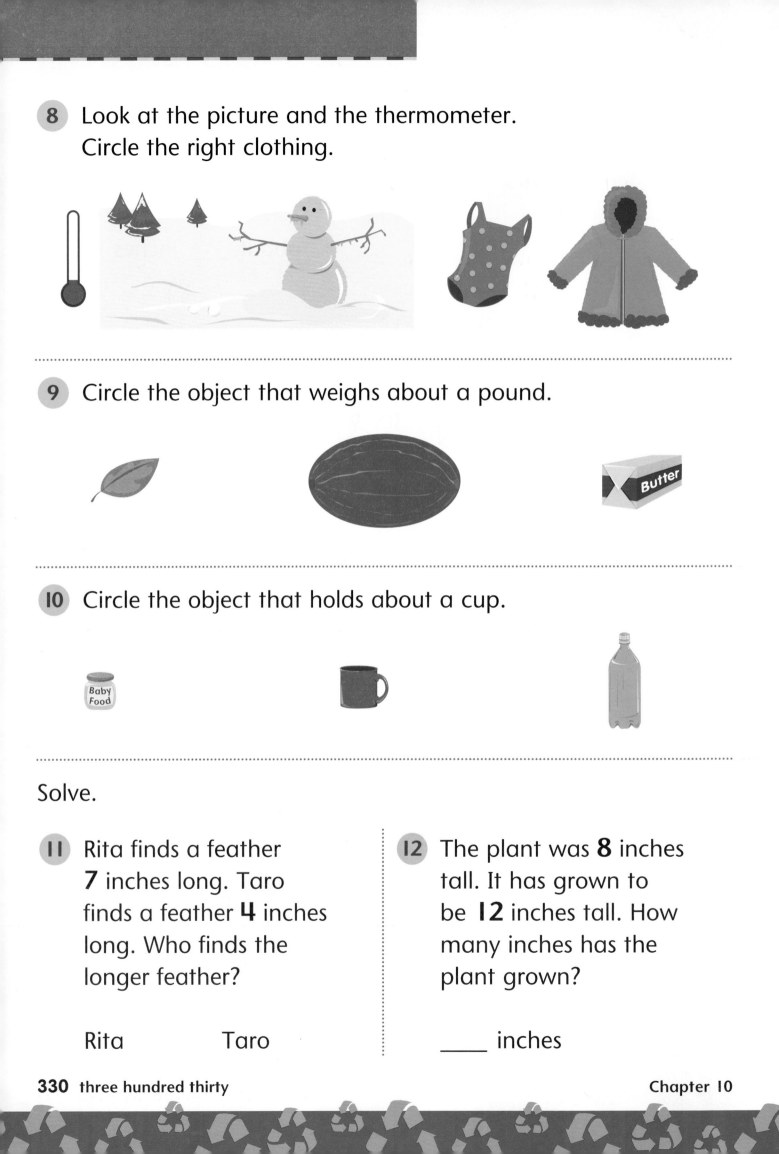

9 Circle the object that weighs about a pound.

10 Circle the object that holds about a cup.

Baby
Food

Solve.

11 Rita finds a feather
7 inches long. Taro
finds a feather **4** inches
long. Who finds the
longer feather?

Rita   Taro

12 The plant was **8** inches
tall. It has grown to
be **12** inches tall. How
many inches has the
plant grown?

_____ inches

How Long Is Baby Bear's Bed?

Name _____

Fill in the chart. Write your name.
Write how long your bear bed is.

Ask three friends how long their bear
beds are. Write each friend's name.
Write how long their bear beds are.

Name	How long is Baby Bear's bed?

Are the numbers in the chart different?
Why? Write or draw your answer.

Draw a bed that is just the right size for a mouse.
Measure the bed. Use cubes.

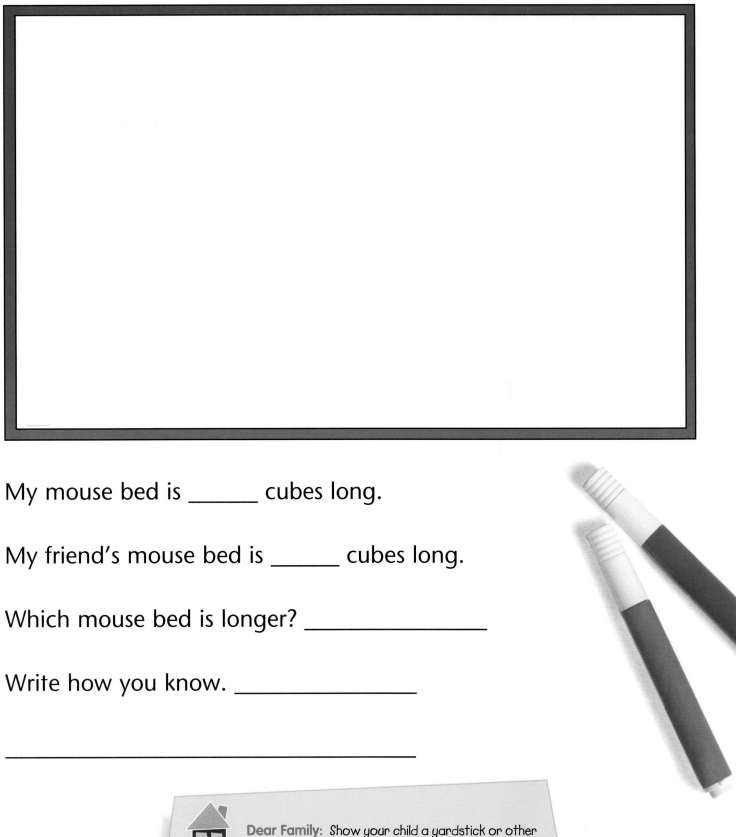

My mouse bed is _____ cubes long.

My friend's mouse bed is _____ cubes long.

Which mouse bed is longer? _____

Write how you know. _____

_____

Dear Family: Show your child a yardstick or other tools you use to measure around the house.

Readiness for Multiplication and Division

Literature
two friends
By Nikki Giovanni

Read Aloud Anthology p. 108
Theme Connection
Fun with Friends

See what I can do by the end of this chapter.

Use What You Know

How many friends are in each group?
How many groups are there?
How can you find out how many friends there are in all?

© Houghton Mifflin Company

three hundred thirty-three **333**

Listen to the stories.
Use counters to act out each story.

Dear Family: Share the pie. Ask your child how to divide the pie with 1, 2, or even 3 friends. Help your child draw to show how they might divide this pie to serve 8 friends.

Name _____

Write how many.

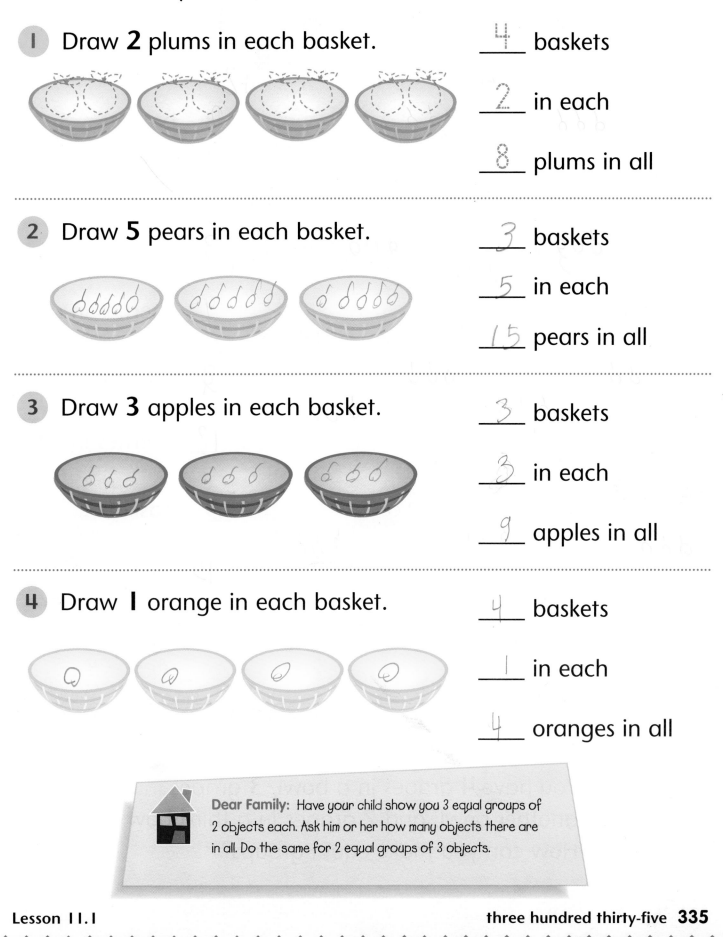

1   Draw **2** plums in each basket.

_4_ baskets

_2_ in each

_8_ plums in all

2   Draw **5** pears in each basket.

_3_ baskets

_5_ in each

_15_ pears in all

3   Draw **3** apples in each basket.

_3_ baskets

_3_ in each

_9_ apples in all

4   Draw **1** orange in each basket.

_4_ baskets

_1_ in each

_4_ oranges in all

Dear Family: Have your child show you 3 equal groups of 2 objects each. Ask him or her how many objects there are in all. Do the same for 2 equal groups of 3 objects.

Draw **3** cherries in each basket.
Write how many.

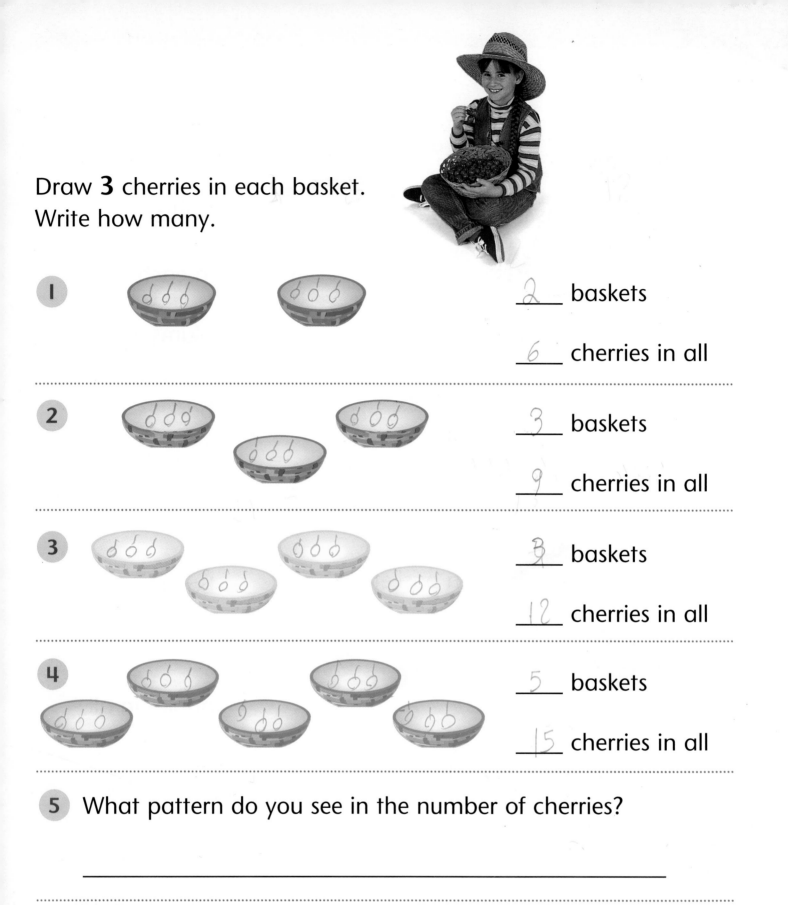

1. __2__ baskets

    __6__ cherries in all

2. __3__ baskets

    __9__ cherries in all

3. __3__ baskets

    __12__ cherries in all

4. __5__ baskets

    __15__ cherries in all

5. What pattern do you see in the number of cherries?

_____

Communication

Write about it

You have **4** grapes in a bowl, **3** grapes in another bowl, and **2** grapes in a third bowl. How can you make equal groups?

Lesson 11.1

Name _____

__4__ + __4__ + __4__ = __12__

__3__ groups of __4__ = __12__

How do counters help you find equal groups?

You may use counters. Write how many.

1

__3__ + __3__ + __3__ = __9__

__3__ groups of __3__ = __9__

2

__5__ + __5__ = __10__

__2__ groups of __5__ = __10__

3

__3__ + __3__ = __6__

__2__ groups of __3__ = __6__

4

__1__ + __1__ + __1__ = __3__

__1__ groups of __3__ = __3__

Dear Family: Ask your child how many plums you have if you take 4 handfuls of 3 plums each. Count other equal groups of things, such as shoes.

▶ **More Practice, page 422**

© Houghton Mifflin Company

Lesson 11.2

three hundred thirty-seven **337**

Write how many.

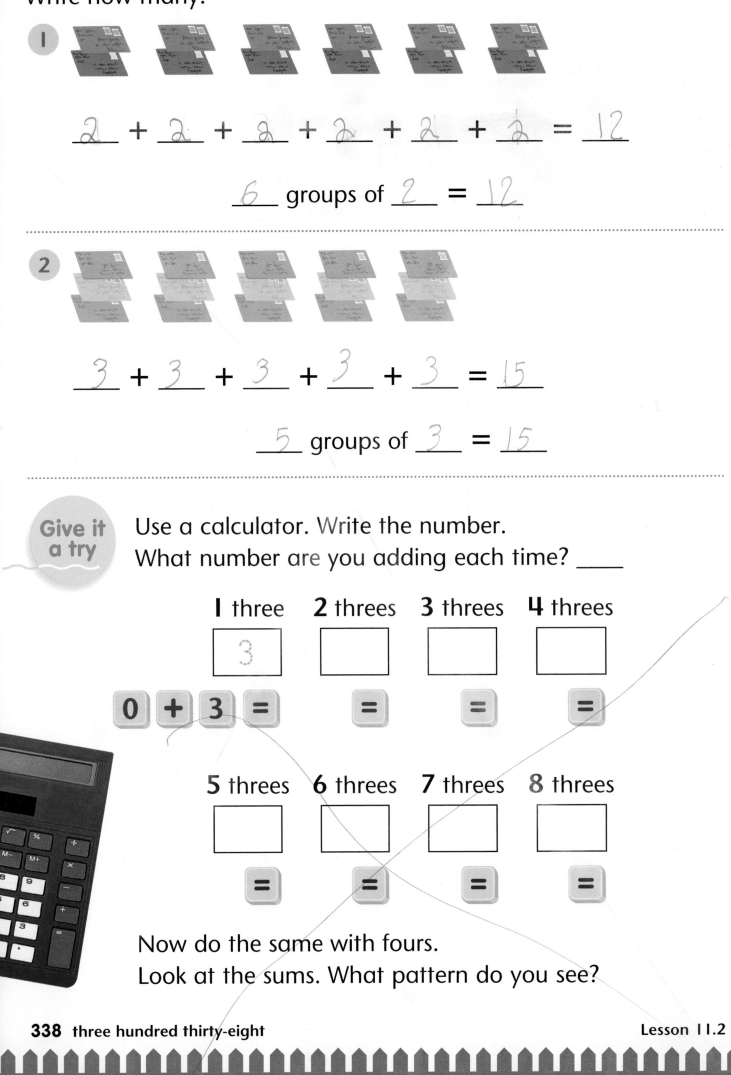

1

$\underline{2} + \underline{2} + \underline{2} + \underline{2} + \underline{2} + \underline{2} = \underline{12}$

$\underline{6}$ groups of $\underline{2} = \underline{12}$

2

$\underline{3} + \underline{3} + \underline{3} + \underline{3} + \underline{3} = \underline{15}$

$\underline{5}$ groups of $\underline{3} = \underline{15}$

Give it a try

Use a calculator. Write the number.
What number are you adding each time? ____

1 three	**2** threes	**3** threes	**4** threes
3			
`0` `+` `3` `=`	`=`	`=`	`=`

5 threes	**6** threes	**7** threes	**8** threes
`=`	`=`	`=`	`=`

Now do the same with fours.
Look at the sums. What pattern do you see?

Name _____

Use a calculator to add.

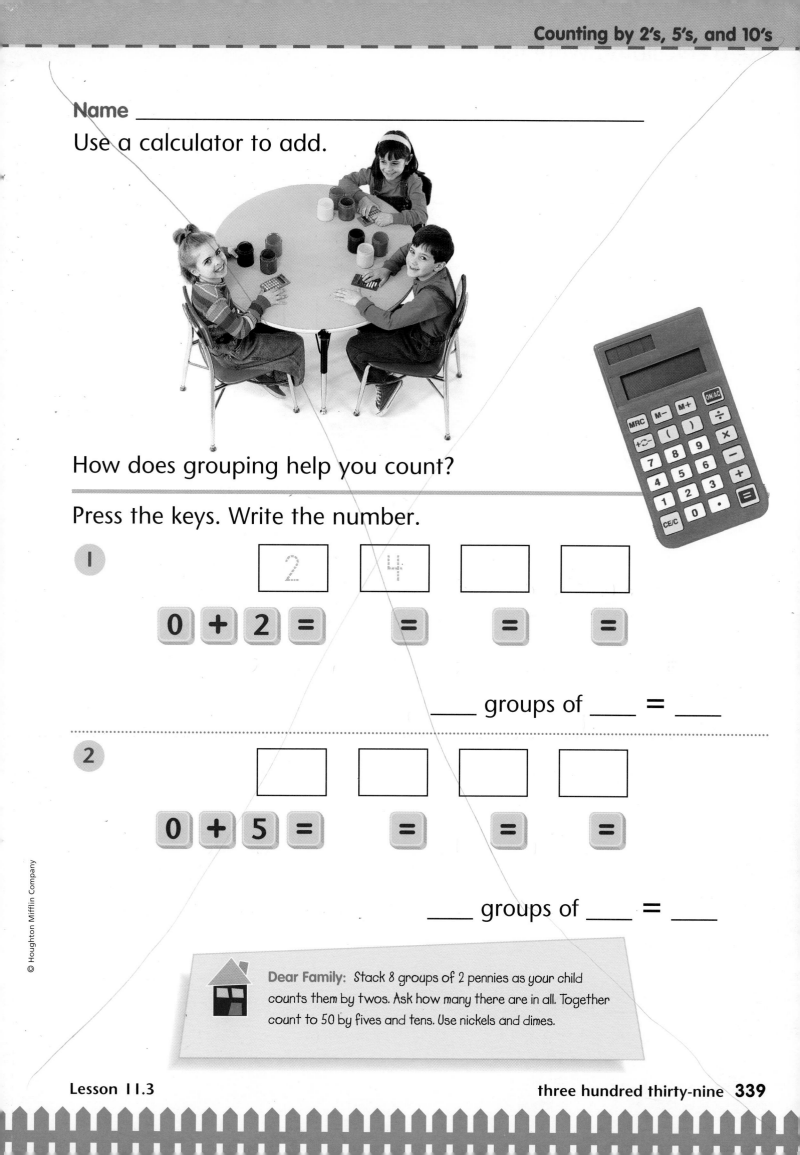

How does grouping help you count?

Press the keys. Write the number.

1

| 2 | 4 | | |

0 + 2 =   =   =   =

_____ groups of _____ = _____

2

| | | | |

0 + 5 =   =   =   =

_____ groups of _____ = _____

Dear Family: Stack 8 groups of 2 pennies as your child counts them by twos. Ask how many there are in all. Together count to 50 by fives and tens. Use nickels and dimes.

Use a calculator. Write the numbers.

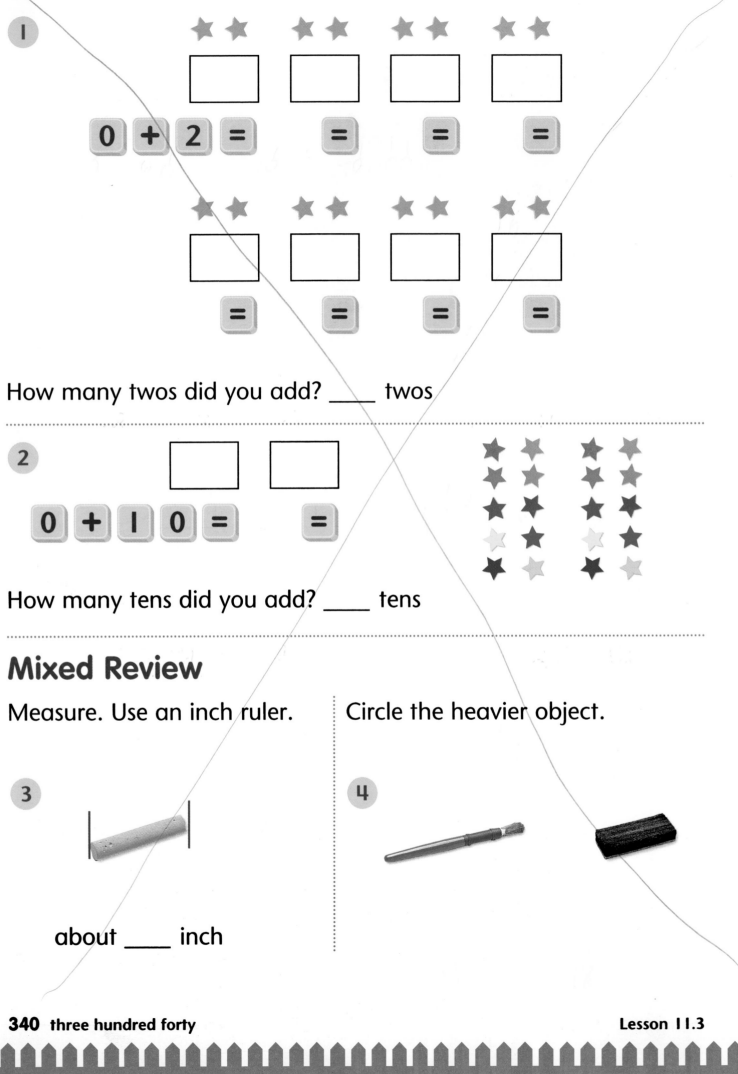

1

☆ ☆ ☆ ☆ ☆ ☆ ☆ ☆

[ ] [ ] [ ] [ ]

[0] [+] [2] [=] [=] [=] [=]

☆ ☆ ☆ ☆ ☆ ☆ ☆ ☆

[ ] [ ] [ ] [ ]

[=] [=] [=] [=]

How many twos did you add? ____ twos

2

[ ] [ ]

[0] [+] [1] [0] [=] [=]

How many tens did you add? ____ tens

Mixed Review

Measure. Use an inch ruler.

Circle the heavier object.

3

about ____ inch

4

Name _____

Circle groups of **2**.

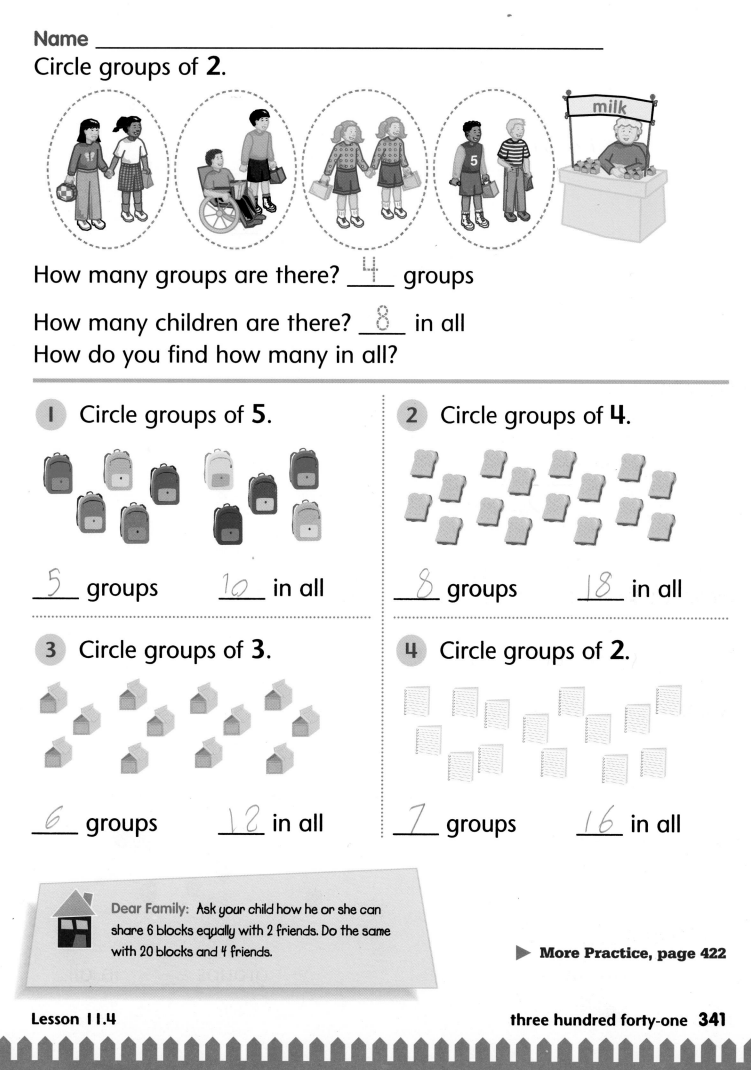

How many groups are there? __4__ groups

How many children are there? __8__ in all

How do you find how many in all?

---

1 Circle groups of **5**.

__5__ groups   __10__ in all

2 Circle groups of **4**.

__8__ groups   __18__ in all

3 Circle groups of **3**.

__6__ groups   __12__ in all

4 Circle groups of **2**.

__7__ groups   __16__ in all

Dear Family: Ask your child how he or she can share 6 blocks equally with 2 friends. Do the same with 20 blocks and 4 friends.

▶ **More Practice, page 422**

Write how many.

1 Draw **4** apples in each basket.

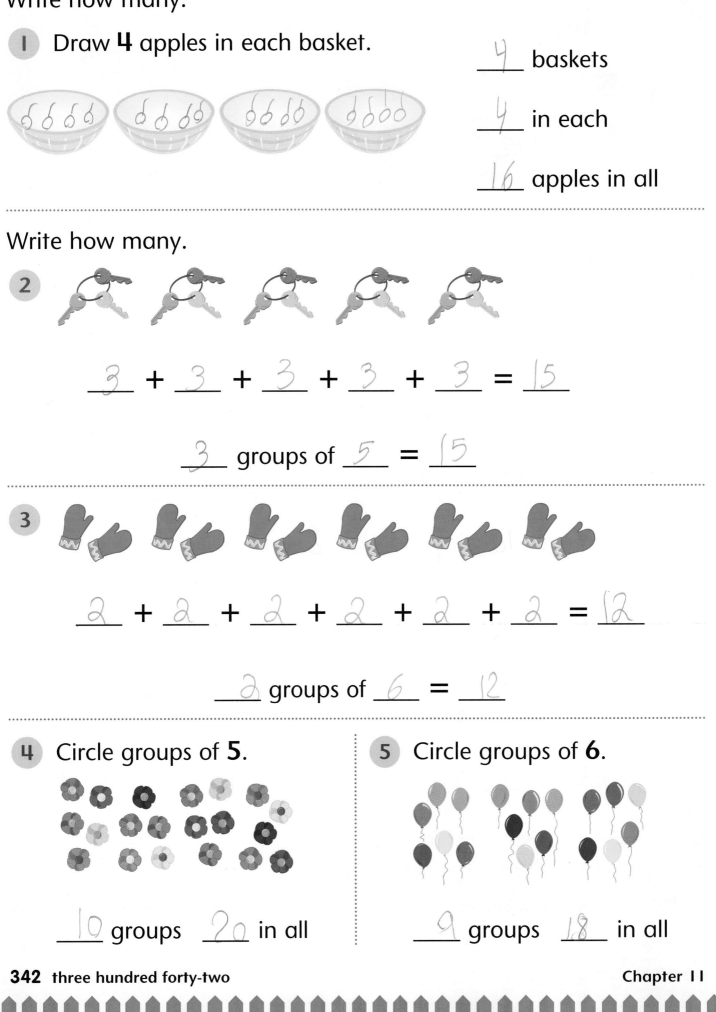

___4___ baskets

___4___ in each

___16___ apples in all

Write how many.

2

___3___ + ___3___ + ___3___ + ___3___ + ___3___ = ___15___

___3___ groups of ___5___ = ___15___

3

___2___ + ___2___ + ___2___ + ___2___ + ___2___ + ___2___ = ___12___

___2___ groups of ___6___ = ___12___

4 Circle groups of **5**.

___10___ groups   ___20___ in all

5 Circle groups of **6**.

___9___ groups   ___18___ in all

Name _____

Math World

In Ghana beautiful patterns cover Adinkra cloth.

People in **Ghana** decorate **Adinkra** cloth by stamping groups of designs in squares.

To make the designs, people make squares on a piece of cloth. Then they use stamps to put several simple patterns in each square.

Internet

Explore Houghton Mifflin's
Education Place Math Center.
http://www.eduplace.com

© Houghton Mifflin Company

▶ **Turn the page for directions.**

You need:
- cloth
- pencil
- styrofoam tray
- craft sticks
- acrylic paints
- scissors
- glue

Try this!

Make your own **Adinkra** cloth.

A Use a pencil to draw a pattern on the styrofoam meat tray. Use scissors to cut out your design.

B Glue your stencil to a craft stick. Use your stencil and paint to make patterns on your cloth.

Dear Family: To help your child prepare for multiplication, discuss "Adinkra" (ah DINK rah) designs.

- Ask your child to show you his or her Adinkra designs and then describe how he or she made the designs.

- Ask your child how many patterns are stamped into the cloth. Encourage him or her to count the number of patterns in each square.

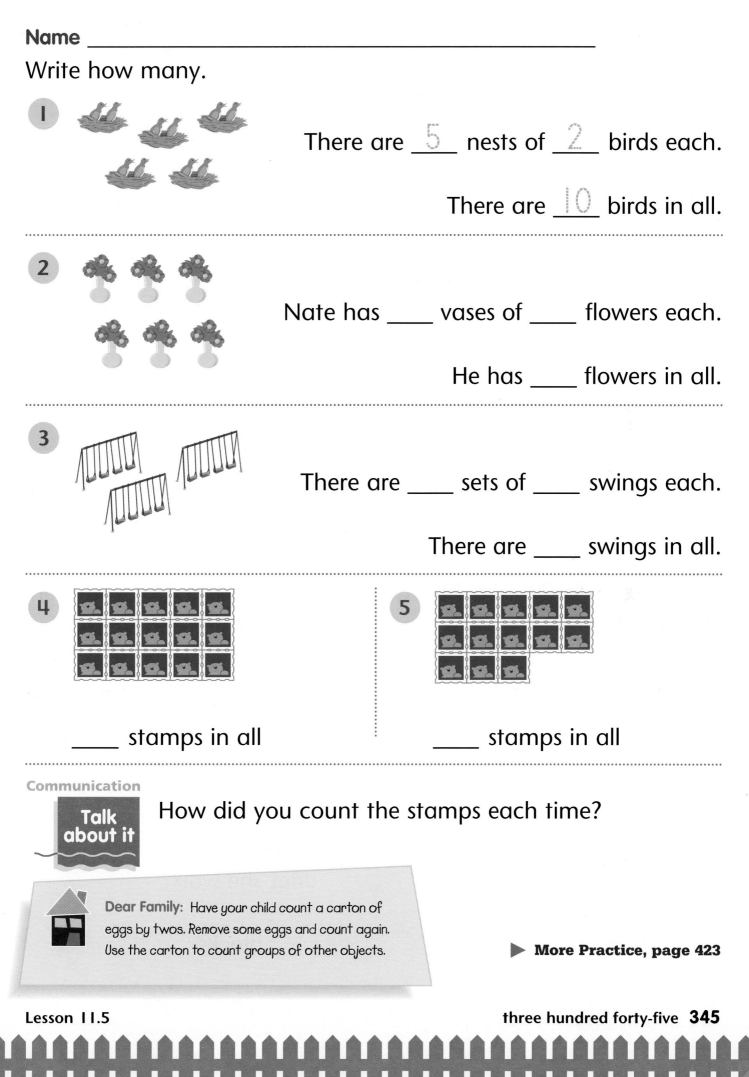

Name _____

Write how many.

1   There are __5__ nests of __2__ birds each.

There are __10__ birds in all.

2   Nate has ____ vases of ____ flowers each.

He has ____ flowers in all.

3   There are ____ sets of ____ swings each.

There are ____ swings in all.

4   ____ stamps in all

5   ____ stamps in all

Communication

Talk about it

How did you count the stamps each time?

Dear Family: Have your child count a carton of eggs by twos. Remove some eggs and count again. Use the carton to count groups of other objects.

▶ **More Practice, page 423**

© Houghton Mifflin Company

Problem Solving

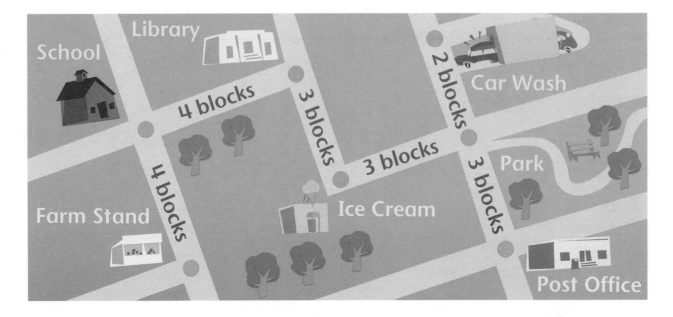

Use the map to solve.

1 Kizza walks from the library to the park.
How far is that?

___6___ blocks

2 Tor walks from the farm stand to the library.
How far is that?

_____ blocks

3 How far is it from the farm stand to the park?

_____ blocks

4 Cole buys stamps and then walks to the library. How far does he walk?

_____ blocks

5 Leilani walks from the library to the farm stand and then back to school. How far does she walk?

_____ blocks

6 Nell goes from the library to the post office and then to the car wash. How far does she walk?

_____ blocks

Lesson 11.5

Name _____

The children have **6** cans of water.
Each can will water **3** bushes.
How many bushes can the children water?

▶ **Understand**

I must find out how many bushes they can water.

▶ **Plan**

I can make a table to help me see a pattern.

▶ **Try it**

Cans	1	2	3	4	5	6
Bushes	3	6	9	12	15	18

The children can water **18** bushes.

▶ **Look back**

$$3 + 3 + 3 + 3 + 3 + 3 = 18$$

6 threes make **18**. My answer makes sense.

Solve.

There are **5** children. They each need **2** pencils.
How many pencils do they need in all?

_____ pencils

Children	1	2	3	4		
Pencils	2	4	6			

Lesson 11.6

Use the table to solve.

1 It takes **4** beads to make a bracelet.
Shani and Cory have **24** beads in all.
How many bracelets can they make? ____ bracelets

 Beads	4	8	12			
Bracelets	1	2	3			

2 There are **18** tulips. Each pot holds **3** tulips.
How many pots of tulips are there? ____ pots

Tulips	3	6				
Pots	1	2				

3 There are **7** boxes of books. Each box holds **5**.
How many books are there in all? ____ books

Boxes	1	2	3	4			
Books	5	10	15				

Communication

 Share Tell a partner what patterns you see and how using a table helps you find how many in all.

 Dear Family: Ask your child how he or she solved these problems. Talk about the patterns in each table and how your child used them to find the answer.

Lesson 11.6

Cooperative Learning

Name _____

Make **2** equal parts
to find one half of a set.

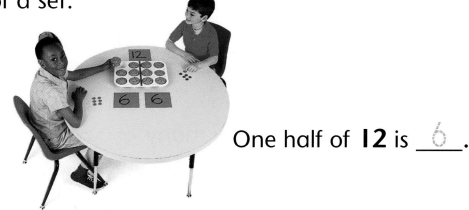

One half of **12** is __6__.

How do you know the parts are equal?

Work with a partner. You may use counters.
Circle two equal parts. Write how many.

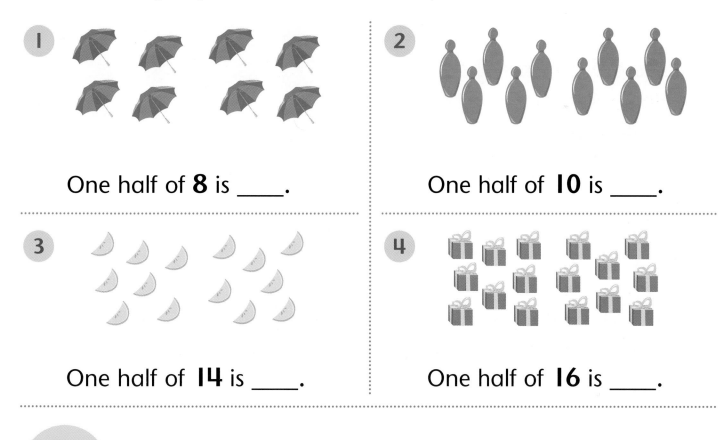

① One half of **8** is ____.

② One half of **10** is ____.

③ One half of **14** is ____.

④ One half of **16** is ____.

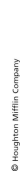
© Houghton Mifflin Company

Give it a try Jake has **16** baseball cards. He shares one half
with Mosi. Mosi gives one half of those to Yuma.
How many cards does Mosi give to Yuma?

Make 3 equal parts.

Make 4 equal parts.

One third of **12** is __4__.

One fourth of **12** is __3__.

Work with a partner. You may use counters.
Circle equal parts. Write how many.

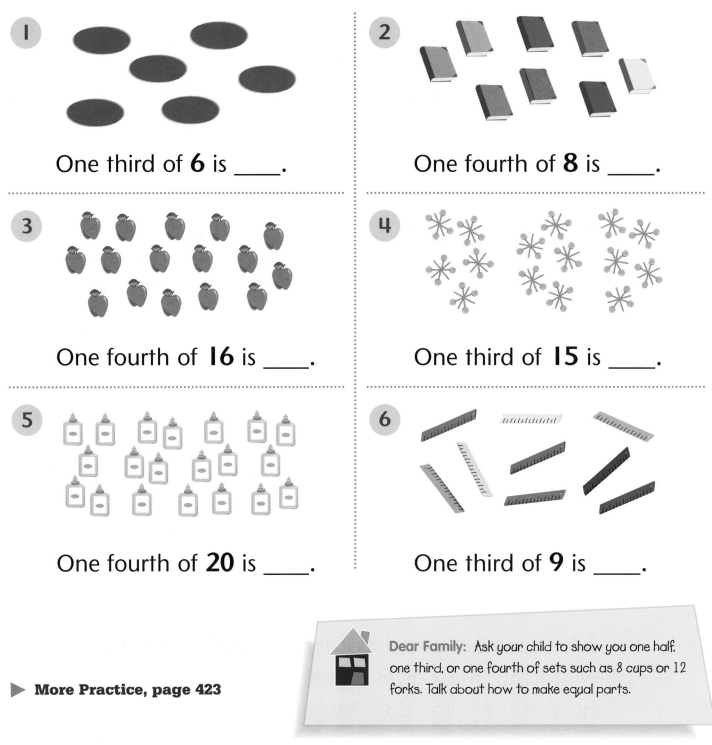

1

One third of **6** is ____.

2

One fourth of **8** is ____.

3

One fourth of **16** is ____.

4

One third of **15** is ____.

5

One fourth of **20** is ____.

6

One third of **9** is ____.

Dear Family: Ask your child to show you one half, one third, or one fourth of sets such as 8 cups or 12 forks. Talk about how to make equal parts.

▶ **More Practice, page 423**

Name _____

There are **8** cards.
Alicia shares **4** of them with Chen.

There are **2** groups of **4** in **8**.

How does making equal groups help you?

Work with a partner. Use cubes.
Write how many groups.

	Start with	Make groups of	Number of groups
1	8	4	2
2	12	3	
3	14	2	
4	15	3	
5	10	2	
6	9	3	

Communication

Share   Tell a friend what other equal groups you can make from each number.

There are **9** tacos. Circle groups of **2**.

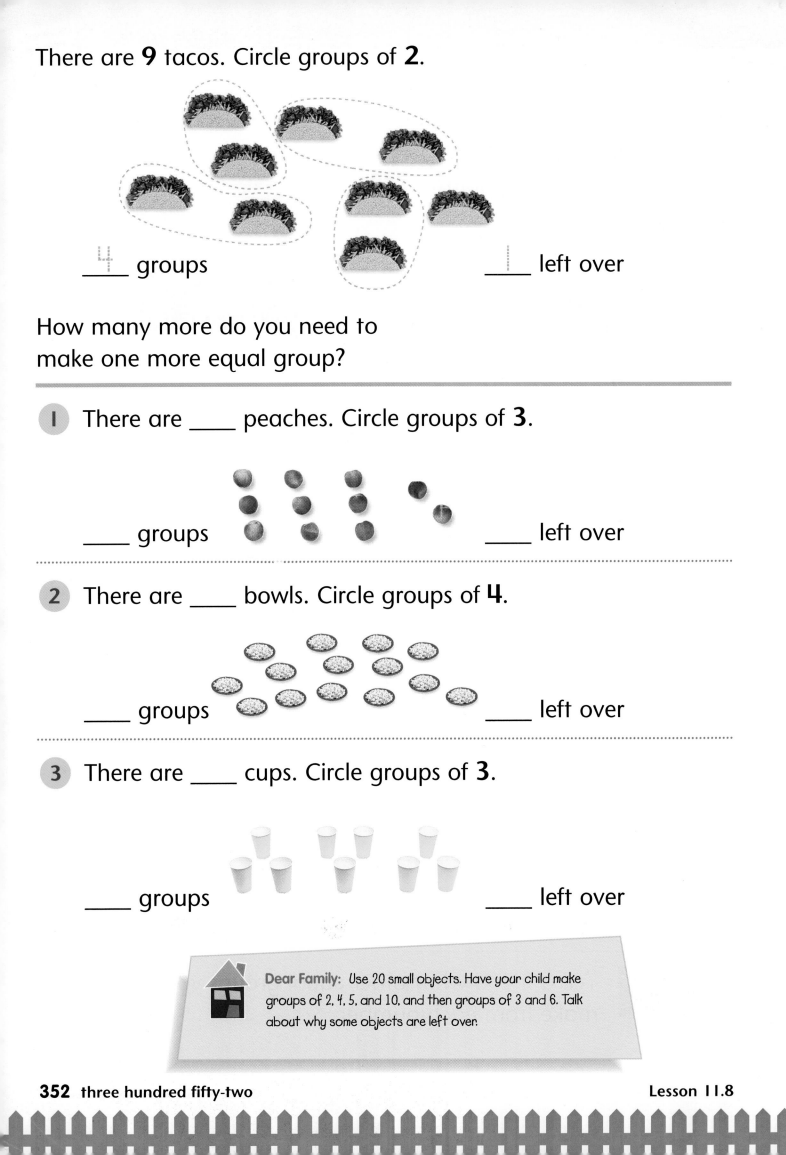

____ groups

____ left over

How many more do you need to make one more equal group?

---

1 There are ____ peaches. Circle groups of **3**.

____ groups

____ left over

....

2 There are ____ bowls. Circle groups of **4**.

____ groups

____ left over

....

3 There are ____ cups. Circle groups of **3**.

____ groups

____ left over

Dear Family: Use 20 small objects. Have your child make groups of 2, 4, 5, and 10, and then groups of 3 and 6. Talk about why some objects are left over.

Lesson 11.8

Cooperative Learning

Name _____

The children have **16** stickers.
They need **3** equal groups.
How many are in each group?
How many are left over?

How do you know how
many are left over?

Work with a partner. Use counters.
Fill in the table.

	Start with	Number of equal groups	How many are in each group?	How many are left?
1	16	3	5	1
2	11	2		
3	13	3		
4	12	5		
5	15	7		
6	8	4		

Communication

Compare tables with your partner. Talk about
how your answers are the same or different.

Work with a partner. Use counters.
Make different numbers of equal groups.
Fill in the table.

	Start with	Number of equal groups	How many are in each group?	How many are left?
1	13			
2	13			
3	14			
4	14			
5	14			
6	15			
7	15			

Mixed Review

Solve.

8 $14 - 7 =$ ____ $12 + 7 =$ ____

9 $13 - 4 =$ ____ $8 + 5 =$ ____

10 ____ $- 6 = 6$ ____ $+$ ____ $= 12$

Dear Family: Ask your child how he or she can share 12 crackers equally with 3 friends. What if there are 19 crackers? How many will be left over?

Name _____

Solve.

1 There are **3** slides at the park. Taro sees **5** children waiting for each slide. How many children are waiting to slide?

_____ children

2 Zina has **16** stamps. Max has one half as many. How many stamps does Max have?

_____ stamps

3 Rance and **6** friends are playing on the swings. Now **3** more children join them. How many children are swinging?

_____ children

4 Brent, Khalil, and Reta meet at the park **3** times each week. Each time they play for **2** hours. How many hours do they play together each week?

_____ hours

Communication

Share Share with a friend how you solve each problem. Talk about which strategies you use.

Solve.

1 There are **18** children and **3** picnic tables. The same number of children sit down at each table. How many children are at each table?

_____ children

2 Alex, Kofi, and Azi each need **3** marbles to play a game. They have **7** marbles in all. How many more marbles do they need?

_____ marbles

3 There are **3** new signs at the park. Circle the signs that have the same shape.

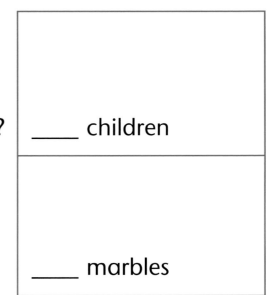

To Harper Street

Drinking Water

Do Not Litter

Susan's House

Leah's House

3 blocks

2 blocks

2 blocks

2 blocks

3 blocks

Coconino National Park

Post Office

Use the map.

4 Who lives closer to the Post Office, Susan or Leah?

_____

5 How much closer is Susan's house to the park than Leah's?

_____ blocks closer

Dear Family: Ask your child how he or she solved each problem. Then make a map to show places in your neighborhood. Create new problems to work out together.

Name _____

Write how many birds.

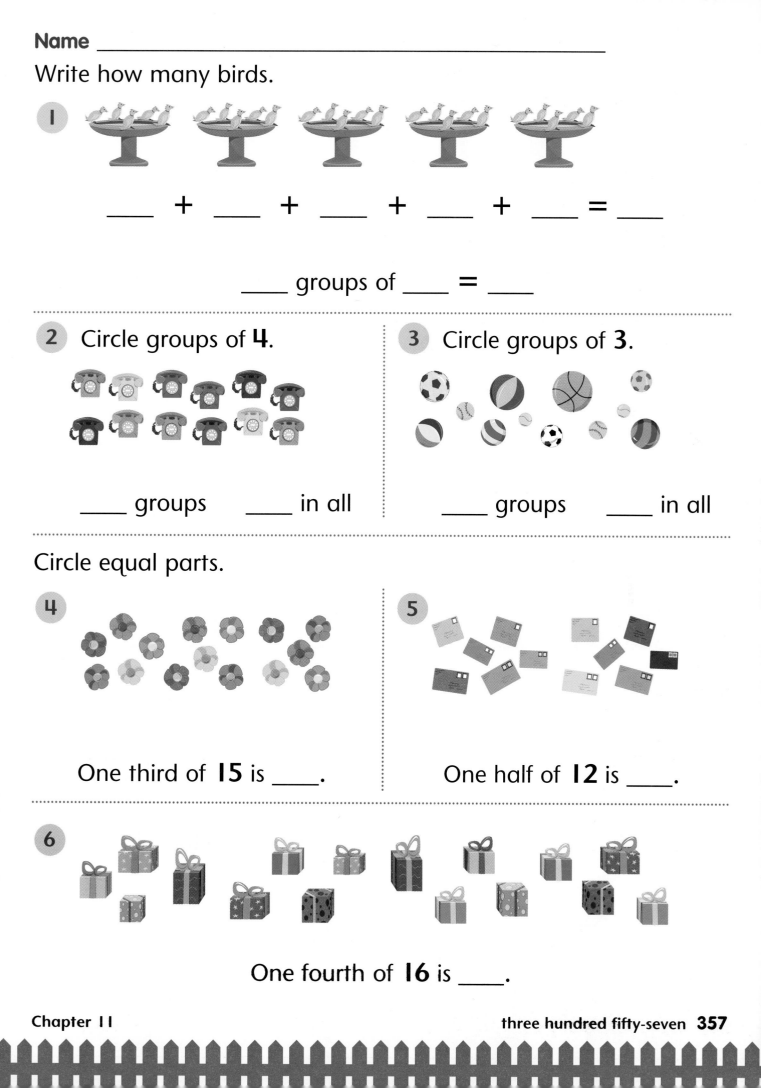

1

___ + ___ + ___ + ___ + ___ = ___

___ groups of ___ = ___

2 Circle groups of **4**.

___ groups   ___ in all

3 Circle groups of **3**.

___ groups   ___ in all

Circle equal parts.

4

One third of **15** is ___.

5

One half of **12** is ___.

6

One fourth of **16** is ___.

7 There are ____ jars of paint. Circle groups of **5**.

____ groups 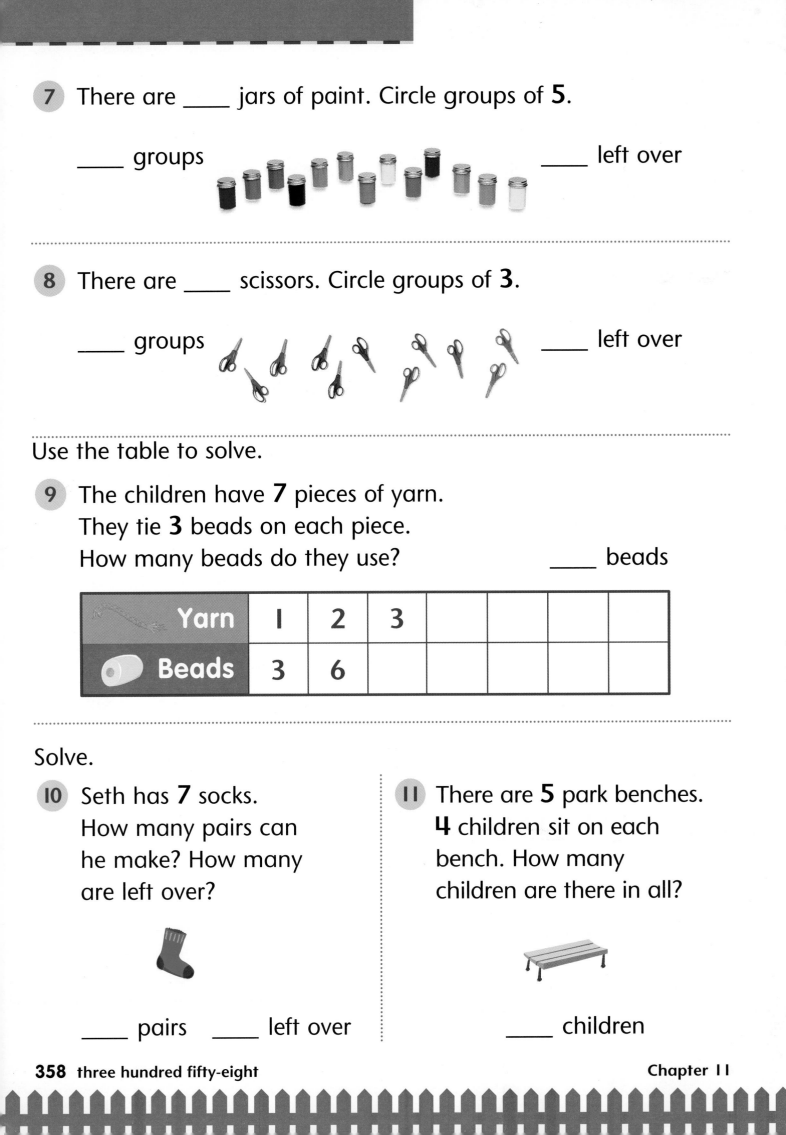 ____ left over

8 There are ____ scissors. Circle groups of **3**.

____ groups ____ left over

Use the table to solve.

9 The children have **7** pieces of yarn.
They tie **3** beads on each piece.
How many beads do they use?   ____ beads

Yarn	1	2	3			
Beads	3	6				

Solve.

10 Seth has **7** socks. How many pairs can he make? How many are left over?

____ pairs ____ left over

11 There are **5** park benches. **4** children sit on each bench. How many children are there in all?

____ children

Name _____

Look at the chart. It shows how many children put two pennies in the bank.

How many pennies are in the bank?

Write your answers in the chart.

How many children?	How many pennies?
1	
2	
3	
4	
5	
6	
7	

What pattern do you see?

_____

_____

_____

Internet
Visit Houghton Mifflin's
Education Place Math Center.
http://www.eduplace.com

Solve the problem.

There are **10** children.
Each child puts **5** pennies in the bank.
How many pennies are in the bank? _____

Write or draw how you solved the problem.

Dear Family: Practice counting pennies by 2's and 5's. You may count into a bank if you have one.

Addition and Subtraction of 2-Digit Numbers

Literature

We're Racing, Racing Down the Walk
By Phyllis McGinley

Read Aloud Anthology p. 34
Theme Connection
Sports and Games

Scoreboard

Lions	27
Bears	6

Charlie finds 10 marbles. Then he finds 12 more. Cornelia finds 29 marbles. Then she loses 14. Who has more marbles?

See what I can do by the end of this chapter.

Use What You Know

How many points does each team have?
Who is winning the game?
How can you find out which team is winning?

Listen to the stories.
Use cubes to race down the walk.

Dear Family: Use the workmat to keep track of your family's favorite teams and players. Place a penny on the workmat for each team or player. See how many groups of ten your child can find.

Name _____

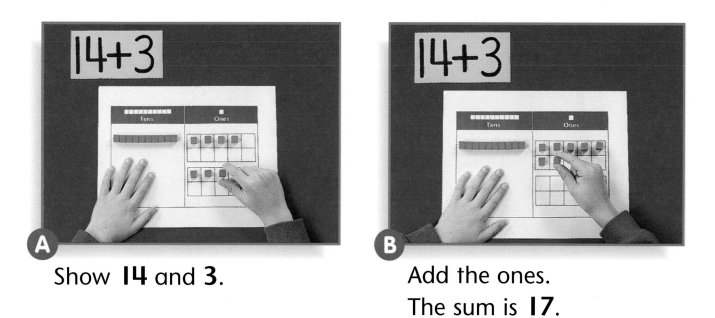

A Show **14** and **3**.

B Add the ones.
The sum is **17**.

How does using blocks and the workmat help you add?

Work with a partner. Use blocks and a workmat.
Write the sum.

① **25 + 2**
Show **25**.

Add **2**.

Tens	Ones

The sum is _____.

② **32 + 7**
Show **32**.

Add **7**.

Tens	Ones

The sum is _____.

③ **13 + 6**
Show **13**.

Add **6**.

Tens	Ones

The sum is _____.

④ **21 + 5**
Show **21**.

Add **5**.

Tens	Ones

The sum is _____.

Work with a partner.
Use blocks and a workmat.
Write the sum.

	Show	Add	Sum
1	11	7	18
2	43	5	
3	20	9	
4	37	0	
5	24	1	
6	15	4	
7	38	0	

Mixed Review

Solve.

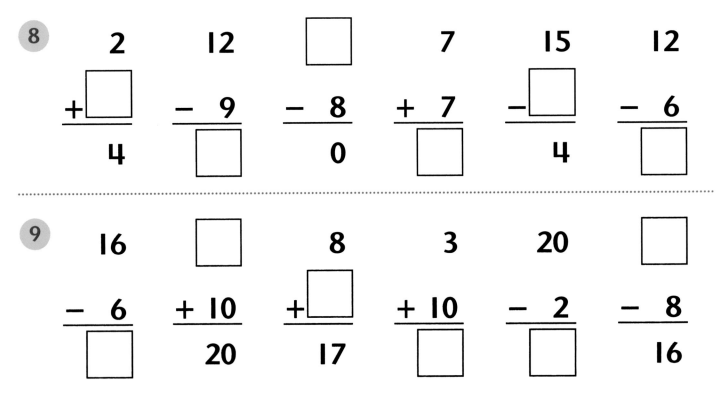

8.

$$2 + \square = 4$$ $$12 - 9 = \square$$ $$\square - 8 = 0$$ $$7 + 7 = \square$$ $$15 - \square = 4$$ $$12 - 6 = \square$$

9.

$$16 - 6 = \square$$ $$\square + 10 = 20$$ $$8 + \square = 17$$ $$3 + 10 = \square$$ $$20 - 2 = \square$$ $$\square - 8 = 16$$

▶ **More Practice, page 424**

 Dear Family: Have your child show you how to solve addition problems with greater numbers, similar to the examples on this page.

Name _____

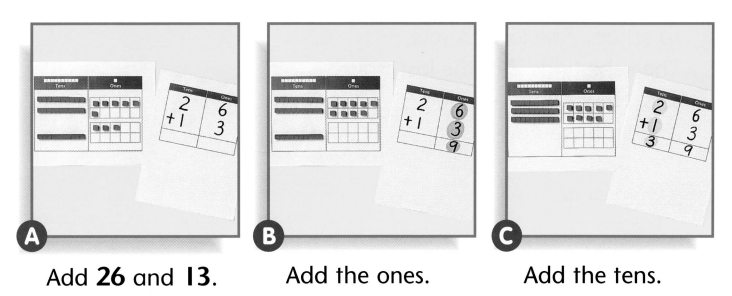

A Add **26** and **13**.

B Add the ones.

C Add the tens.

Use blocks and a workmat.
Write the sum.

1

Tens	Ones
3	5
+ 1	2

2

Tens	Ones
1	2
+ 1	7

3

Tens	Ones
2	1
+ 2	4

4

Tens	Ones
4	8
+ 1	0

5

Tens	Ones
5	1
+ 1	6

6

Tens	Ones
6	1
+ 0	8

Communication

Write about it What is another name for **10** ones?

Problem Solving

You may use blocks. Solve.

1 Angela takes **7** sets of jacks to school. She loses **3** sets. Then she finds **2** of the lost sets. How many sets does Angela have now?

_____ sets

2 Jiro and Leah have the same number of soccer balls. Jiro gives **4** away. Who has more soccer balls now?

_____

Use a calculator to solve.
Write your answer.

3 3 2 + 1 7 = ☐

4 2 6 + 3 1 = ☐

5 4 0 + 5 8 = ☐

▶ **More Practice, page 424**

Dear Family: Have your child read some of the word problems to you and explain how to solve them.

Name _____

Add **15** and **7**.

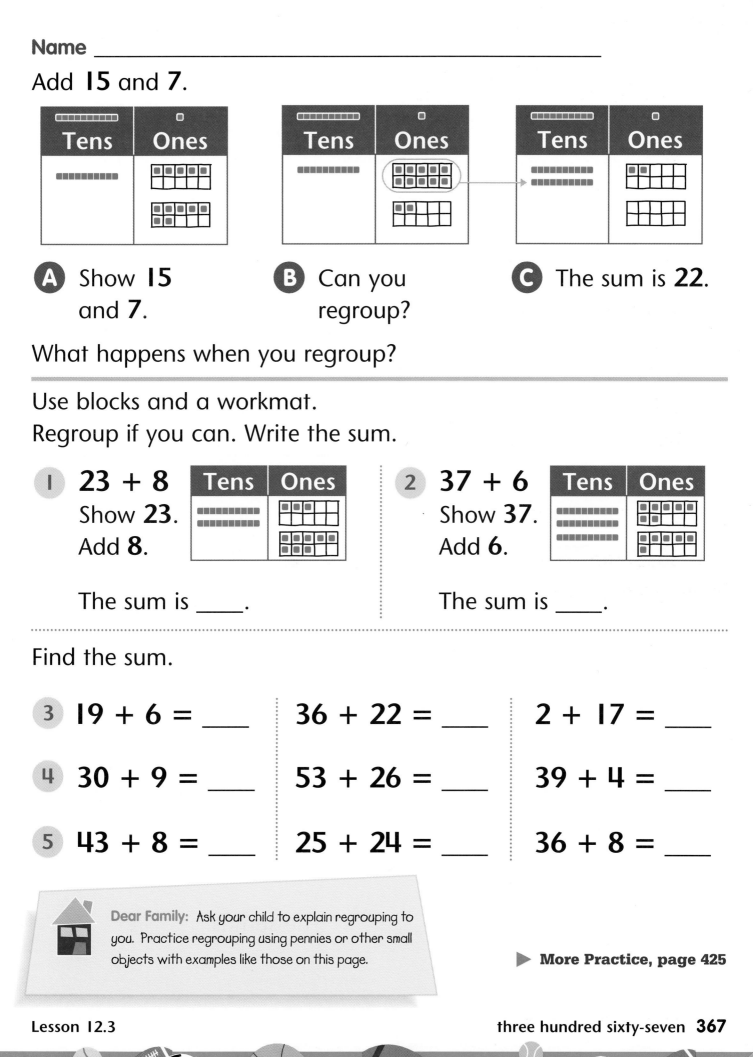

A Show **15** and **7**.

B Can you regroup?

C The sum is **22**.

What happens when you regroup?

Use blocks and a workmat.
Regroup if you can. Write the sum.

1 **23 + 8**
Show **23**.
Add **8**.

Tens	Ones

The sum is ____.

2 **37 + 6**
Show **37**.
Add **6**.

Tens	Ones

The sum is ____.

Find the sum.

3 $19 + 6 =$ ___ $36 + 22 =$ ___ $2 + 17 =$ ___

4 $30 + 9 =$ ___ $53 + 26 =$ ___ $39 + 4 =$ ___

5 $43 + 8 =$ ___ $25 + 24 =$ ___ $36 + 8 =$ ___

Dear Family: Ask your child to explain regrouping to you. Practice regrouping using pennies or other small objects with examples like those on this page.

▶ **More Practice, page 425**

Use blocks and the workmat.
Regroup if you can. Write the sum.

1 **26 + 32**
Show **26**.

Add **32**.

The sum is _____.

Tens	Ones
2	6
+ 3	2

---

2 **27 + 14**
Show **27**.

Add **14**.

The sum is _____.

3

Tens	Ones
3	4
+ 0	5

4

Tens	Ones
1	2
+ 2	7

5

Tens	Ones
4	3
+ 1	6

---

6 **26 + 28**
Show **26**.
Add **28**.

The sum is _____.

7 **19 + 18**
Show **19**.
Add **18**.

The sum is _____.

Name _____

Math World

Around the world, children play games with spinning tops.

This game from **Italy** is called **Turbo**. Children spin tops on a circle of numbers.

To play **Turbo**, children spin a top on a number circle. They add the numbers of the spaces where the top stops spinning. Children add each new score to the sum of their earlier scores.

Internet

Explore Houghton Mifflin's **Education Place Math Center.** http://www.eduplace.com

▶ **Turn the page for directions.**

Did you know?

The name **Turbo** comes from the Latin word for spinning top.

You need:
- pipe cleaner cut in half
- oaktag
- scissors
- paper plate
- markers

Try this!

Make your own **Turbo** game.

A Make the top. Cut a circle out of oaktag. Poke a tiny hole in the center of the circle. Push a pipe cleaner through the hole.

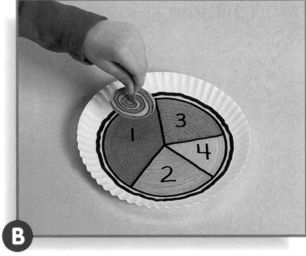

B Make a Turbo board by writing numbers on a paper plate. Use the picture to help you.

Dear Family: Use the following directions to play "Turbo." Give your child a chance to practice adding two-digit numbers by marking spaces on the plate with numbers above nine.

- To play, set the top on the plate and spin. Each player spins twice per turn. Record the numbers the top stops spinning on. After each spin, players use the sum of their previous turn, adding it to their current number to find a new sum. The player with the most points starts the next game.

- To change the game, add a challenge number. Example: The first player to hit 200 starts the next game.

Name _____

Cross out the information that you do not
need to answer the question.
Solve the problem.

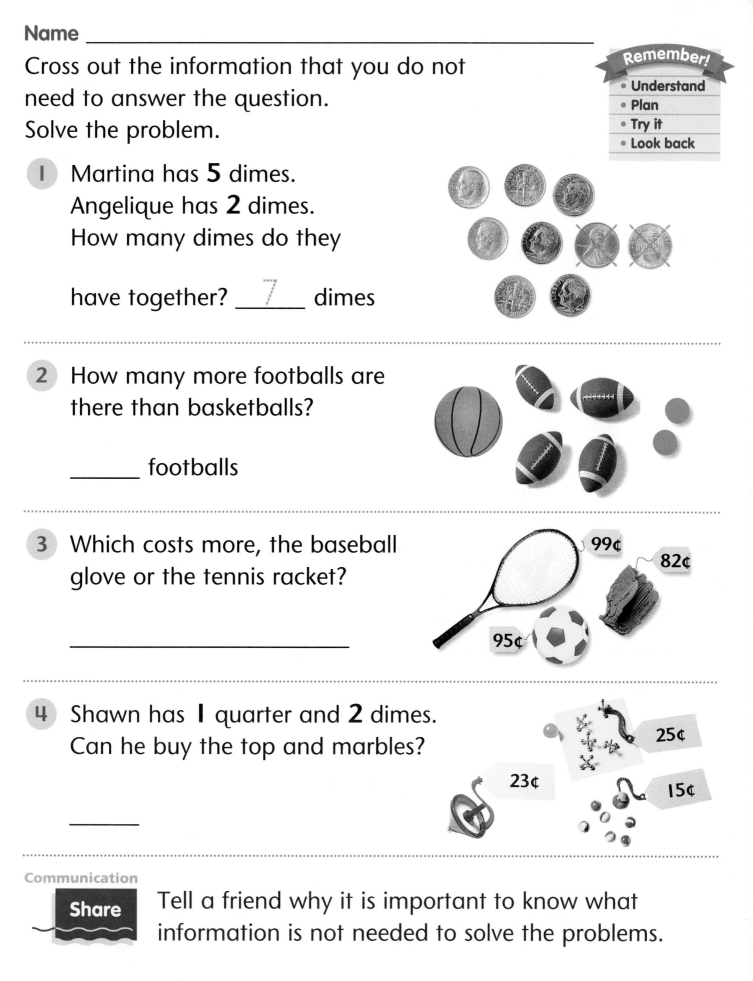

1   Martina has **5** dimes.
    Angelique has **2** dimes.
    How many dimes do they

    have together? __7__ dimes

2   How many more footballs are
    there than basketballs?

    _____ footballs

3   Which costs more, the baseball
    glove or the tennis racket?

    99¢   82¢   95¢

    _____

4   Shawn has **1** quarter and **2** dimes.
    Can he buy the top and marbles?

    25¢   23¢   15¢

    _____

Communication

Share   Tell a friend why it is important to know what
information is not needed to solve the problems.

© Houghton Mifflin Company

Cross out the information that you do not need.
Solve.

1. Janine has 13 trading cards.
   She gives Derek 4 cards.
   ~~Paul has 11 cards.~~ How many
   cards does Janine have left?

   __9__ trading cards

2. Matilda goes home at 4:00.
   Rose goes home at 6:00.
   They ate lunch at 12:00.
   Who went home first?

   _____

3. Jenny's ball bounces 25 times.
   Greg's ball bounces 14 times.
   Jenny's ball is purple.
   Whose ball bounces more?

   _____

4. Tadeo has 60¢. A box of
   playground chalk costs 75¢.
   He buys 4 stickers for 10¢ each.
   Does he have any money left?

   _____

Dear Family: Have your child explain to you what information was not needed to solve the word problems and how the questions were answered.

Lesson 12.4

Cooperative Learning

Name _____

A

Show **27**.

B

Subtract **5**.
The difference is **22**.

How does using blocks and the workmat help you subtract?

Use blocks and the workmat to find the difference.

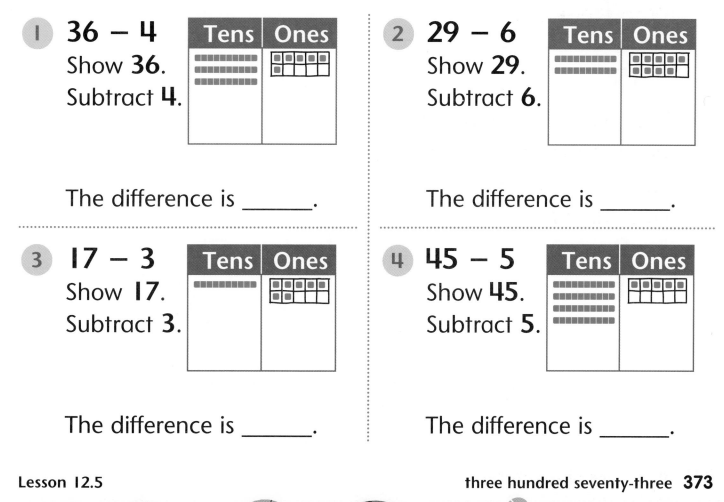

1 **36 − 4**

Tens	Ones

Show **36**.
Subtract **4**.

The difference is _____.

2 **29 − 6**

Tens	Ones

Show **29**.
Subtract **6**.

The difference is _____.

3 **17 − 3**

Tens	Ones

Show **17**.
Subtract **3**.

The difference is _____.

4 **45 − 5**

Tens	Ones

Show **45**.
Subtract **5**.

The difference is _____.

Work with a partner.
Use blocks and a workmat.
Write the difference.

	Show	Subtract	Difference
1	43	1	42
2	27	6	
3	34	1	
4	16	6	
5	25	3	
6	43	2	
7	32	0	
8	19	8	

Mixed Review

Solve.

9

$$8 + \square = 15$$

$$12 + 4 = \square$$

$$19 - \square = 10$$

$$\square + 6 = 12$$

$$10 - \square = 6$$

$$\square - 7 = 9$$

10

$$\square - 6 = 1$$

$$5 + 5 = \square$$

$$20 - \square = 13$$

$$4 + 2 = \square$$

$$13 - \square = 9$$

$$\square - 5 = 11$$

▶ **More Practice, page 425**

Dear Family: Ask your child to show you how to subtract with household items, such as paper clips or buttons.

Lesson 12.5

Cooperative Learning

Name _____

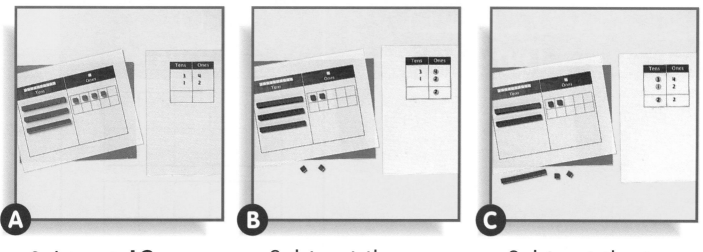

A Subtract **12** from **34**.

B Subtract the ones.

C Subtract the tens.

How does using blocks and a workmat help you to subtract greater numbers?

Work with a partner. Use blocks and a workmat.
Write the difference.

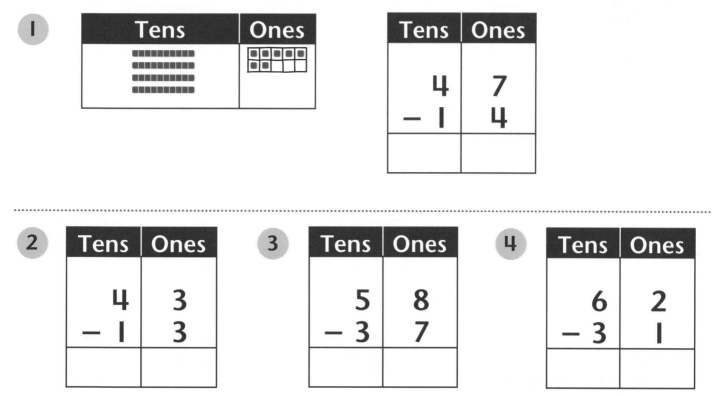

1

Tens	Ones

Tens	Ones
4	7
− 1	4

2

Tens	Ones
4	3
− 1	3

3

Tens	Ones
5	8
− 3	7

4

Tens	Ones
6	2
− 3	1

Work with a partner.
Use blocks and the workmat.
Write the difference.

Tens	Ones

1

43	26	62	29	44	57
− 11	− 15	− 10	− 27	− 22	− 37

2

38	15	28	51	39	65
− 16	− 13	− 12	− 30	− 14	− 24

Give it a try

Use a calculator.
Start with your age.
Add or subtract.

☐ + 28 = ☐ − 16 = ☐ + 17 = ☐ − 29 = ☐

▶ **More Practice, page 426**

Dear Family: Practice 2-digit subtraction with your child by asking questions, such as: You have 48 cards. If you lose 16 of them, how many do you have left?

Lesson 12.6

Name _____

Subtract **8** from **32**.

A Show **32**.
Are there enough
ones to subtract?

B Regroup **1** ten
as **10** ones.

C Subtract **8**.
The difference
is **24**.

How does regrouping help to solve the problem?

Use blocks and a workmat. Regroup if you need to.
Write the difference.

① **23 − 9**
Show **23**.
Subtract **9**.

Tens	Ones

The difference is _____.

② **35 − 16**
Show **35**.
Subtract **16**.

Tens	Ones

The difference is _____.

③

18	64	27	36	72
− 9	− 7	− 8	− 9	− 4

Lesson 12.7

Problem Solving

Solve. Use dimes and pennies.
Trade **1** dime for **10** pennies to regroup.

1. Raymond has **4** dimes.
He buys a trading card for **15¢**.
How many dimes and
pennies does he have left?

____ dimes ____ pennies

2. Lucille has **3** dimes and **5** pennies.
Russell has **1** dime and **16** pennies.
Who has more money?

_____

3. Darcy has **5** dimes.
A baseball card costs **25¢**.
How many baseball cards
can she buy?

____ baseball cards

4. Casey and Mark each have **7** dimes.
Casey gives Mark **2** dimes.
Who has more money now?

_____

Communication

Talk about it   Did you regroup in each example? Why?

▶ **More Practice, page 426**

Dear Family: Ask your child to explain to you when regrouping is necessary in subtraction.

Name _____

Finding a pattern can help you add or subtract.

Solve.

1

17	16	15
+ 3	+ 4	+ 5
20	20	20

2

| 67 | 67 | 67 |
| + 4 | + 5 | + 6 |

3

| 65 | 45 | 25 |
| − 10 | − 10 | − 10 |

4

| 34 | 24 | 14 |
| + 10 | + 10 | + 10 |

5

| 21 | 22 | 23 |
| − 1 | − 2 | − 3 |

6

| 62 | 62 | 62 |
| − 2 | − 3 | − 4 |

Give it a try

You may use blocks.
Write the number.
40 is my double. What number am I? _____

What is one half of me? _____

Use crayons.
Solve.
Use the key to color
the picture.

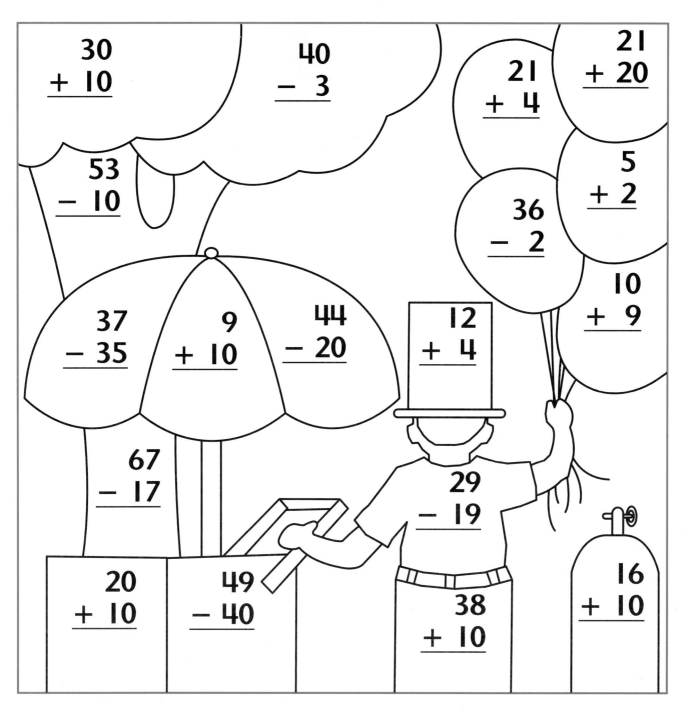

Key

blue	1 to 10	green	31 to 40
yellow	11 to 20	brown	41 to 50
red	21 to 30		

$$30 + 10$$

$$40 - 3$$

$$21 + 4$$

$$21 + 20$$

$$53 - 10$$

$$5 + 2$$

$$36 - 2$$

$$37 - 35$$

$$9 + 10$$

$$44 - 20$$

$$12 + 4$$

$$10 + 9$$

$$67 - 17$$

$$29 - 19$$

$$20 + 10$$

$$49 - 40$$

$$38 + 10$$

$$16 + 10$$

Dear Family: Help your child practice number patterns in addition and subtraction by solving problems such as: 55 + 10, 65 + 10, 75 + 10; or 36 – 2, 36 – 3, 36 – 4.

Lesson 12.8

Name _____

Nicole has **2** dimes and **13** pennies.
She wants to buy **2** trading cards.
They cost **16¢** each.
Does she have enough money?

▶ **Understand**

I need to know if Nicole has enough
money to buy the trading cards.

▶ **Plan**

I can act it out.

▶ **Try it**

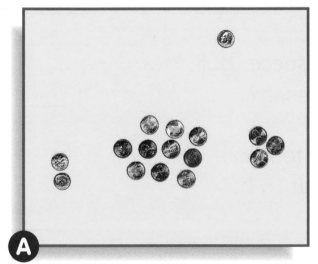

A

I use dimes and pennies.
I can regroup.

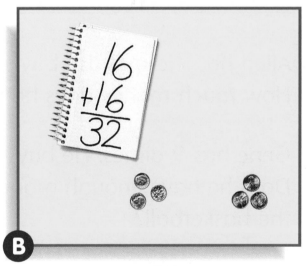

B

Nicole has **33¢**. Two
trading cards cost **32¢**.
She can buy the cards.

▶ **Look back**

33¢ is more than **32¢**. My answer makes sense.

Lesson 12.9

Look at the picture.
Use dimes and pennies.

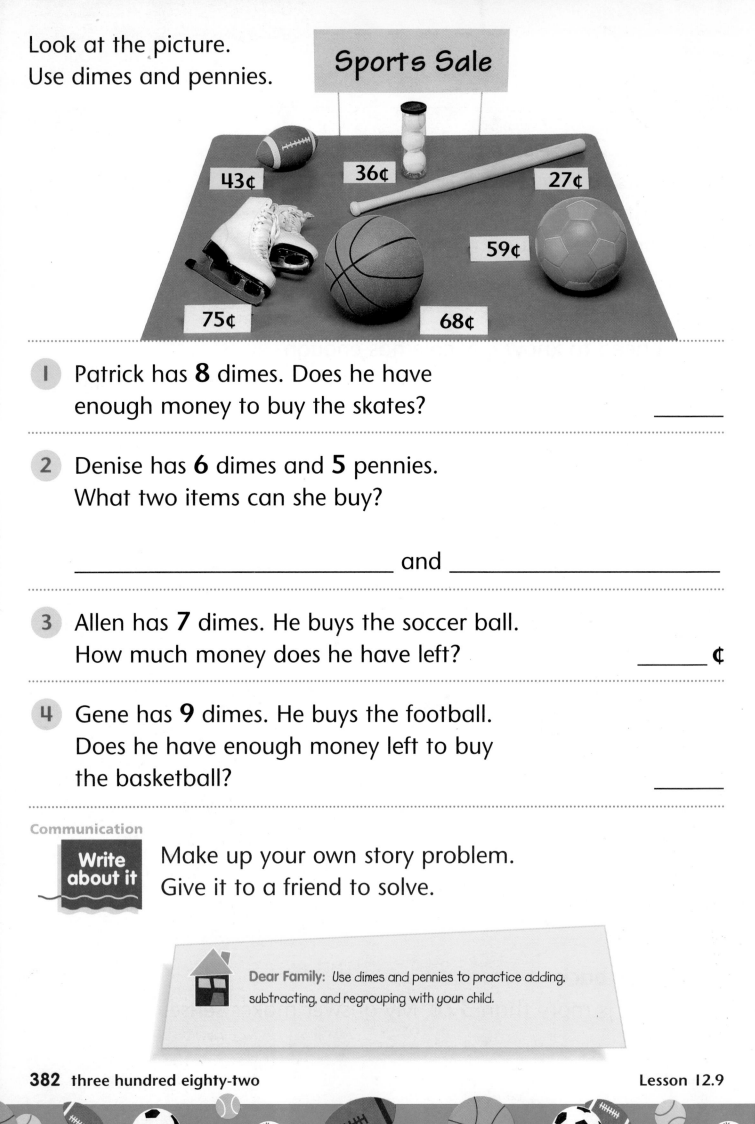

Sports Sale

43¢   36¢   27¢

59¢

75¢   68¢

1 Patrick has **8** dimes. Does he have
enough money to buy the skates?   _____

2 Denise has **6** dimes and **5** pennies.
What two items can she buy?

_____ and _____

3 Allen has **7** dimes. He buys the soccer ball.
How much money does he have left?   _____ ¢

4 Gene has **9** dimes. He buys the football.
Does he have enough money left to buy
the basketball?   _____

Communication

Write about it   Make up your own story problem.
Give it to a friend to solve.

Dear Family: Use dimes and pennies to practice adding,
subtracting, and regrouping with your child.

Name _____

Use blocks and a workmat. Add.
Regroup as needed. Write the sum.

| 1 | 27 + 2 | 2 | 31 + 7 | 3 | 24 + 4 | 4 | 26 + 32 |

| 5 | 45 + 33 | 6 | 52 + 21 | 7 | 22 + 7 | 8 | 14 + 23 |

	Show	Add	Sum
9	34	28	
10	62	17	
11	43	10	
12	28	27	
13	48	35	
14	21	18	
15	37	19	
16	25	25	

Use blocks and a workmat. Subtract.
Regroup as needed. Write the difference.

17   39
     − 8
     ___

18   47
     − 27
     ___

19   57
     − 46
     ___

20   63
     − 19
     ___

	Show	Subtract	Difference
21	42	36	
22	24	15	
23	36	13	
24	51	23	

Solve.

25 Nadia and Scott have the same
    number of trading cards.
    Nadia gives **6** to her brother.
    Who has more now?

    _____

26 Rachelle has **19** marbles.
    She buys **18** more marbles.
    How many marbles does she have now?

    _____ marbles

Name _____

Write your answer.

Charlie has 16 marbles.
Cornelia has 21 marbles.

Who has more marbles? _____

How many more marbles does the winner have? ____

Write or draw how you solved the problem.

Internet

Visit Houghton Mifflin's
Education Place Math Center.
http://www.eduplace.com

Make up your own story problem
about Charlie and Cornelia.

_____

_____

_____

_____

_____

Who wins the contest? _____
Write or draw how you know.

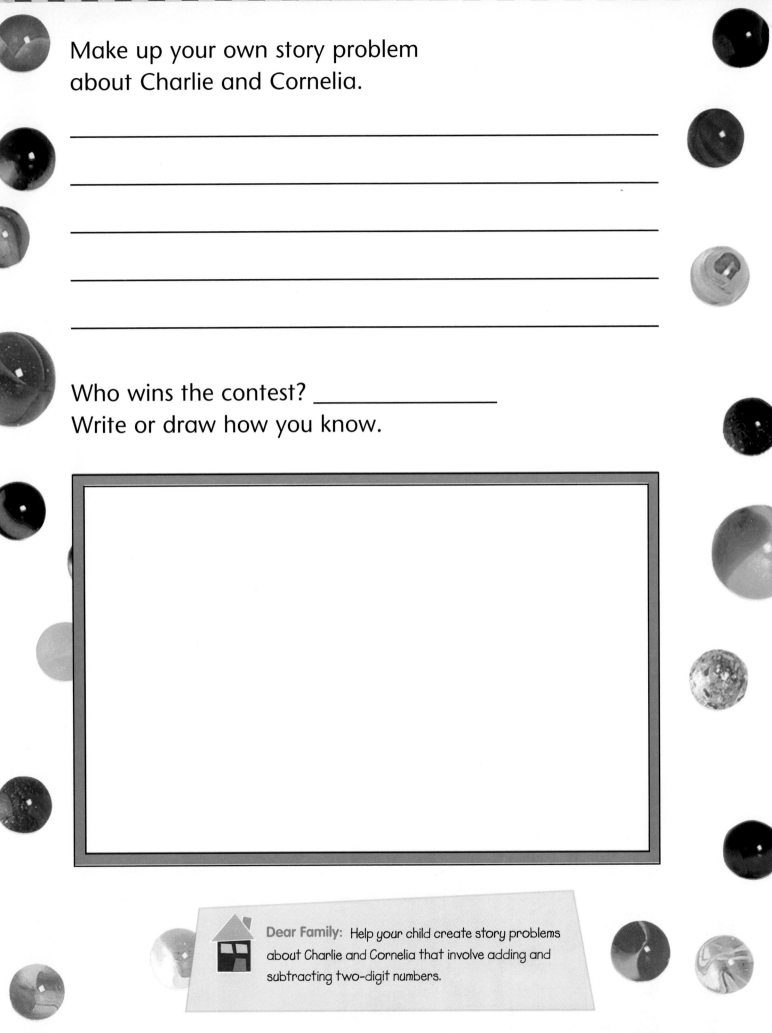

Dear Family: Help your child create story problems
about Charlie and Cornelia that involve adding and
subtracting two-digit numbers.

Name _____

Circle the doubles.

Write the sum or the difference.

1.
```
   20
 − 10
```

2.
```
   17
 +  2
```

3.
```
   15
 −  4
```

4.
```
    8
 +  8
```

5.
```
   16
 −  3
```

6.
```
    9
 +  9
```

7.
```
    7
 +  9
```

8.
```
   18
 −  5
```

9.
```
    7
 −  7
```

10.
```
   11
 +  6
```

Measure. Use a centimeter ruler.

11.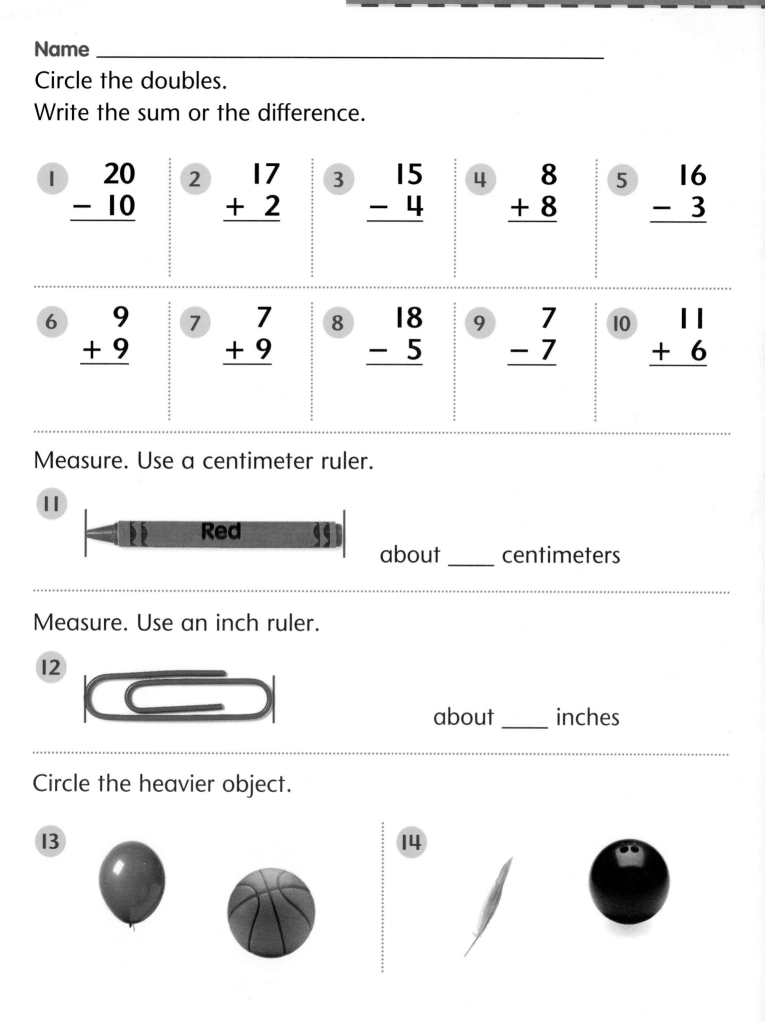

about ____ centimeters

Measure. Use an inch ruler.

12.

about ____ inches

Circle the heavier object.

13.

14.

15 Circle how you measure how long.

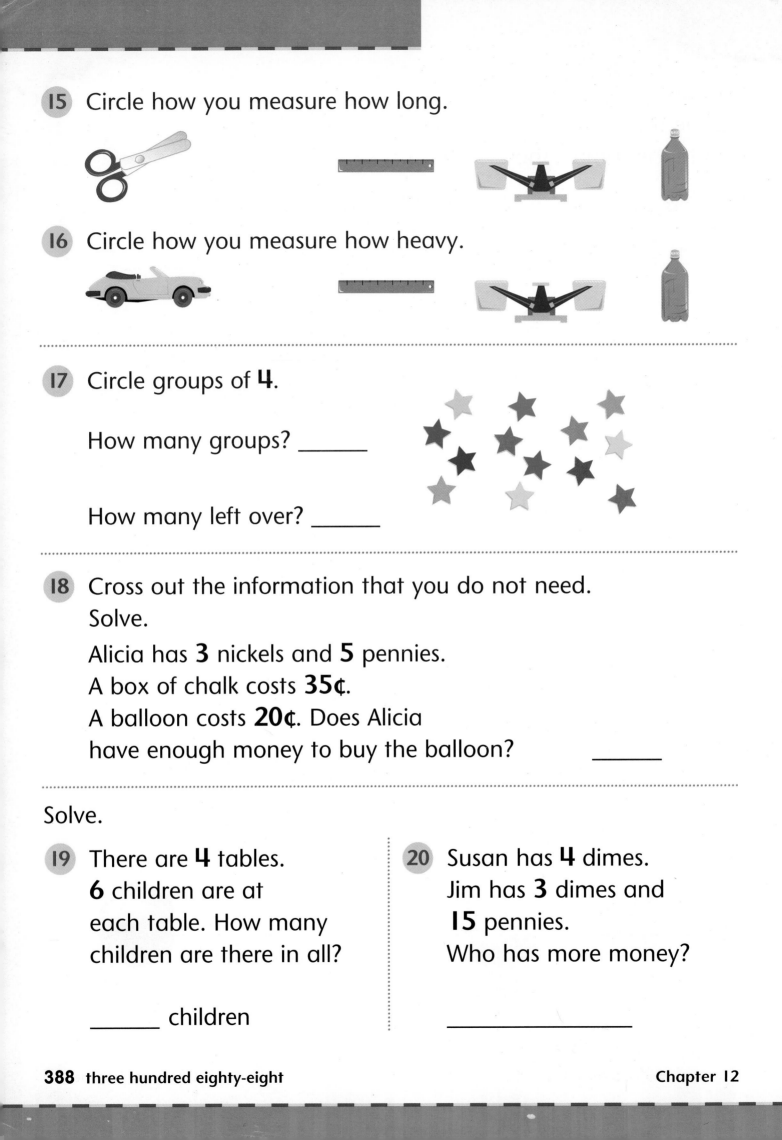

16 Circle how you measure how heavy.

17 Circle groups of **4**.

How many groups? _____

How many left over? _____

18 Cross out the information that you do not need. Solve.

Alicia has **3** nickels and **5** pennies.
A box of chalk costs **35¢**.
A balloon costs **20¢**. Does Alicia
have enough money to buy the balloon? _____

Solve.

19 There are **4** tables.
6 children are at
each table. How many
children are there in all?

_____ children

20 Susan has **4** dimes.
Jim has **3** dimes and
15 pennies.
Who has more money?

_____

Name _____

Set 1.1   Use with pages 3–4. •••

Draw a line to match. Circle which has more.

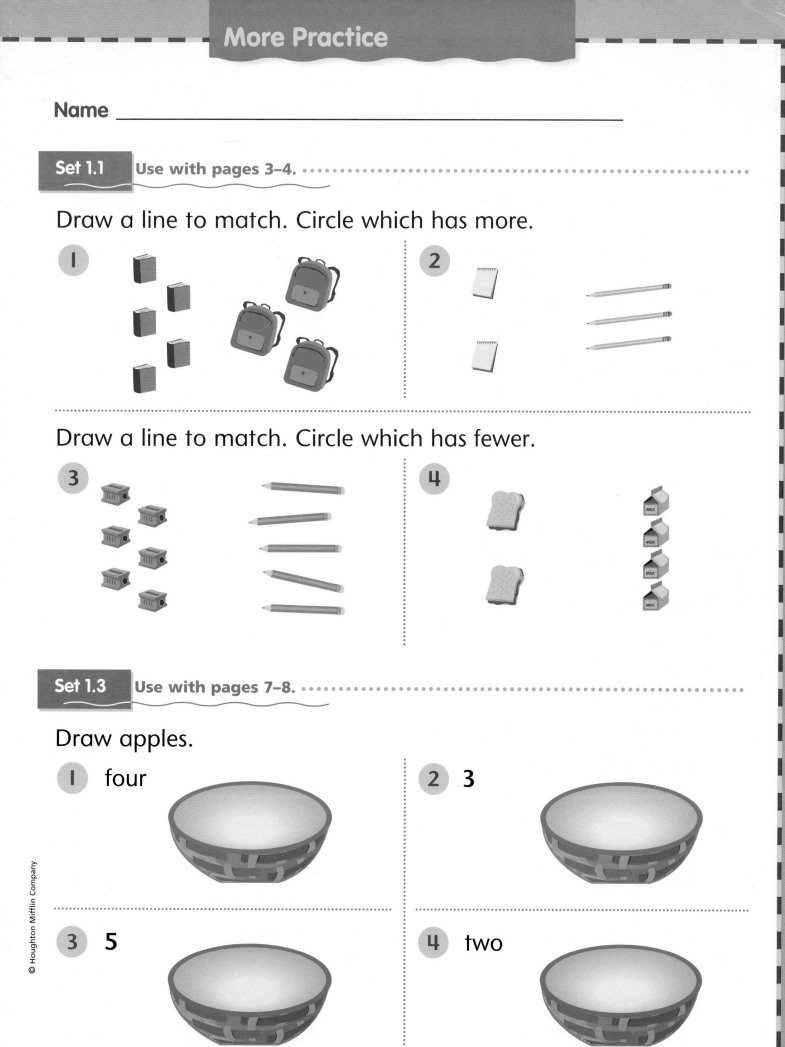

1

2

Draw a line to match. Circle which has fewer.

3

4

Set 1.3   Use with pages 7–8. •••

Draw apples.

1 four

2 3

3 5

4 two

Count the fish. Circle the number that tells how many.

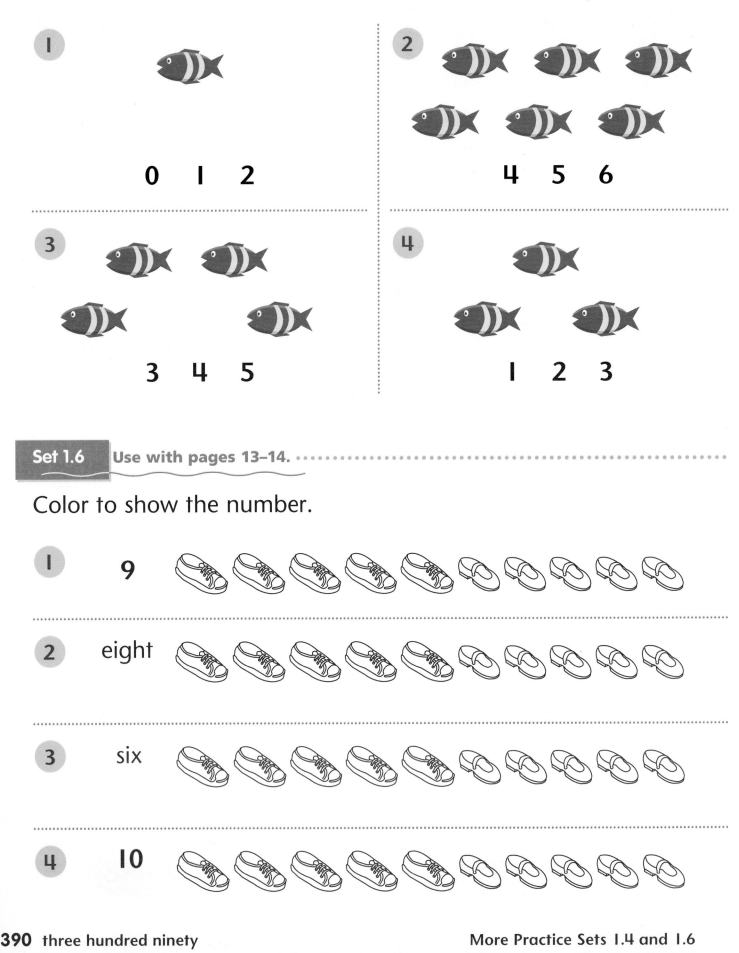

1

0   I   2

2

4   5   6

3

3   4   5

4

I   2   3

Color to show the number.

1   9

2   eight

3   six

4   10

More Practice Sets 1.4 and 1.6

Name _____

Set 1.11 Use with pages 25–26. ....

Write how many. Circle the group that has **more**.

1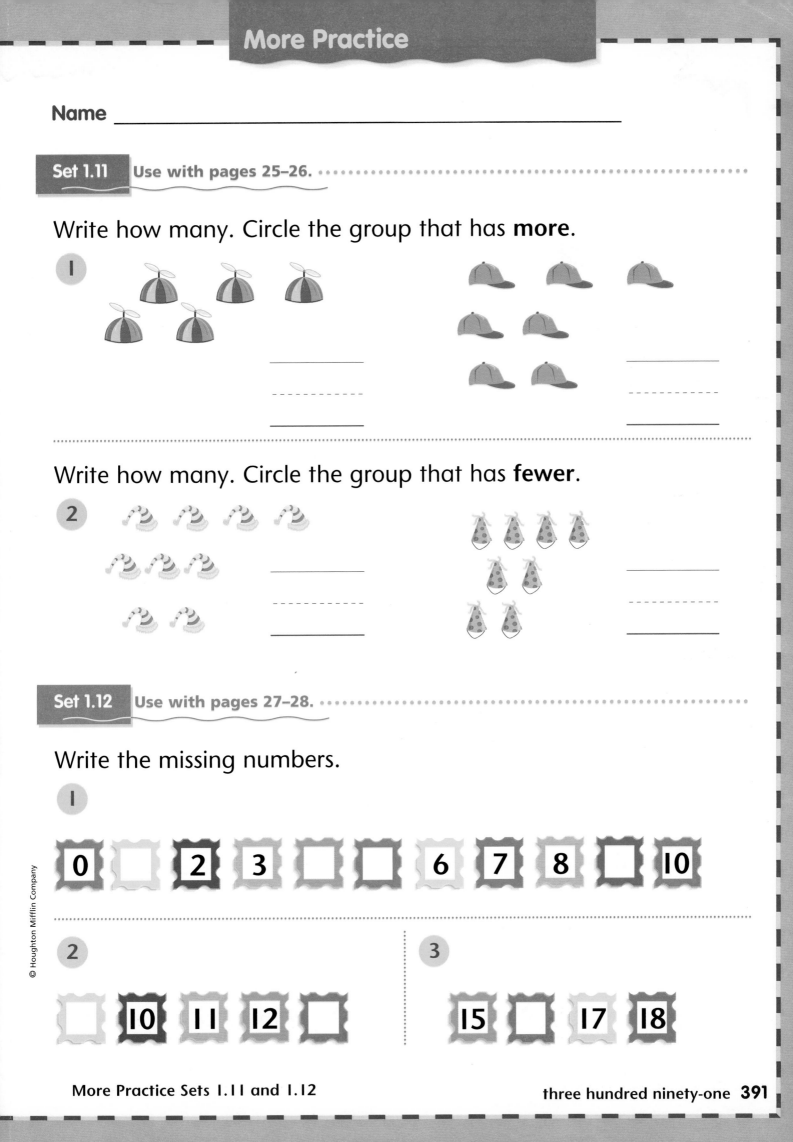

_____

- - - - - - - - -

_____

Write how many. Circle the group that has **fewer**.

2

_____

- - - - - - - - -

_____

Set 1.12 Use with pages 27–28. ....

Write the missing numbers.

1

| 0 | | 2 | 3 | | | 6 | 7 | 8 | | 10 |

2

| | 10 | 11 | 12 | |

3

| 15 | | 17 | 18 |

© Houghton Mifflin Company

Use cubes. Build the train.
Add the missing cubes. Draw them. Write the sum.

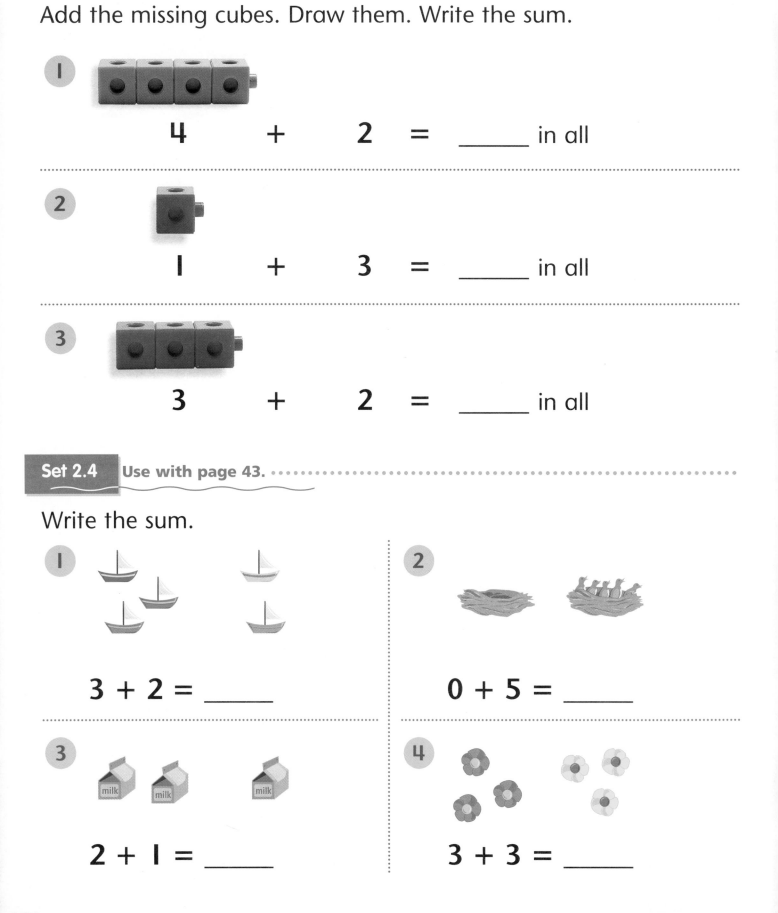

1   4   +   2   = _____ in all

2   1   +   3   = _____ in all

3   3   +   2   = _____ in all

Set 2.4 Use with page 43.

Write the sum.

1   3 + 2 = _____

2   0 + 5 = _____

3   2 + 1 = _____

4   3 + 3 = _____

Name _____

Set 2.5 Use with pages 47–48. ···

Write the sum.

1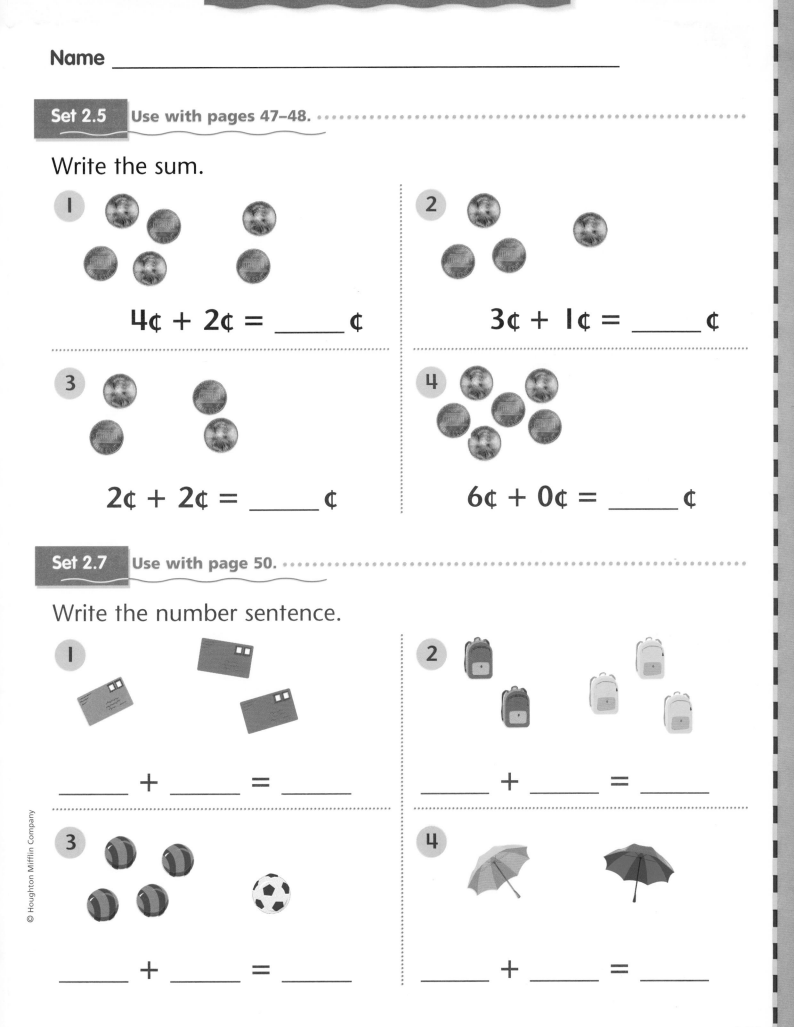
$$4¢ + 2¢ = \underline{\hspace{2em}} ¢$$

2
$$3¢ + 1¢ = \underline{\hspace{2em}} ¢$$

3
$$2¢ + 2¢ = \underline{\hspace{2em}} ¢$$

4
$$6¢ + 0¢ = \underline{\hspace{2em}} ¢$$

Set 2.7 Use with page 50. ···

Write the number sentence.

1
$$\underline{\hspace{3em}} + \underline{\hspace{3em}} = \underline{\hspace{3em}}$$

2
$$\underline{\hspace{3em}} + \underline{\hspace{3em}} = \underline{\hspace{3em}}$$

3
$$\underline{\hspace{3em}} + \underline{\hspace{3em}} = \underline{\hspace{3em}}$$

4
$$\underline{\hspace{3em}} + \underline{\hspace{3em}} = \underline{\hspace{3em}}$$

Make the whole with cubes.
Take part away. Cross out.
Write how many are left.

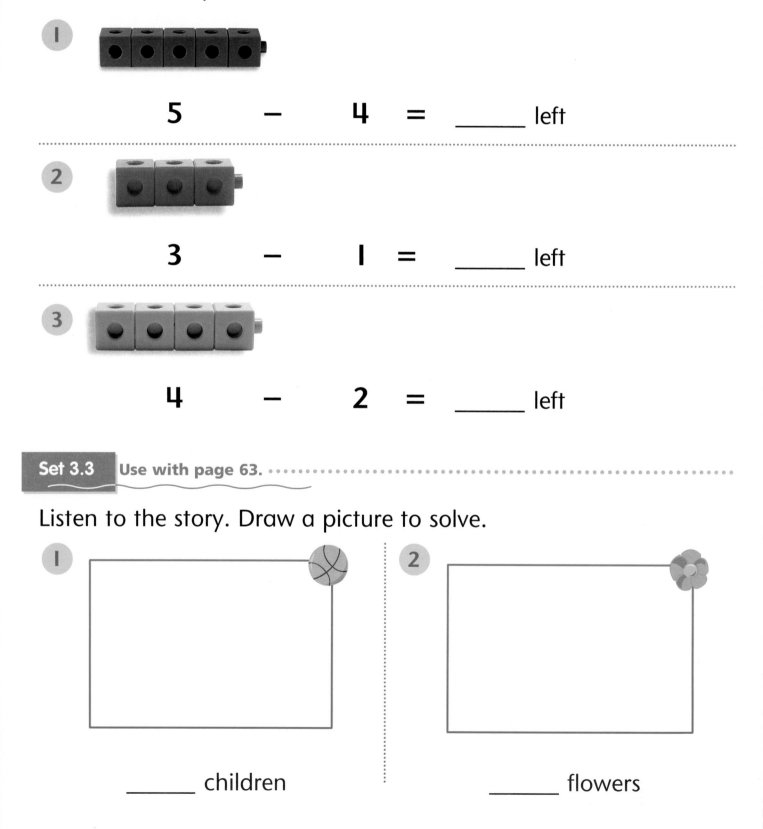

1

5 – 4 = _____ left

2

3 – 1 = _____ left

3

4 – 2 = _____ left

Set 3.3 Use with page 63.

Listen to the story. Draw a picture to solve.

1

_____ children

2

_____ flowers

Name _____

Set 3.4   Use with pages 67–68. ••••••••••••••••••••••••••••••••••••

Match. Write how many more.

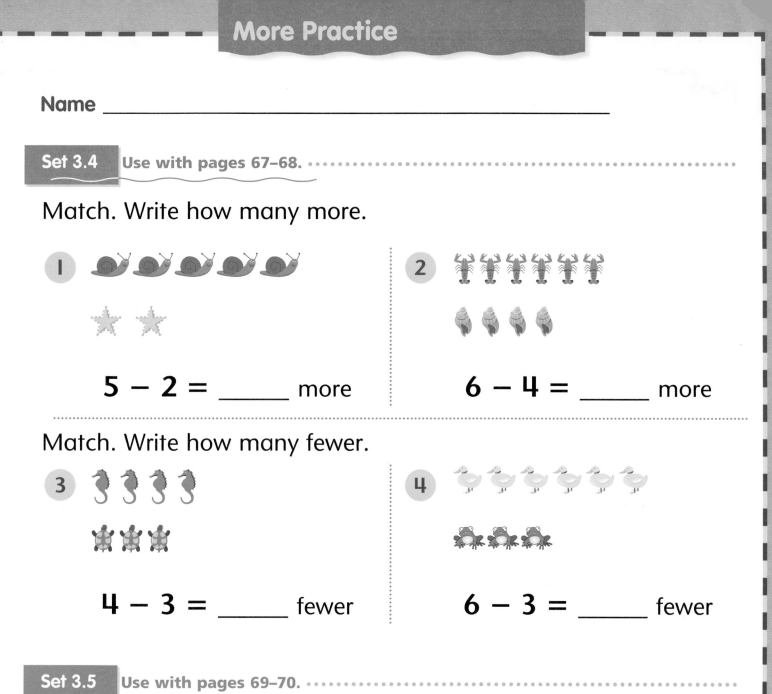

1   5 – 2 = _____ more

2   6 – 4 = _____ more

Match. Write how many fewer.

3   4 – 3 = _____ fewer

4   6 – 3 = _____ fewer

Set 3.5   Use with pages 69–70. ••••••••••••••••••••••••••••••••••••

Write how many pennies. Cross out pennies to buy
each toy. Write the subtraction sentence.

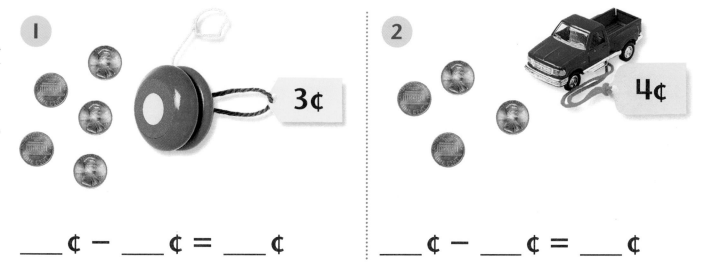

1   3¢

2   4¢

1   ___¢ – ___¢ = ___¢

2   ___¢ – ___¢ = ___¢

© Houghton Mifflin Company

Write the number of flowers in each vase.
How many flowers should be in the last vase?
Draw the flowers.

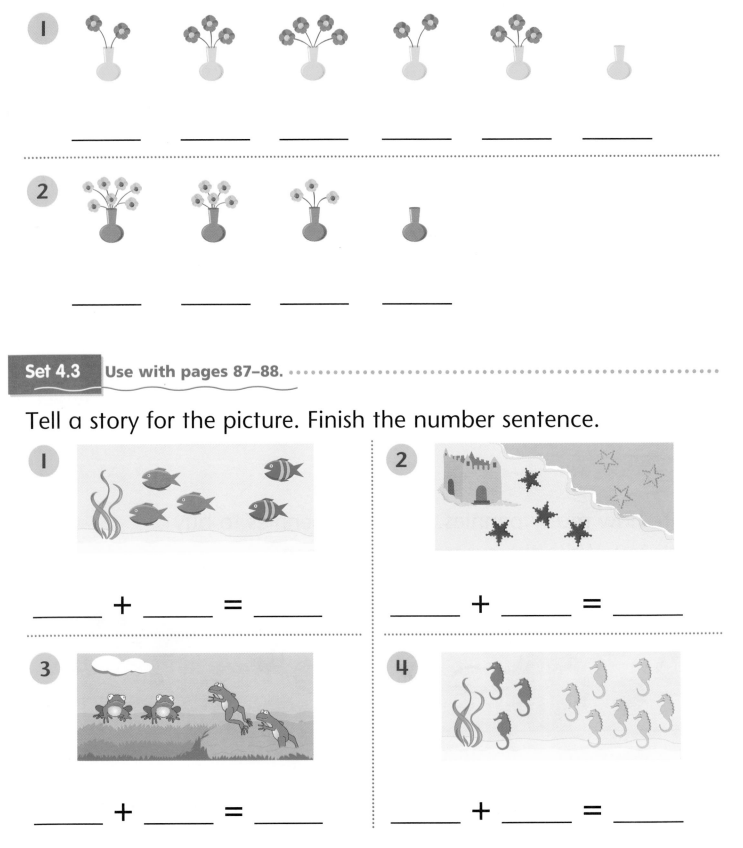

1 _____ _____ _____ _____ _____ _____

2 _____ _____ _____ _____

Set 4.3 Use with pages 87–88. ●●

Tell a story for the picture. Finish the number sentence.

1

_____ + _____ = _____

2

_____ + _____ = _____

3

_____ + _____ = _____

4

_____ + _____ = _____

Name _____

Set 4.4 Use with pages 89–90. ●

Look at each picture. Write the sum.

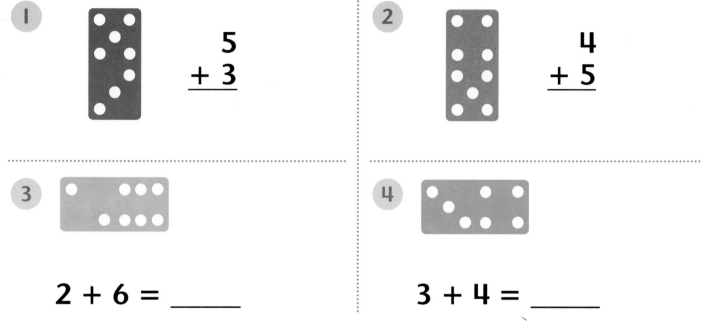

1

$$\begin{array}{r} 5 \\ +\ 3 \\ \hline \end{array}$$

2

$$\begin{array}{r} 4 \\ +\ 5 \\ \hline \end{array}$$

3

$2 + 6 =$ _____

4

$3 + 4 =$ _____

Set 4.6 Use with page 93. ●

Draw leaves to fill in the ten frame.
Finish the number sentence.

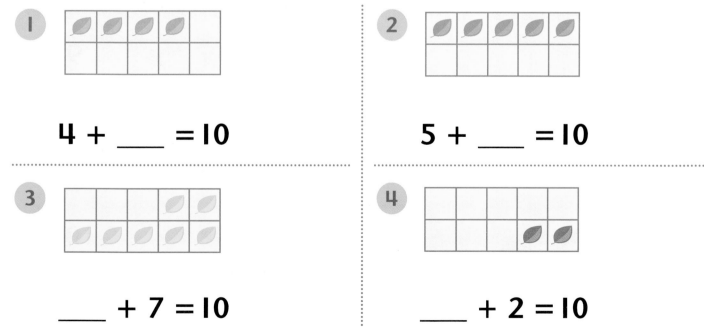

1

$4 +$ ___ $= 10$

2

$5 +$ ___ $= 10$

3

___ $+ 7 = 10$

4

___ $+ 2 = 10$

Match. Write how many more or fewer.

1

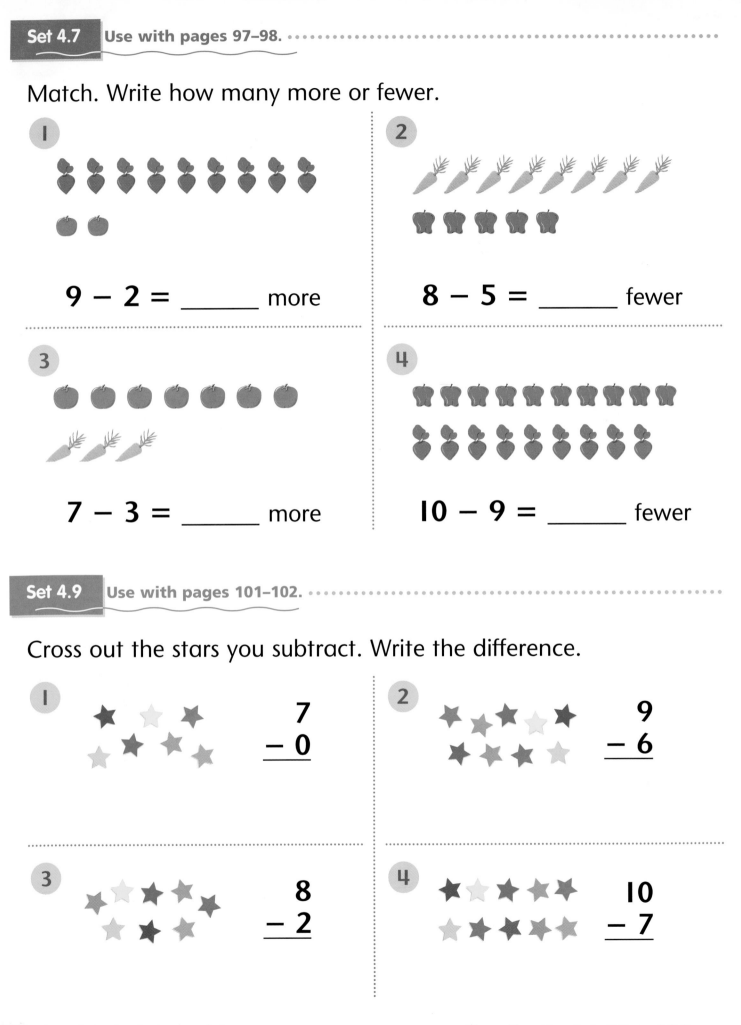

$9 - 2 =$ _____ more

2

$8 - 5 =$ _____ fewer

3

$7 - 3 =$ _____ more

4

$10 - 9 =$ _____ fewer

Cross out the stars you subtract. Write the difference.

1

$$\begin{array}{r} 7 \\ -\ 0 \\ \hline \end{array}$$

2

$$\begin{array}{r} 9 \\ -\ 6 \\ \hline \end{array}$$

3

$$\begin{array}{r} 8 \\ -\ 2 \\ \hline \end{array}$$

4

$$\begin{array}{r} 10 \\ -\ 7 \\ \hline \end{array}$$

Name _____

Set 4.11 Use with pages 105–106. ···

Write the number sentences for each fact family.

1

___1___ + ___5___ = ___6___

_____ + _____ = _____

_____ − _____ = _____

_____ − _____ = _____

2

_____ + _____ = _____

_____ + _____ = _____

_____ − _____ = _____

_____ − _____ = _____

Set 4.12 Use with pages 107–108. ···

Read the story. Write the number sentence.

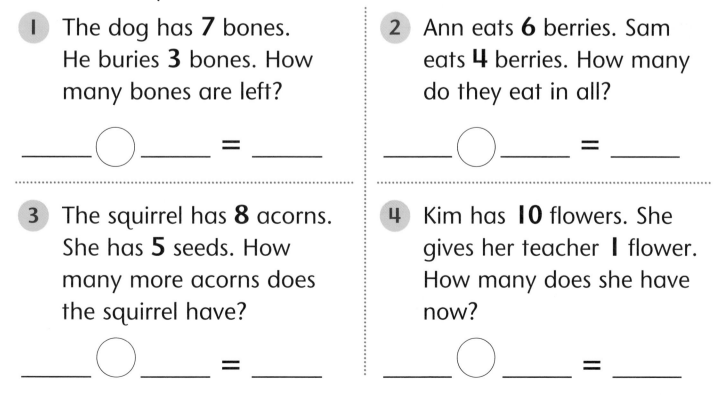

1 The dog has **7** bones. He buries **3** bones. How many bones are left?

_____ ◯ _____ = _____

2 Ann eats **6** berries. Sam eats **4** berries. How many do they eat in all?

_____ ◯ _____ = _____

3 The squirrel has **8** acorns. She has **5** seeds. How many more acorns does the squirrel have?

_____ ◯ _____ = _____

4 Kim has **10** flowers. She gives her teacher **1** flower. How many does she have now?

_____ ◯ _____ = _____

© Houghton Mifflin Company

Circle the number that is greater.

1

18 14   13 17   15 16

2

19 12   11 13   10 8

Circle the number that is less.

3

7 13   16 19   14 12

4

11 12   18 13   15 17

Use cubes. Write the missing number.

1 __8__ , __9__ , _____

2 __11__ , _____ , __13__

3 _____ , __15__ , __16__

4 __17__ , _____ , __19__

5 Write two numbers that come between **12** and **17**.

_____ and _____

6 Write three numbers that come before **18**.

_____ , _____ , _____

More Practice Sets 5.2 and 5.3

Name _____

Set 5.4 Use with pages 123–124.

Write how many tens. Write the number.

1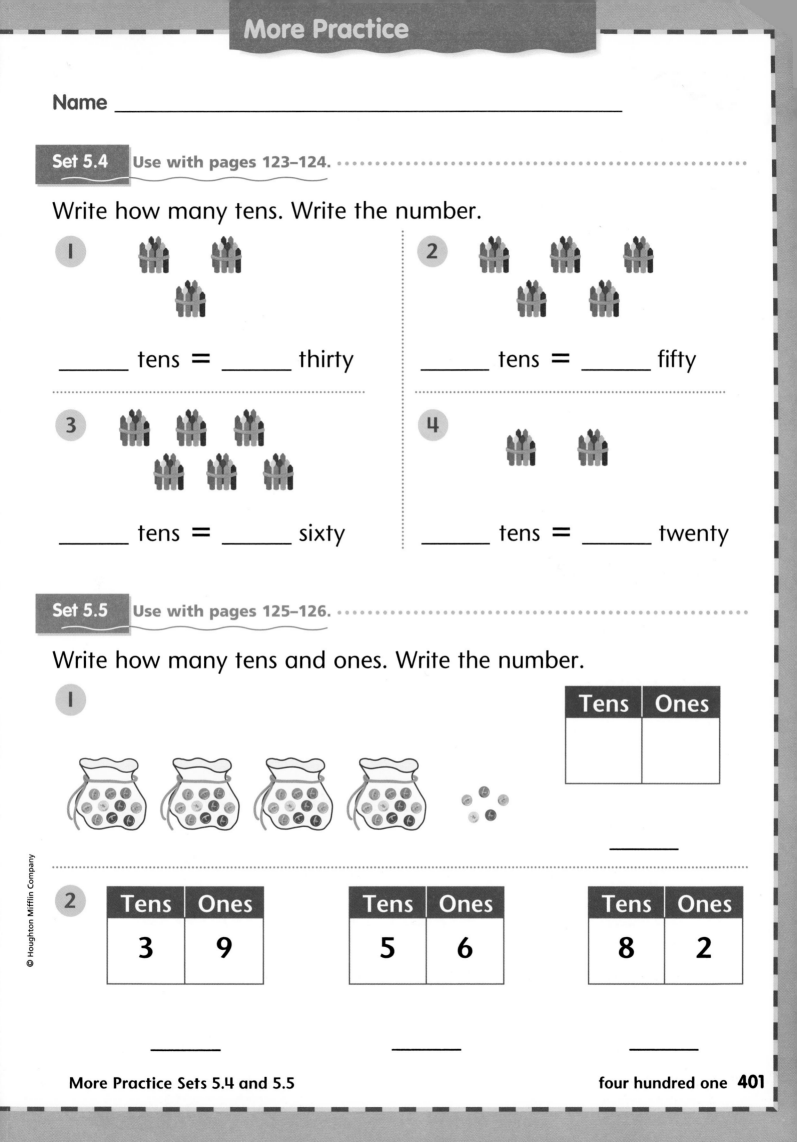

_____ tens = _____ thirty

2

_____ tens = _____ fifty

3

_____ tens = _____ sixty

4

_____ tens = _____ twenty

Set 5.5 Use with pages 125–126.

Write how many tens and ones. Write the number.

1

Tens	Ones

_____

2

Tens	Ones
3	9

_____

Tens	Ones
5	6

_____

Tens	Ones
8	2

_____

Circle the number that is greater.

1 (47   43)   (27   38)   15   18

2 (27   32)   (49   41)   23   32

3 (31   21)   (46   36)   15   5

Circle the number that is less.

4 (7   9)   36   23   28   38

5 (11   13)   41   27   46   16

6 (15   19)   25   29   34   35

Write the missing numbers.

Just Before   Between   Just After

1 _____, 15, 16   21, _____, 23   26, 27, _____

2 _____, 31, 32   42, _____, 44   48, 49, _____

3 _____, 23, 24   10, _____, 12   27, 28, _____

4 _____, 7, 8   29, _____, 31   17, 18, _____

5 _____, 49, 50   14, _____, 16   39, 40, _____

6 33 ☐ ☐ 36 ☐ ☐ 39 ☐ ☐ ☐

More Practice Sets 5.6 and 5.7

Name _____

Set 5.10 Use with pages 135–136. ·····························

Circle the number that is greater.

1   56   65   92   72   45   43

2   31   13   70   80   58   38

Circle the number that is less.

3   37   31   76   78   19   21

4   66   69   13   15   50   40

Set 5.12 Use with page 138. ·····························

Circle groups of **2**. Circle odd or even.

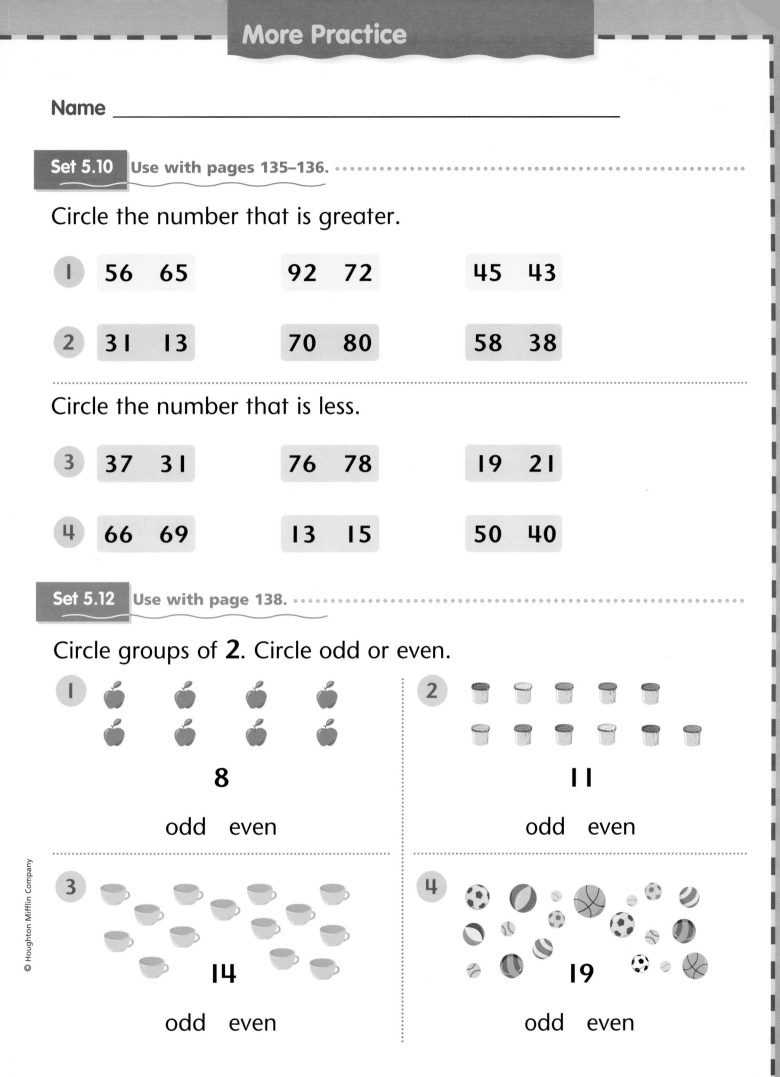

1
8
odd   even

2
11
odd   even

3
14
odd   even

4
19
odd   even

Count by twos. Write the numbers.

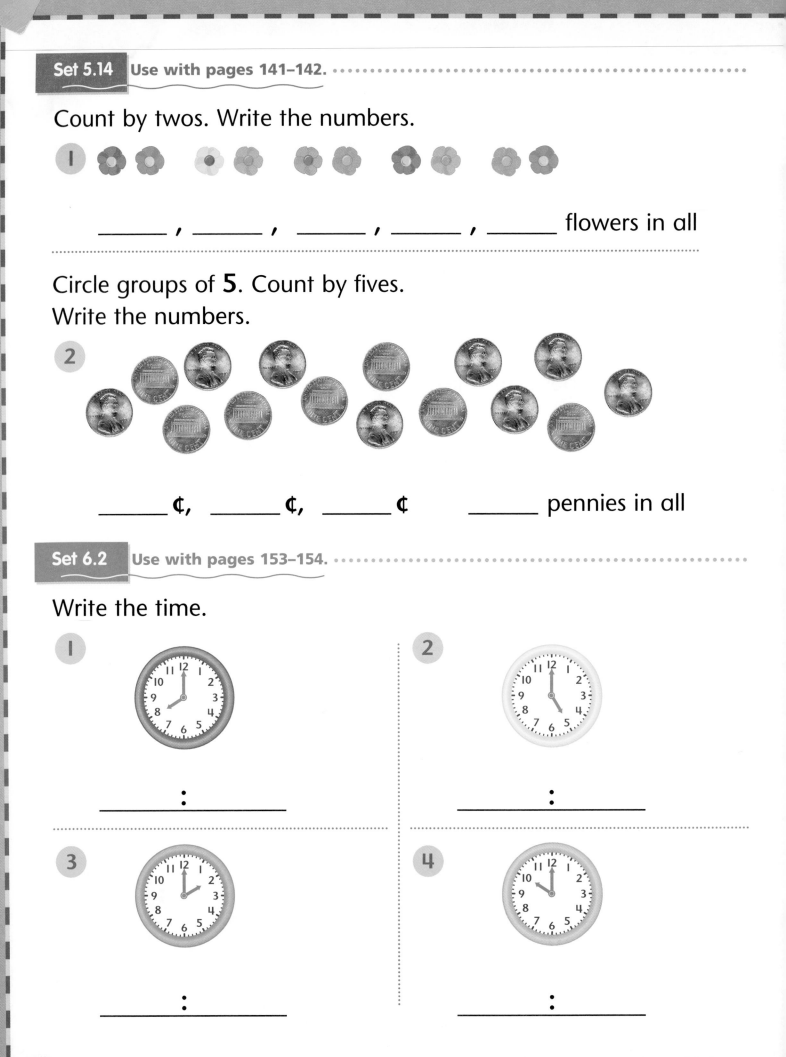

1

_____ , _____ , _____ , _____ , _____ flowers in all

Circle groups of **5**. Count by fives.
Write the numbers.

2

_____ ¢, _____ ¢, _____ ¢　　　_____ pennies in all

Write the time.

1

_____ : _____

2

_____ : _____

3

_____ : _____

4

_____ : _____

Name _____

Set 6.4   Use with pages 157–158. •••••••••••••••••••••••••••••••••••••

Write the time.

1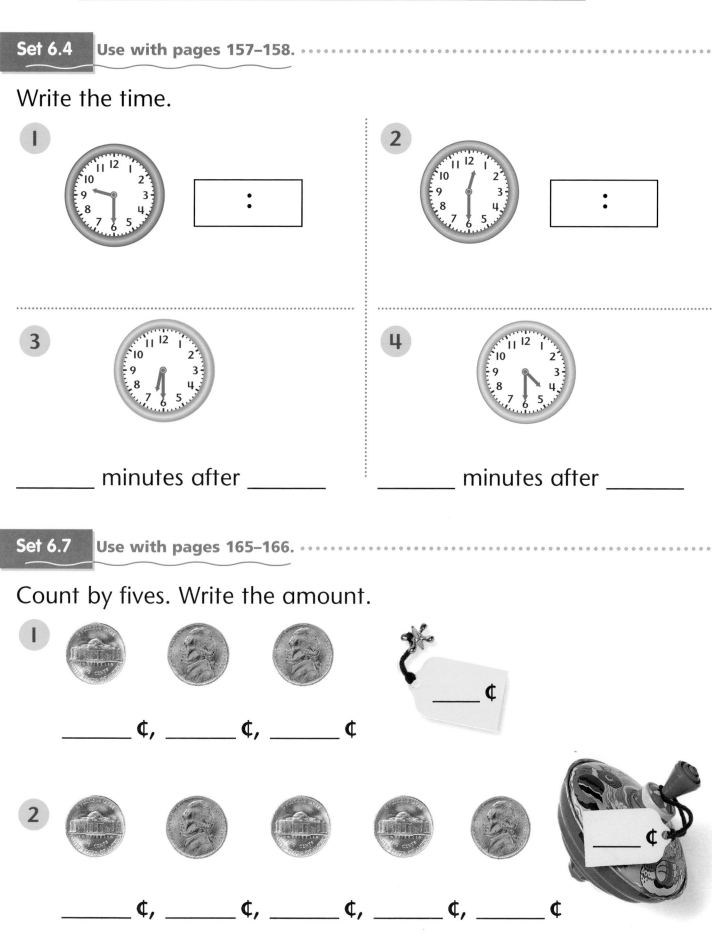

☐ **:** ☐

2

☐ **:** ☐

3

_____ minutes after _____

4

_____ minutes after _____

Set 6.7   Use with pages 165–166. ••••••••••••••••••••••••••••••••••••••

Count by fives. Write the amount.

1

_____ ¢, _____ ¢, _____ ¢

_____ ¢

2

_____ ¢, _____ ¢, _____ ¢, _____ ¢, _____ ¢

_____ ¢

Count by tens. Write the amount.

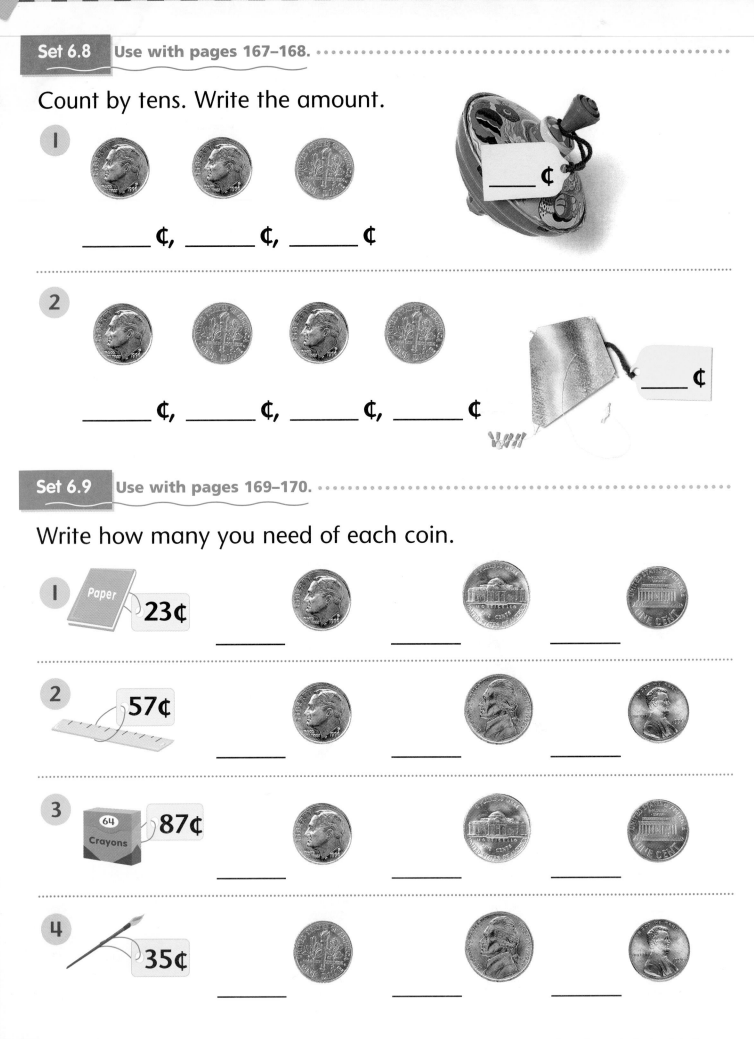

1 _____ ¢, _____ ¢, _____ ¢

_____ ¢

2 _____ ¢, _____ ¢, _____ ¢, _____ ¢

_____ ¢

Write how many you need of each coin.

1 Paper **23¢** _____ _____ _____

2 **57¢** _____ _____ _____

3 64 Crayons **87¢** _____ _____ _____

4 **35¢** _____ _____ _____

Name _____

Set 6.11 **Use with pages 173–174.** •••••••••••••••••••••••••••••••

Count the money. Write the amounts.

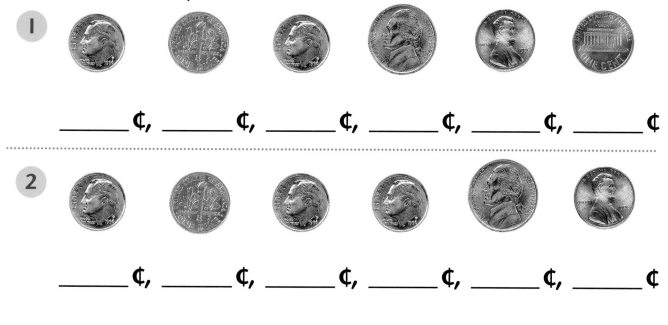

1   _____ ¢, _____ ¢, _____ ¢, _____ ¢, _____ ¢, _____ ¢

2   _____ ¢, _____ ¢, _____ ¢, _____ ¢, _____ ¢, _____ ¢

Set 6.12 **Use with pages 175–176.** ••••••••••••••••••••••••••••

Guess. Circle the amounts more than **25¢**.
Count the money. Write the amount.

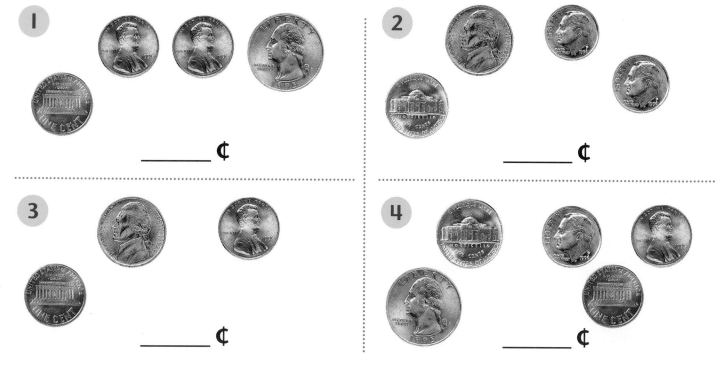

1   _____ ¢

2   _____ ¢

3   _____ ¢

4   _____ ¢

Solve.

1.
$$3 + 4 \qquad 8 - 1 \qquad 7 + 2 \qquad 3 - 2 \qquad 6 + 4 \qquad 9 - 6$$

2.
$$5 + 3 \qquad 9 - 2 \qquad 6 + 3 \qquad 8 - 6 \qquad 7 - 5 \qquad 8 + 2$$

3.
$$3 + 7 \qquad 9 - 4 \qquad 5 + 5 \qquad 5 - 3 \qquad 8 - 5 \qquad 4 + 5$$

Write the addition sentence.

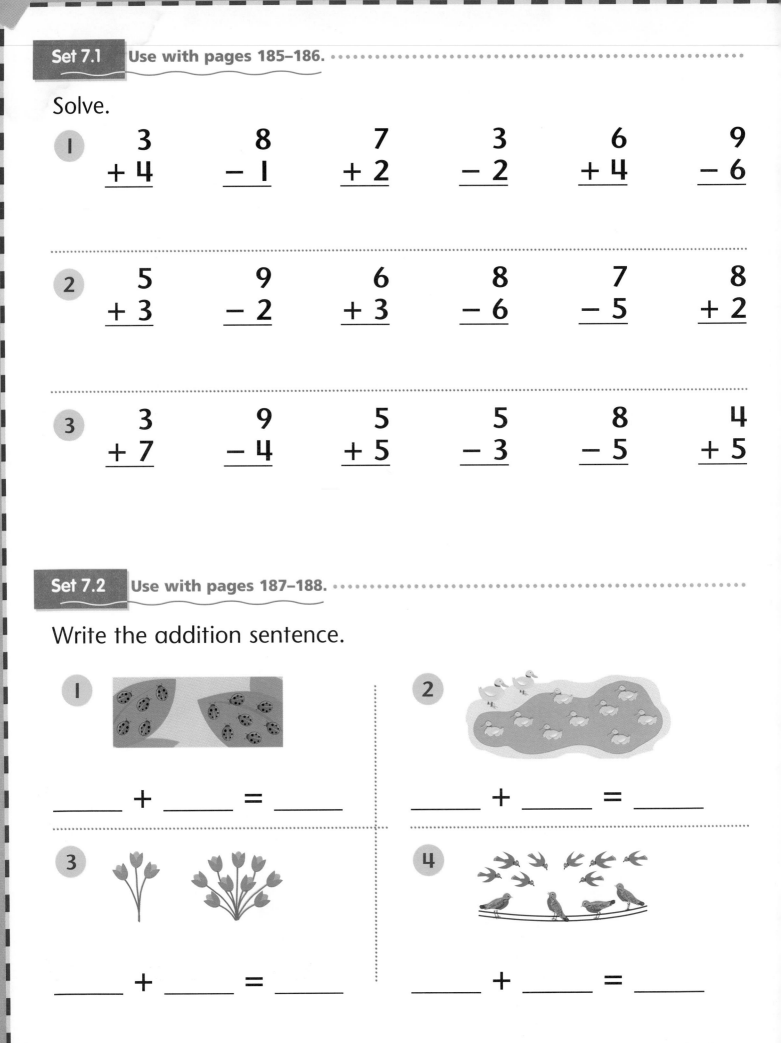

1. ____ + ____ = ____

2. ____ + ____ = ____

3. ____ + ____ = ____

4. ____ + ____ = ____

More Practice Sets 7.1 and 7.2

Name _____

Set 7.4 Use with pages 191–192. ••

Add.

① $\begin{array}{r} 3 \\ + 3 \\ \hline \end{array}$ $\begin{array}{r} 5 \\ + 6 \\ \hline \end{array}$ $\begin{array}{r} 7 \\ + 2 \\ \hline \end{array}$ $\begin{array}{r} 6 \\ + 6 \\ \hline \end{array}$ $\begin{array}{r} 10 \\ + 1 \\ \hline \end{array}$ $\begin{array}{r} 9 \\ + 3 \\ \hline \end{array}$

② $\begin{array}{r} 11 \\ + 1 \\ \hline \end{array}$ $\begin{array}{r} 8 \\ + 4 \\ \hline \end{array}$ $\begin{array}{r} 4 \\ + 4 \\ \hline \end{array}$ $\begin{array}{r} 5 \\ + 7 \\ \hline \end{array}$ $\begin{array}{r} 8 \\ + 3 \\ \hline \end{array}$ $\begin{array}{r} 9 \\ + 2 \\ \hline \end{array}$

Set 7.5 Use with pages 193–194. ••

Add. Use the number line if you need to.

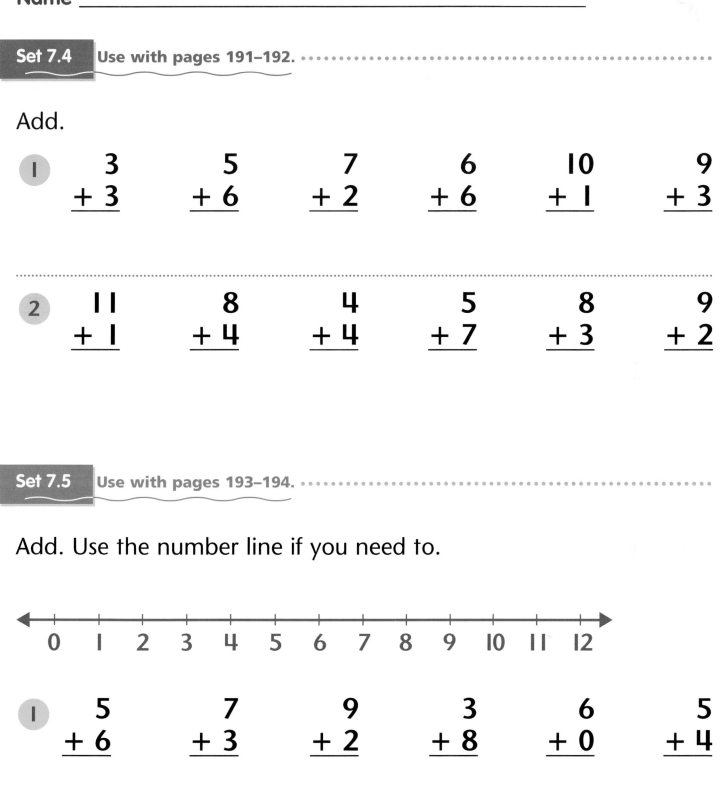

0 1 2 3 4 5 6 7 8 9 10 11 12

① $\begin{array}{r} 5 \\ + 6 \\ \hline \end{array}$ $\begin{array}{r} 7 \\ + 3 \\ \hline \end{array}$ $\begin{array}{r} 9 \\ + 2 \\ \hline \end{array}$ $\begin{array}{r} 3 \\ + 8 \\ \hline \end{array}$ $\begin{array}{r} 6 \\ + 0 \\ \hline \end{array}$ $\begin{array}{r} 5 \\ + 4 \\ \hline \end{array}$

② $\begin{array}{r} 9 \\ + 3 \\ \hline \end{array}$ $\begin{array}{r} 5 \\ + 5 \\ \hline \end{array}$ $\begin{array}{r} 2 \\ + 7 \\ \hline \end{array}$ $\begin{array}{r} 7 \\ + 5 \\ \hline \end{array}$ $\begin{array}{r} 8 \\ + 4 \\ \hline \end{array}$ $\begin{array}{r} 6 \\ + 6 \\ \hline \end{array}$

Use cubes. Add. Circle the two numbers you add first.

1
3	6	2	8	4	3
6	2	5	0	1	2
+ 1	+ 4	+ 2	+ 3	+ 5	+ 7

2
9	4	6	4	3	7
0	5	4	4	3	1
+ 1	+ 2	+ 0	+ 4	+ 5	+ 2

Write the sum.

1
| 3 | 8 | 6 | 9 | 3 | 10 |
| + 7 | + 4 | + 3 | + 2 | + 8 | + 1 |

2
| 8 | 4 | 7 | 11 | 5 | 9 |
| + 2 | + 7 | + 3 | + 1 | + 7 | + 3 |

3
6	2	5	2	4	4
3	9	4	3	1	4
+ 2	+ 1	+ 3	+ 4	+ 3	+ 4

Name _____

Set 7.13   Use with pages 211–212. ....

Subtract. Use the number line if you need to.

```
←—+——+——+——+——+——+——+——+——+——+——+——+——→
   0   1   2   3   4   5   6   7   8   9  10  11  12
```

1.
12	9	11	8	10	6
− 4	− 5	− 9	− 3	− 7	− 2

2.
9	10	12	11	10	11
− 9	− 4	− 6	− 7	− 0	− 5

Set 7.15   Use with pages 215–216. ....

Solve.

1.
11	3	9	12	3	10
− 6	+ 7	+ 2	− 4	+ 3	− 5

2.
5	4	12	10	11	3
+ 4	+ 8	− 6	− 8	− 7	+ 5

Use counters.

Show each fact. Write the number sentences
for each fact family.

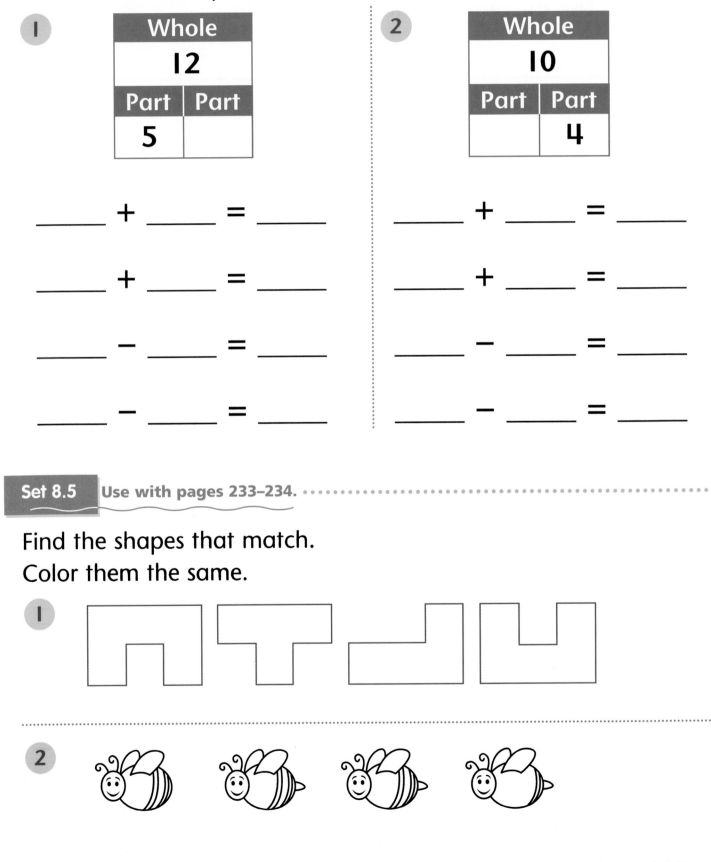

1

Whole	
12	
Part	Part
5	

____ + ____ = ____

____ + ____ = ____

____ − ____ = ____

____ − ____ = ____

2

Whole	
10	
Part	Part
	4

____ + ____ = ____

____ + ____ = ____

____ − ____ = ____

____ − ____ = ____

Find the shapes that match.
Color them the same.

1

2

Name _____

Set 8.8   Use with pages 239–240. ···

Draw and color the missing shape.

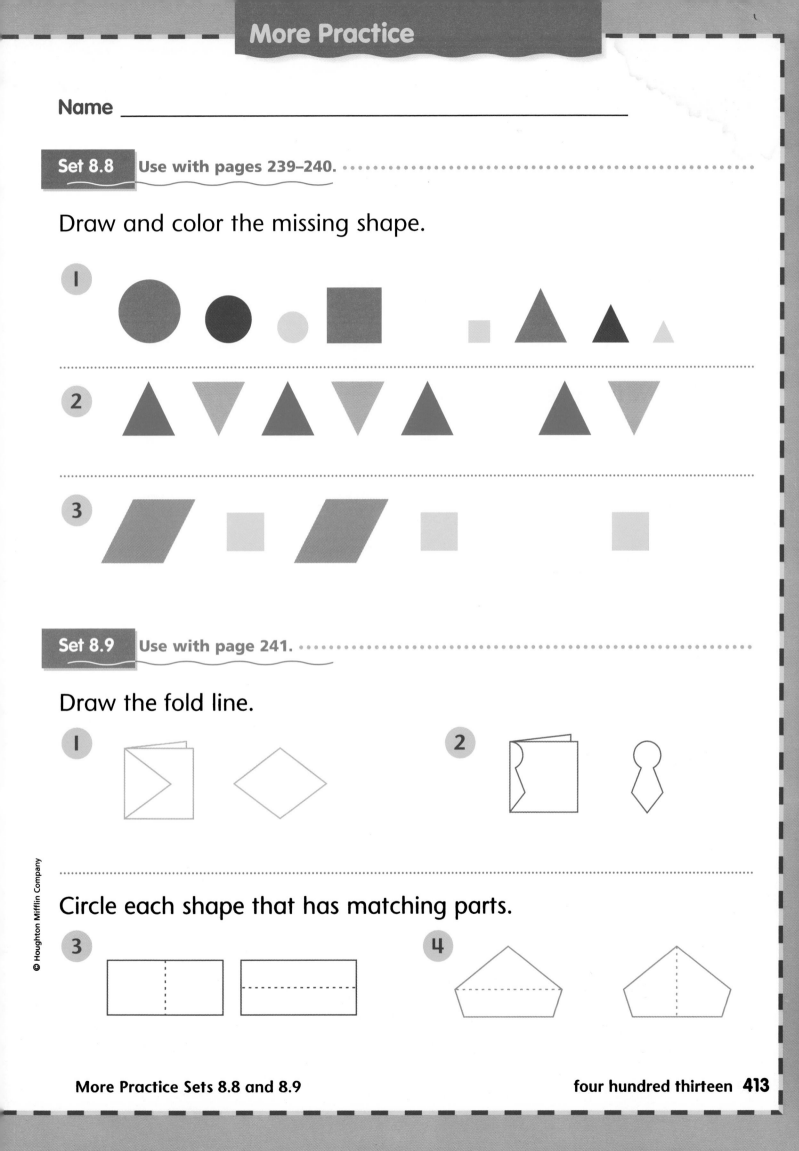

Set 8.9   Use with page 241. ···

Draw the fold line.

Circle each shape that has matching parts.

Color one of the equal parts.

1

2

3

Write how many equal parts.

4

5

6

_____   _____   _____

Color one half if the shape has equal parts.

1

2

3

Color one third if the shape has equal parts.

4

5

6

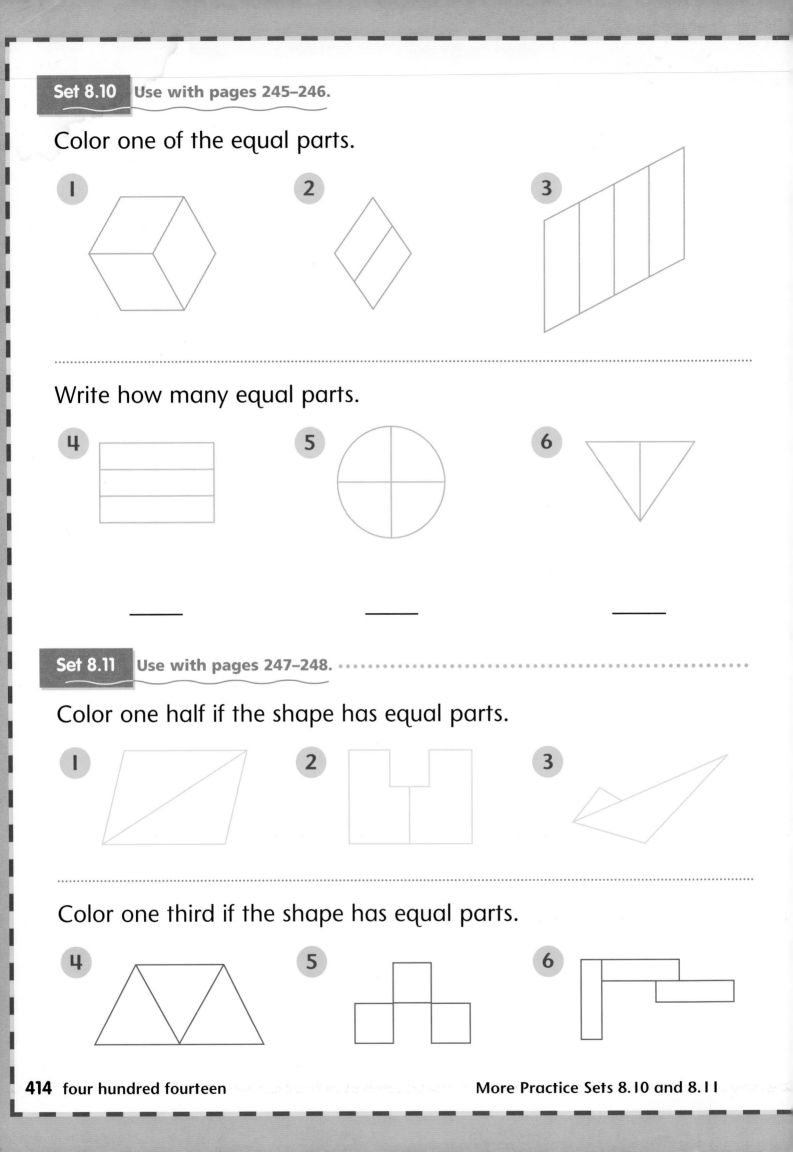

Name _____

Set 8.12 Use with pages 249–250. •

Color one fourth if the shape has equal parts.

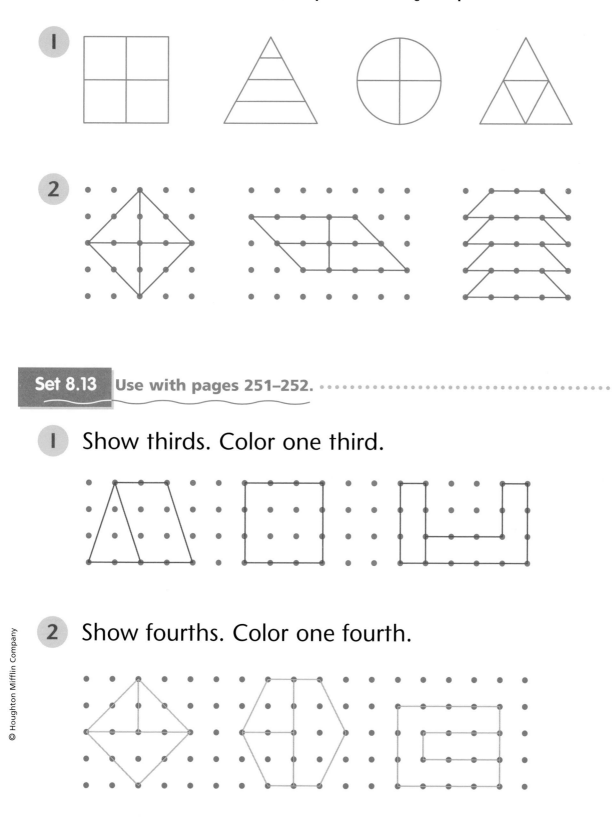

Set 8.13 Use with pages 251–252.

1 Show thirds. Color one third.

2 Show fourths. Color one fourth.

© Houghton Mifflin Company

Problem Solving

1 Shayna got **12** gifts. She opened **5**.
   How many gifts are left to open?

_____ gifts

2 Melanie had **8** shells. Her aunt gave
   her **3** more. How many shells does
   she have now?

_____ shells

3 There were **7** muffins on a plate. Jared put
   4 more muffins on the plate. How many muffins
   are on the plate now?

_____ muffins

Use ten frames and counters. Write the sum.

1
$$\begin{array}{r}7\\+8\end{array}\qquad\begin{array}{r}6\\+9\end{array}\qquad\begin{array}{r}8\\+6\end{array}\qquad\begin{array}{r}9\\+7\end{array}\qquad\begin{array}{r}10\\+5\end{array}\qquad\begin{array}{r}4\\+7\end{array}$$

2
$$\begin{array}{r}8\\+4\end{array}\qquad\begin{array}{r}10\\+7\end{array}\qquad\begin{array}{r}7\\+5\end{array}\qquad\begin{array}{r}4\\+6\end{array}\qquad\begin{array}{r}6\\+5\end{array}\qquad\begin{array}{r}7\\+7\end{array}$$

3
$$\begin{array}{r}9\\+4\end{array}\qquad\begin{array}{r}6\\+8\end{array}\qquad\begin{array}{r}10\\+3\end{array}\qquad\begin{array}{r}5\\+8\end{array}\qquad\begin{array}{r}7\\+6\end{array}\qquad\begin{array}{r}9\\+5\end{array}$$

Name _____

Set 9.4 Use with pages 269–270. ·····································

Double the smaller number.
Then add one more. Write the sum.

1.
$$6 \atop + 5$$ $$8 \atop + 9$$ $$1 \atop + 2$$ $$4 \atop + 5$$ $$9 \atop + 10$$ $$3 \atop + 2$$

2.
$$4 \atop + 3$$ $$6 \atop + 7$$ $$5 \atop + 6$$ $$8 \atop + 7$$ $$2 \atop + 3$$ $$9 \atop + 8$$

3.
$$7 \atop + 8$$ $$10 \atop + 9$$ $$7 \atop + 6$$ $$3 \atop + 4$$ $$4 \atop + 5$$ $$2 \atop + 1$$

Set 9.7 Use with pages 277–278. ·····································

Write how much is left.

		Has	Spends	Has left
1	Rhonda	13¢	10¢	_____ ¢
2	Sheldon	19¢	10¢	_____ ¢
3	Pearl	11¢	10¢	_____ ¢

More Practice Sets 9.4 and 9.7

Use ten frames and counters.
Subtract.

1.
15	14	16	12	13	17
− 7	− 5	− 8	− 9	− 7	− 5

2.
16	18	13	14	19	15
− 6	− 7	− 6	− 8	− 4	− 9

Solve.

1.
7	9	12	15	20	8
+ 8	+ 8	− 9	− 8	− 9	+ 8

2.
5	12	6	10	11	19
+ 8	− 7	+ 8	+ 4	− 5	− 3

3.
14	9	17	9	18	4
− 6	+ 9	− 8	+ 6	− 7	+ 9

More Practice Sets 9.8 and 9.10

Name _____

Set 9.11 Use with pages 285–286. ·····························

Write the missing number.

1. 8 + ___ = 13   6 + ___ = 16   9 + ___ = 15

2. 9 + ___ = 18   5 + ___ = 13   7 + ___ = 16

3. 8 + ___ = 17   7 + ___ = 13   6 + ___ = 12

4. 6 + ___ = 14   3 + ___ = 12   9 + ___ = 19

Set 9.12 Use with pages 287–288. ·····························

Use cubes. Show each fact.
Write the number sentences for each fact family.

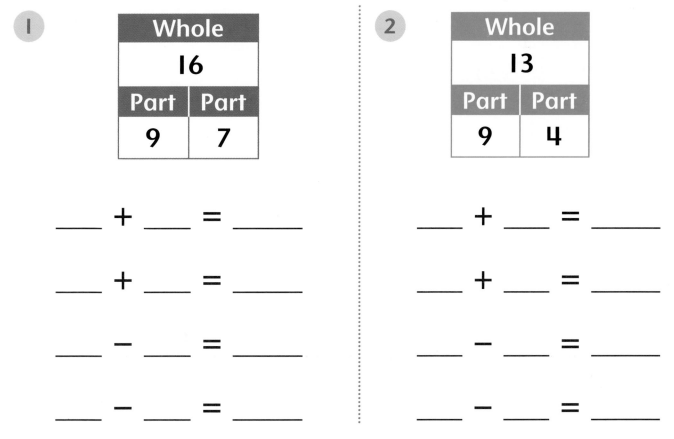

1.

Whole	
16	
Part	Part
9	7

___ + ___ = ___

___ + ___ = ___

___ − ___ = ___

___ − ___ = ___

2.

Whole	
13	
Part	Part
9	4

___ + ___ = ___

___ + ___ = ___

___ − ___ = ___

___ − ___ = ___

Estimate how many inches long or tall. Measure.
Use an inch ruler.

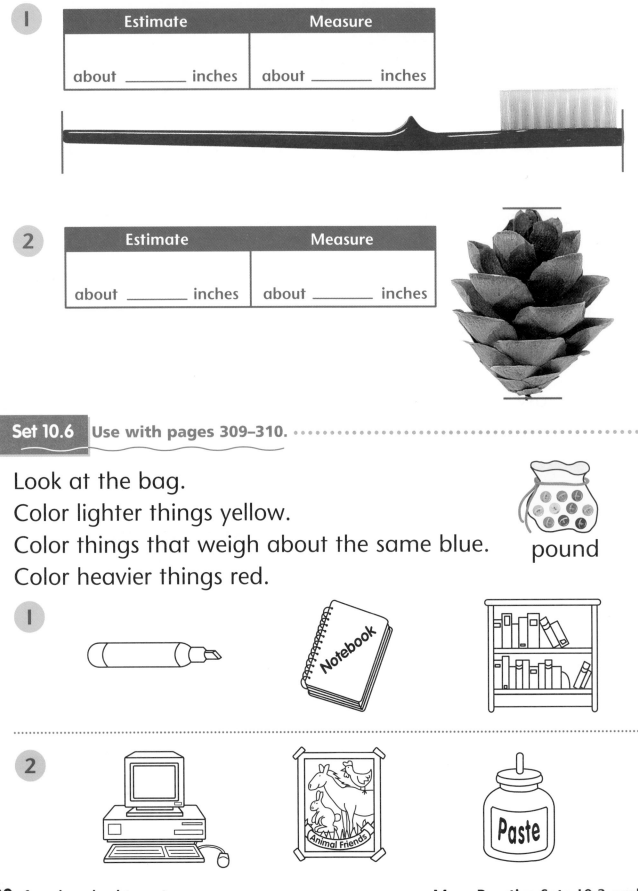

1

Estimate	Measure
about _____ inches	about _____ inches

2

Estimate	Measure
about _____ inches	about _____ inches

Look at the bag.
Color lighter things yellow.
Color things that weigh about the same blue.
Color heavier things red.

pound

1

2

Name _____

Set 10.10 Use with pages 319–320. •••

Look at the container.
Color things that hold less green.
Color things that hold about the same orange.
Color things that hold more purple.

quart

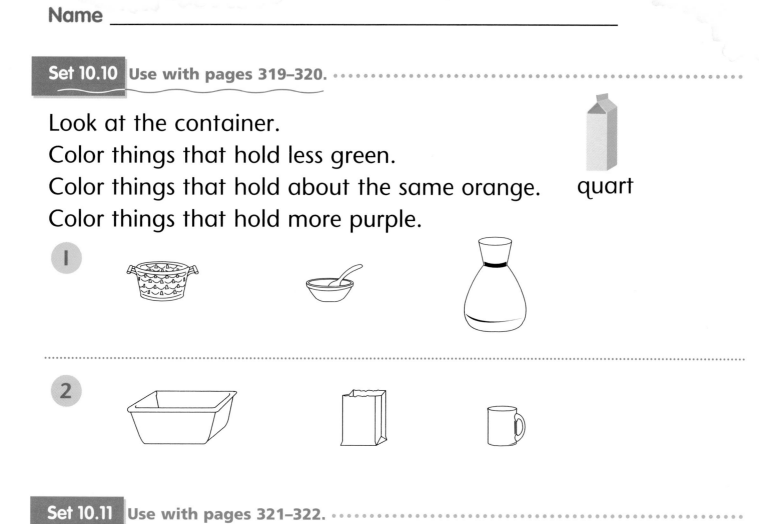

1

2

Set 10.11 Use with pages 321–322. •••

Estimate how many centimeters long. Measure.
Use a centimeter ruler.

	Object	Estimate	Measure
1		about ___ centimeters	about ___ centimeters
2	S O A P	about ___ centimeters	about ___ centimeters
3		about ___ centimeters	about ___ centimeters

© Houghton Mifflin Company

Write how many.

1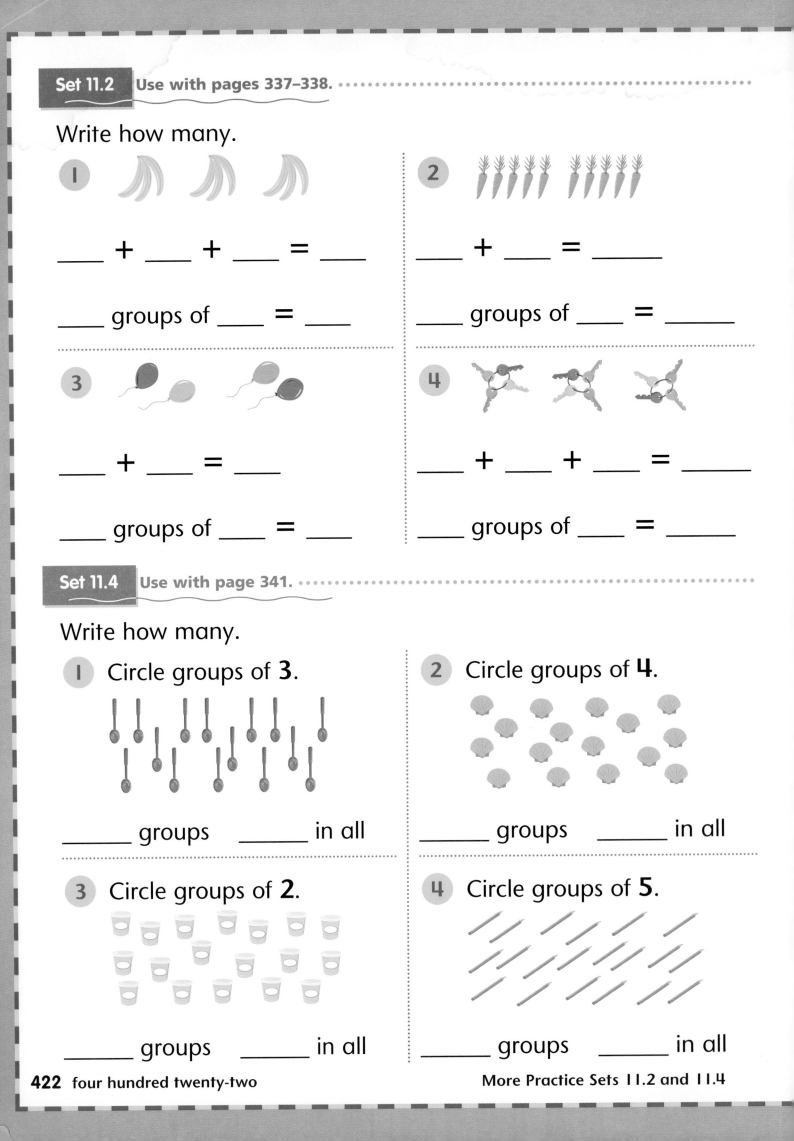

___ + ___ + ___ = ___

____ groups of ____ = ___

2

___ + ___ = _____

____ groups of ____ = _____

3

___ + ___ = ___

____ groups of ____ = ___

4

___ + ___ + ___ = _____

____ groups of ____ = _____

Write how many.

1 Circle groups of **3.**

_____ groups   _____ in all

2 Circle groups of **4.**

_____ groups   _____ in all

3 Circle groups of **2.**

_____ groups   _____ in all

4 Circle groups of **5.**

_____ groups   _____ in all

Name _____

Set 11.5 Use with pages 345–346. ···

Write how many.

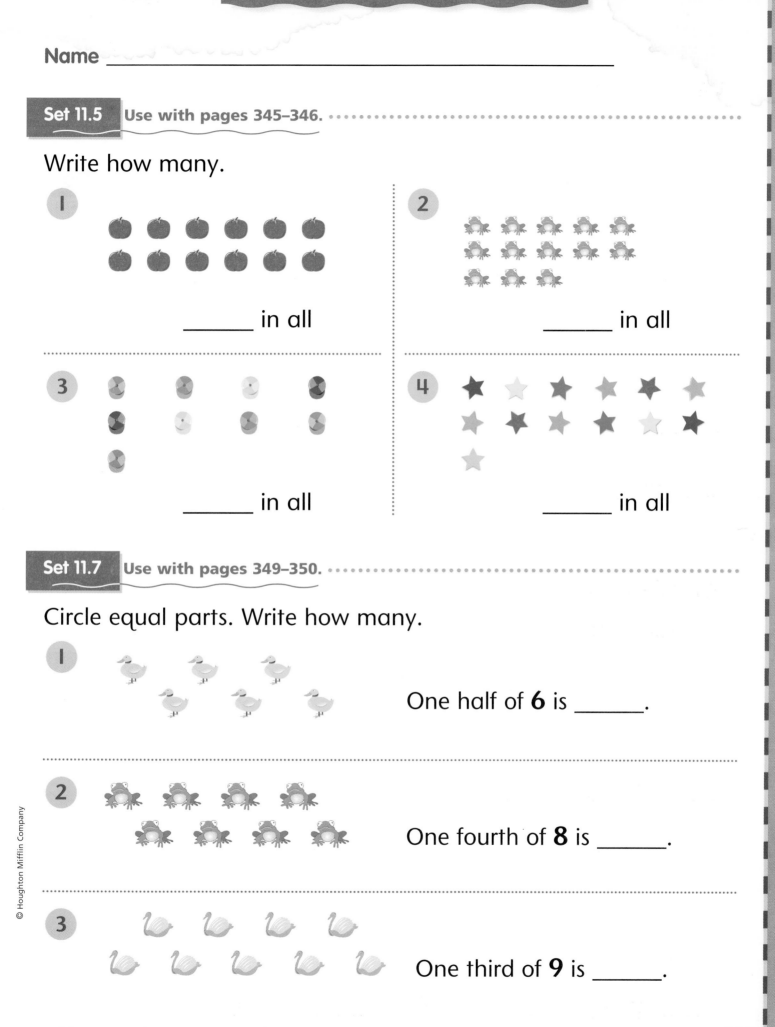

1

_____ in all

2

_____ in all

3

_____ in all

4

_____ in all

Set 11.7 Use with pages 349–350. ···

Circle equal parts. Write how many.

1

One half of **6** is _____.

2

One fourth of **8** is _____.

3

One third of **9** is _____.

Use blocks and a workmat. Write the sum.

1 **24 + 4**

Show **24**.
Add **4**.

Tens	Ones

The sum is _____.

2 **35 + 3**

Show **35**.
Add **3**.

Tens	Ones

The sum is _____.

3 12 + 7 = _____

4 21 + 5 = _____

5 43 + 2 = _____

6 31 + 6 = _____

7 37 + 2 = _____

8 23 + 3 = _____

Use blocks and a workmat. Write the sum.

1 **43 + 12**

Show **43**.
Add **12**.

Tens	Ones

The sum is _____.

2 **36 + 23**

Show **36**.
Add **23**.

Tens	Ones

The sum is _____.

3 12 + 36 = _____

4 36 + 33 = _____

5 21 + 17 = _____

6 61 + 12 = _____

7 52 + 16 = _____

8 20 + 14 = _____

More Practice Sets 12.1 and 12.2

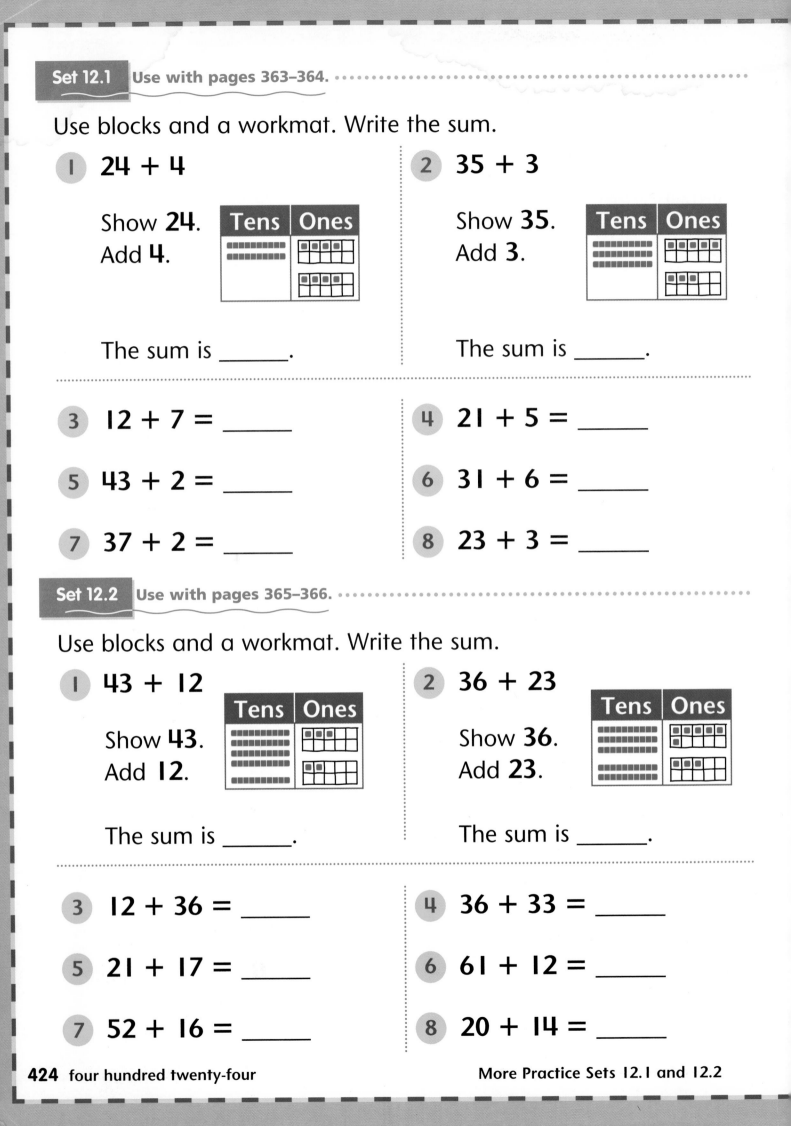

Name _____

Set 12.3 Use with page 367. ●●●

Use blocks and a workmat.
Regroup if you can. Write the sum.

① **34 + 16**

Show **34**.
Add **16**.

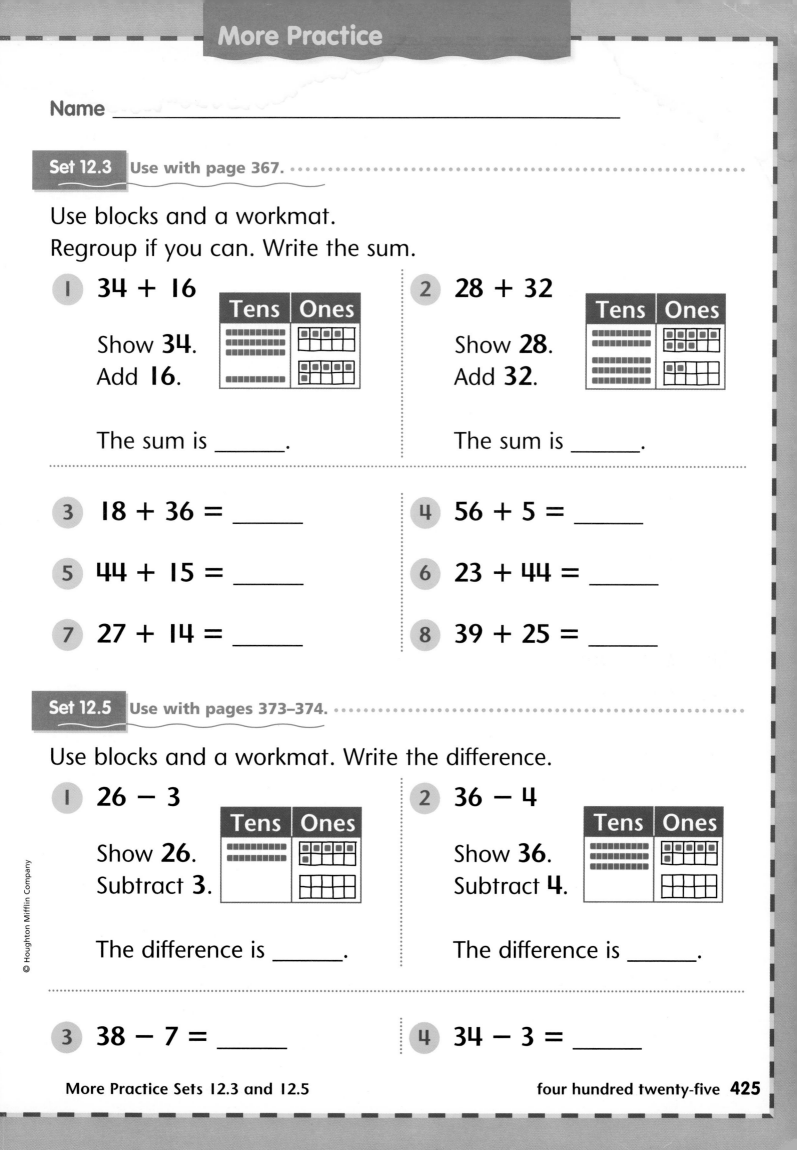

The sum is _____.

② **28 + 32**

Show **28**.
Add **32**.

The sum is _____.

③ **18 + 36 = _____**

④ **56 + 5 = _____**

⑤ **44 + 15 = _____**

⑥ **23 + 44 = _____**

⑦ **27 + 14 = _____**

⑧ **39 + 25 = _____**

Set 12.5 Use with pages 373–374. ●●

Use blocks and a workmat. Write the difference.

① **26 − 3**

Show **26**.
Subtract **3**.

The difference is _____.

② **36 − 4**

Show **36**.
Subtract **4**.

The difference is _____.

③ **38 − 7 = _____**

④ **34 − 3 = _____**

Use blocks and a workmat. Write the difference.

1 **21 − 11**

Show **21**.
Subtract **11**.

Tens	Ones

The difference is _____.

2 **38 − 17**

Show **38**.
Subtract **17**.

Tens	Ones

The difference is _____.

3 **49 − 12 = _____**

4 **58 − 17 = _____**

5 **64 − 14 = _____**

6 **68 − 35 = _____**

7 **27 − 14 = _____**

8 **36 − 25 = _____**

Use blocks and a workmat. Write the difference.

1 **24 − 9**

Show **24**.
Subtract **9**.

Tens	Ones

The difference is _____.

2 **28 − 18**

Show **28**.
Subtract **18**.

Tens	Ones

The difference is _____.

3 **72 − 28 = _____**

4 **36 − 29 = _____**

5 **52 − 35 = _____**

6 **69 − 17 = _____**

7 **43 − 37 = _____**

8 **74 − 48 = _____**

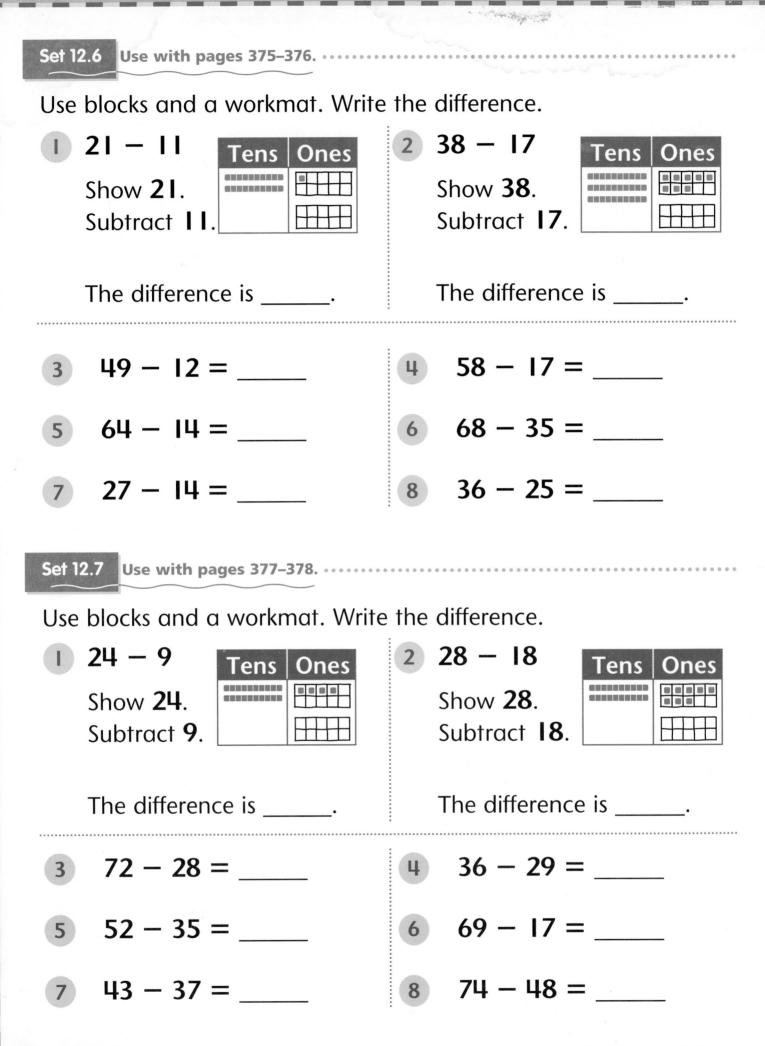

Picture Glossary

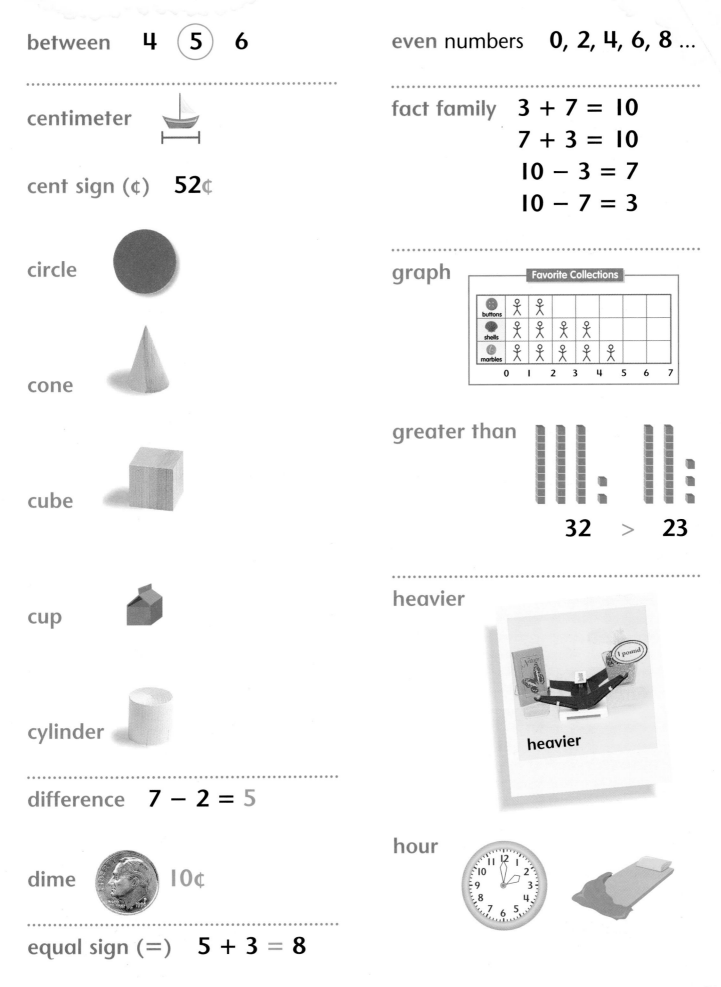

between   4   (5)   6

centimeter

cent sign (¢)   **52¢**

circle

cone

cube

cup

cylinder

difference   **7 − 2 = 5**

dime   10¢

equal sign (=)   **5 + 3 = 8**

even numbers   **0, 2, 4, 6, 8 ...**

fact family   **3 + 7 = 10**
             7 + 3 = 10
             10 − 3 = 7
             10 − 7 = 3

graph

Favorite Collections

	0	1	2	3	4	5	6	7
buttons								
shells								
marbles								

greater than

32 > 23

heavier

heavier

hour

hour hand

inch

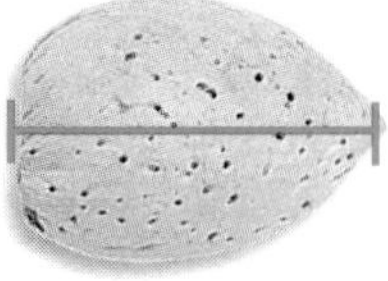

less than

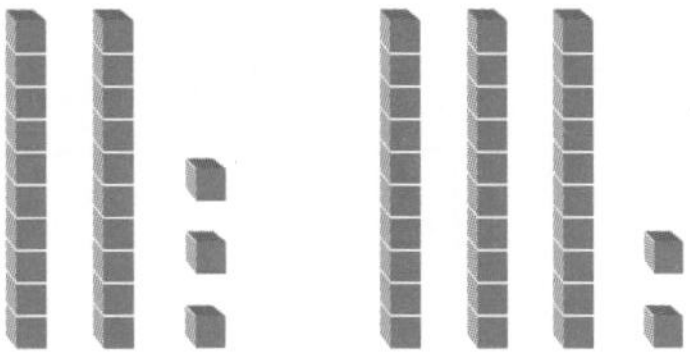

$$23 \quad < \quad 32$$

liter

minus sign (−) $8 - 3 = 5$

minute hand

more/fewer

more   fewer

more than

more than **30¢**

nickel   5¢

number   **7, 11, 56**

number line

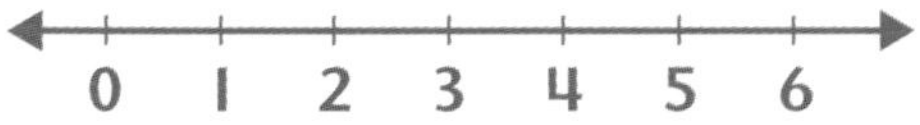

0 1 2 3 4 5 6

o'clock

5:00   5 o'clock

odd numbers **1, 3, 5, 7, 9 ...**

one fourth

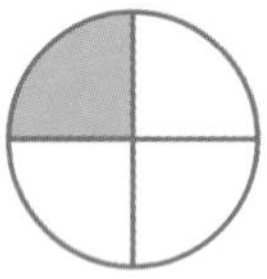

one half

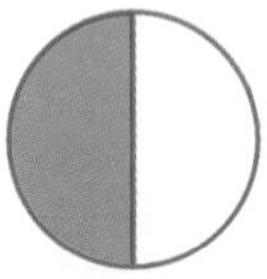

one third

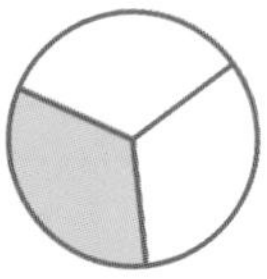

Picture Glossary

pattern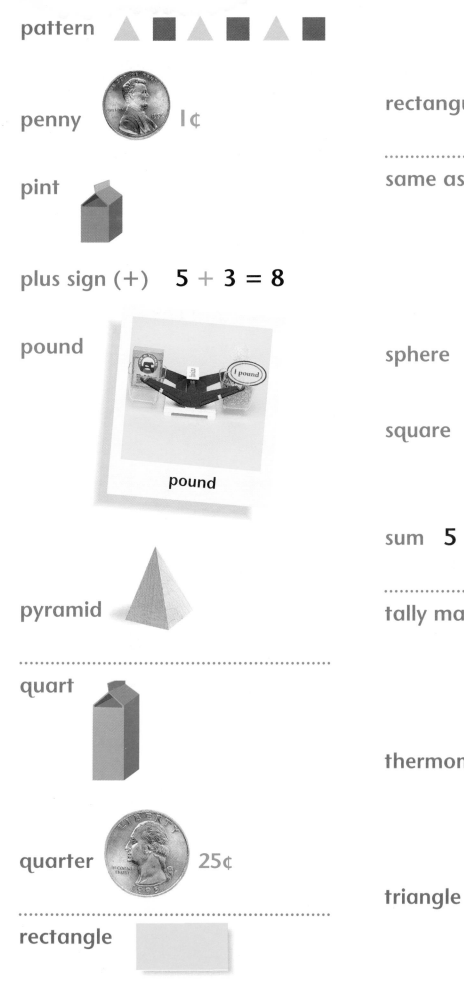

penny 1¢

pint

plus sign (+) **5 + 3 = 8**

pound

pound

pyramid

quart

quarter 25¢

rectangle

rectangular prism

same as

32 = 32

sphere

square

sum **5 + 2 = 7**

tally marks

Favorite Color	
Blue	ЖЖ ЖЖ |||
Red	ЖЖ ЖЖ ЖЖ ||

thermometer

triangle

Credits